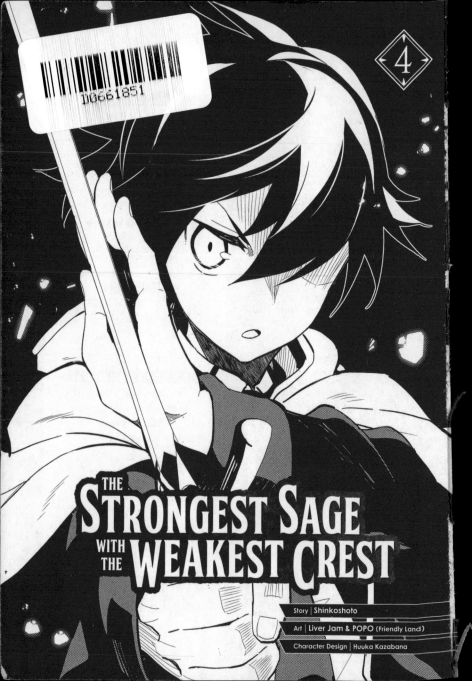

4

THE STRONGEST SAGE
WITH THE WEAKEST CREST

Story | Shinkoshoto

Art | Liver Jam & POPO (Friendly Land)

Character Design | Huuka Kazabana

Contents

THE STRONGEST SAGE WITH THE WEAKEST CREST

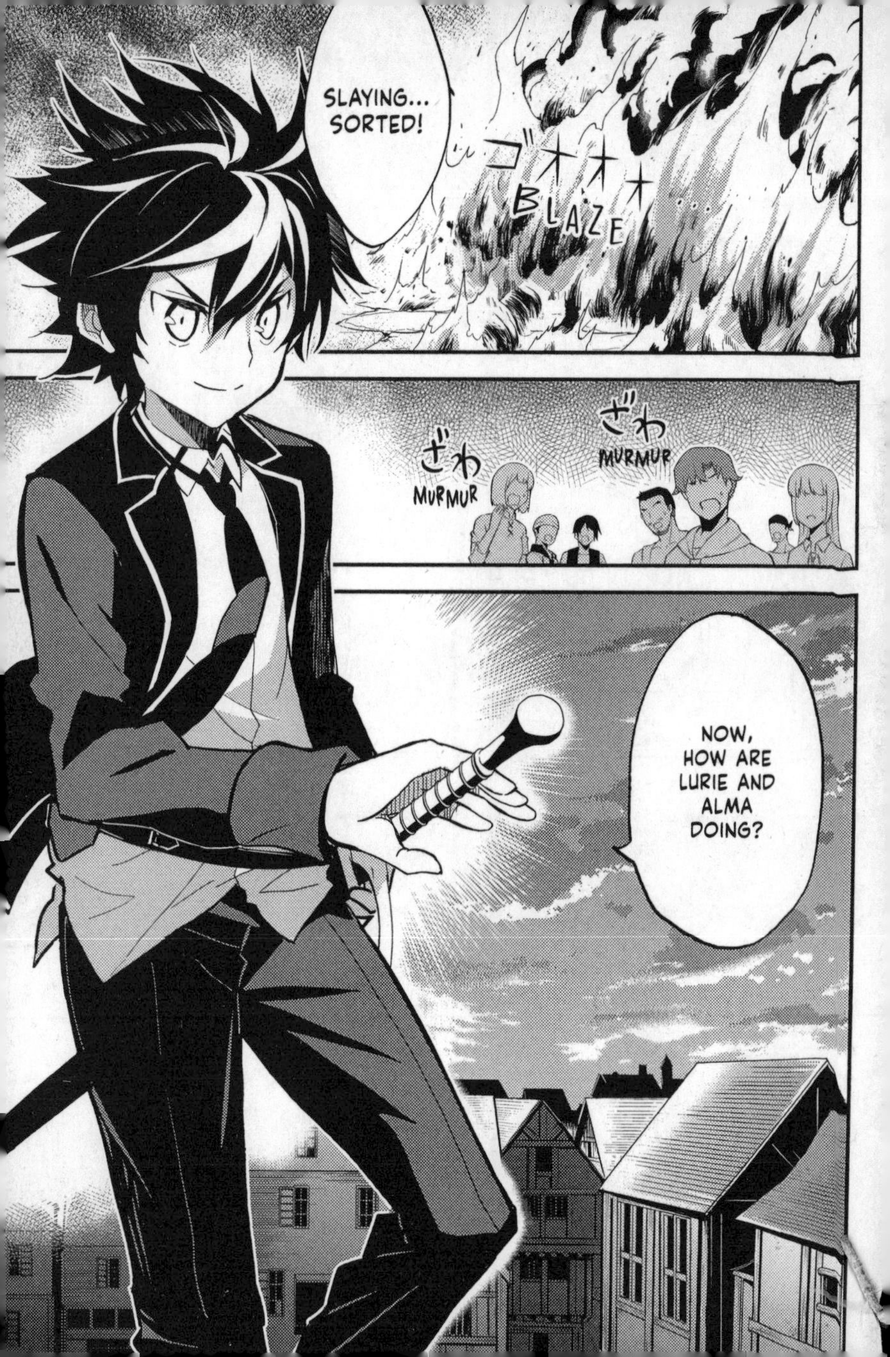
ゴオオオ
BLAZE
SLAYING... SORTED!
ざわ
MURMUR
ざわ
MURMUR
NOW, HOW ARE LURIE AND ALMA DOING?

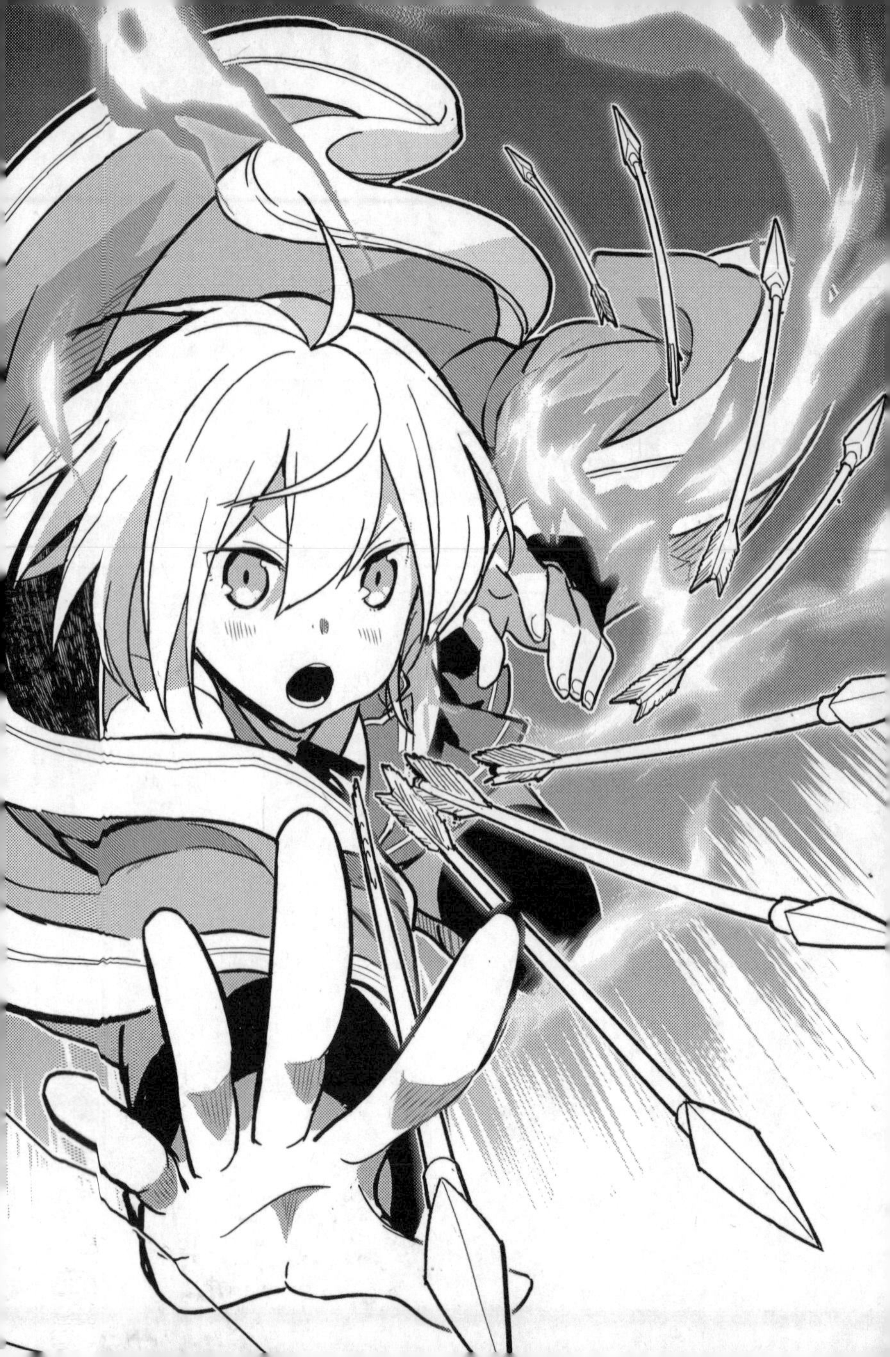

CHAPTER 12 ◆ The Strongest Sage Ends the Invaders

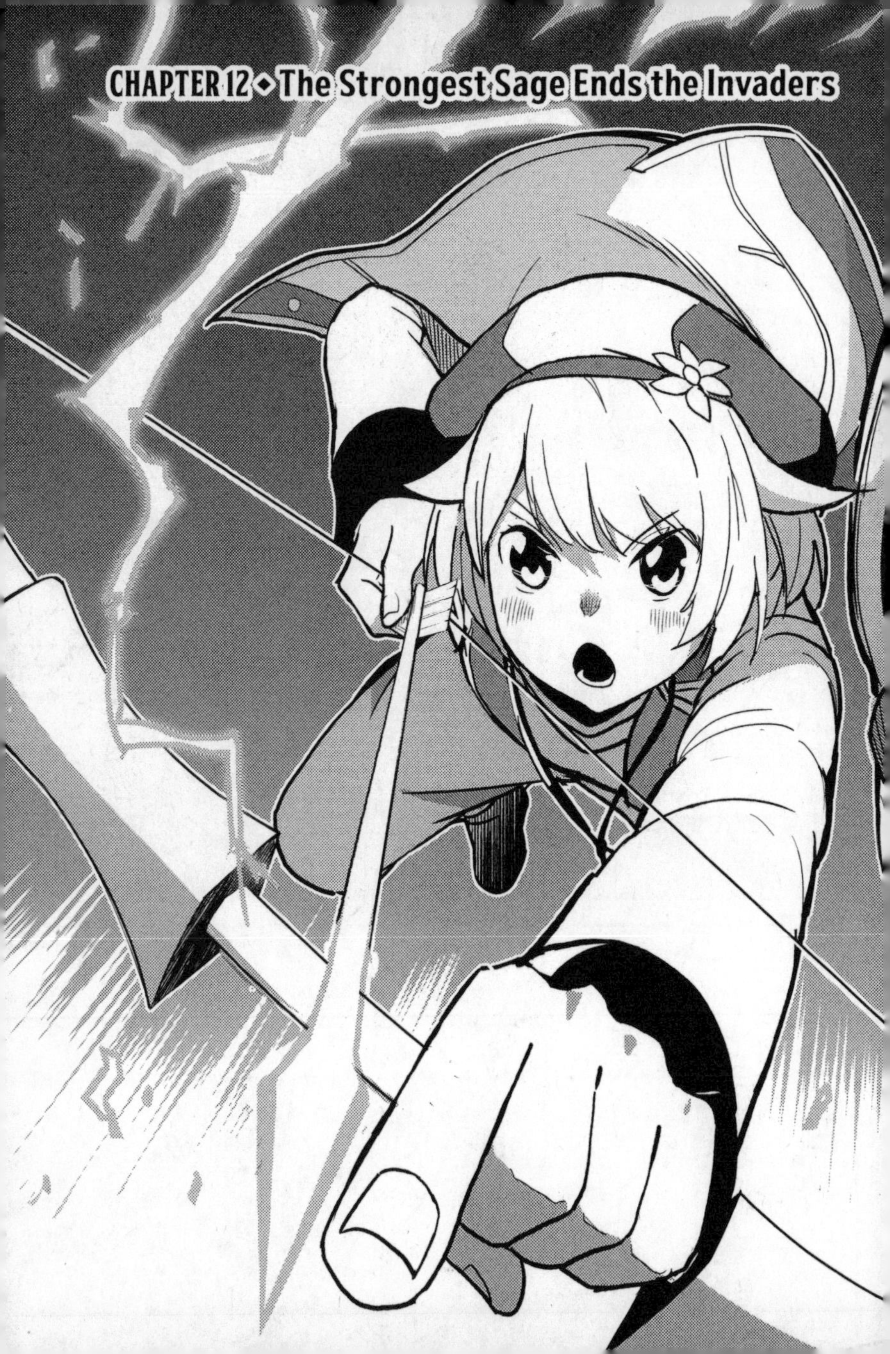

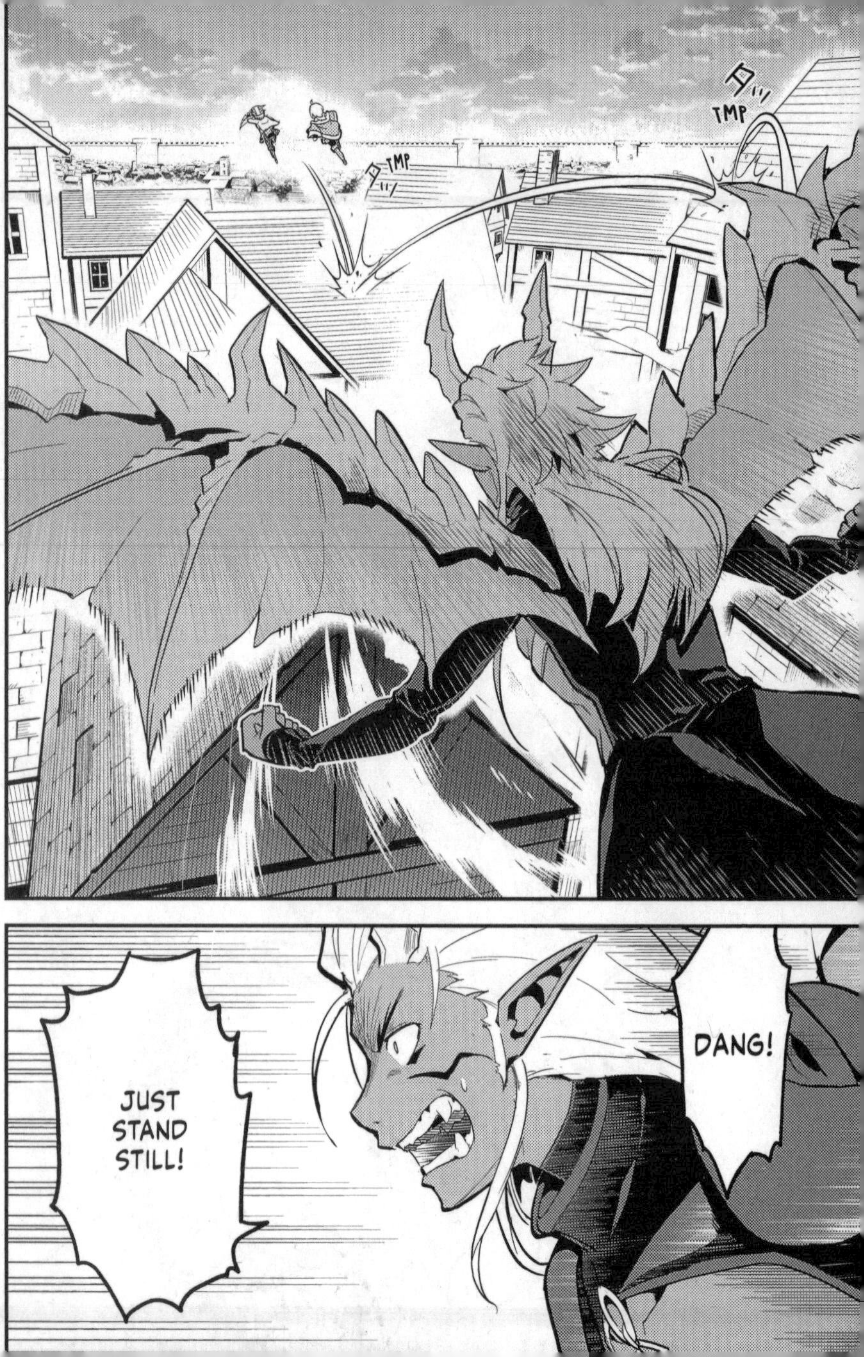

タッ
TMP
タッ
TMP
DANG!
JUST STAND STILL!

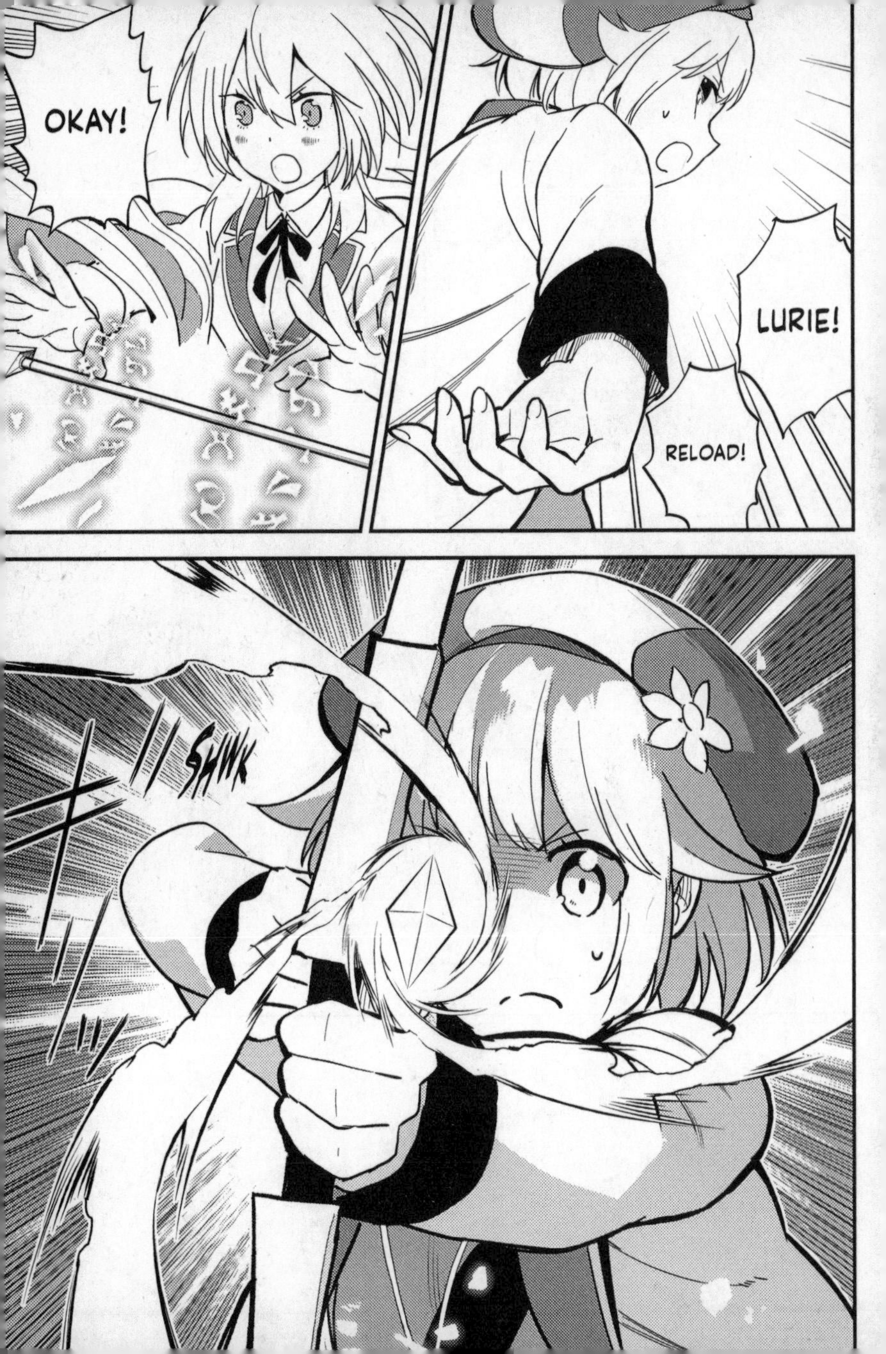
LURIE!
RELOAD!
OKAY!
SHUK

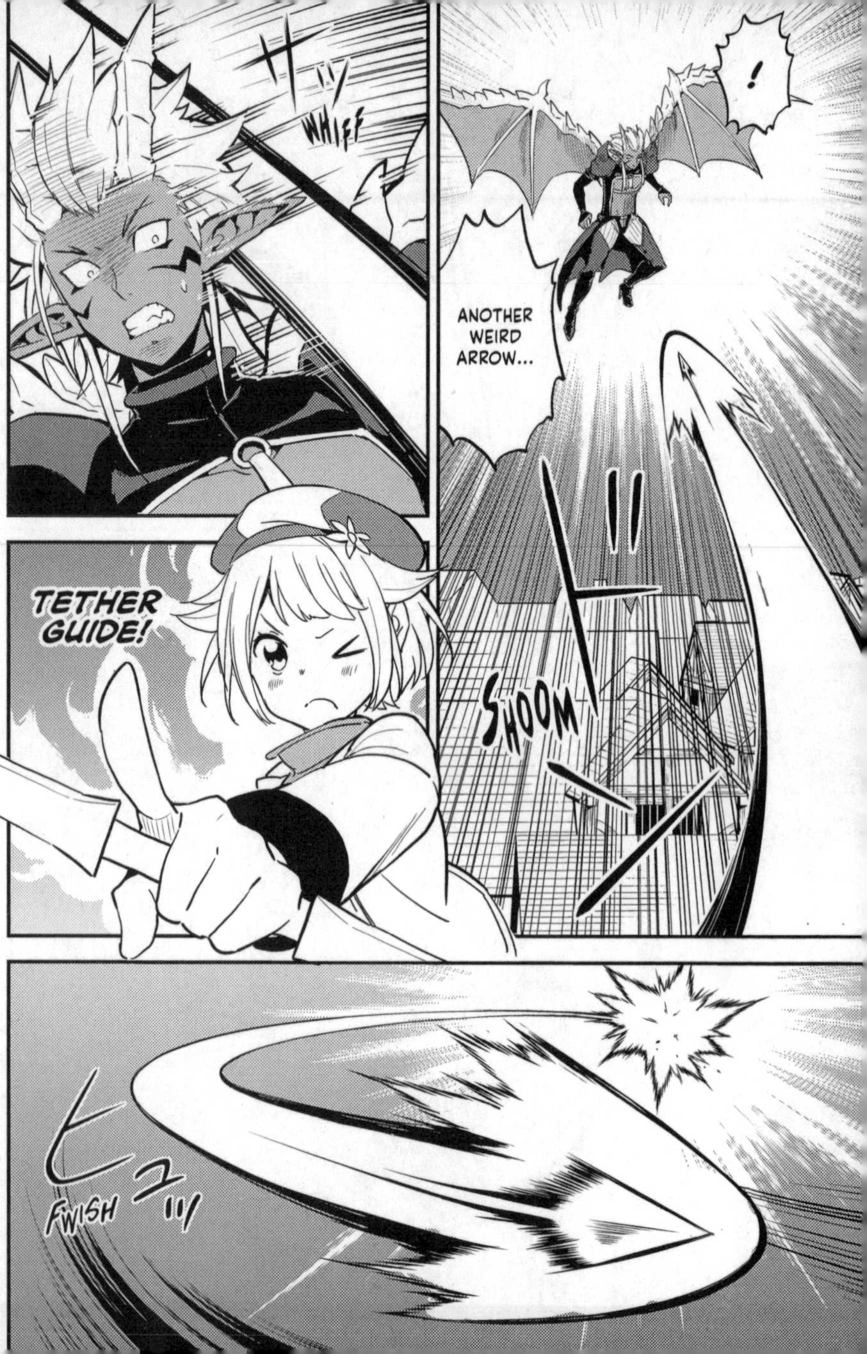
!
ANOTHER WEIRD ARROW...
SHOOM
WHIFF
TETHER GUIDE!
FWISH

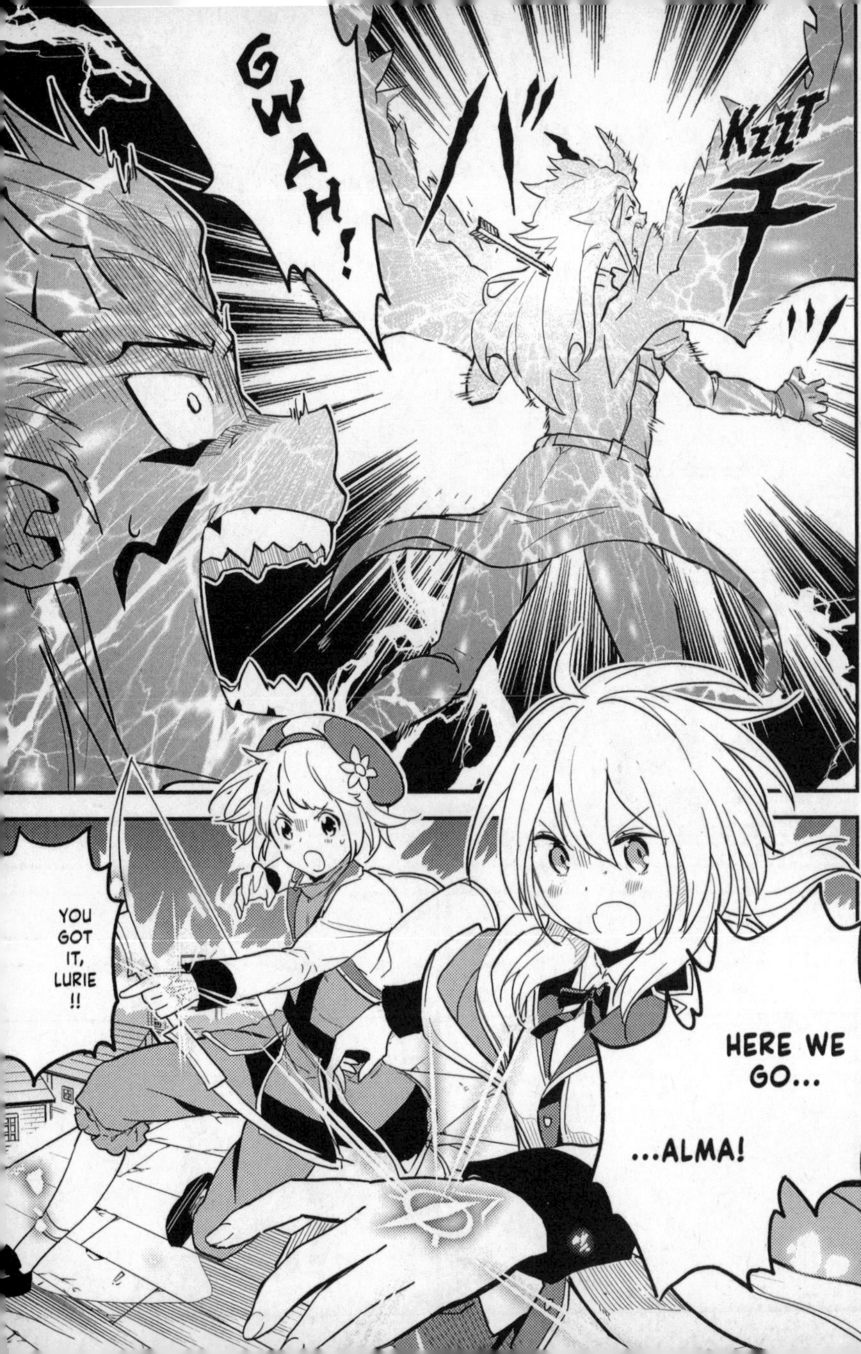
KZZT
バチッ
GWAH!
HERE WE GO...
...ALMA!
YOU GOT IT, LURIE!!

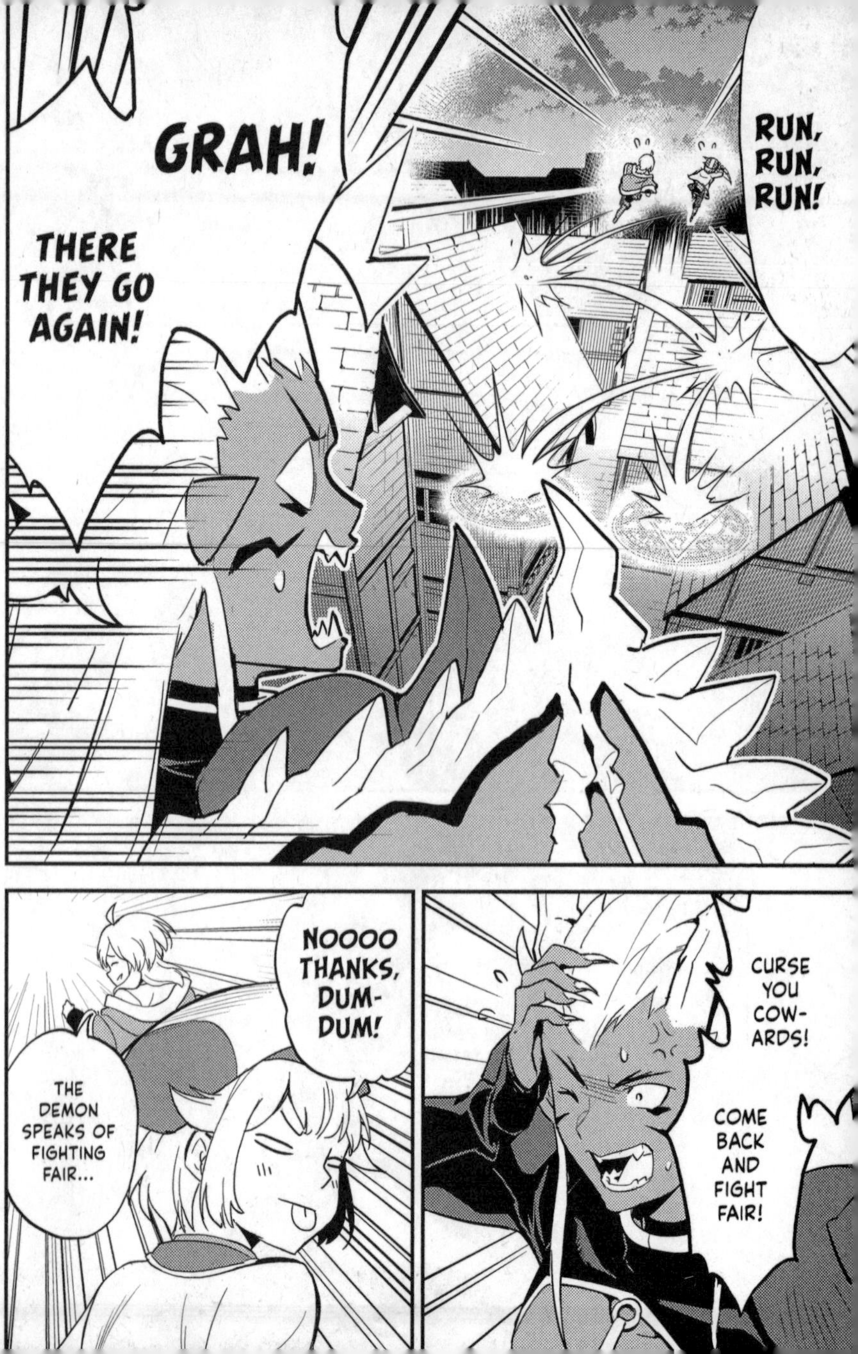
RUN, RUN, RUN!
GRAH!
THERE THEY GO AGAIN!
CURSE YOU COW-ARDS!
COME BACK AND FIGHT FAIR!
NOOOO THANKS, DUM-DUM!
THE DEMON SPEAKS OF FIGHTING FAIR...

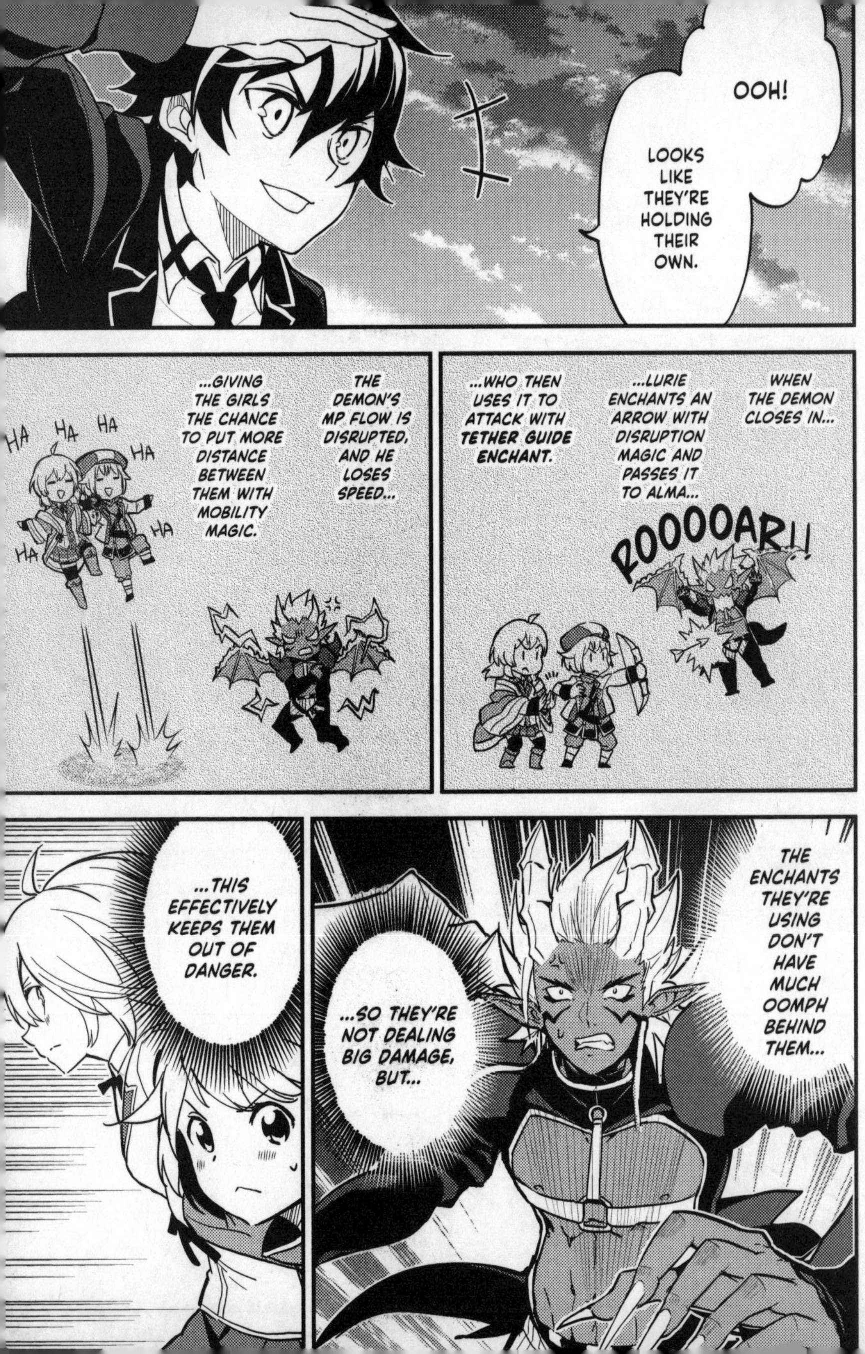
OOH!
LOOKS LIKE THEY'RE HOLDING THEIR OWN.
WHEN THE DEMON CLOSES IN...
...LURIE ENCHANTS AN ARROW WITH DISRUPTION MAGIC AND PASSES IT TO ALMA...
...WHO THEN USES IT TO ATTACK WITH TETHER GUIDE ENCHANT.
ROOOOAR!!
THE DEMON'S MP FLOW IS DISRUPTED, AND HE LOSES SPEED...
...GIVING THE GIRLS THE CHANCE TO PUT MORE DISTANCE BETWEEN THEM WITH MOBILITY MAGIC.
HA HA HA HA HA HA
THE ENCHANTS THEY'RE USING DON'T HAVE MUCH OOMPH BEHIND THEM...
...SO THEY'RE NOT DEALING BIG DAMAGE, BUT...
...THIS EFFECTIVELY KEEPS THEM OUT OF DANGER.

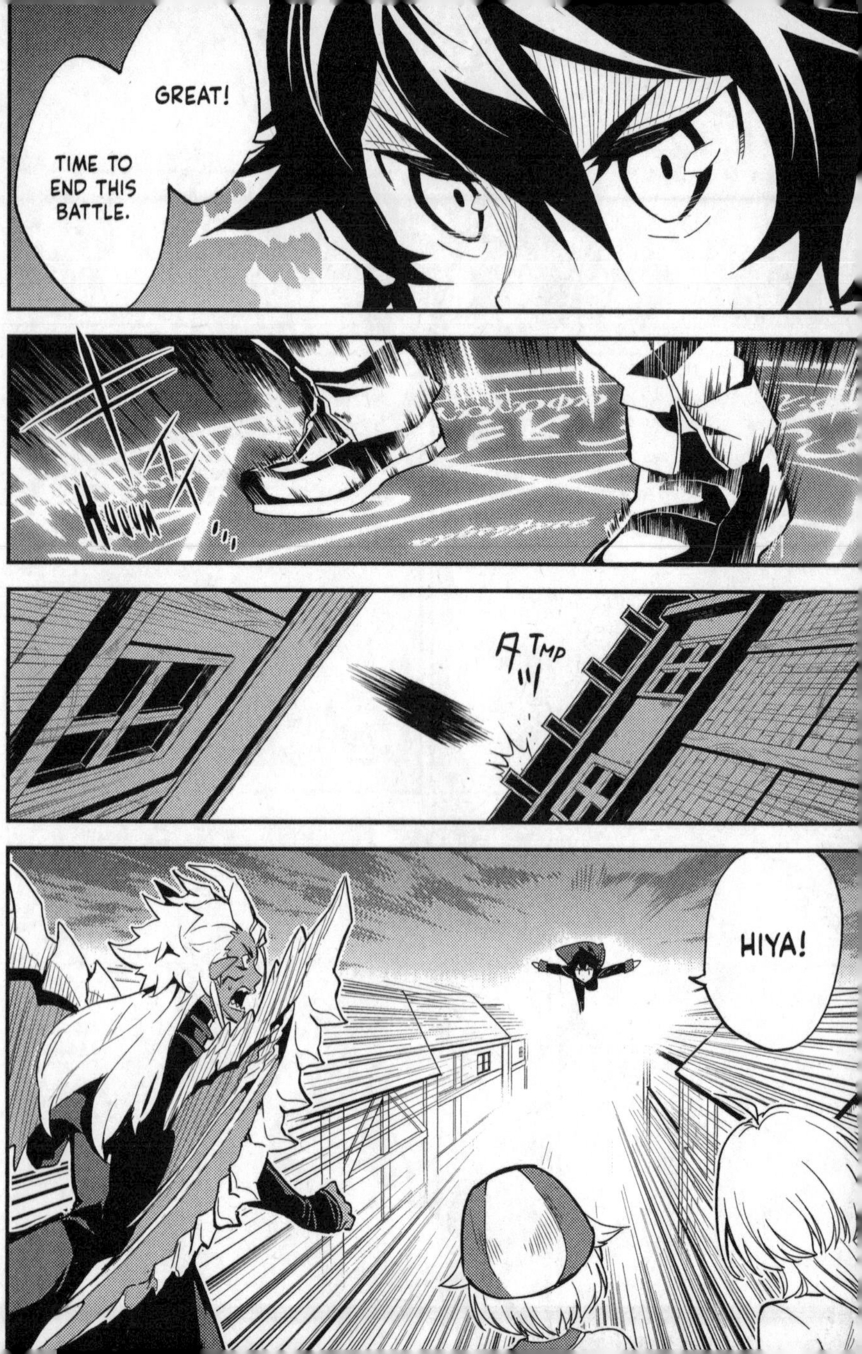
GREAT!
TIME TO END THIS BATTLE.
HUUUM...
TMP
HIYA!

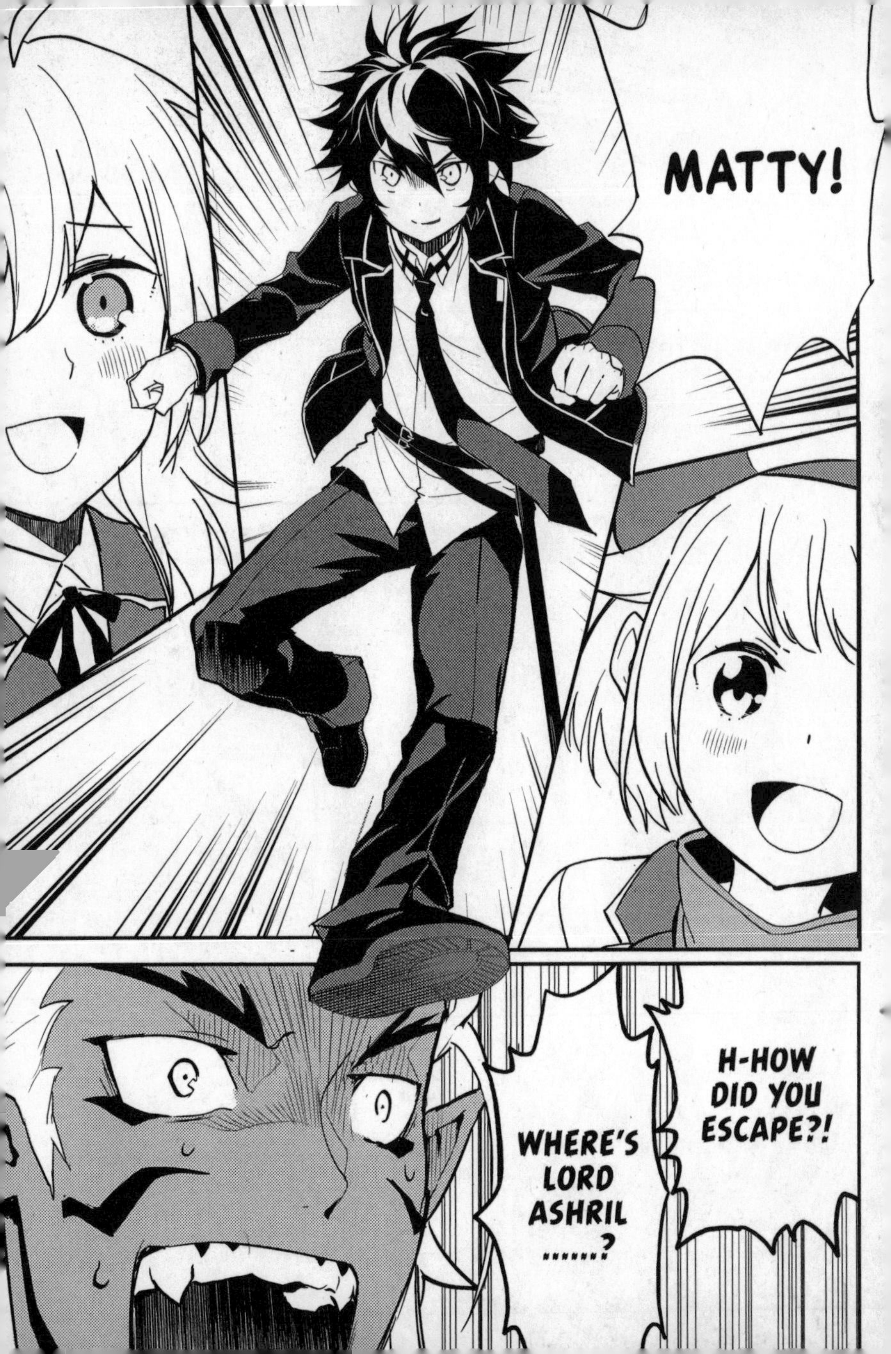
MATTY!
H-HOW DID YOU ESCAPE?!
WHERE'S LORD ASHRIL ....?

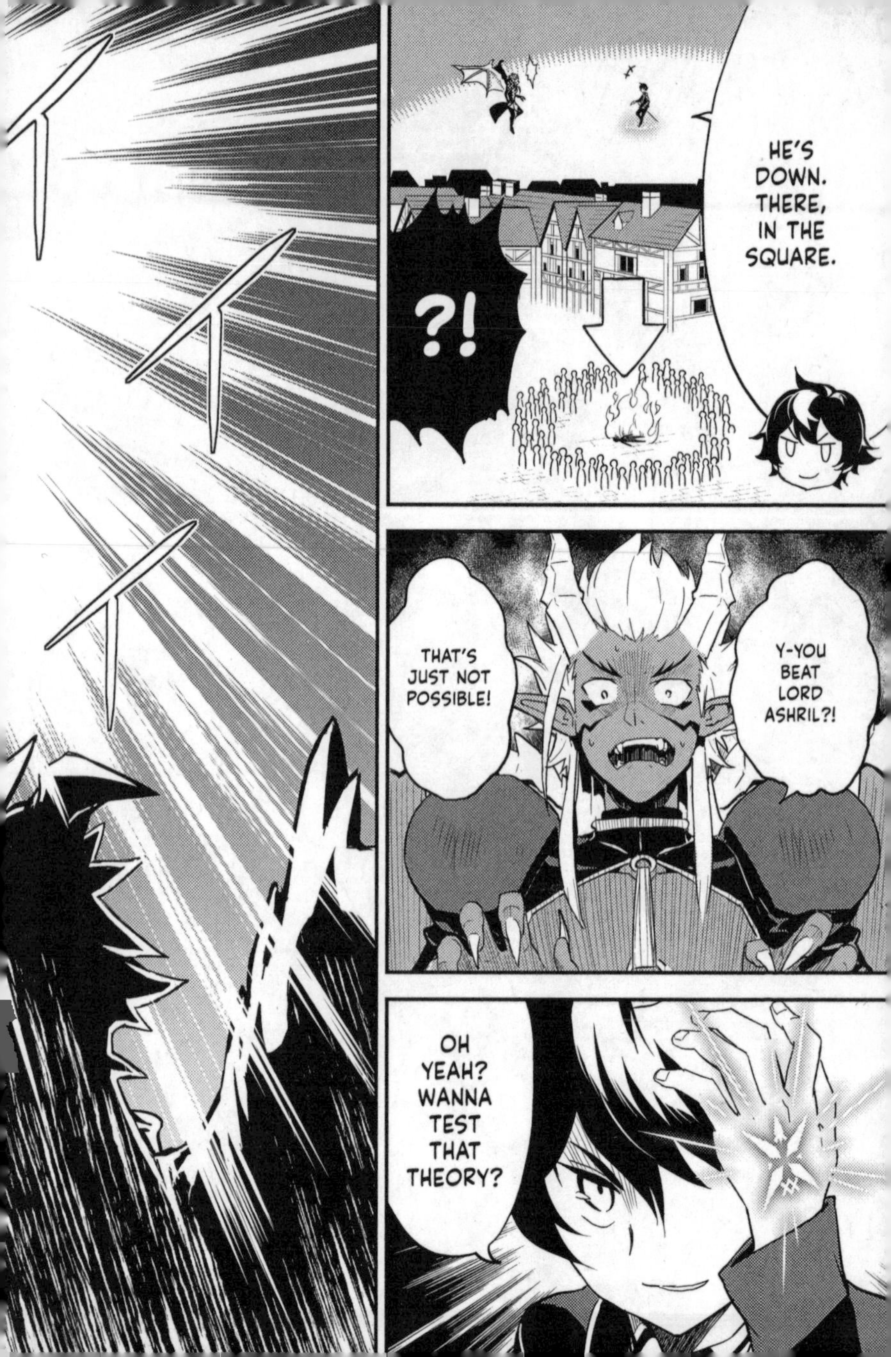
HE'S DOWN. THERE, IN THE SQUARE.
?!
Y-YOU BEAT LORD ASHRIL?!
THAT'S JUST NOT POSSIBLE!
OH YEAH? WANNA TEST THAT THEORY?

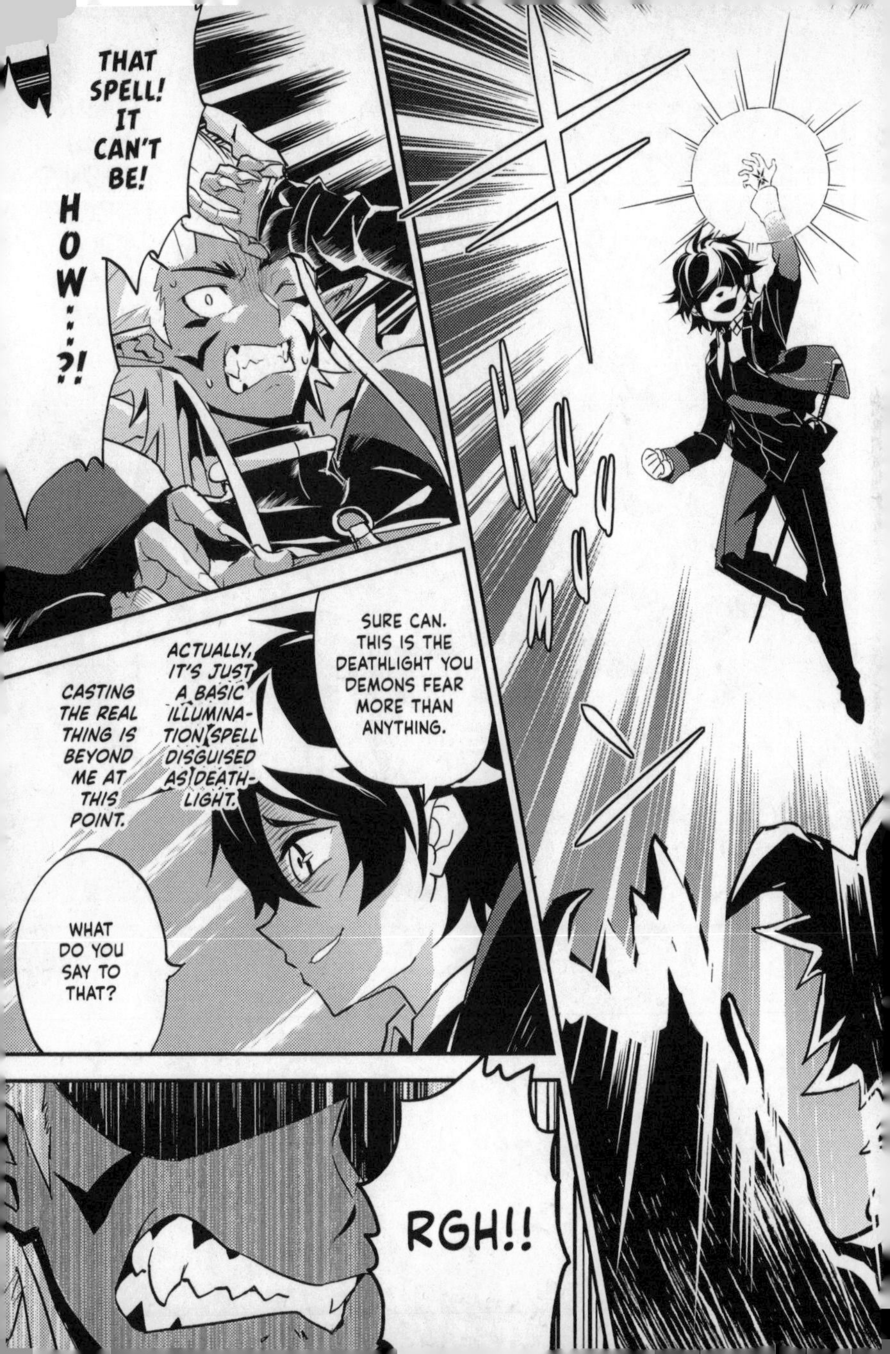
THAT SPELL! IT CAN'T BE!
HOW...?!
SURE CAN. THIS IS THE DEATHLIGHT YOU DEMONS FEAR MORE THAN ANYTHING.
ACTUALLY, IT'S JUST A BASIC ILLUMINATION SPELL DISGUISED AS DEATHLIGHT.
CASTING THE REAL THING IS BEYOND ME AT THIS POINT.
WHAT DO YOU SAY TO THAT?
RGH!!

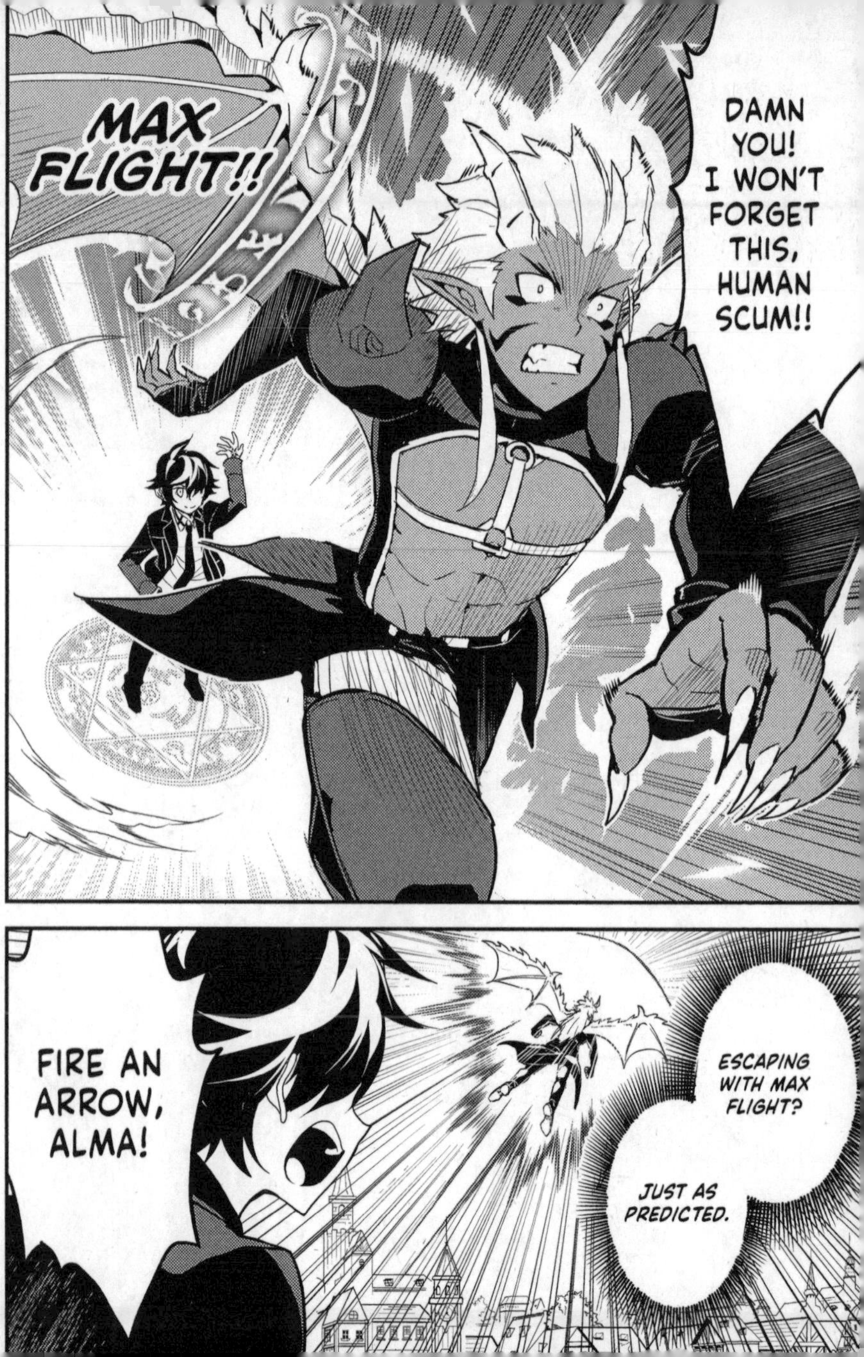
DAMN YOU! I WON'T FORGET THIS, HUMAN SCUM!!
MAX FLIGHT!!
ESCAPING WITH MAX FLIGHT?
JUST AS PREDICTED.
FIRE AN ARROW, ALMA!

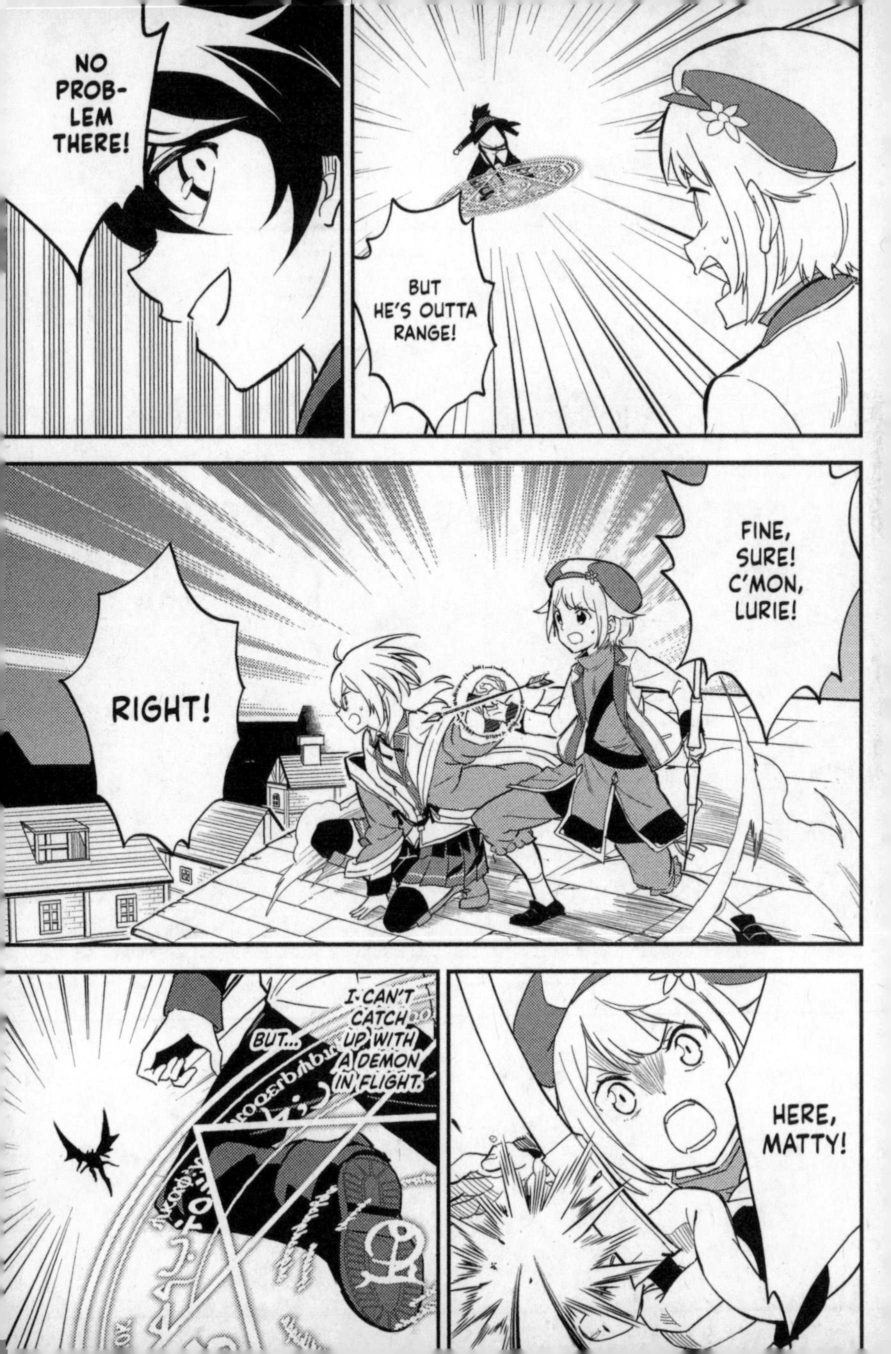
BUT HE'S OUTTA RANGE!
NO PROB-LEM THERE!
FINE, SURE! C'MON, LURIE!
RIGHT!
HERE, MATTY!
I·CAN'T CATCH UP WITH A DEMON IN FLIGHT.
BUT...

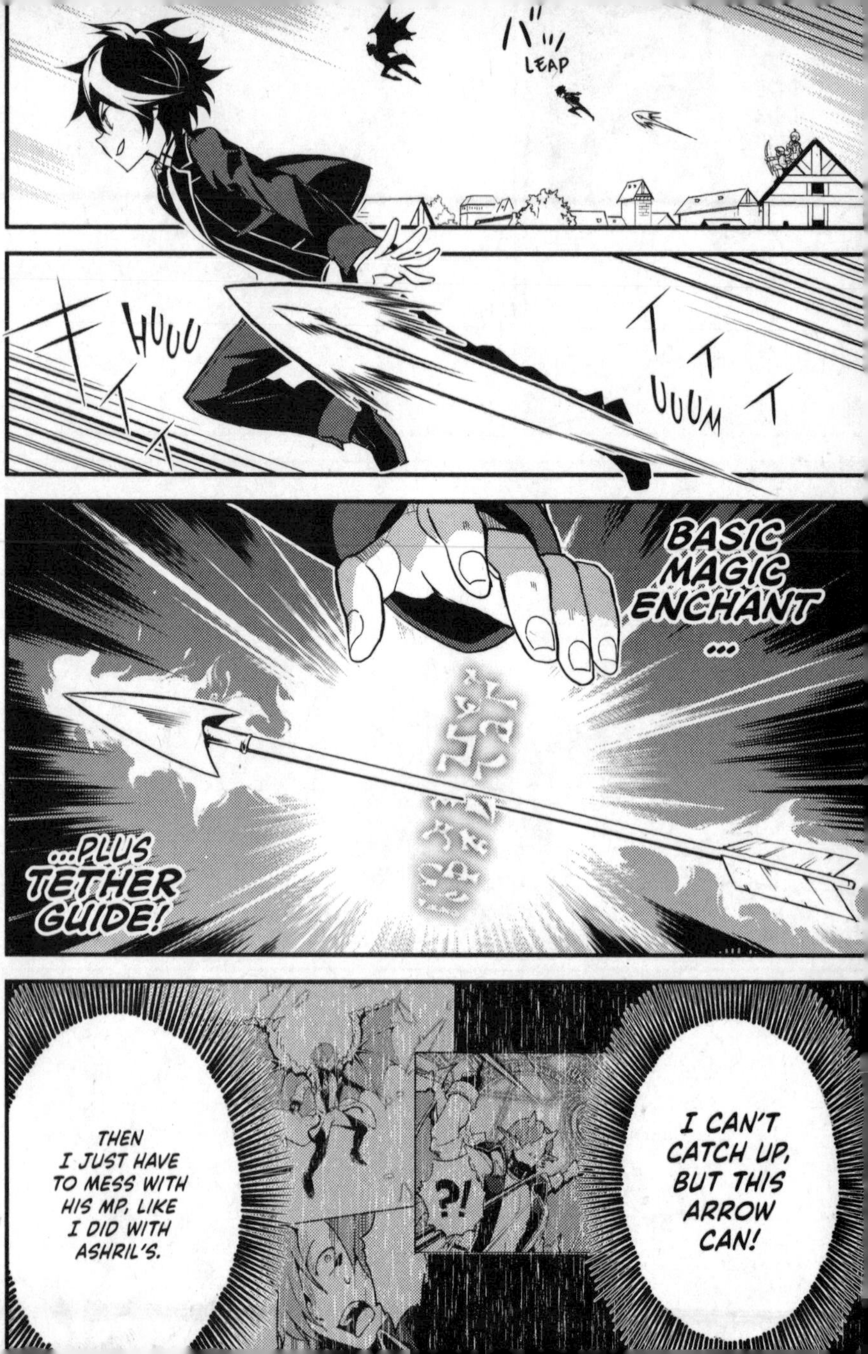
バッ
LEAP
HUUU
UUUM
BASIC MAGIC ENCHANT...
...PLUS TETHER GUIDE!
I CAN'T CATCH UP, BUT THIS ARROW CAN!
?!
THEN I JUST HAVE TO MESS WITH HIS MP, LIKE I DID WITH ASHRIL'S.

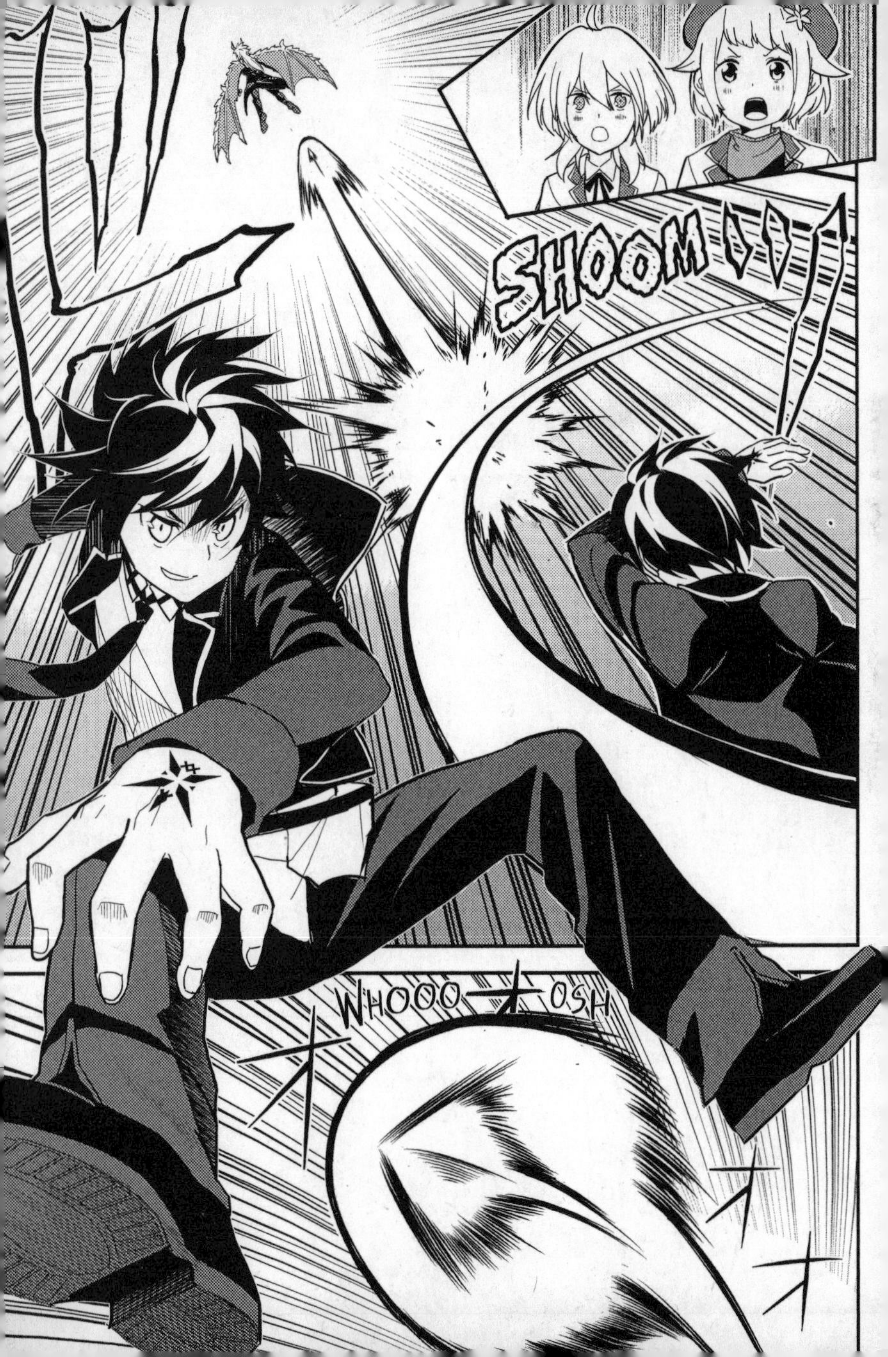
SHOOM
WHOOOOSH

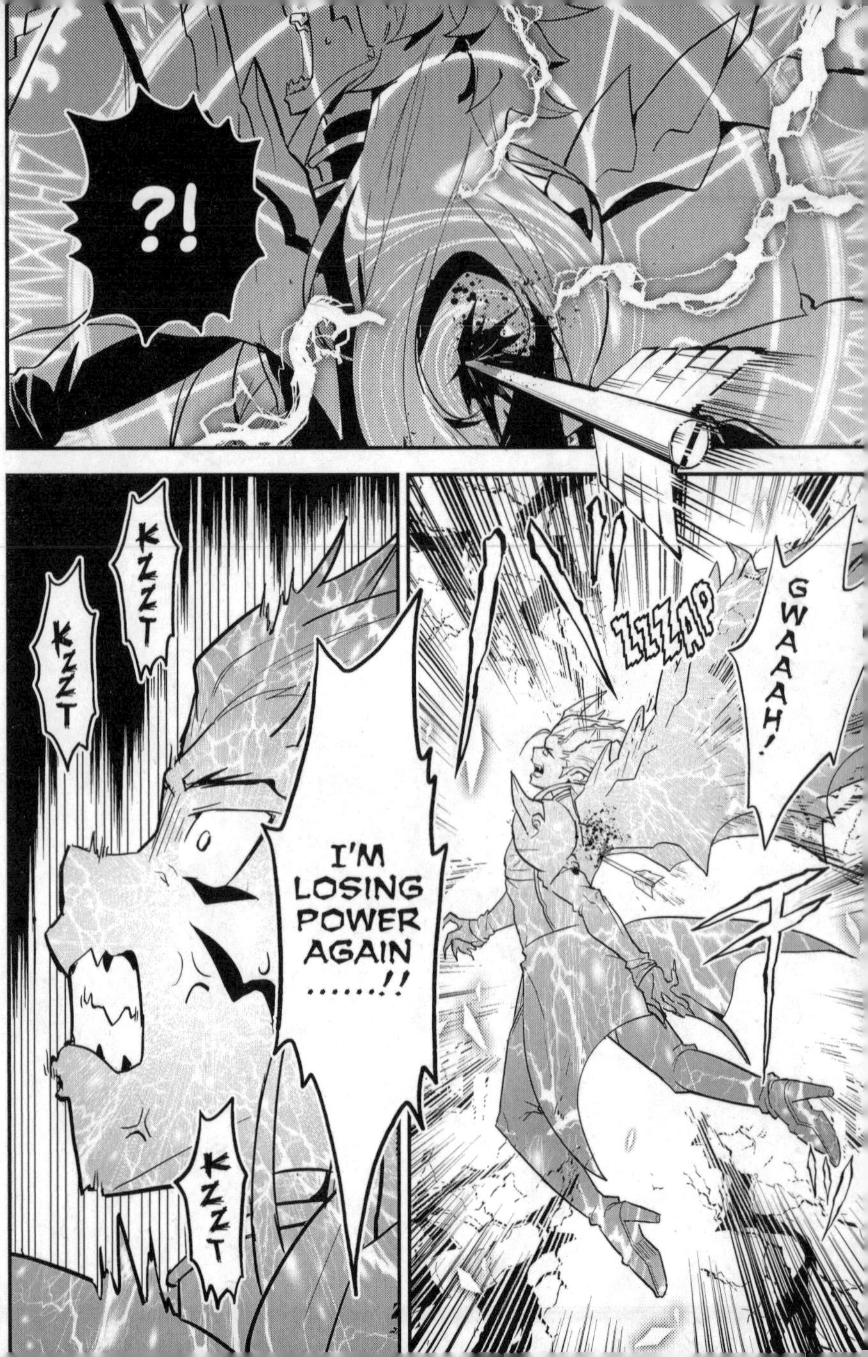
?!
ZZZAP
GWAAAH!
KZZZT
KZZZT
I'M LOSING POWER AGAIN......!!
KZZZT

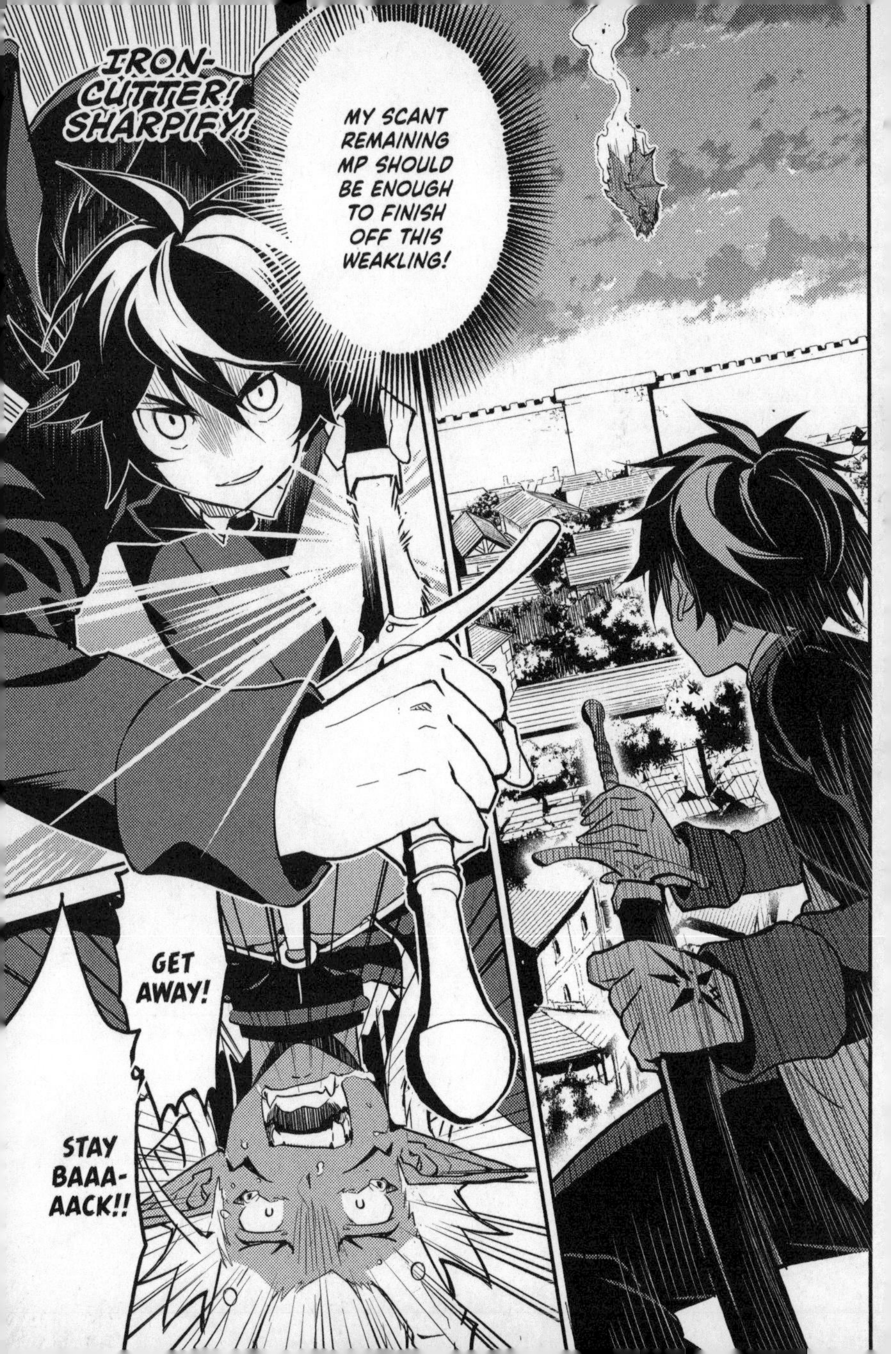
MY SCANT REMAINING MP SHOULD BE ENOUGH TO FINISH OFF THIS WEAKLING!
IRON-CUTTER! SHARPIFY!
GET AWAY!
STAY BAAAA-AACK!!

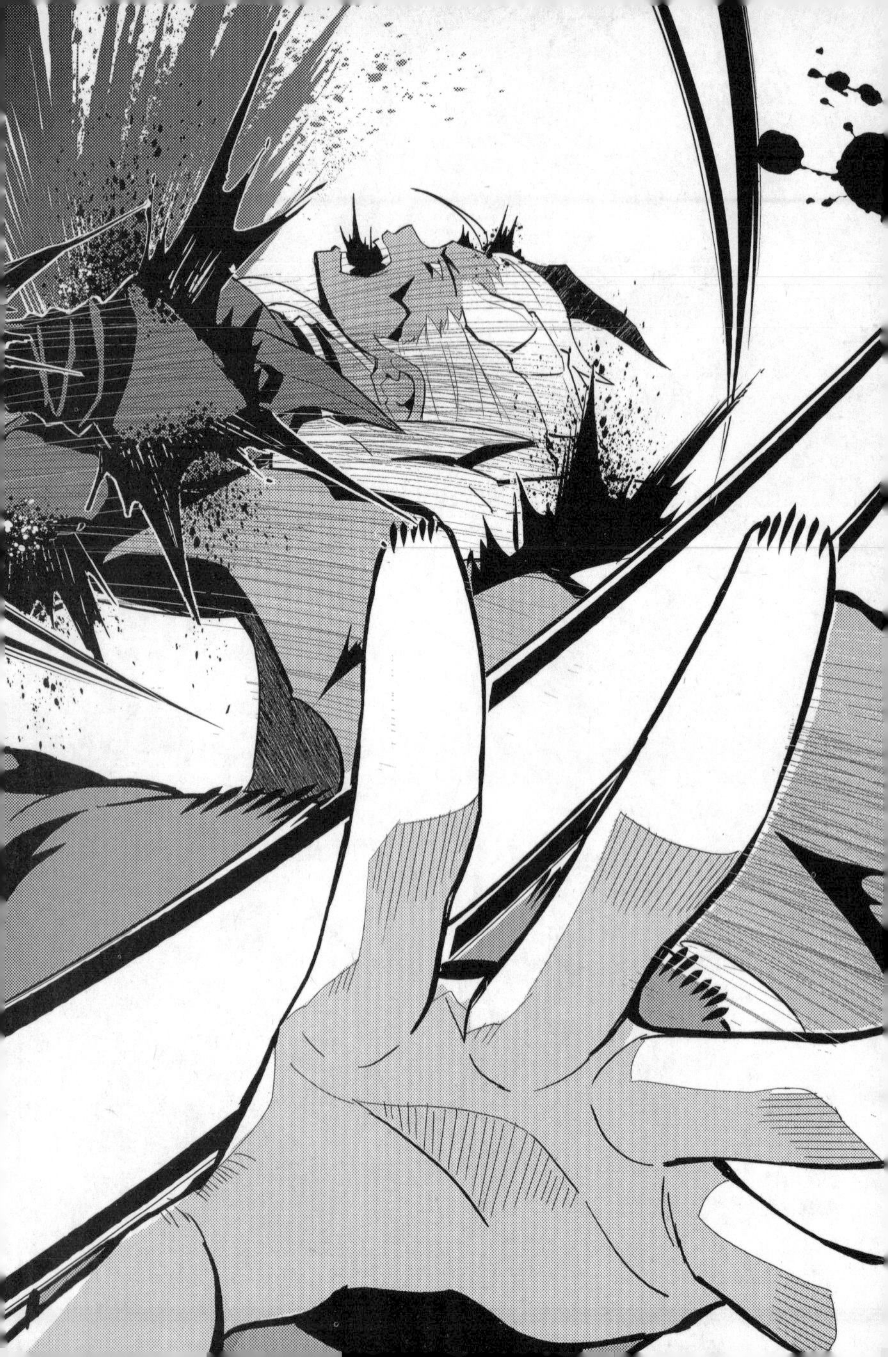

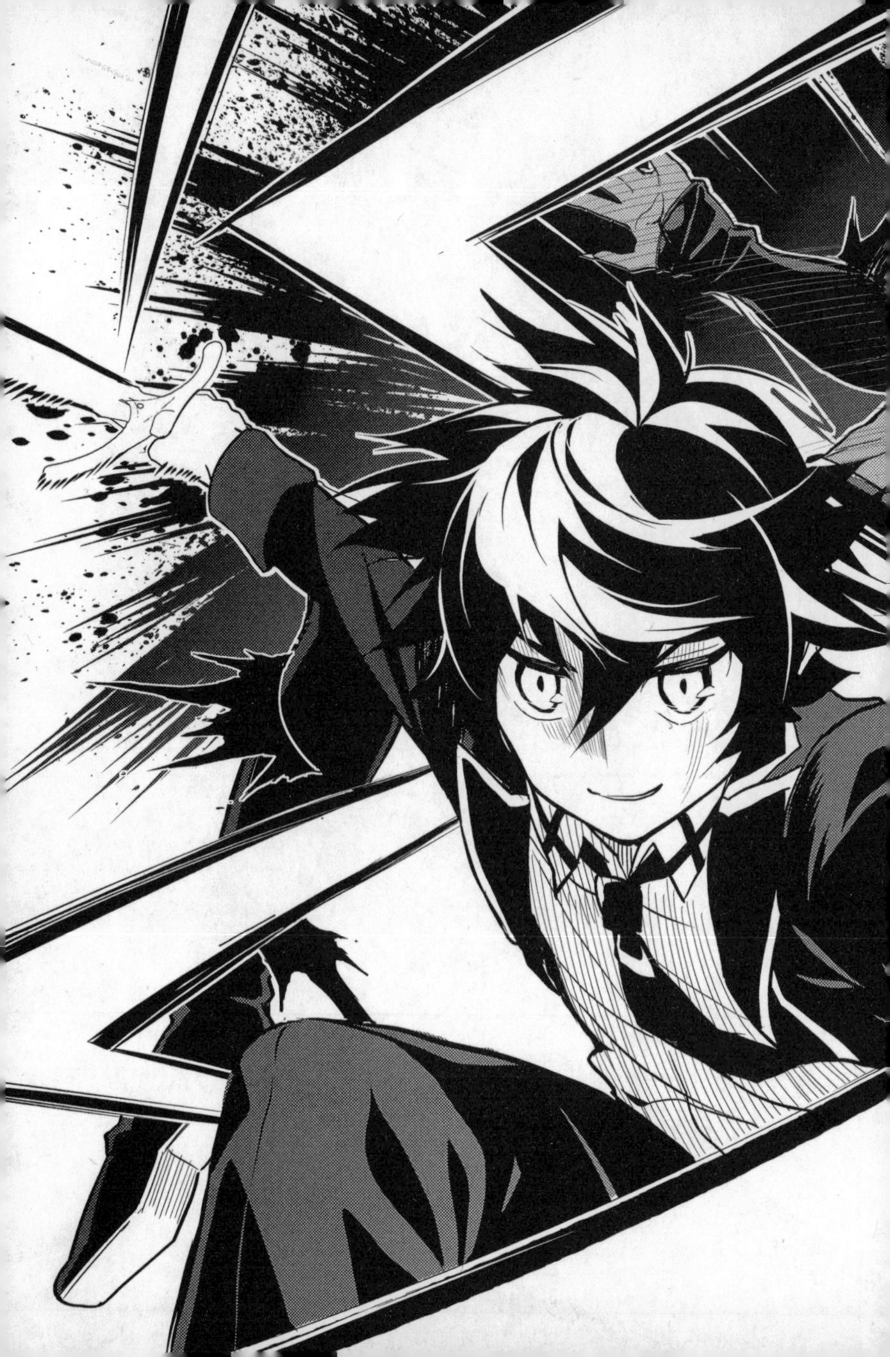

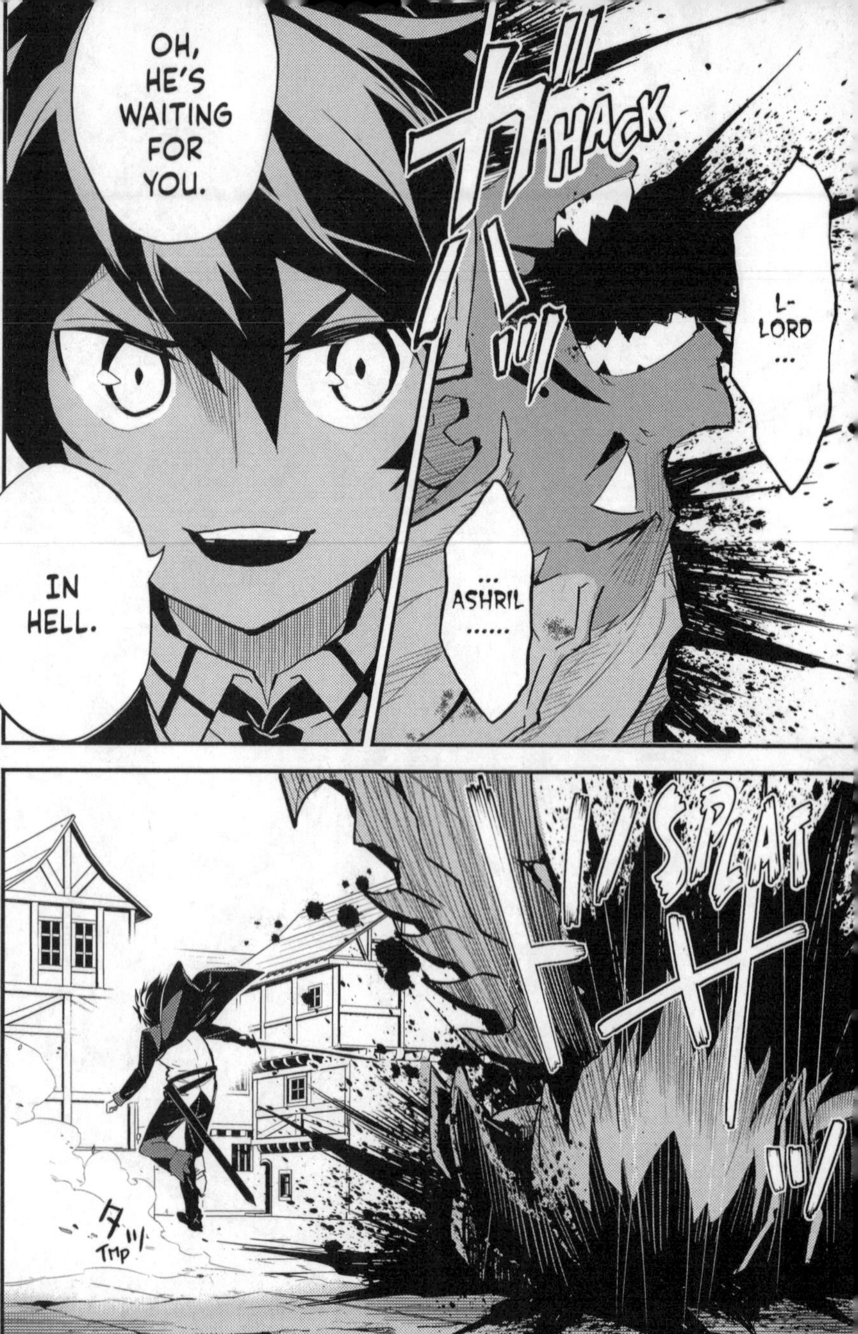
HACK
L-LORD...
...ASHRIL......
OH, HE'S WAITING FOR YOU.
IN HELL.
SPLAT
TMP

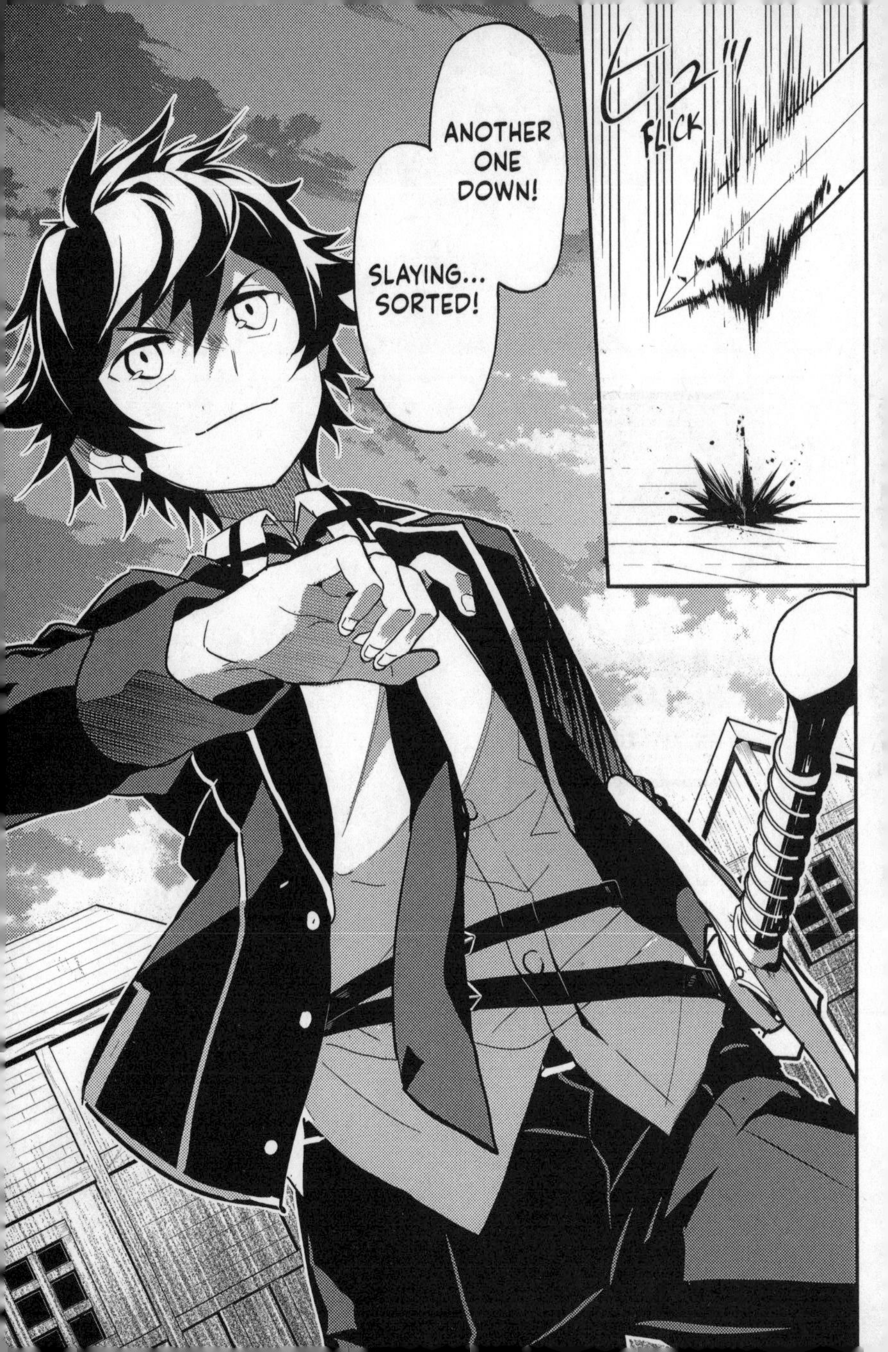
FLICK
ANOTHER ONE DOWN!
SLAYING... SORTED!

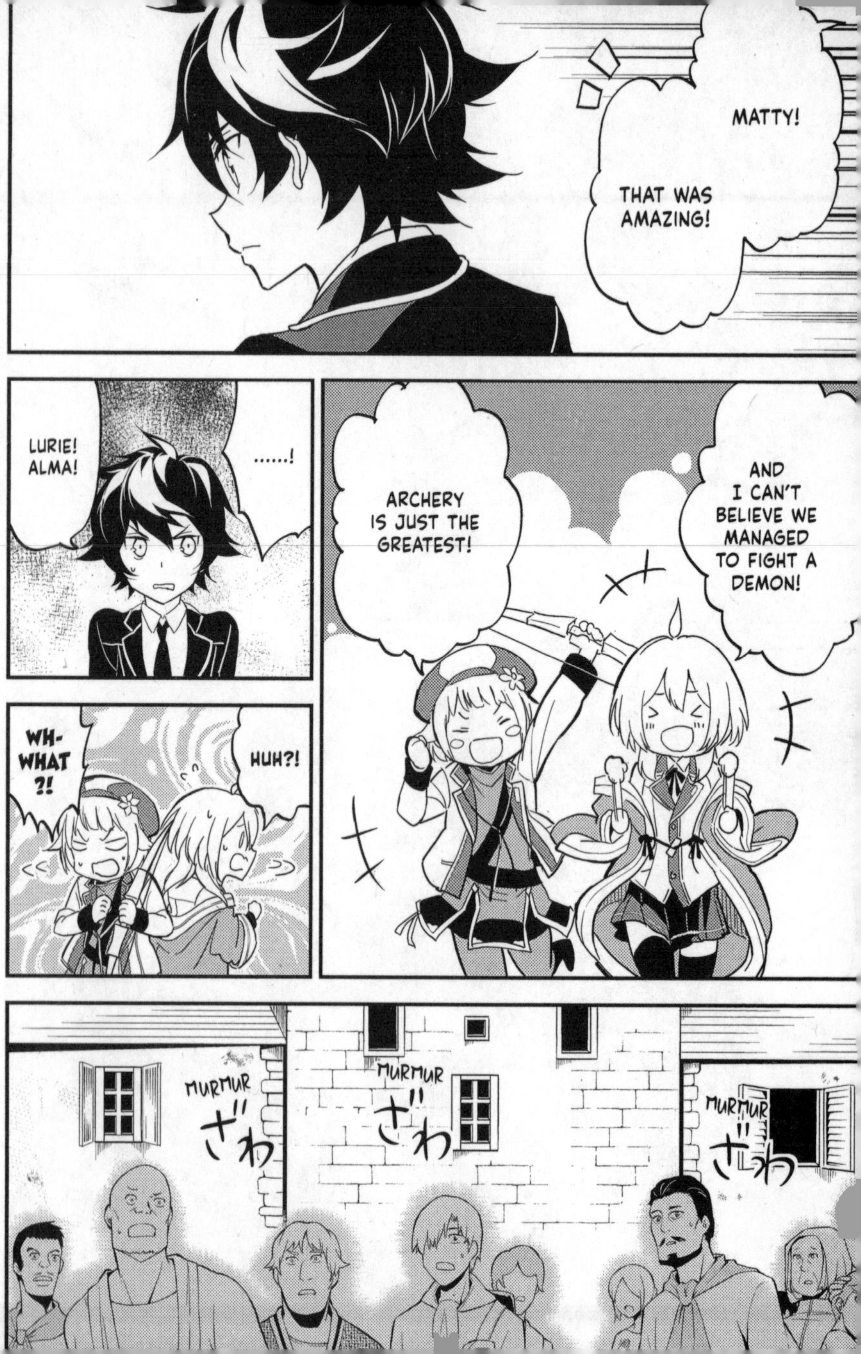
MATTY!
THAT WAS AMAZING!
AND I CAN'T BELIEVE WE MANAGED TO FIGHT A DEMON!
ARCHERY IS JUST THE GREATEST!
......!
LURIE! ALMA!
HUH?!
WH-WHAT?!
MURMUR ざわ
MURMUR ざわ
MURMUR ざわ

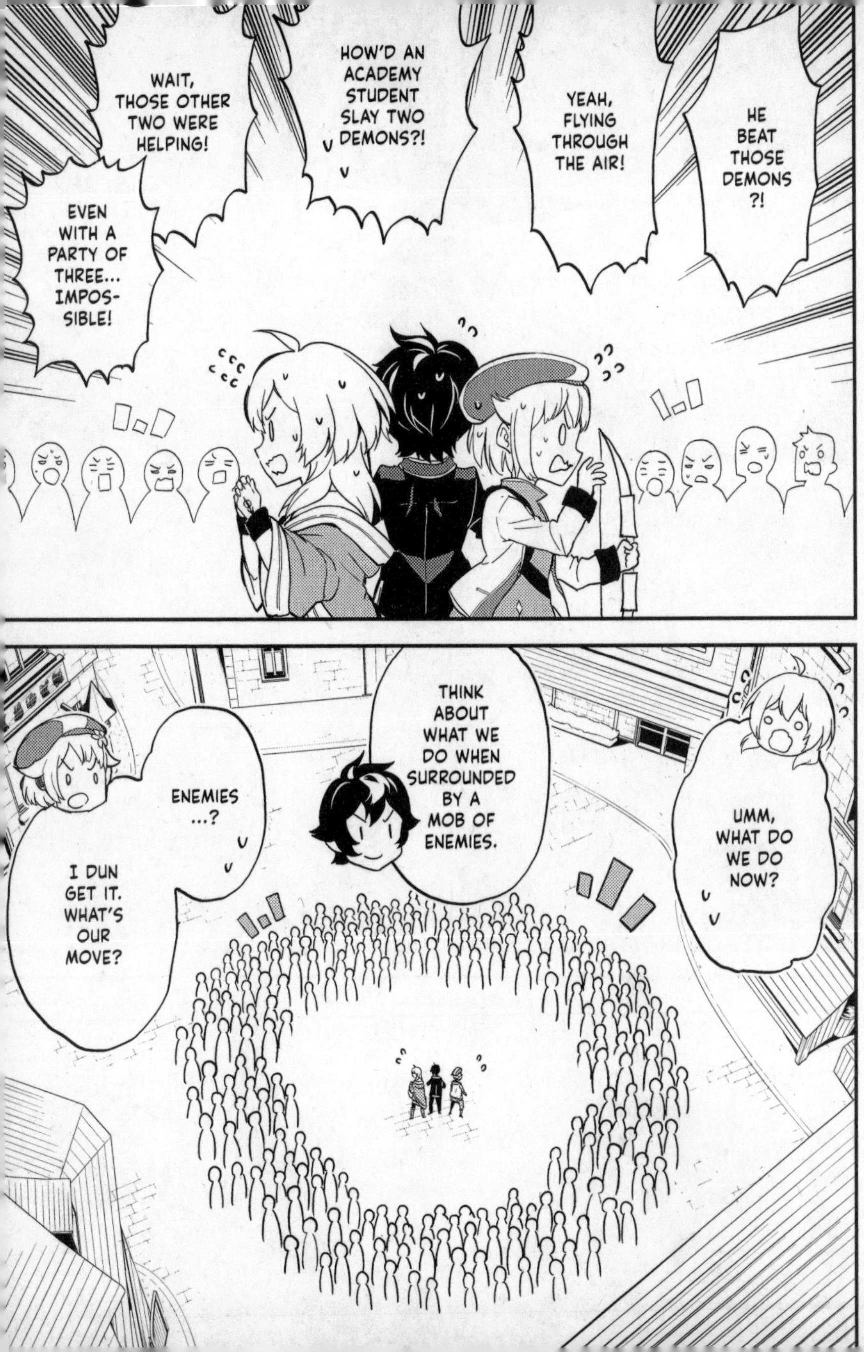
HE BEAT THOSE DEMONS?!
YEAH, FLYING THROUGH THE AIR!
HOW'D AN ACADEMY STUDENT SLAY TWO DEMONS?!
WAIT, THOSE OTHER TWO WERE HELPING!
EVEN WITH A PARTY OF THREE... IMPOSSIBLE!
UMM, WHAT DO WE DO NOW?
THINK ABOUT WHAT WE DO WHEN SURROUNDED BY A MOB OF ENEMIES.
ENEMIES ...?
I DUN GET IT. WHAT'S OUR MOVE?

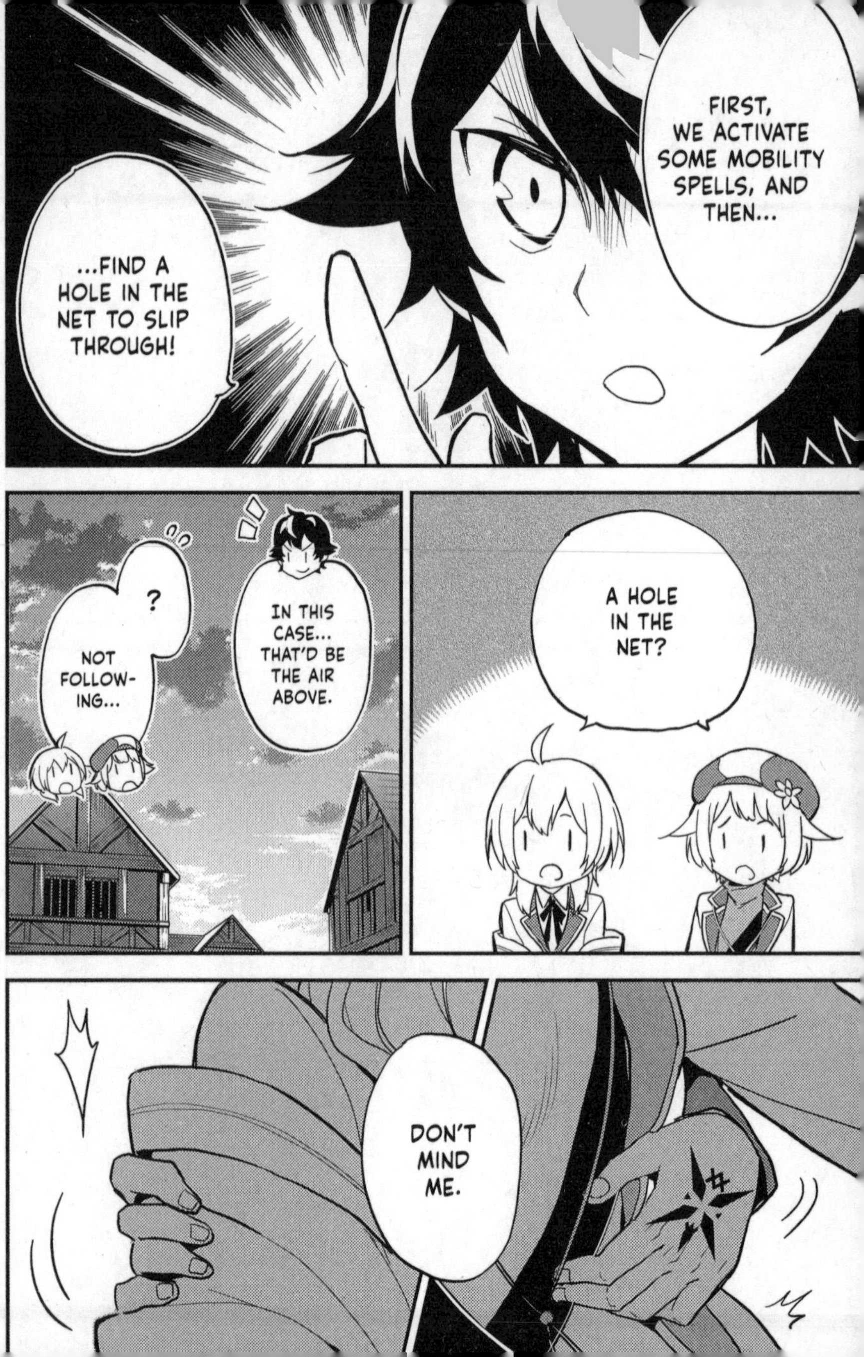
FIRST, WE ACTIVATE SOME MOBILITY SPELLS, AND THEN...
...FIND A HOLE IN THE NET TO SLIP THROUGH!
A HOLE IN THE NET?
IN THIS CASE... THAT'D BE THE AIR ABOVE.
? NOT FOLLOWING...
DON'T MIND ME.

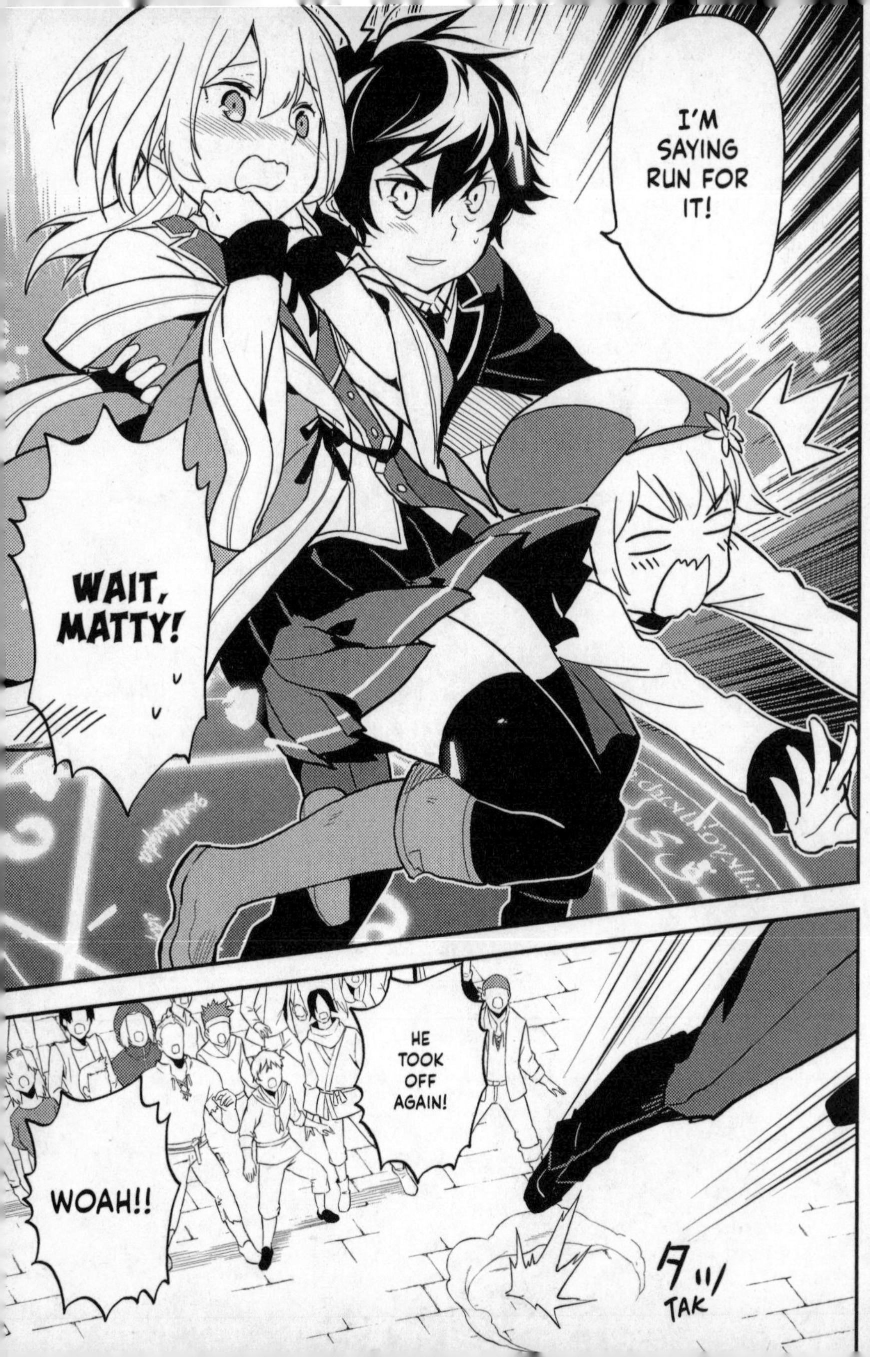
I'M SAYING RUN FOR IT!
WAIT, MATTY!
HE TOOK OFF AGAIN!
タッ
TAK
WOAH!!

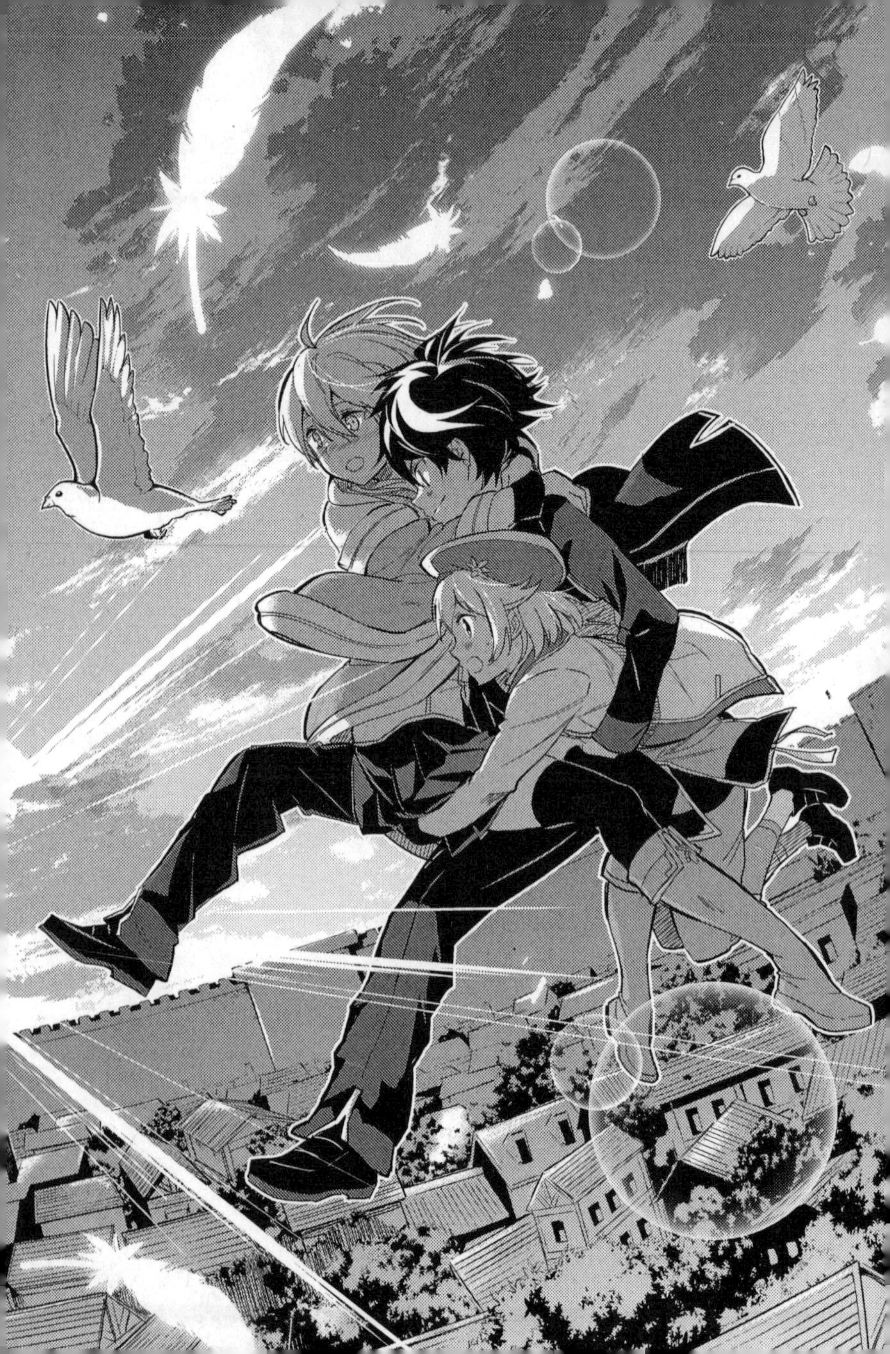

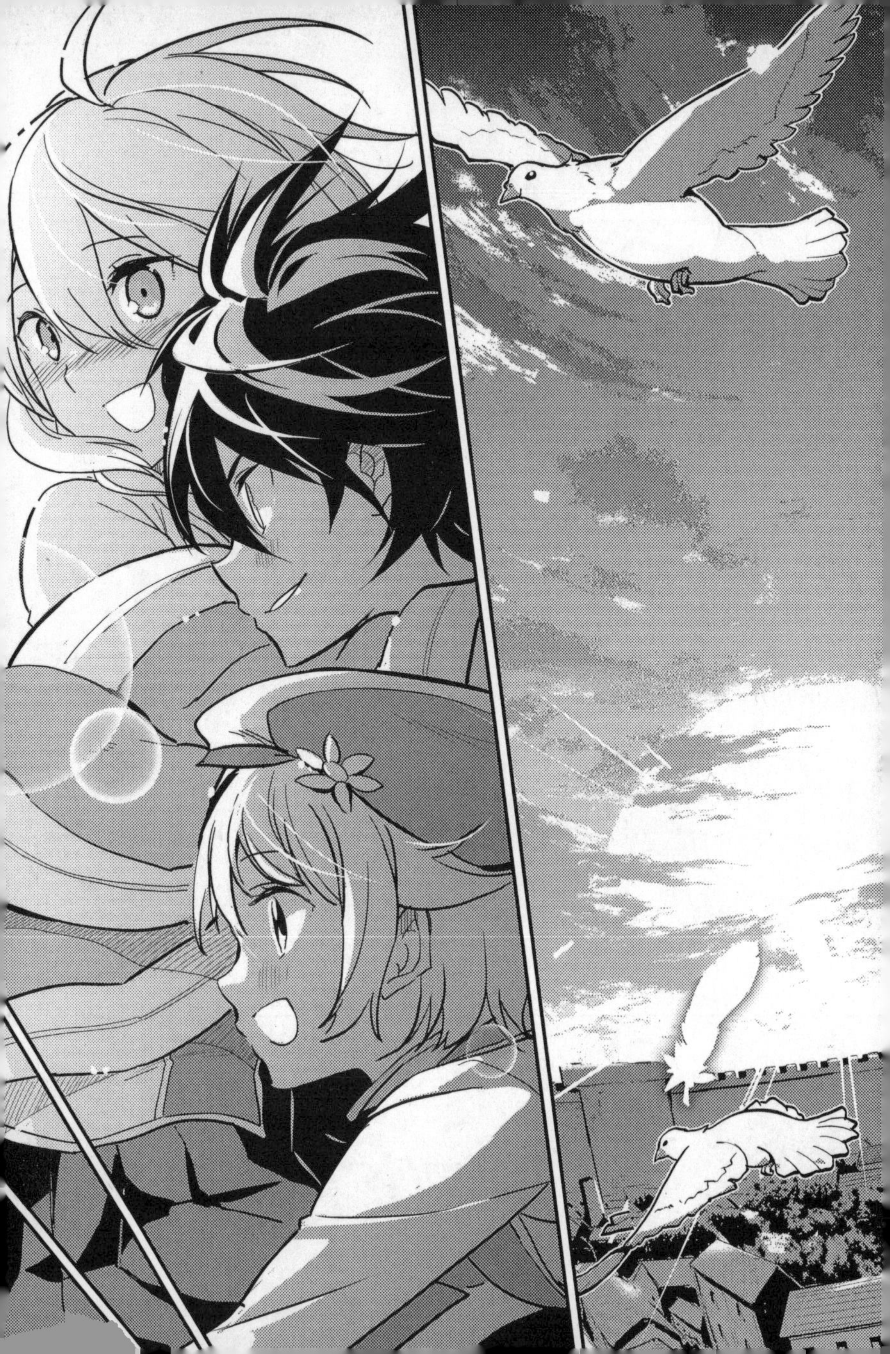

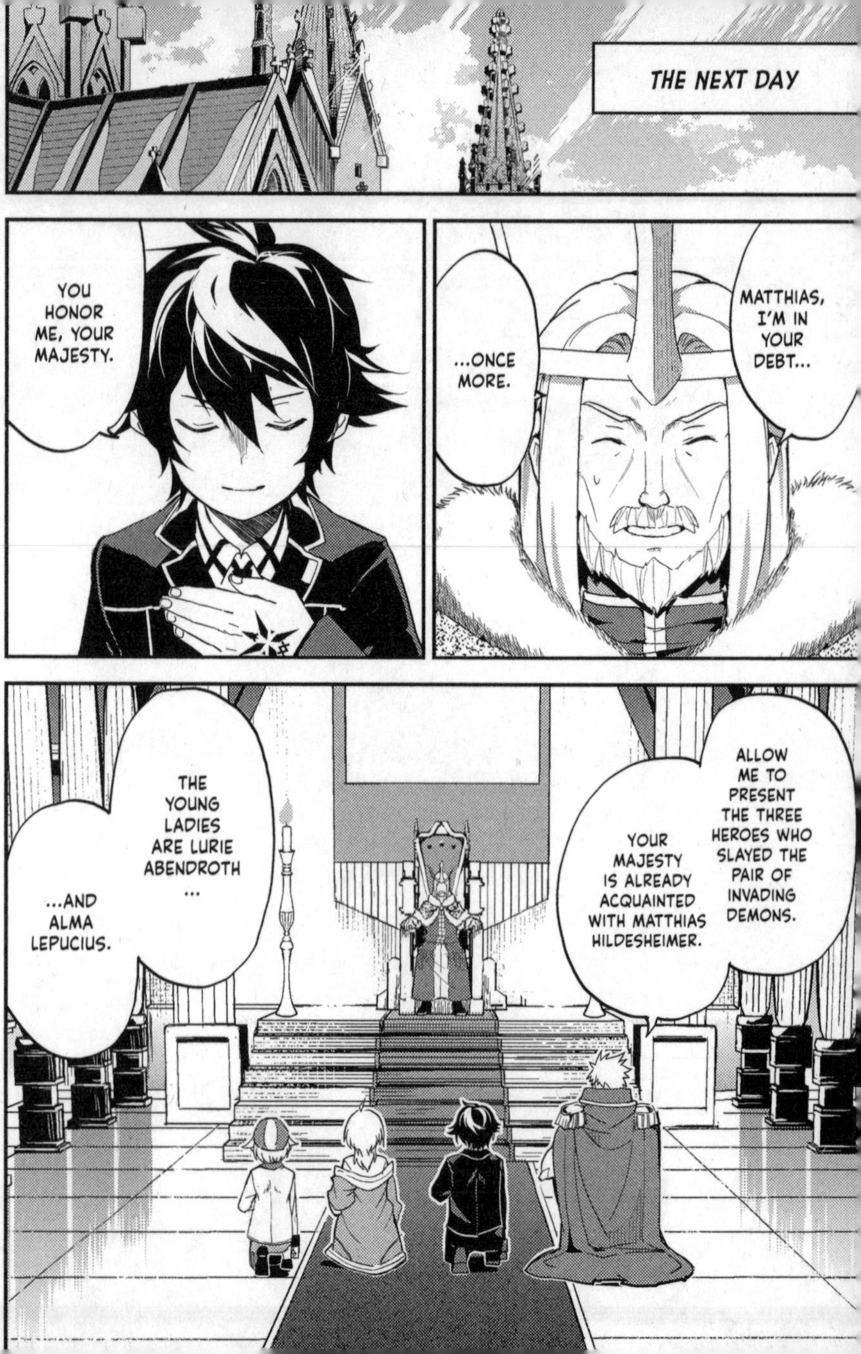
THE NEXT DAY
MATTHIAS, I'M IN YOUR DEBT...
...ONCE MORE.
YOU HONOR ME, YOUR MAJESTY.
ALLOW ME TO PRESENT THE THREE HEROES WHO SLAYED THE PAIR OF INVADING DEMONS.
YOUR MAJESTY IS ALREADY ACQUAINTED WITH MATTHIAS HILDESHEIMER.
THE YOUNG LADIES ARE LURIE ABENDROTH ...
...AND ALMA LEPUCIUS.

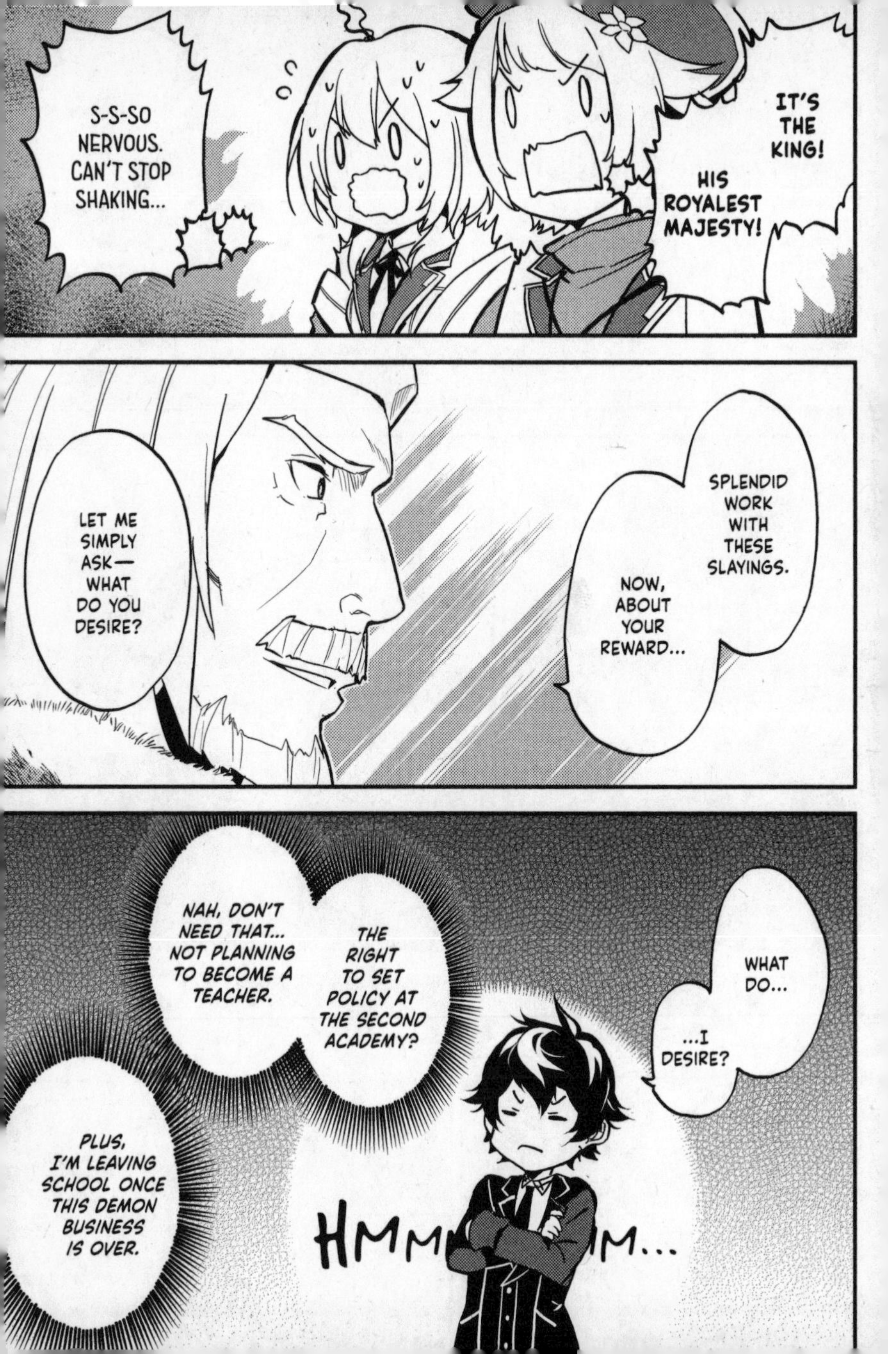
IT'S THE KING!
HIS ROYALEST MAJESTY!
S-S-SO NERVOUS. CAN'T STOP SHAKING...
SPLENDID WORK WITH THESE SLAYINGS.
NOW, ABOUT YOUR REWARD...
LET ME SIMPLY ASK—WHAT DO YOU DESIRE?
WHAT DO...
...I DESIRE?
HMM
MM...
THE RIGHT TO SET POLICY AT THE SECOND ACADEMY?
NAH, DON'T NEED THAT... NOT PLANNING TO BECOME A TEACHER.
PLUS, I'M LEAVING SCHOOL ONCE THIS DEMON BUSINESS IS OVER.

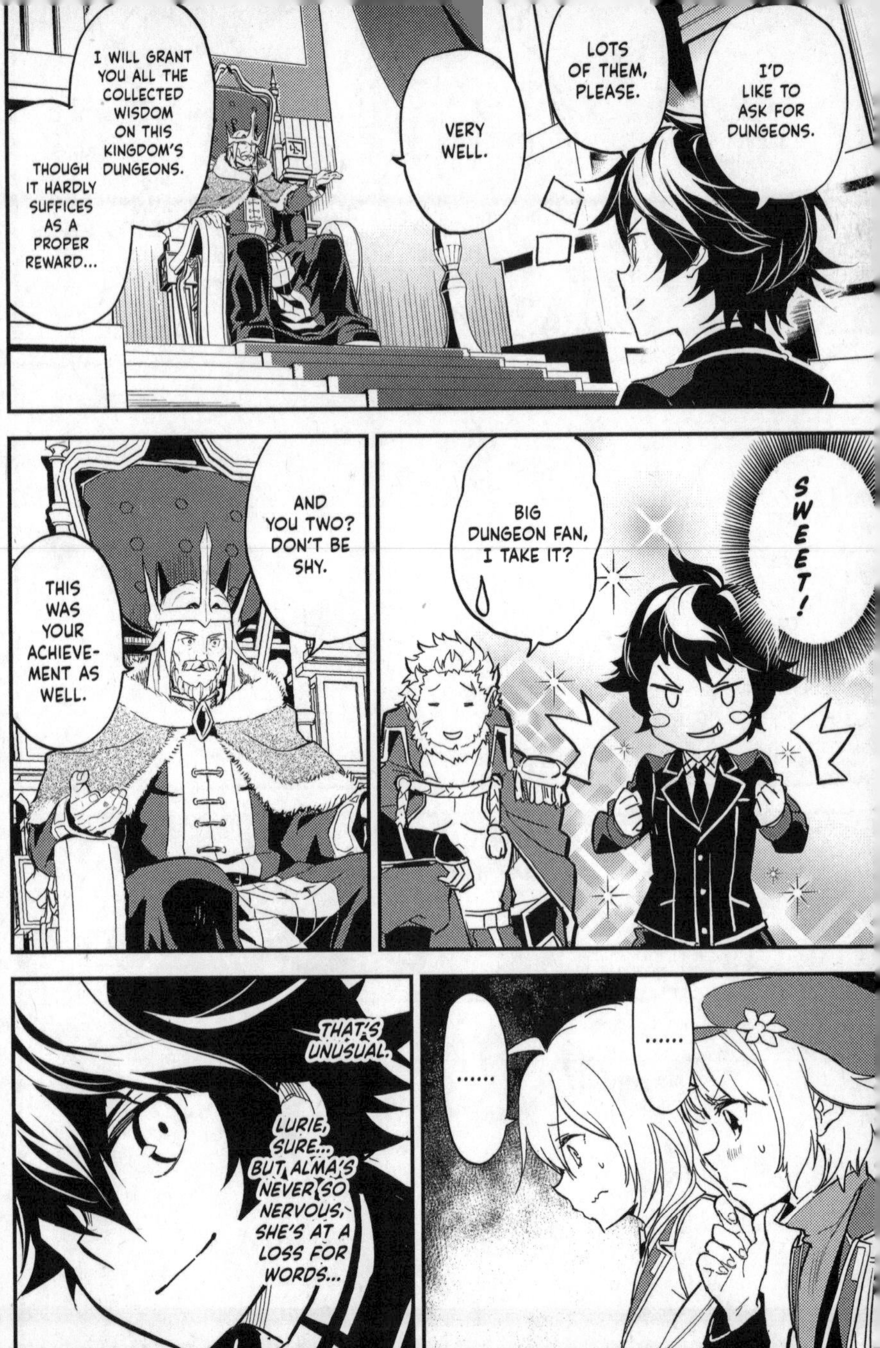
I'D LIKE TO ASK FOR DUNGEONS.
LOTS OF THEM, PLEASE.
VERY WELL.
I WILL GRANT YOU ALL THE COLLECTED WISDOM ON THIS KINGDOM'S DUNGEONS.
THOUGH IT HARDLY SUFFICES AS A PROPER REWARD...
SWEET!
BIG DUNGEON FAN, I TAKE IT?
AND YOU TWO? DON'T BE SHY.
THIS WAS YOUR ACHIEVEMENT AS WELL.
......
......
THAT'S UNUSUAL.
LURIE, SURE... BUT ALMA'S NEVER SO NERVOUS, SHE'S AT A LOSS FOR WORDS...

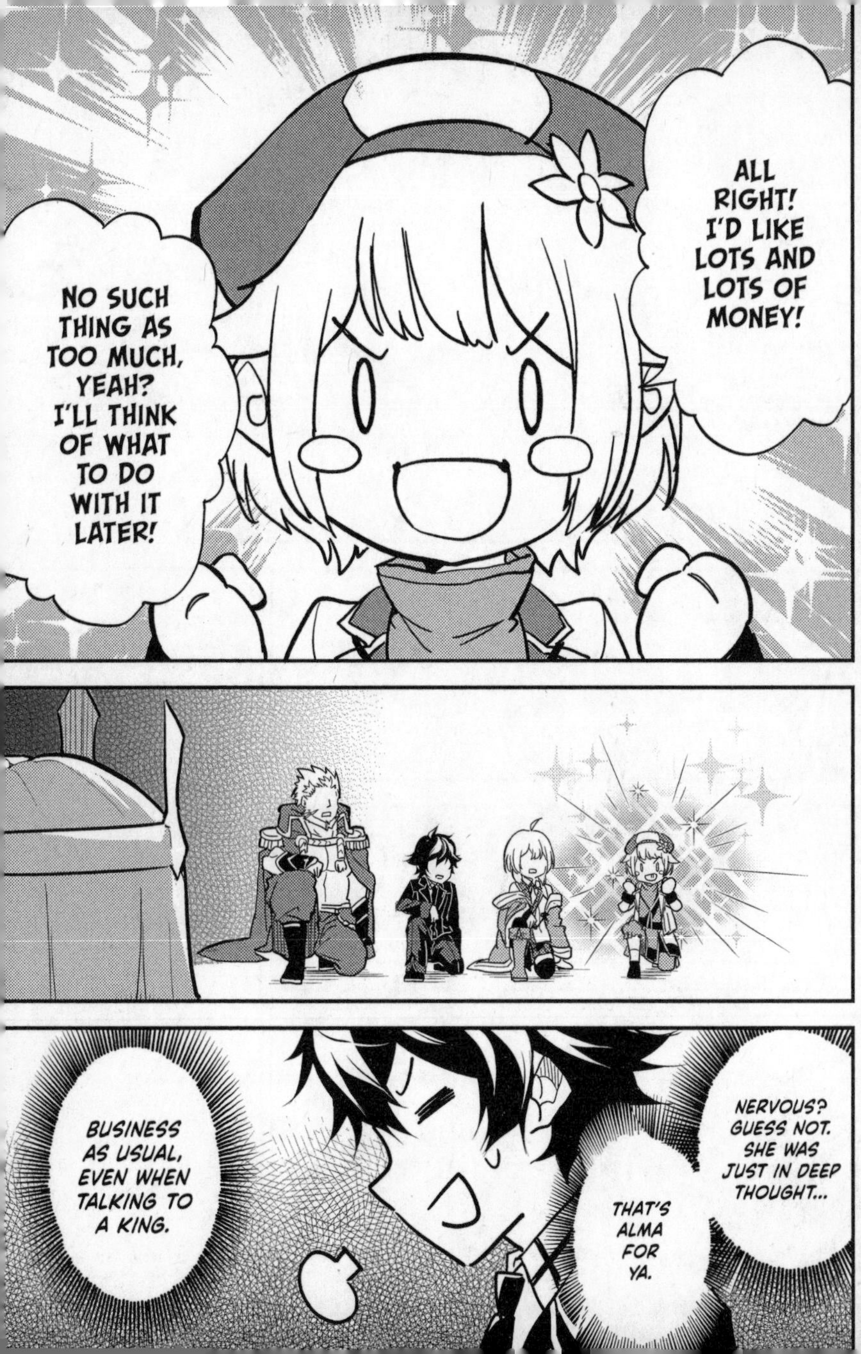
ALL RIGHT! I'D LIKE LOTS AND LOTS OF MONEY!
NO SUCH THING AS TOO MUCH, YEAH? I'LL THINK OF WHAT TO DO WITH IT LATER!
NERVOUS? GUESS NOT. SHE WAS JUST IN DEEP THOUGHT...
BUSINESS AS USUAL, EVEN WHEN TALKING TO A KING.
THAT'S ALMA FOR YA.

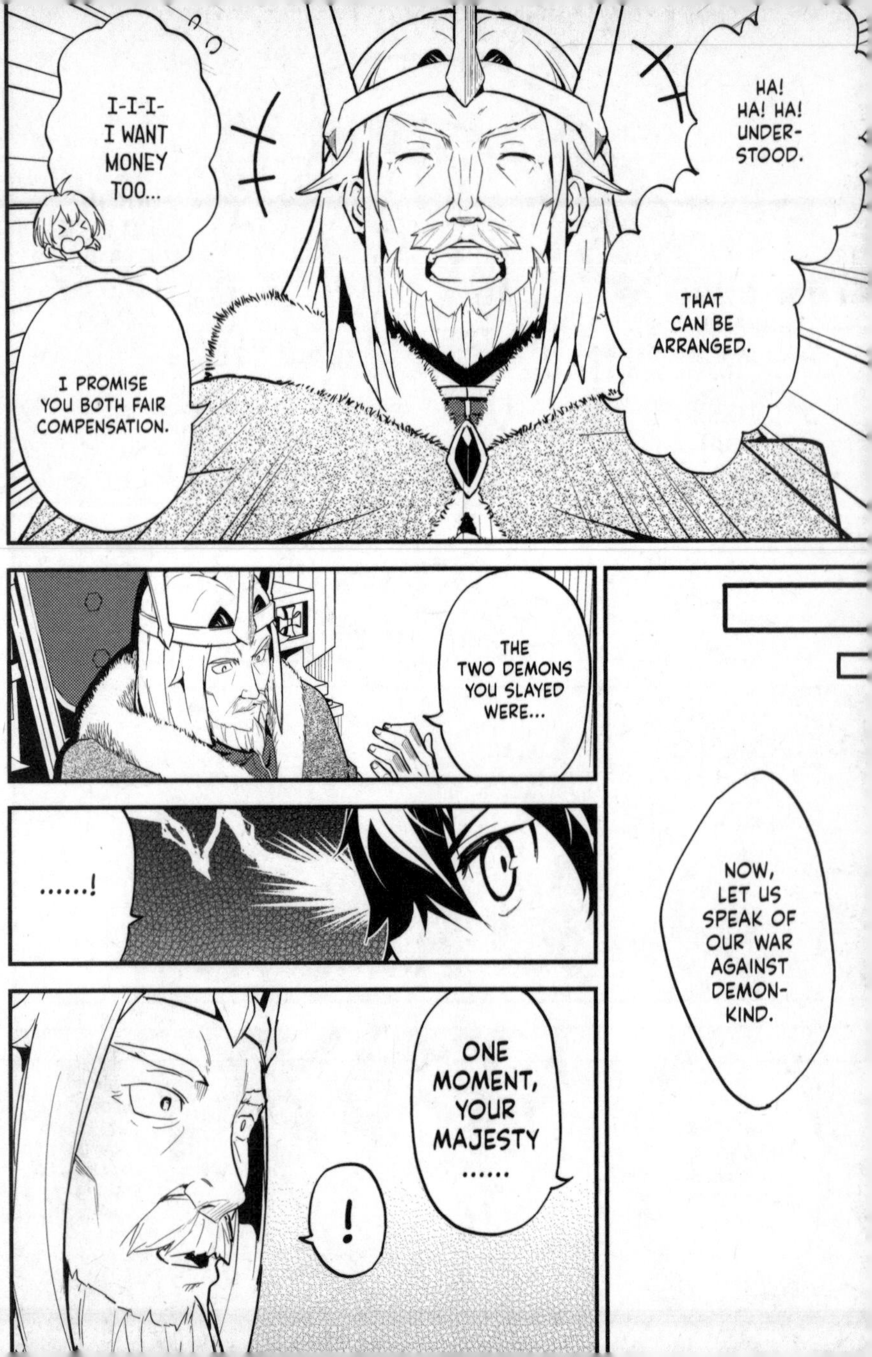
HA! HA! HA! UNDER-STOOD.
THAT CAN BE ARRANGED.
I-I-I- I WANT MONEY TOO...
I PROMISE YOU BOTH FAIR COMPENSATION.
NOW, LET US SPEAK OF OUR WAR AGAINST DEMON-KIND.
THE TWO DEMONS YOU SLAYED WERE...
......!
ONE MOMENT, YOUR MAJESTY ......
!

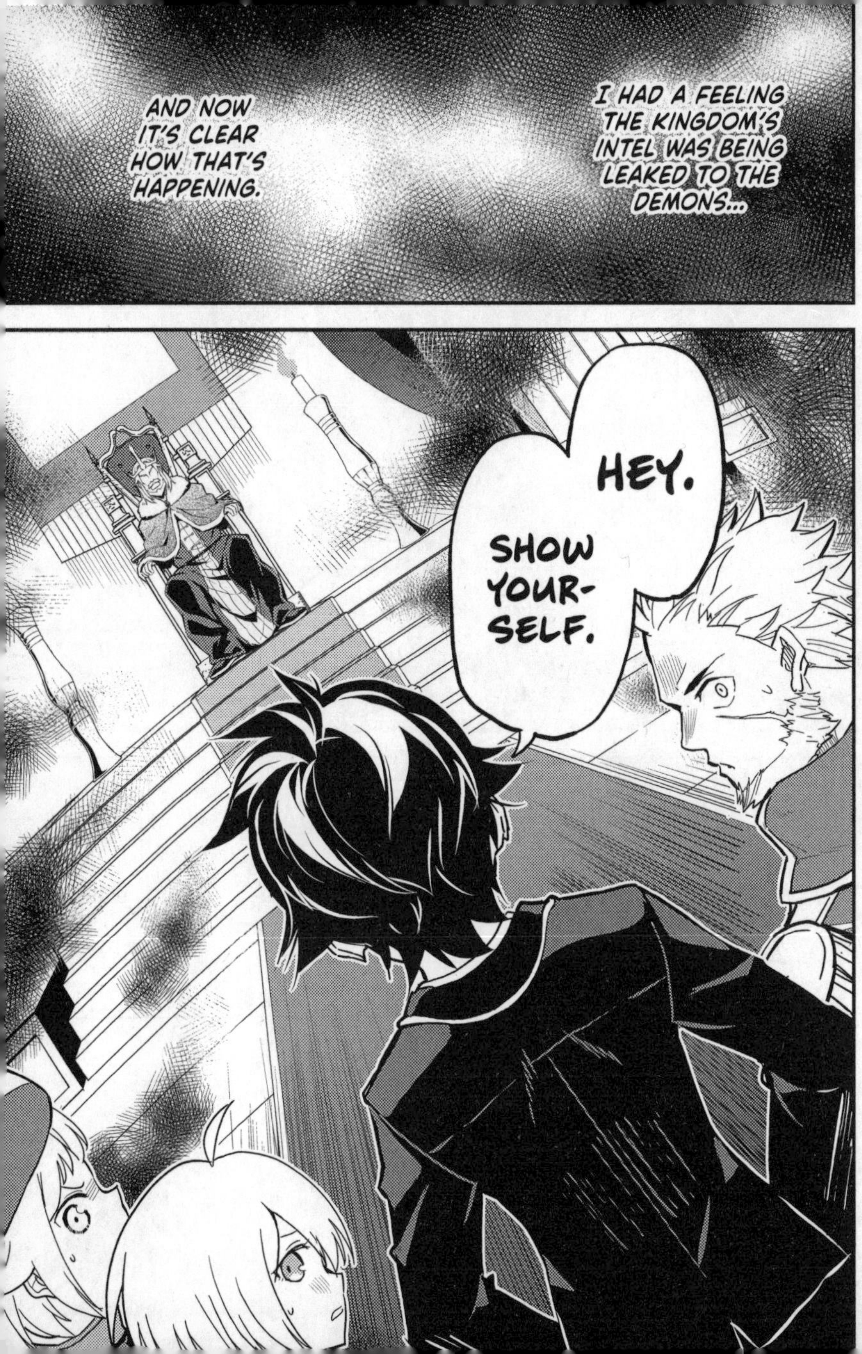
I HAD A FEELING THE KINGDOM'S INTEL WAS BEING LEAKED TO THE DEMONS...
AND NOW IT'S CLEAR HOW THAT'S HAPPENING.
HEY.
SHOW YOURSELF.

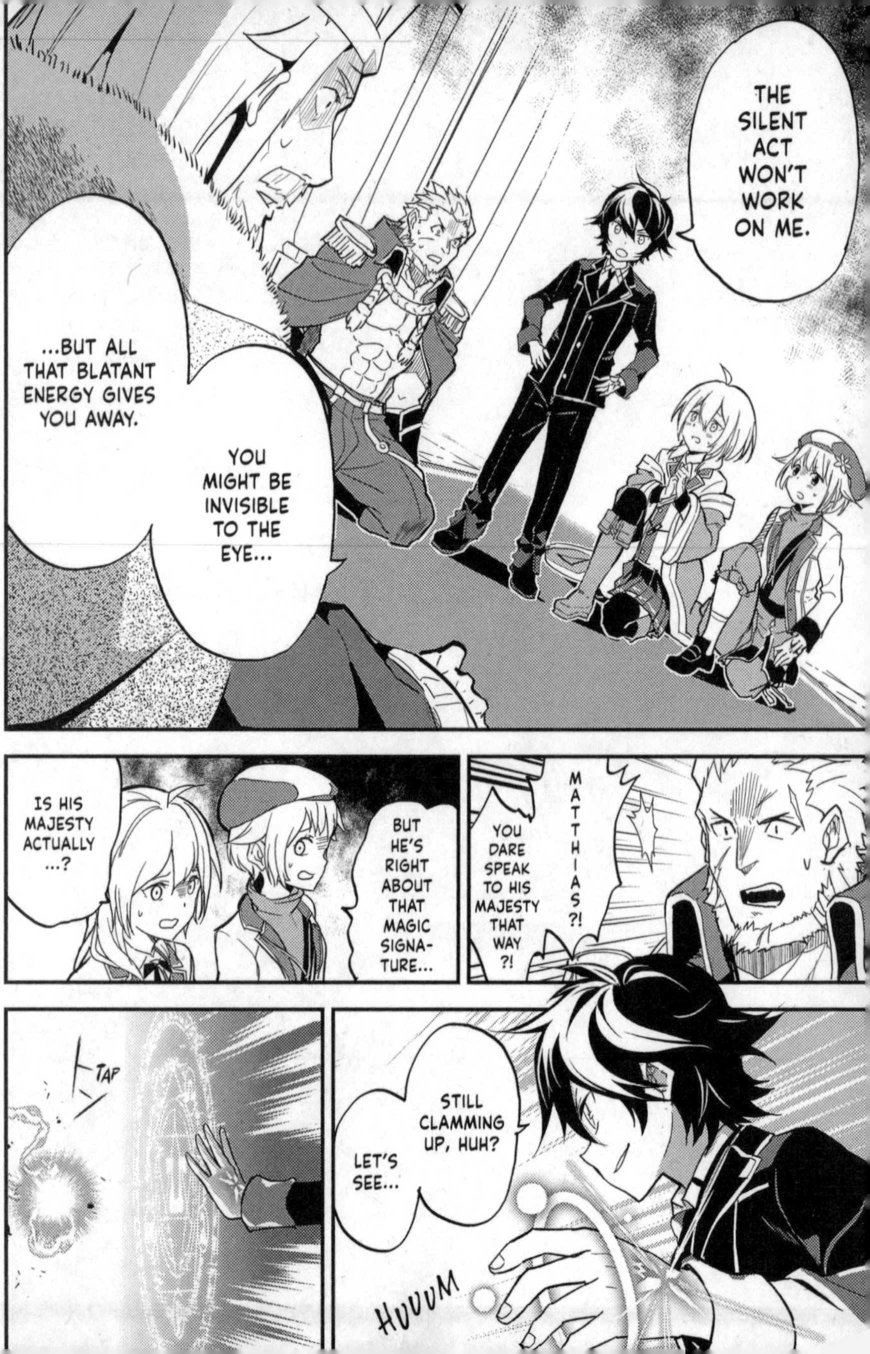
THE SILENT ACT WON'T WORK ON ME.
YOU MIGHT BE INVISIBLE TO THE EYE...
...BUT ALL THAT BLATANT ENERGY GIVES YOU AWAY.
MATTHIAS?!
YOU DARE SPEAK TO HIS MAJESTY THAT WAY?!
BUT HE'S RIGHT ABOUT THAT MAGIC SIGNATURE...
IS HIS MAJESTY ACTUALLY ...?
STILL CLAMMING UP, HUH?
LET'S SEE...
HUUUM
TAP

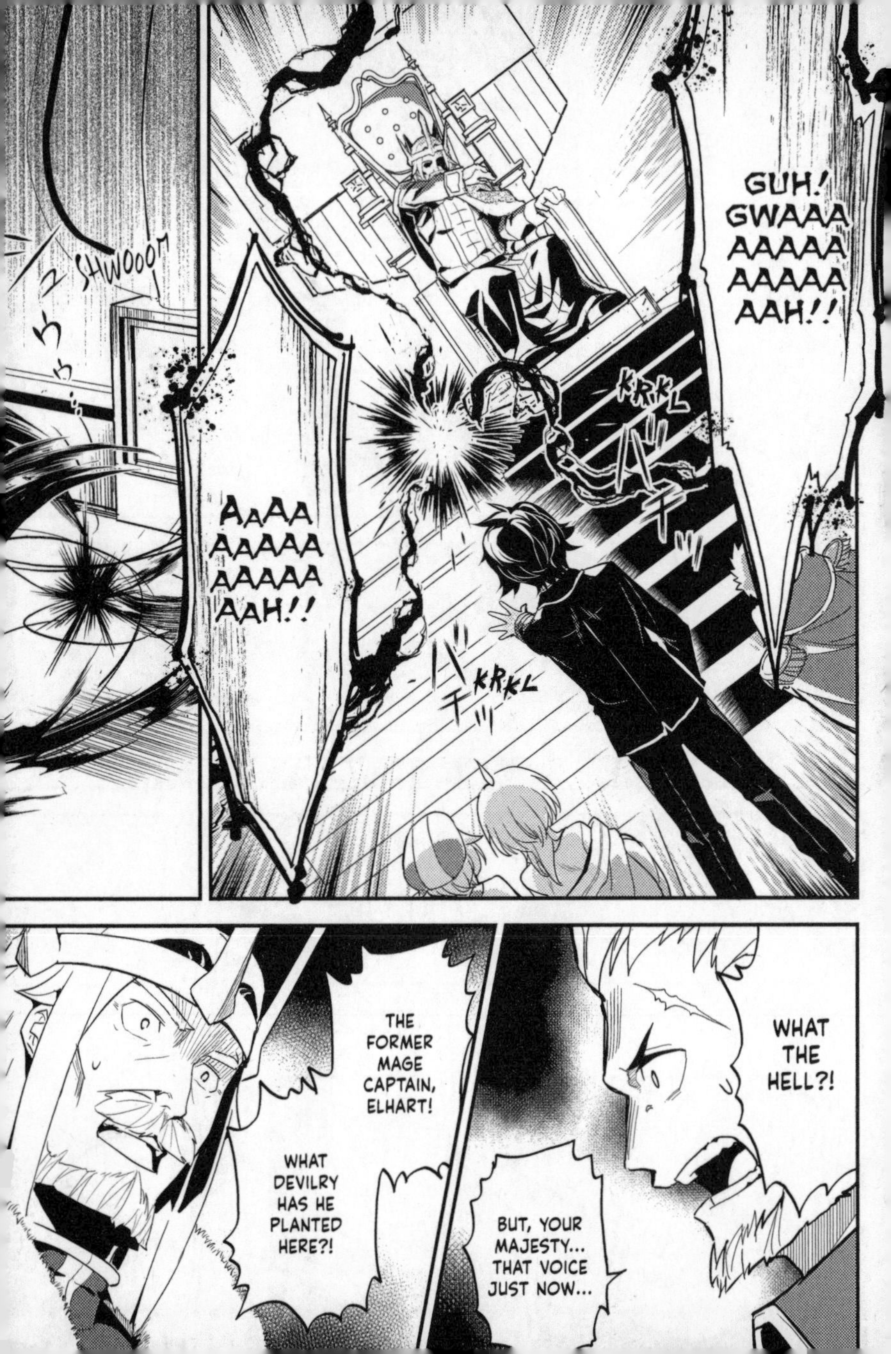
GUH! GWAAA AAAAA AAAAA AAH!!
KRKL
AAAA AAAAA AAAAA AAH!!
KRKL
SHWOOOM
WHAT THE HELL?!
BUT, YOUR MAJESTY... THAT VOICE JUST NOW...
THE FORMER MAGE CAPTAIN, ELHART!
WHAT DEVILRY HAS HE PLANTED HERE?!

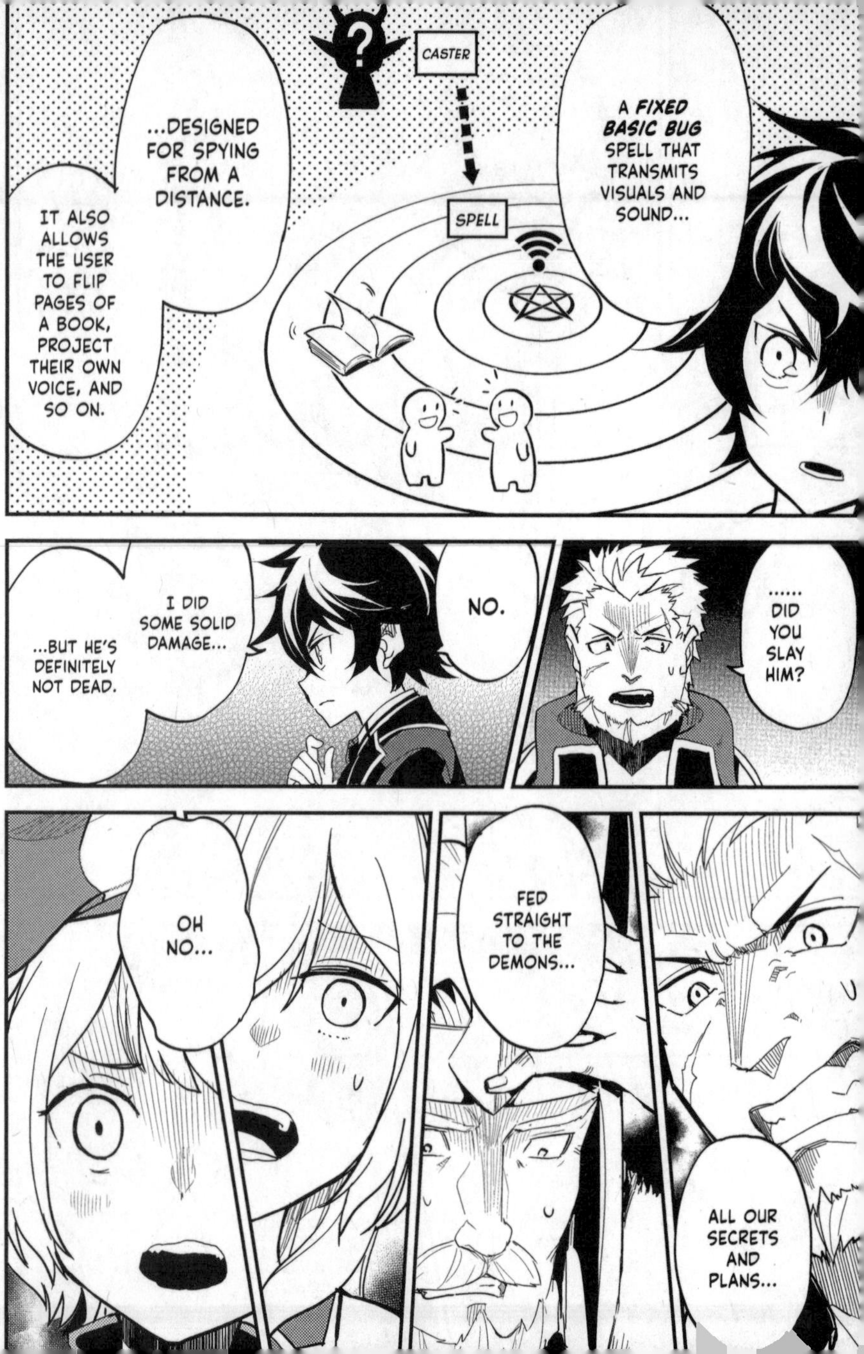
A FIXED BASIC BUG SPELL THAT TRANSMITS VISUALS AND SOUND...
CASTER
SPELL
...DESIGNED FOR SPYING FROM A DISTANCE.
IT ALSO ALLOWS THE USER TO FLIP PAGES OF A BOOK, PROJECT THEIR OWN VOICE, AND SO ON.
...... DID YOU SLAY HIM?
NO.
I DID SOME SOLID DAMAGE...
...BUT HE'S DEFINITELY NOT DEAD.
ALL OUR SECRETS AND PLANS...
FED STRAIGHT TO THE DEMONS...
OH NO...

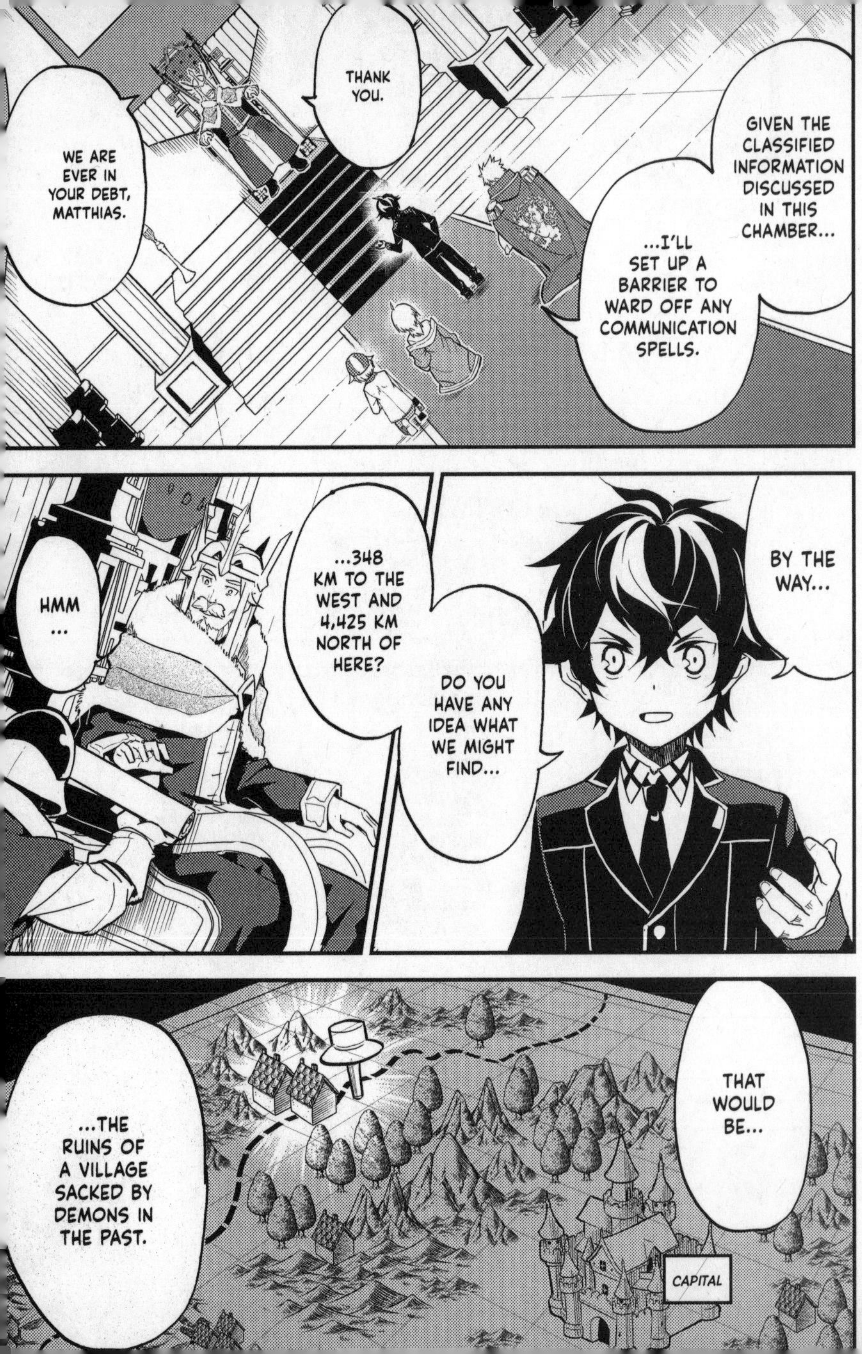
GIVEN THE CLASSIFIED INFORMATION DISCUSSED IN THIS CHAMBER...
...I'LL SET UP A BARRIER TO WARD OFF ANY COMMUNICATION SPELLS.
THANK YOU.
WE ARE EVER IN YOUR DEBT, MATTHIAS.
BY THE WAY...
DO YOU HAVE ANY IDEA WHAT WE MIGHT FIND...
...348 KM TO THE WEST AND 4,425 KM NORTH OF HERE?
HMM ...
THAT WOULD BE...
...THE RUINS OF A VILLAGE SACKED BY DEMONS IN THE PAST.
CAPITAL

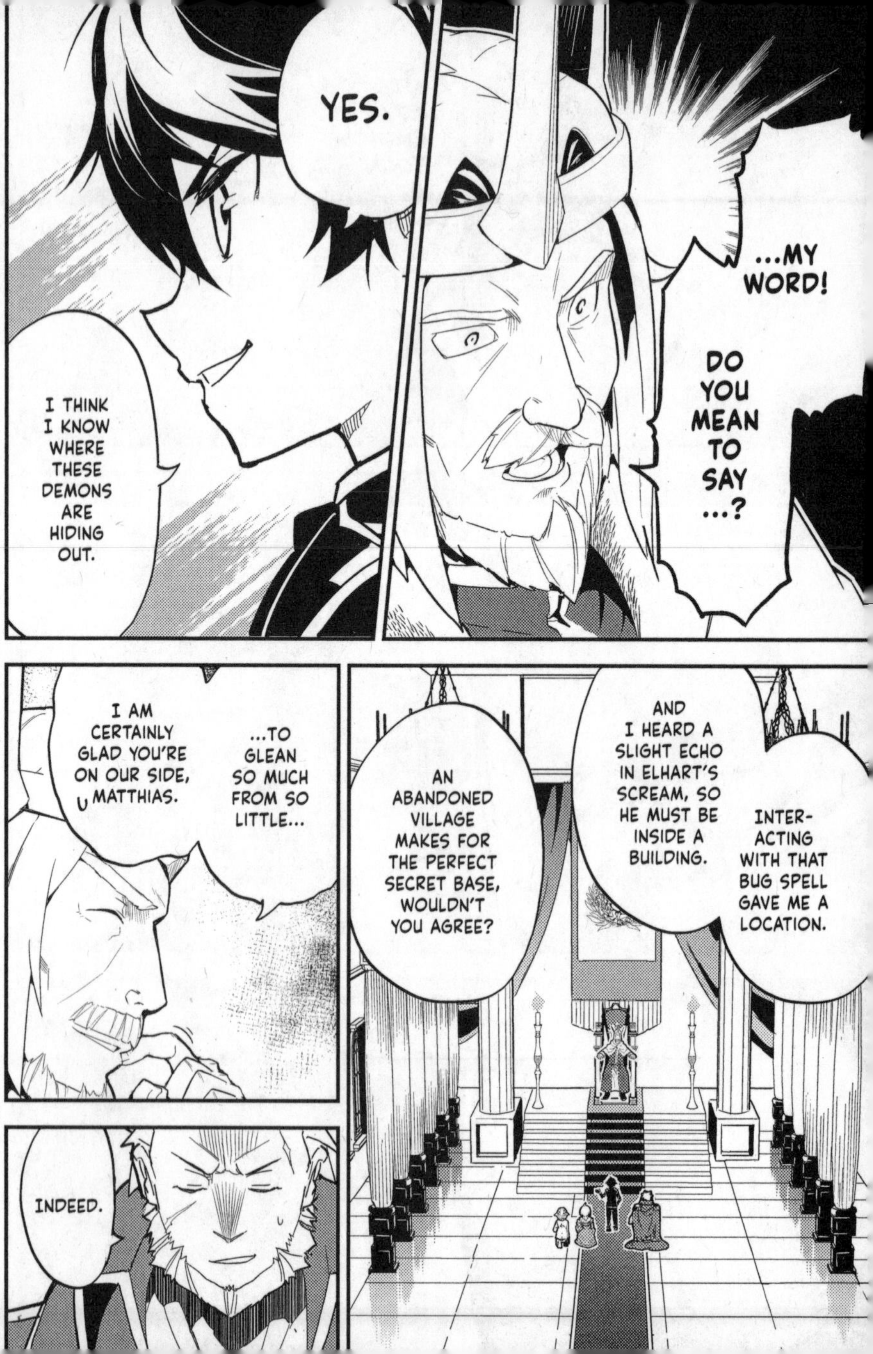
...MY WORD!
DO YOU MEAN TO SAY ...?
YES.
I THINK I KNOW WHERE THESE DEMONS ARE HIDING OUT.
INTER-ACTING WITH THAT BUG SPELL GAVE ME A LOCATION.
AND I HEARD A SLIGHT ECHO IN ELHART'S SCREAM, SO HE MUST BE INSIDE A BUILDING.
AN ABANDONED VILLAGE MAKES FOR THE PERFECT SECRET BASE, WOULDN'T YOU AGREE?
I AM CERTAINLY GLAD YOU'RE ON OUR SIDE, MATTHIAS.
...TO GLEAN SO MUCH FROM SO LITTLE...
INDEED.

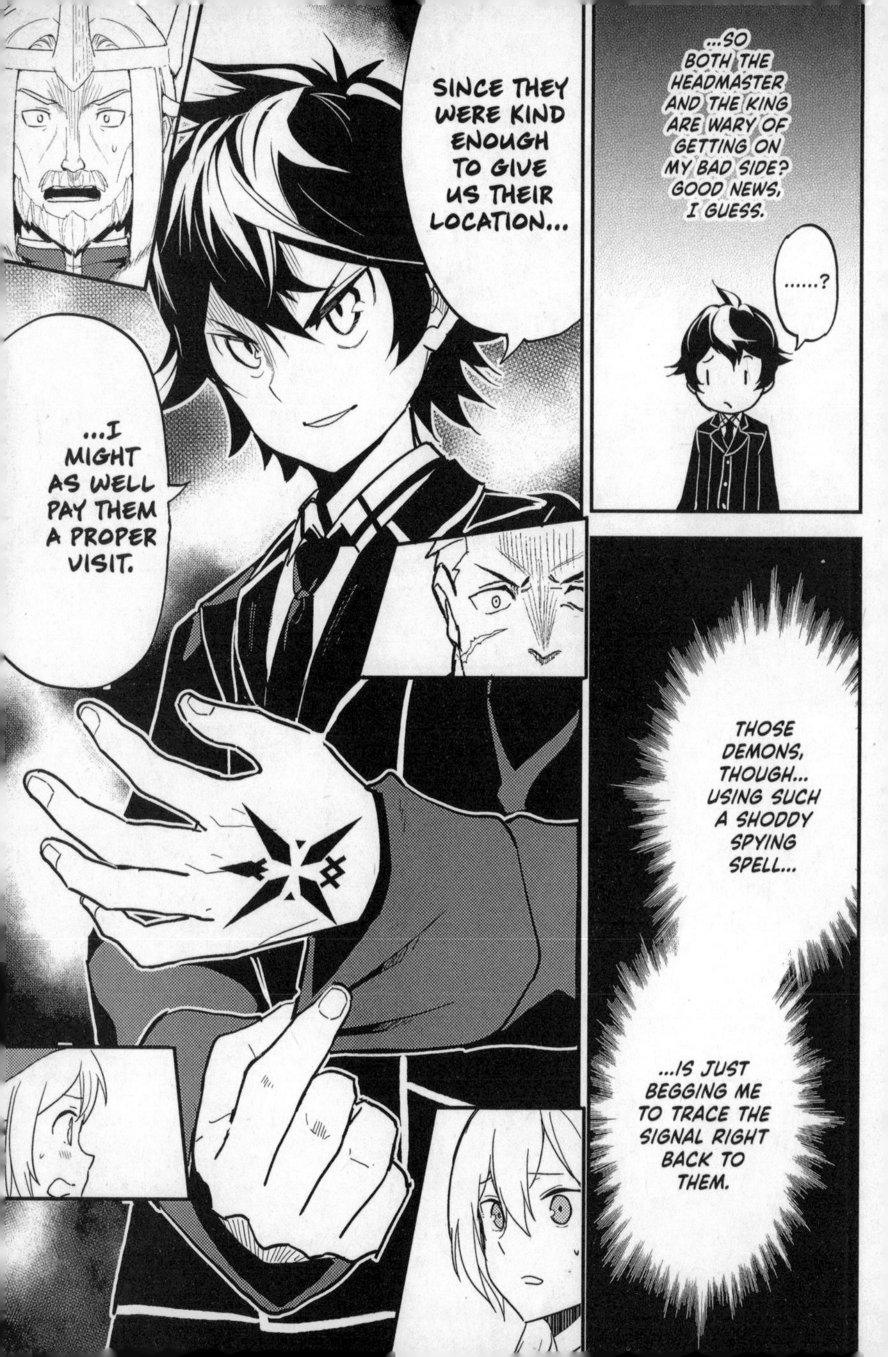
...SO BOTH THE HEADMASTER AND THE KING ARE WARY OF GETTING ON MY BAD SIDE? GOOD NEWS, I GUESS.
......?
THOSE DEMONS, THOUGH... USING SUCH A SHODDY SPYING SPELL...
...IS JUST BEGGING ME TO TRACE THE SIGNAL RIGHT BACK TO THEM.
SINCE THEY WERE KIND ENOUGH TO GIVE US THEIR LOCATION...
...I MIGHT AS WELL PAY THEM A PROPER VISIT.

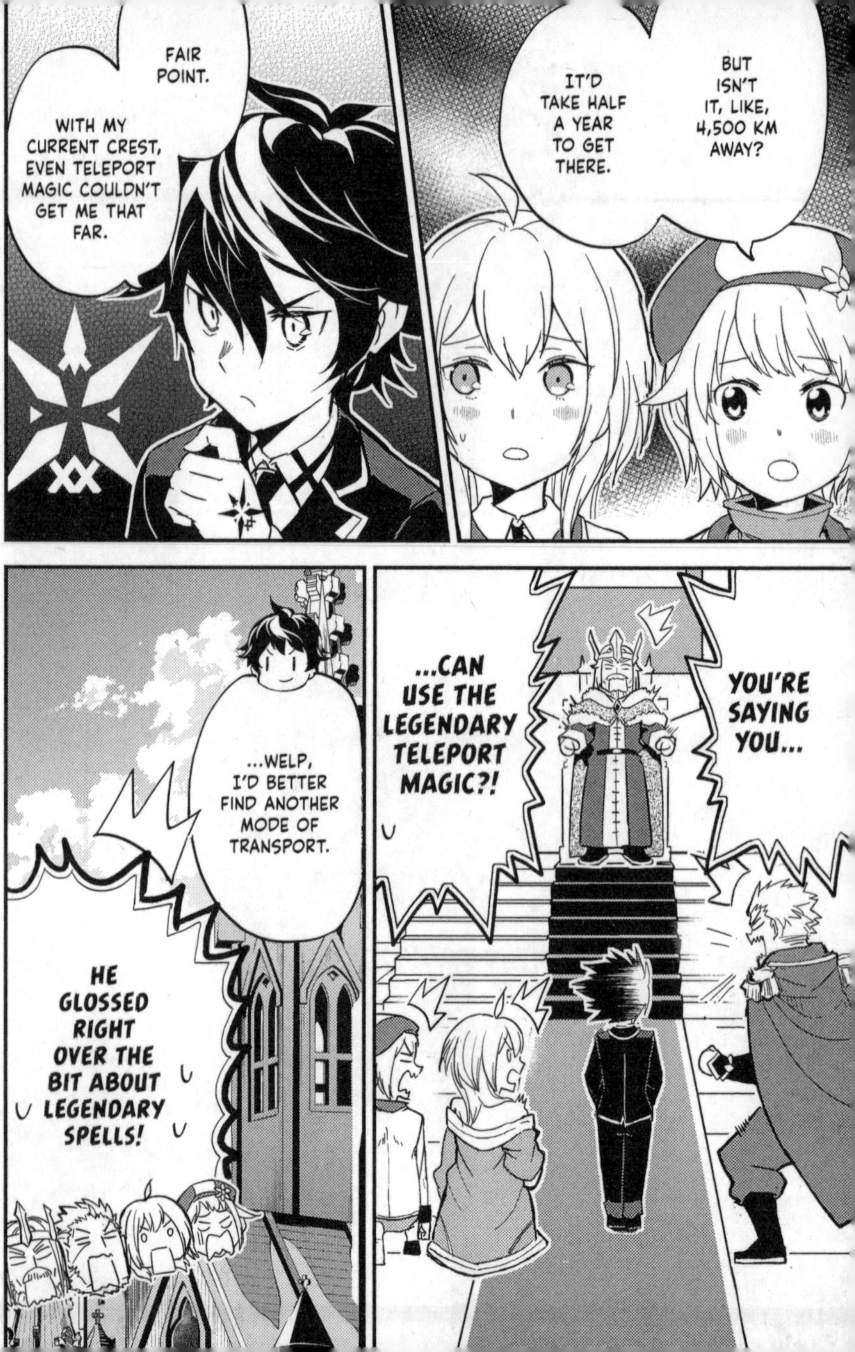
BUT ISN'T IT, LIKE, 4,500 KM AWAY?
IT'D TAKE HALF A YEAR TO GET THERE.
FAIR POINT.
WITH MY CURRENT CREST, EVEN TELEPORT MAGIC COULDN'T GET ME THAT FAR.
YOU'RE SAYING YOU...
...CAN USE THE LEGENDARY TELEPORT MAGIC?!
...WELP, I'D BETTER FIND ANOTHER MODE OF TRANSPORT.
HE GLOSSED RIGHT OVER THE BIT ABOUT LEGENDARY SPELLS!

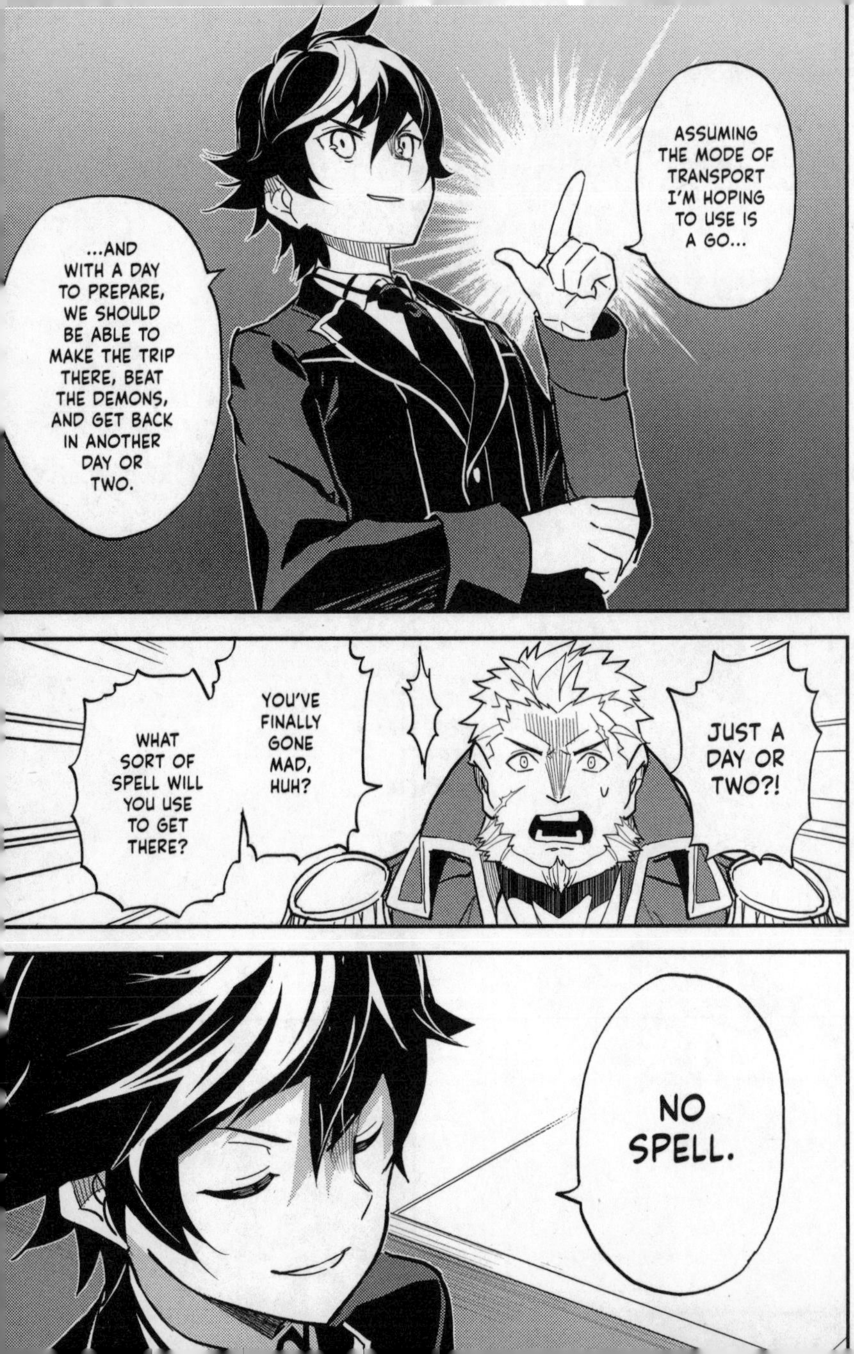
ASSUMING THE MODE OF TRANSPORT I'M HOPING TO USE IS A GO...
...AND WITH A DAY TO PREPARE, WE SHOULD BE ABLE TO MAKE THE TRIP THERE, BEAT THE DEMONS, AND GET BACK IN ANOTHER DAY OR TWO.
JUST A DAY OR TWO?!
YOU'VE FINALLY GONE MAD, HUH?
WHAT SORT OF SPELL WILL YOU USE TO GET THERE?
NO SPELL.

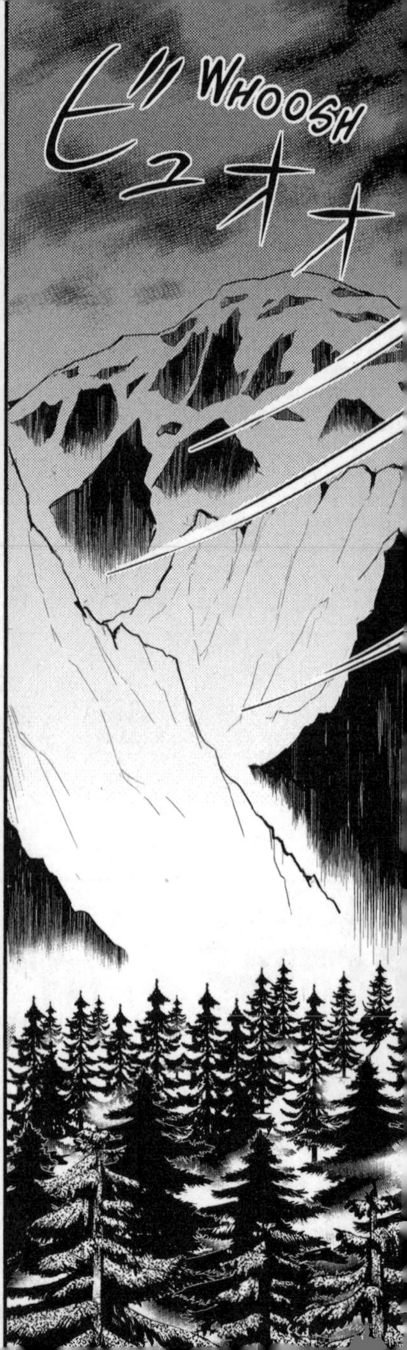
ビュオオ
WHOOSH
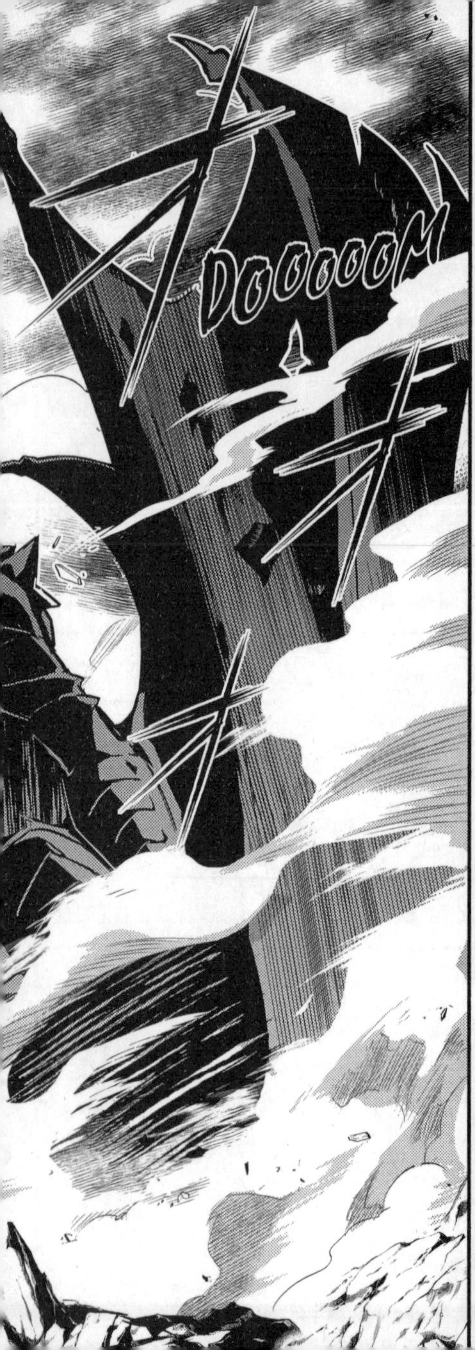
DOOOOOM

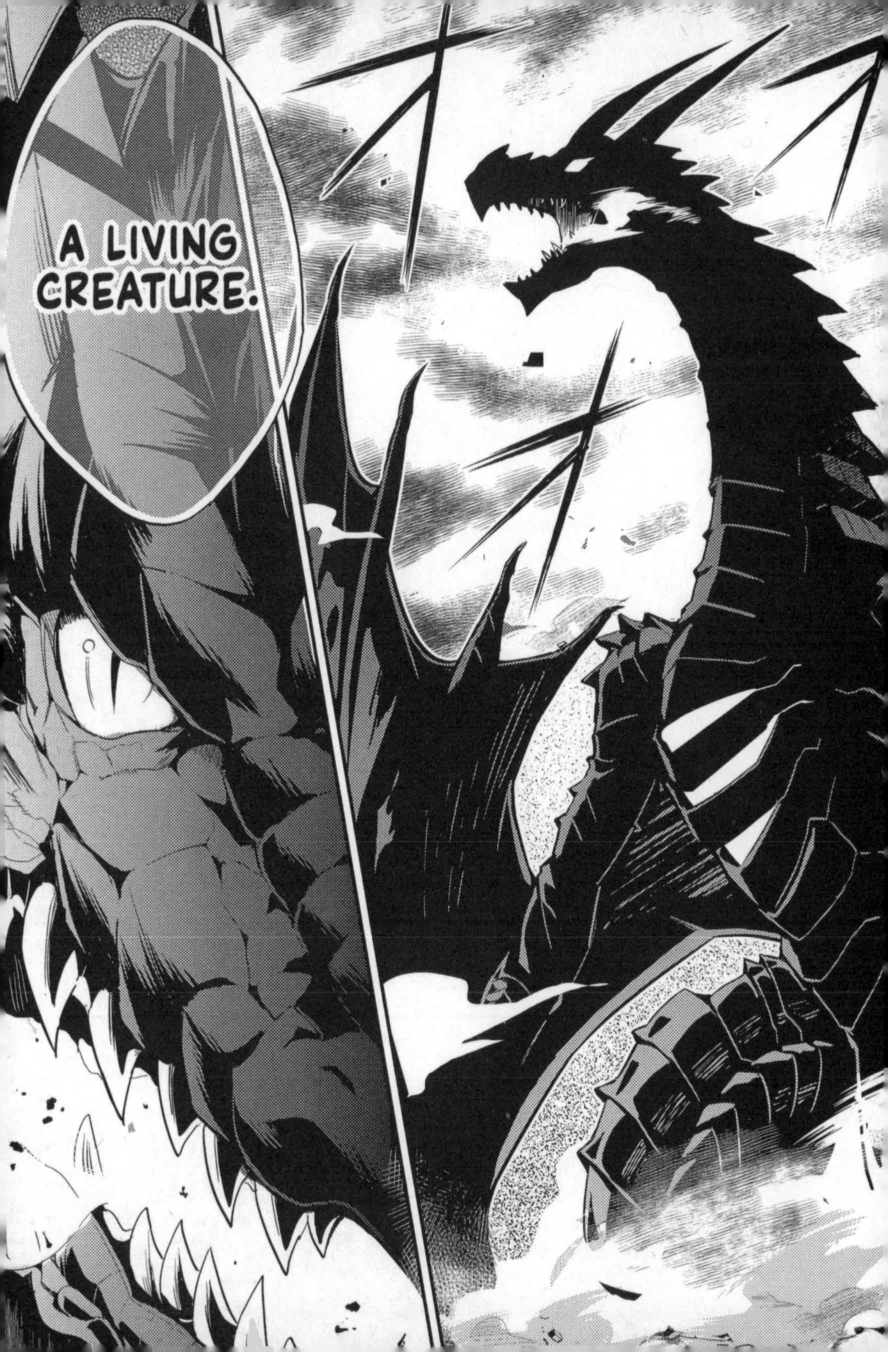
A LIVING CREATURE.

THE
STRONGEST SAGE
WITH
THE WEAKEST CREST

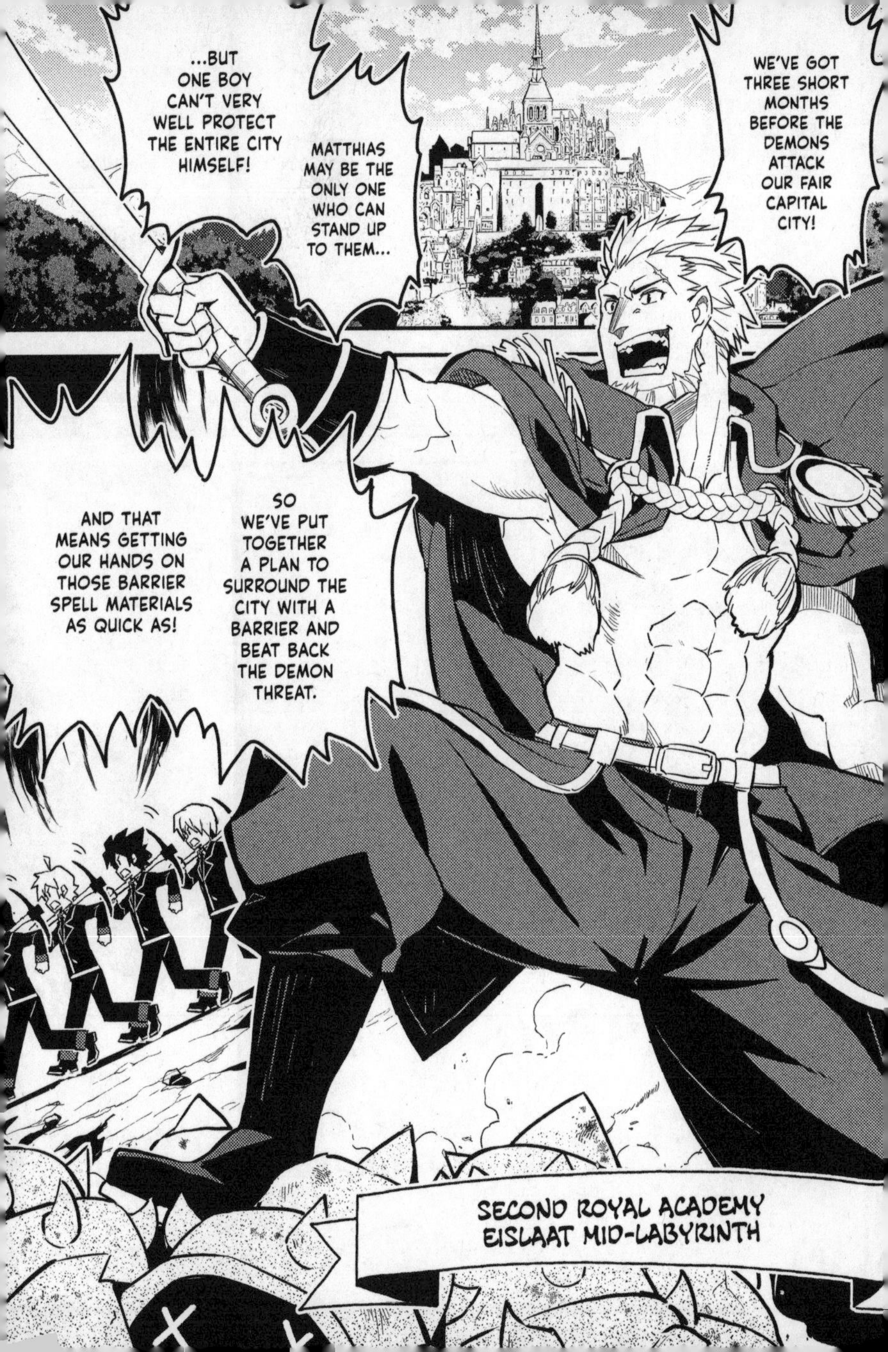
WE'VE GOT THREE SHORT MONTHS BEFORE THE DEMONS ATTACK OUR FAIR CAPITAL CITY!
MATTHIAS MAY BE THE ONLY ONE WHO CAN STAND UP TO THEM...
...BUT ONE BOY CAN'T VERY WELL PROTECT THE ENTIRE CITY HIMSELF!
SO WE'VE PUT TOGETHER A PLAN TO SURROUND THE CITY WITH A BARRIER AND BEAT BACK THE DEMON THREAT.
AND THAT MEANS GETTING OUR HANDS ON THOSE BARRIER SPELL MATERIALS AS QUICK AS!
SECOND ROYAL ACADEMY EISLAAT MID-LABYRINTH

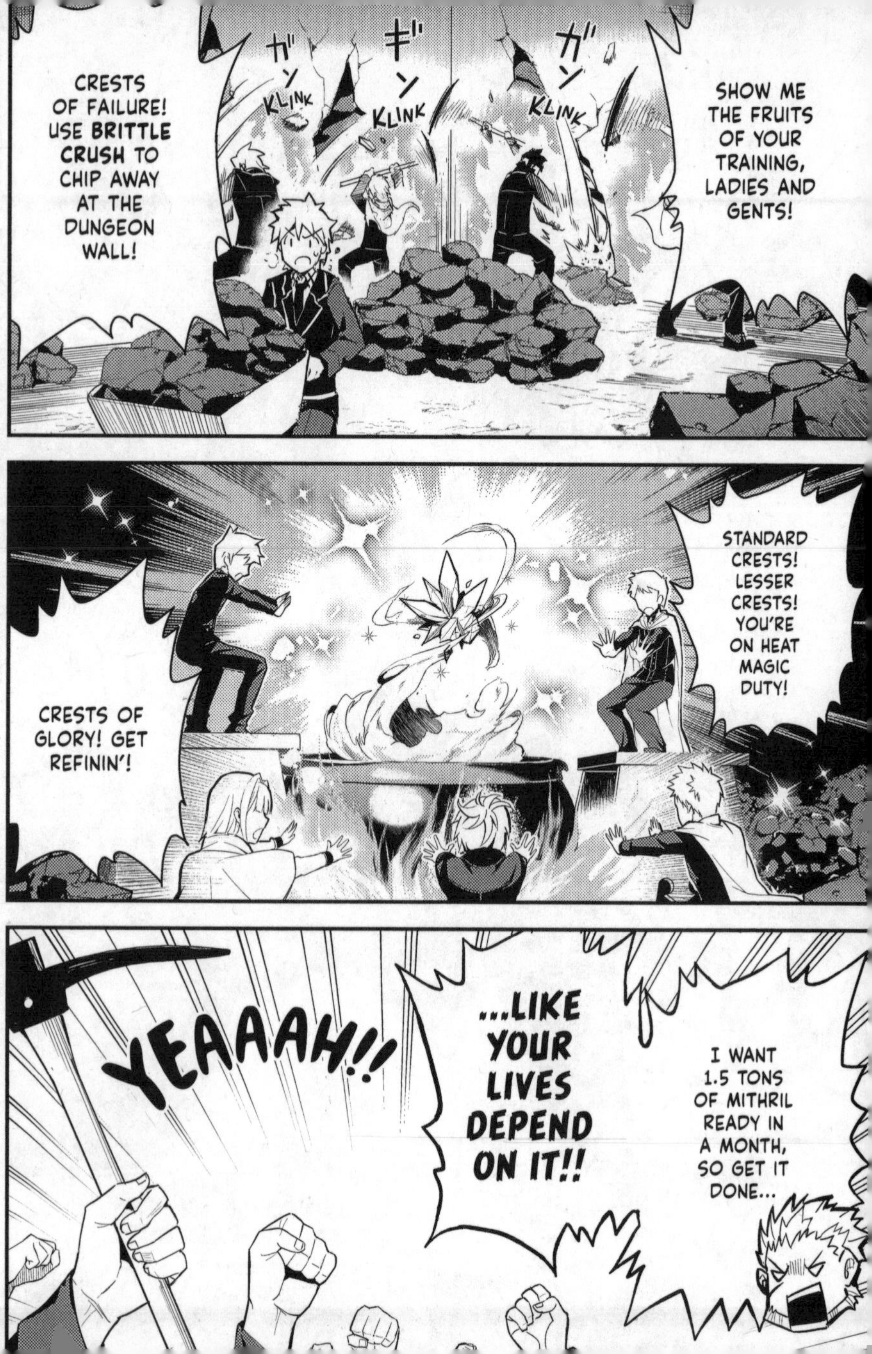
SHOW ME THE FRUITS OF YOUR TRAINING, LADIES AND GENTS!
ガン
KLINK
ギン
KLINK
ガン
KLINK
CRESTS OF FAILURE! USE BRITTLE CRUSH TO CHIP AWAY AT THE DUNGEON WALL!
STANDARD CRESTS! LESSER CRESTS! YOU'RE ON HEAT MAGIC DUTY!
CRESTS OF GLORY! GET REFININ'!
I WANT 1.5 TONS OF MITHRIL READY IN A MONTH, SO GET IT DONE...
...LIKE YOUR LIVES DEPEND ON IT!!
YEAAAH!!

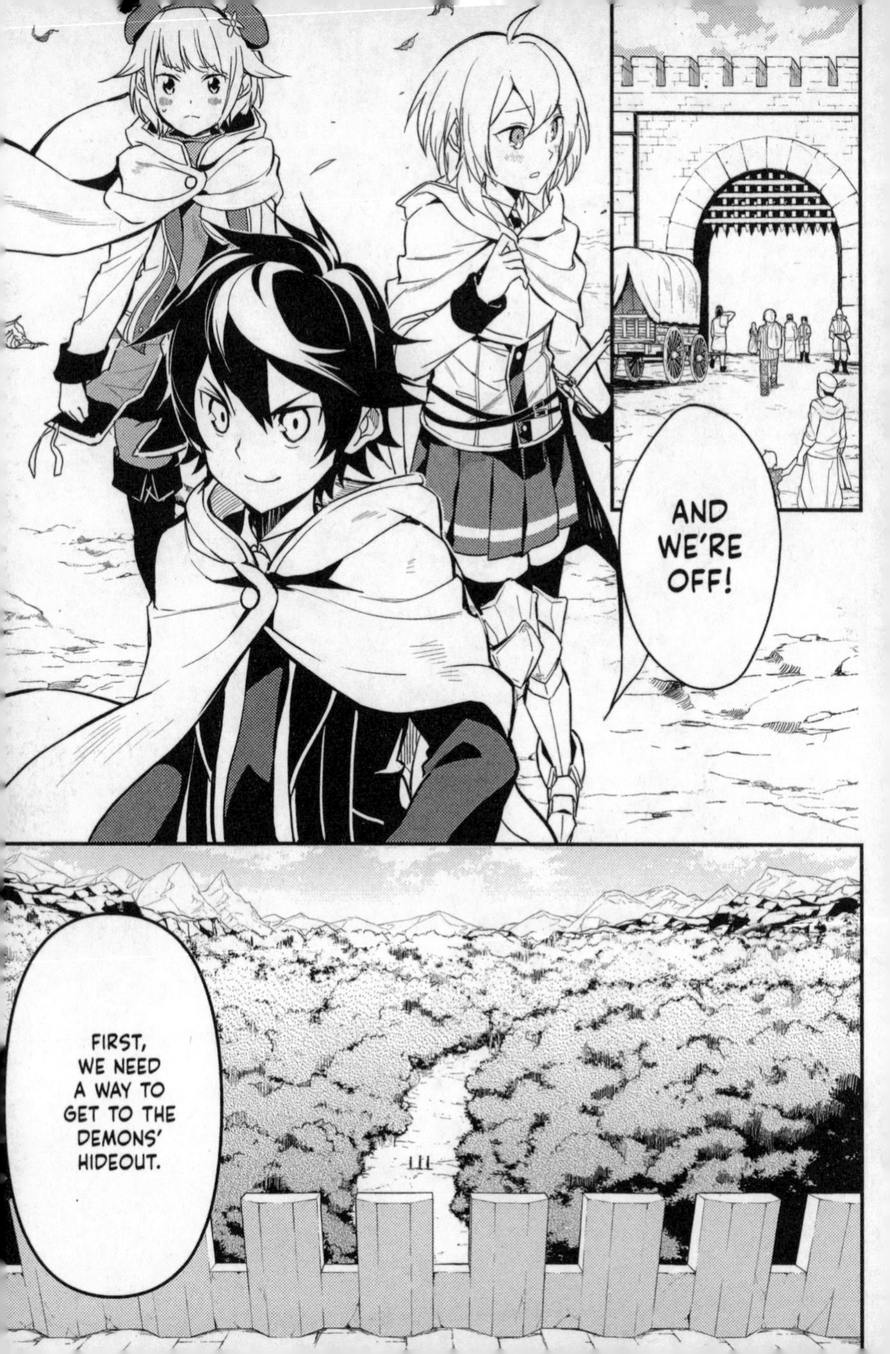
AND WE'RE OFF!
FIRST, WE NEED A WAY TO GET TO THE DEMONS' HIDEOUT.

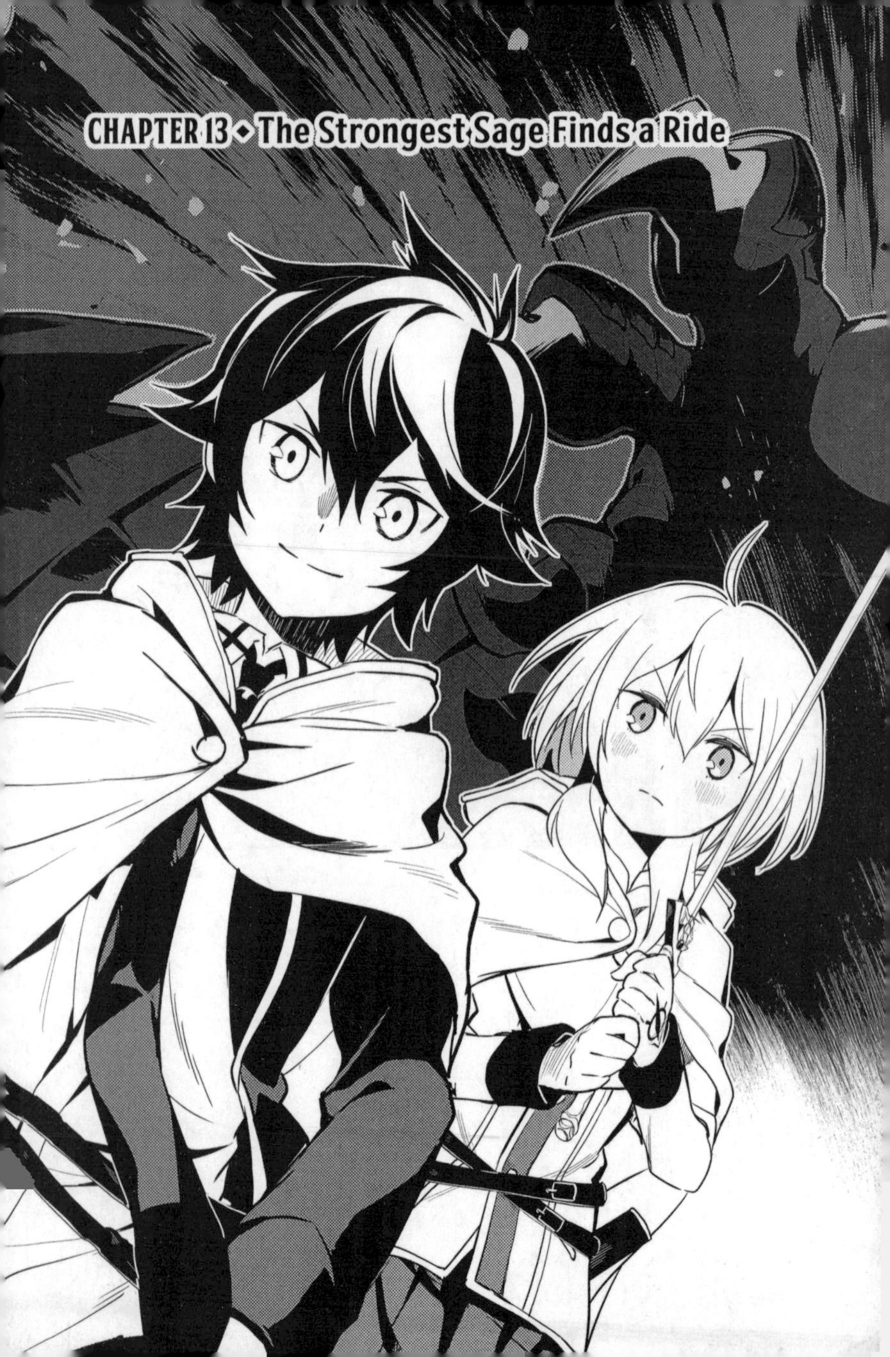
CHAPTER 13 ◆ The Strongest Sage Finds a Ride

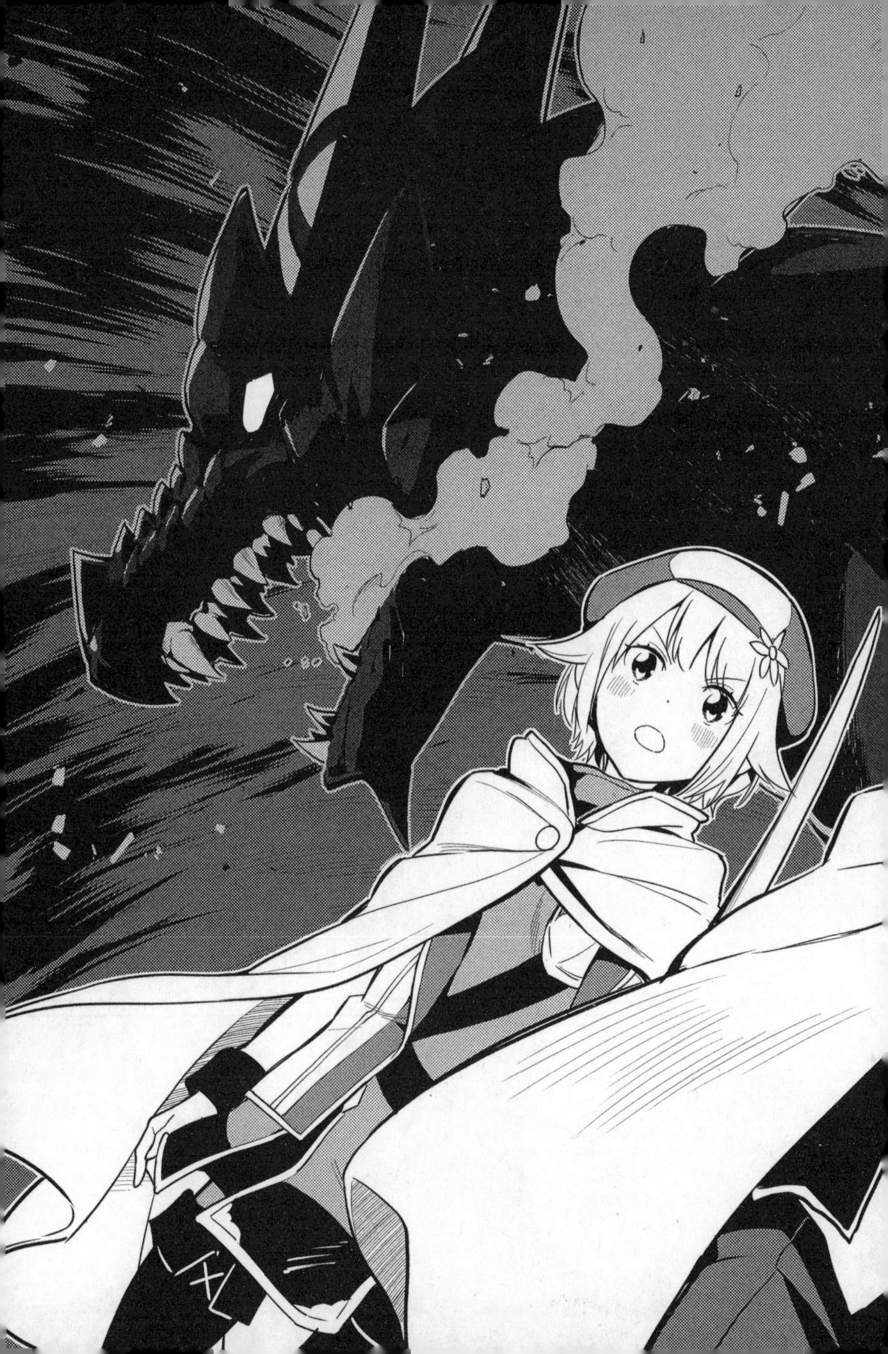

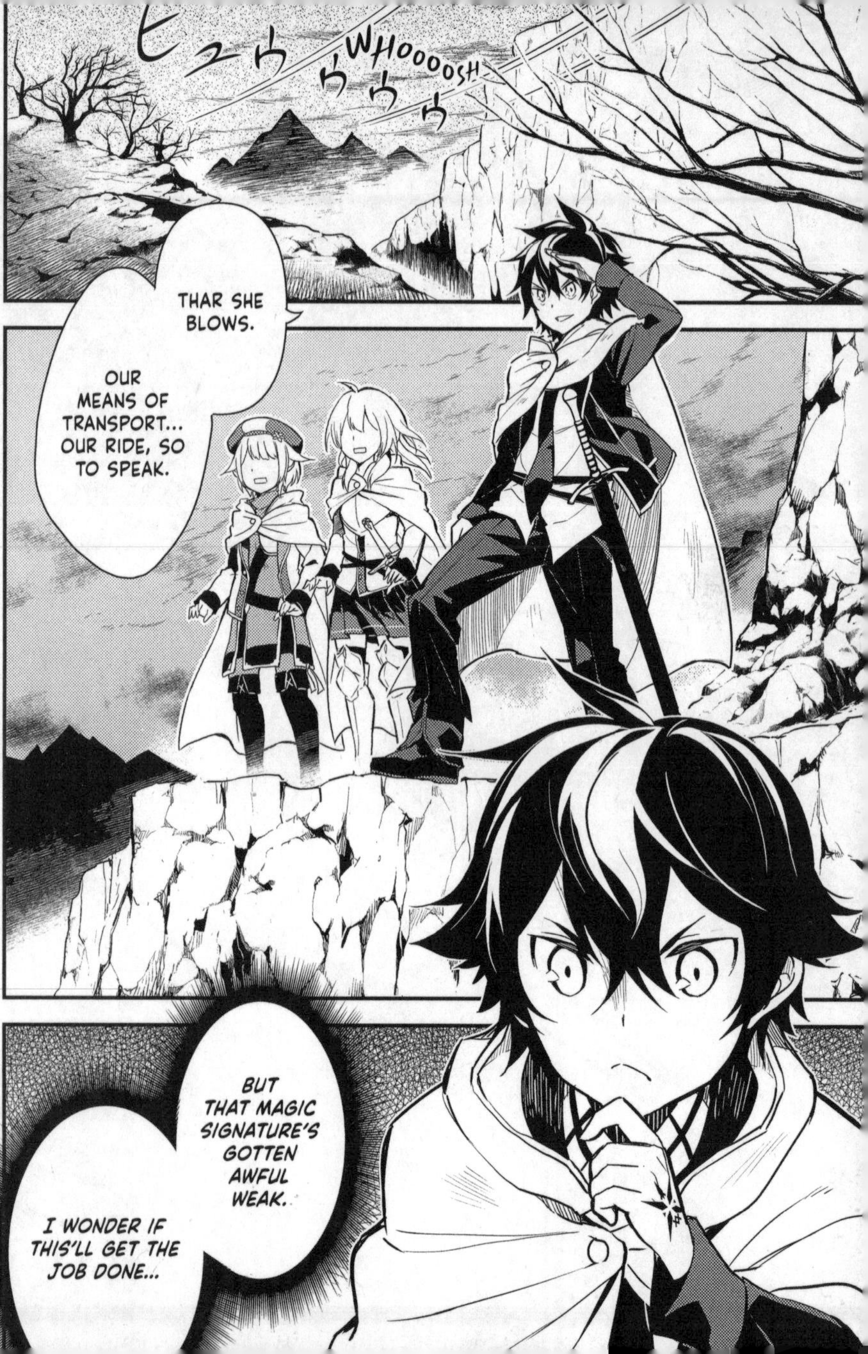
ヒュウウウウウ
WHOOOOSH
THAR SHE BLOWS.
OUR MEANS OF TRANSPORT... OUR RIDE, SO TO SPEAK.
BUT THAT MAGIC SIGNATURE'S GOTTEN AWFUL WEAK.
I WONDER IF THIS'LL GET THE JOB DONE...

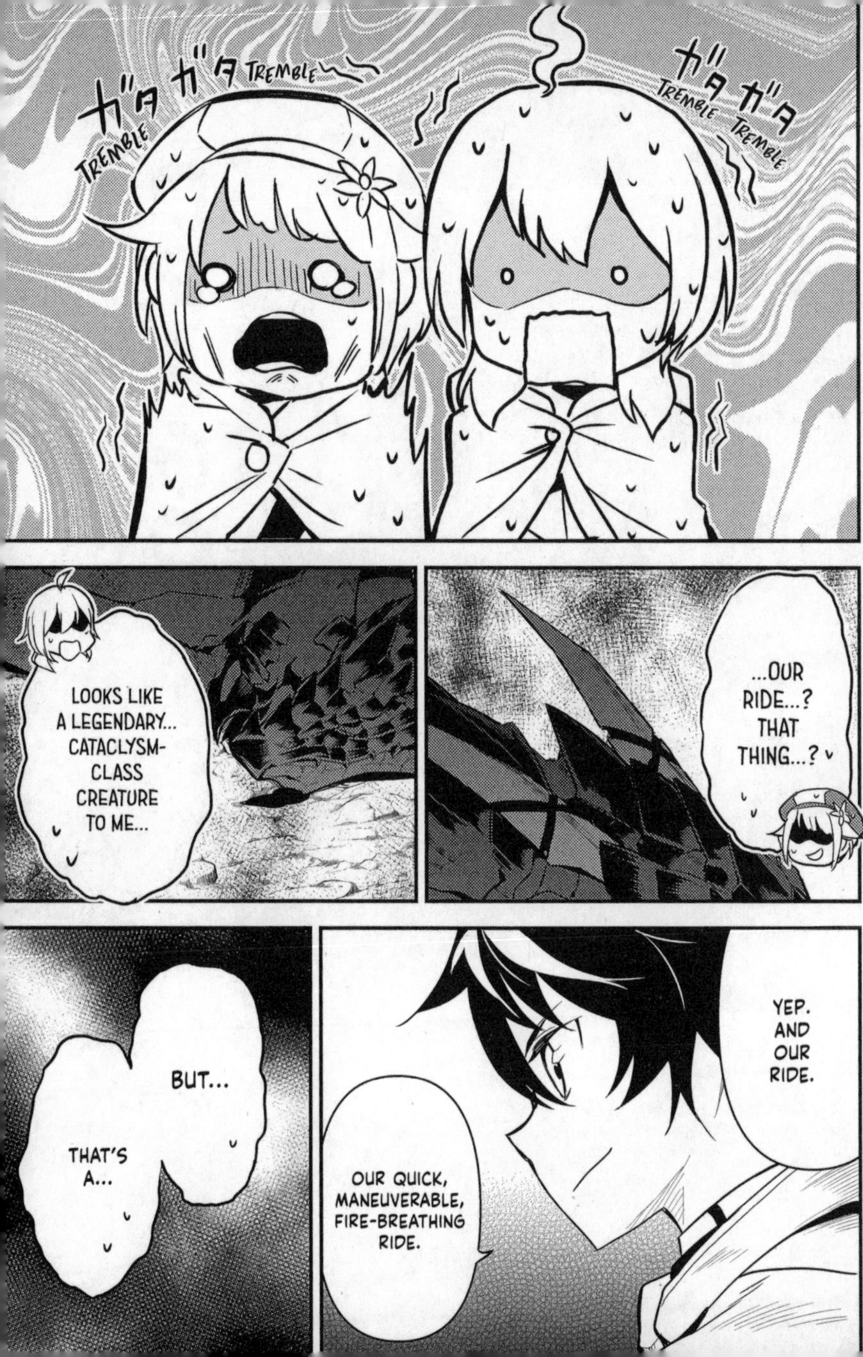
ガタガタ
TREMBLE TREMBLE
ガタガタ
TREMBLE TREMBLE
...OUR RIDE...? THAT THING...?
LOOKS LIKE A LEGENDARY... CATACLYSM-CLASS CREATURE TO ME...
YEP. AND OUR RIDE.
OUR QUICK, MANEUVERABLE, FIRE-BREATHING RIDE.
BUT...
THAT'S A...

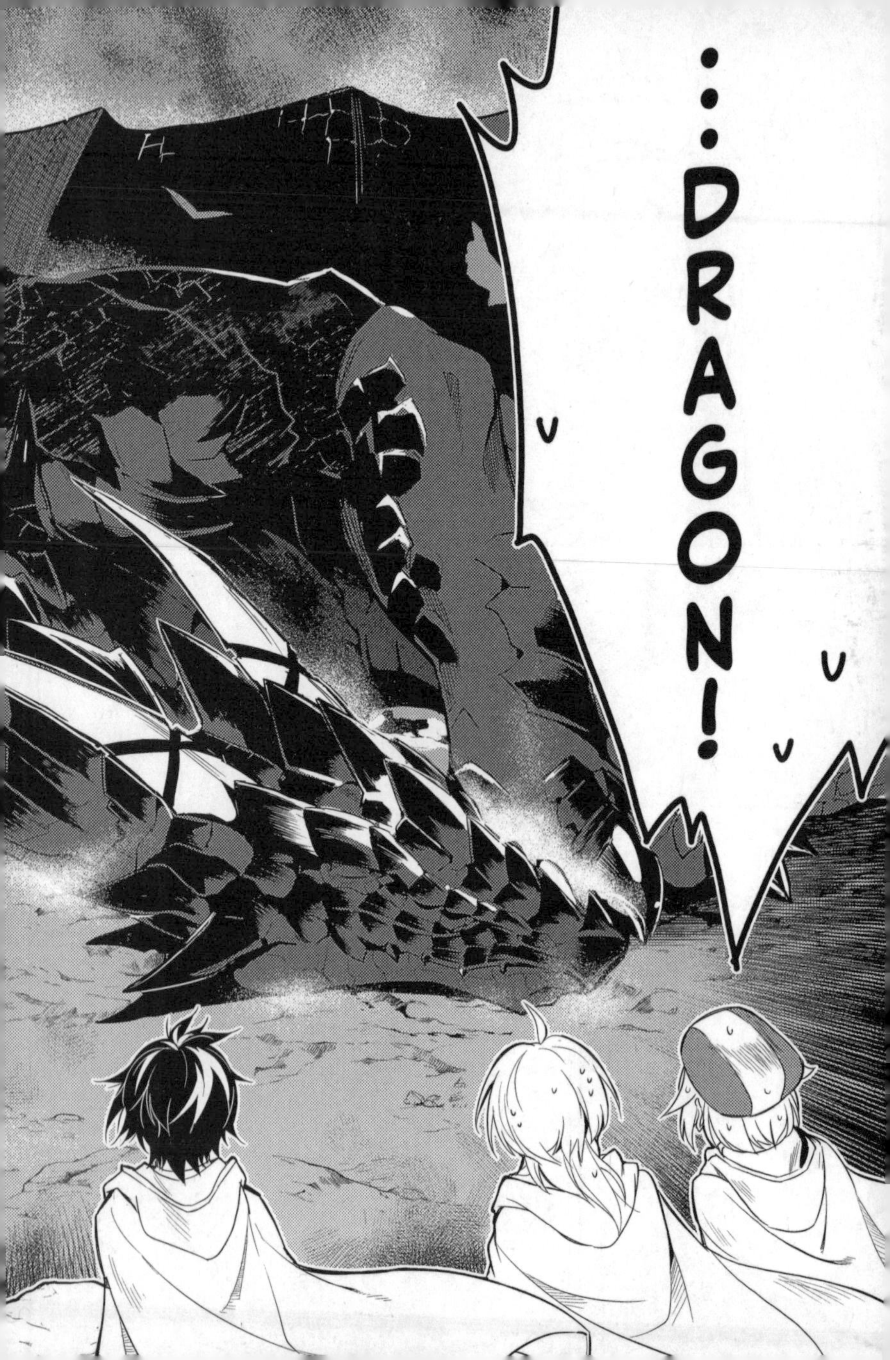
...DRAGON!

THE DARK DRAGON IRIS, TO BE PRECISE.
......!!
ONE OF THE KINGDOM-OBLITERATING DRAGONS OF LEGEND!

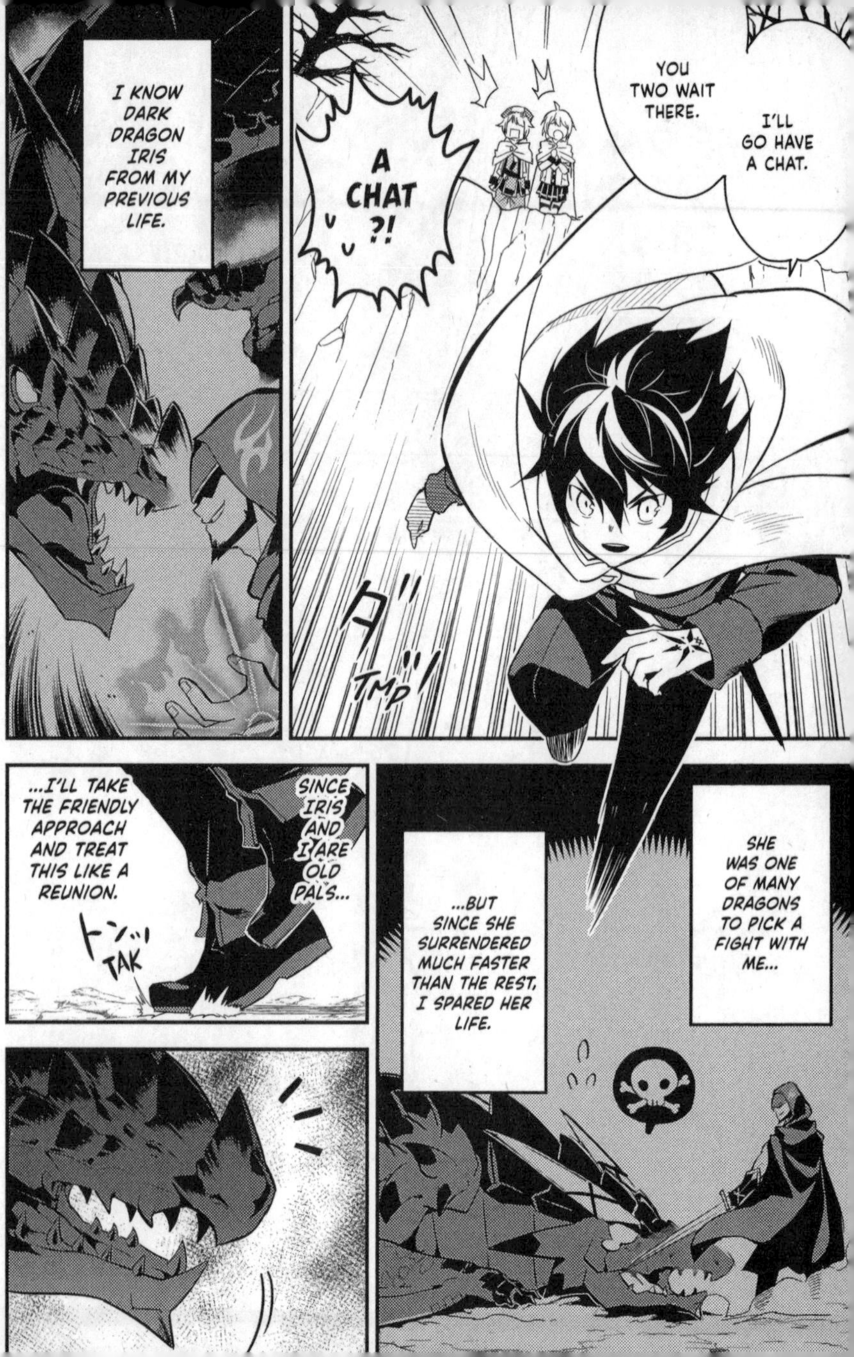
YOU TWO WAIT THERE.
I'LL GO HAVE A CHAT.
A CHAT?!
TMP
I KNOW DARK DRAGON IRIS FROM MY PREVIOUS LIFE.
SHE WAS ONE OF MANY DRAGONS TO PICK A FIGHT WITH ME...
...BUT SINCE SHE SURRENDERED MUCH FASTER THAN THE REST, I SPARED HER LIFE.
SINCE IRIS AND I ARE OLD PALS...
...I'LL TAKE THE FRIENDLY APPROACH AND TREAT THIS LIKE A REUNION.
TAK

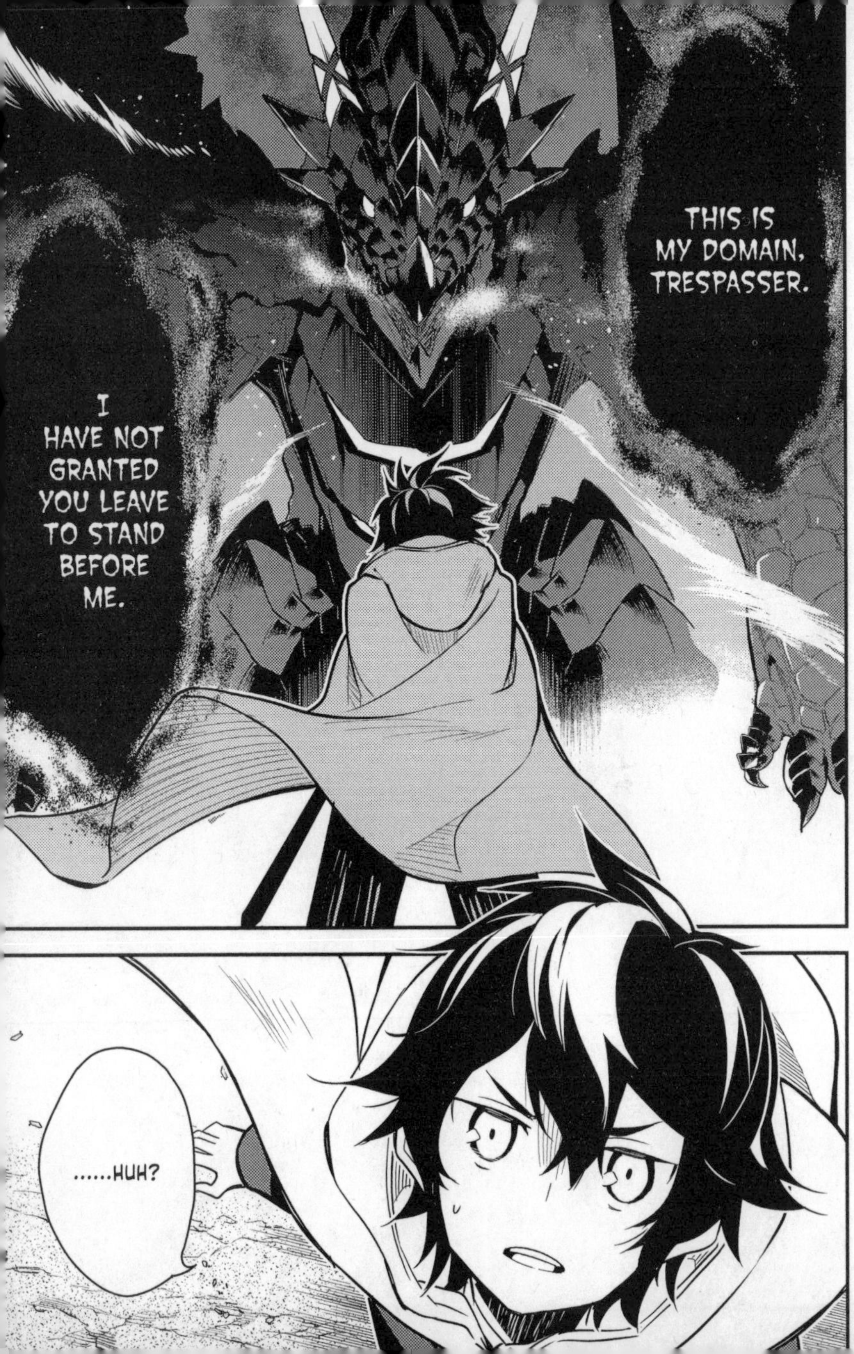
THIS IS MY DOMAIN, TRESPASSER.
I HAVE NOT GRANTED YOU LEAVE TO STAND BEFORE ME.
......HUH?

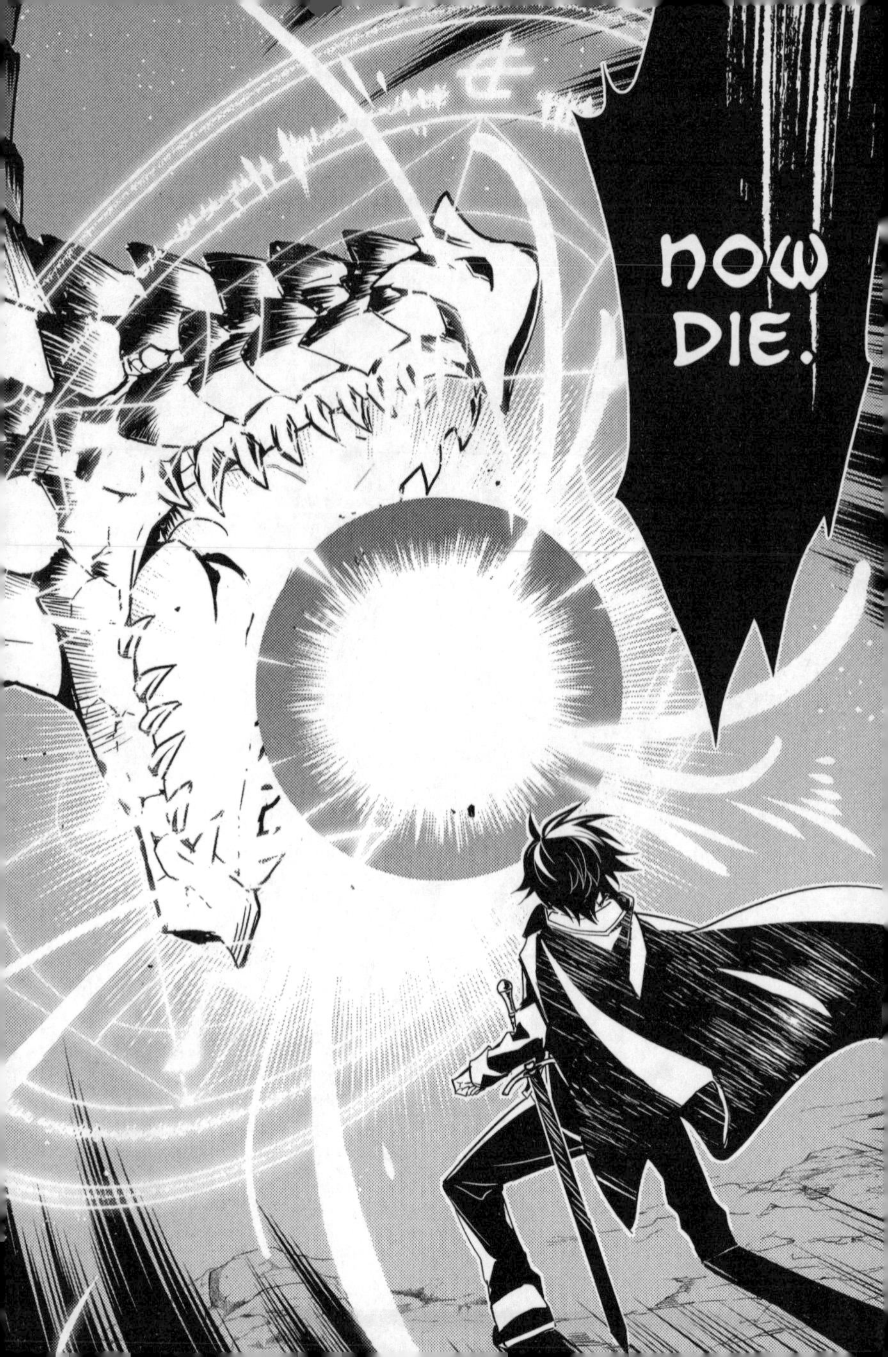
NOW DIE.

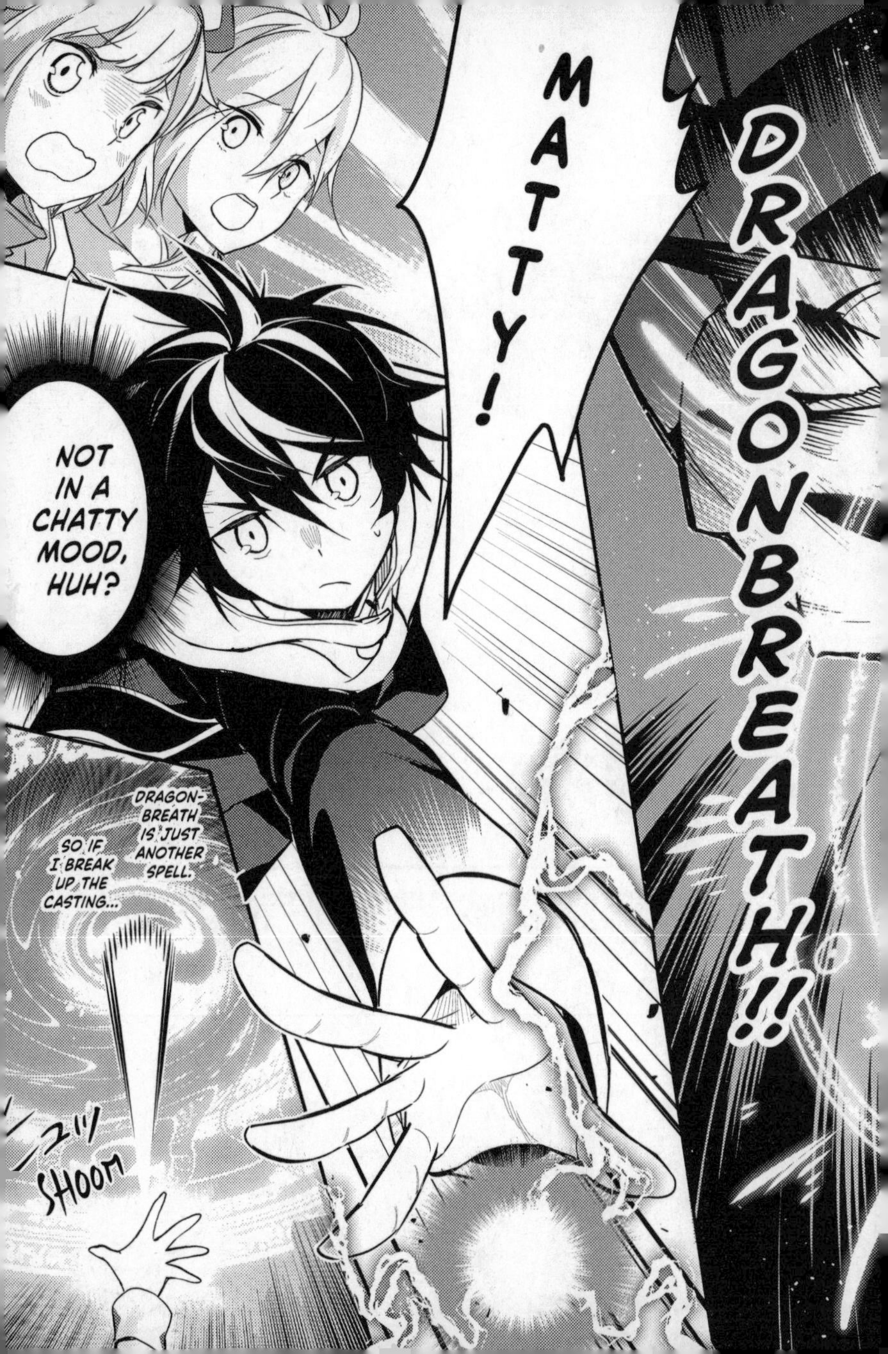
DRAGONBREATH!!
MATTY!
NOT IN A CHATTY MOOD, HUH?
DRAGON-BREATH IS JUST ANOTHER SPELL.
SO IF I BREAK UP THE CASTING...
SHOOM

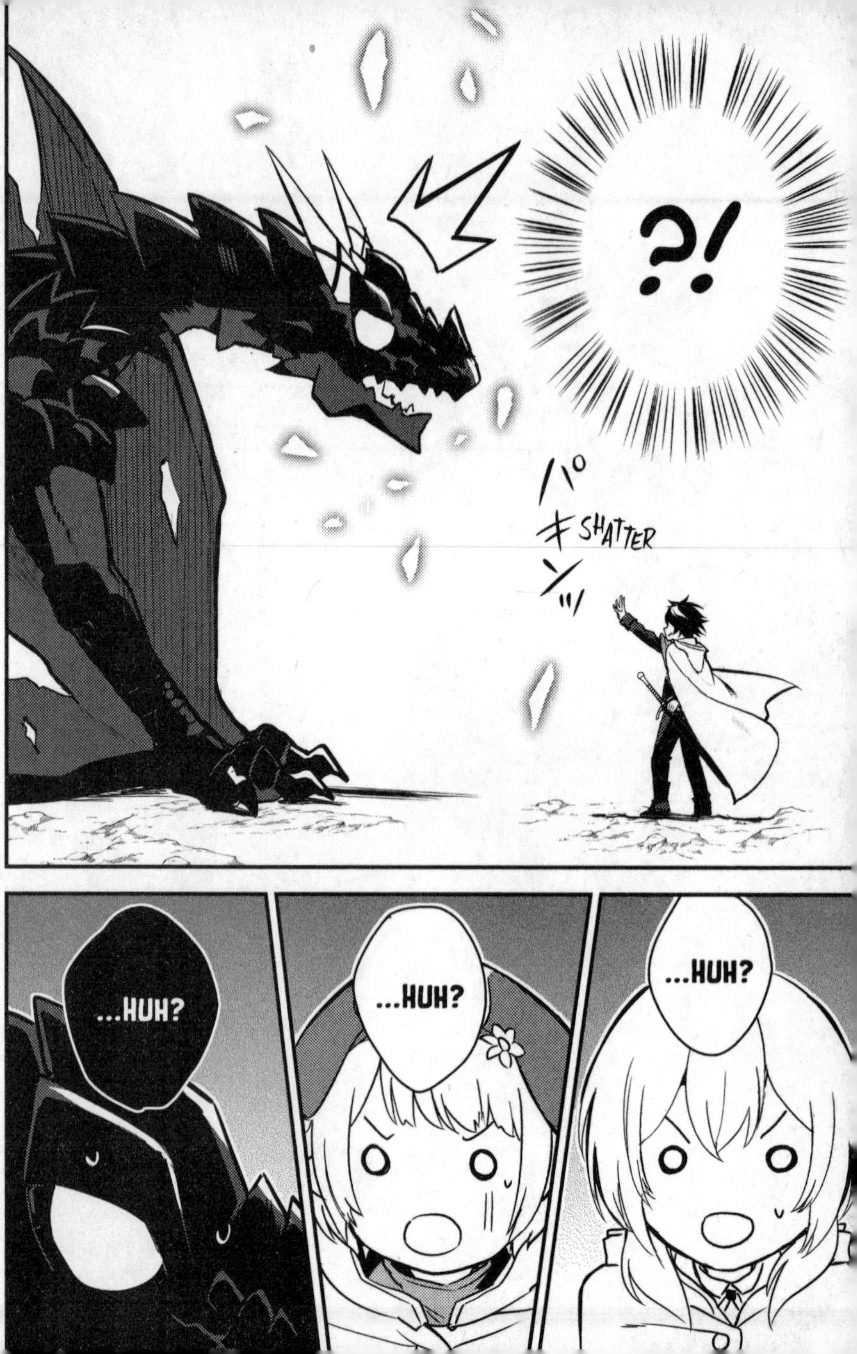
?!
パキンッ
SHATTER
...HUH?
...HUH?
...HUH?

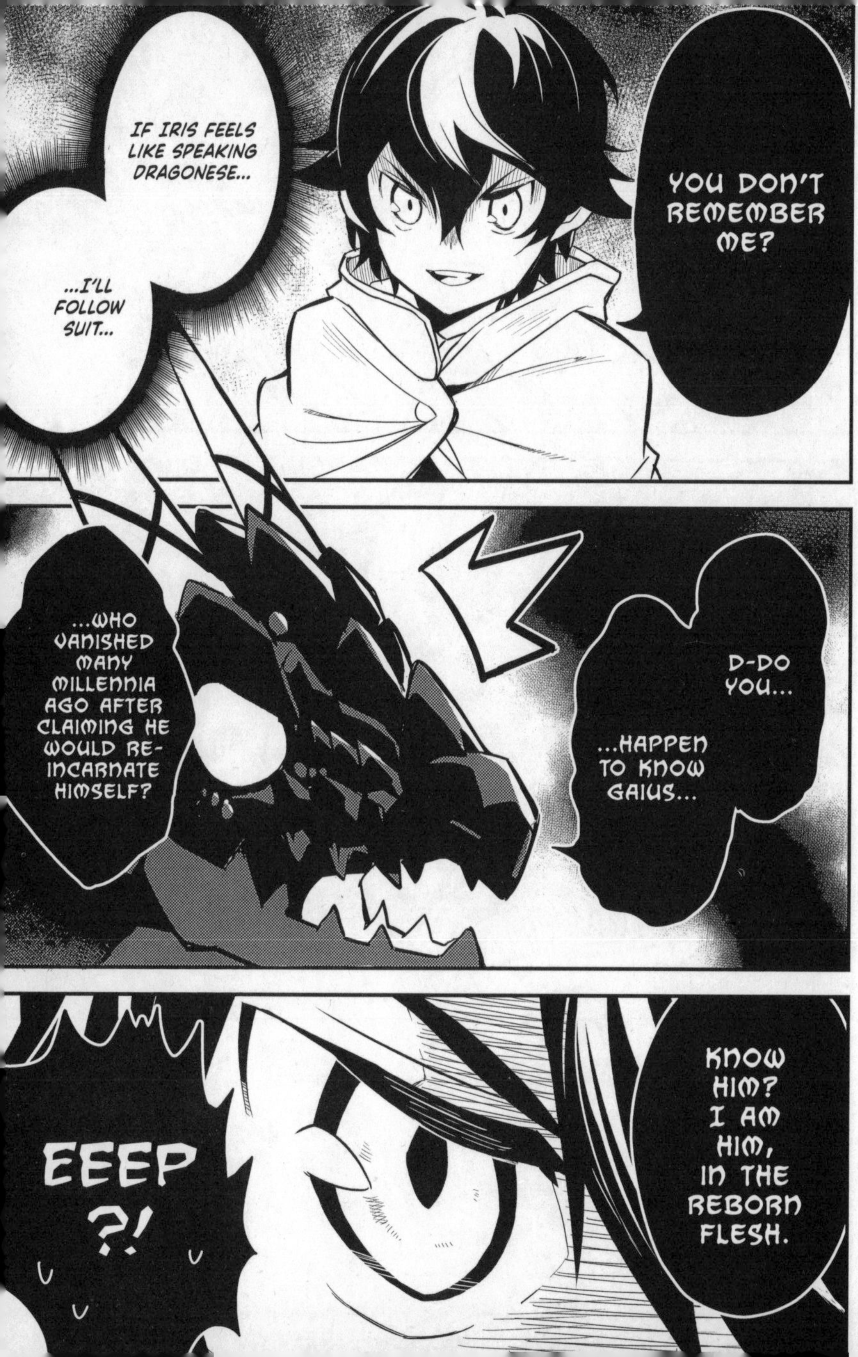
YOU DON'T REMEMBER ME?
IF IRIS FEELS LIKE SPEAKING DRAGONESE...
...I'LL FOLLOW SUIT...
D-DO YOU...
...HAPPEN TO KNOW GAIUS...
...WHO VANISHED MANY MILLENNIA AGO AFTER CLAIMING HE WOULD RE-INCARNATE HIMSELF?
KNOW HIM? I AM HIM, IN THE REBORN FLESH.
EEEP ?!

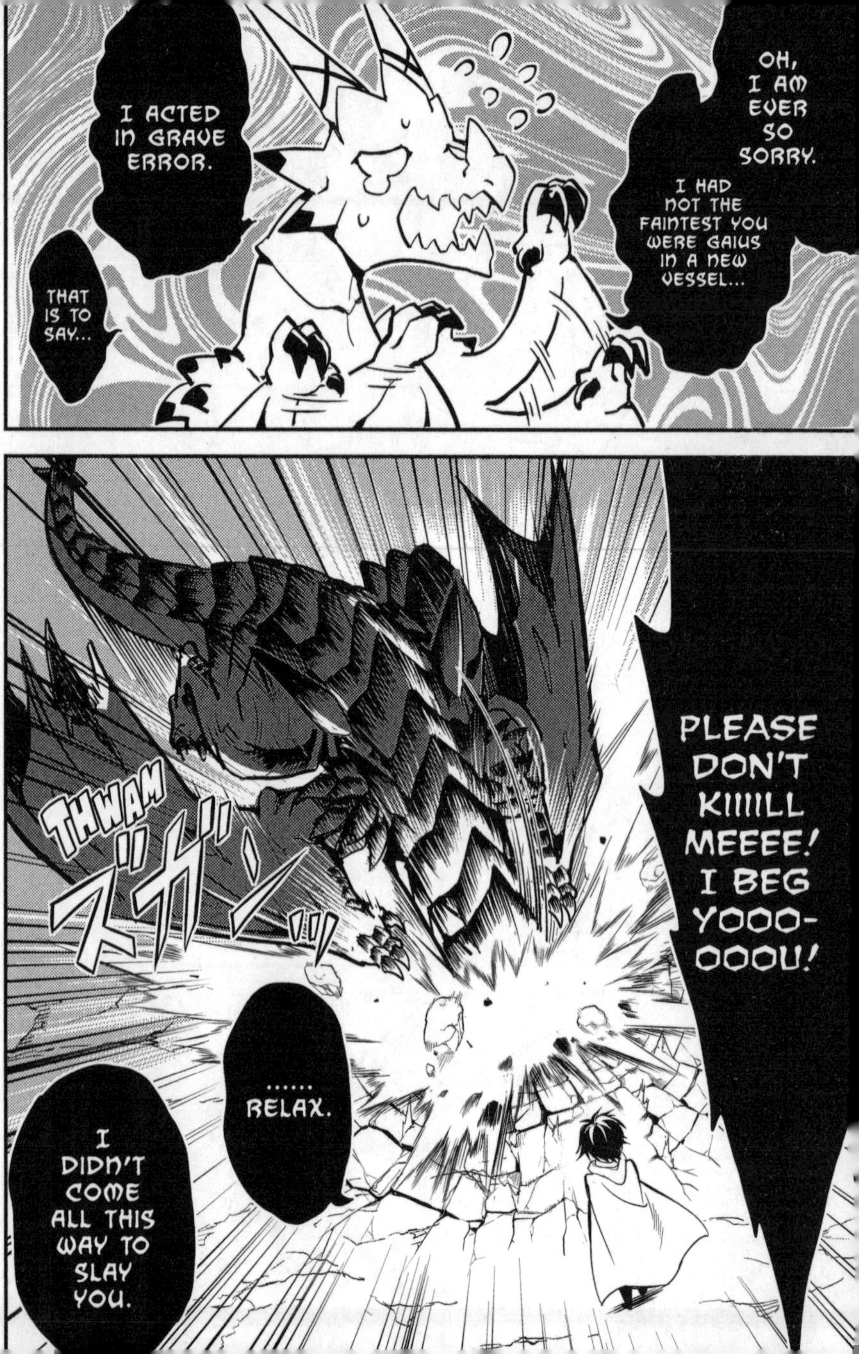
OH, I AM EVER SO SORRY.
I HAD NOT THE FAINTEST YOU WERE GAIUS IN A NEW VESSEL...
I ACTED IN GRAVE ERROR.
THAT IS TO SAY...
PLEASE DON'T KIIIILL MEEEE! I BEG YOOO-OOOU!
THWAM
ズガン!!
...... RELAX.
I DIDN'T COME ALL THIS WAY TO SLAY YOU.

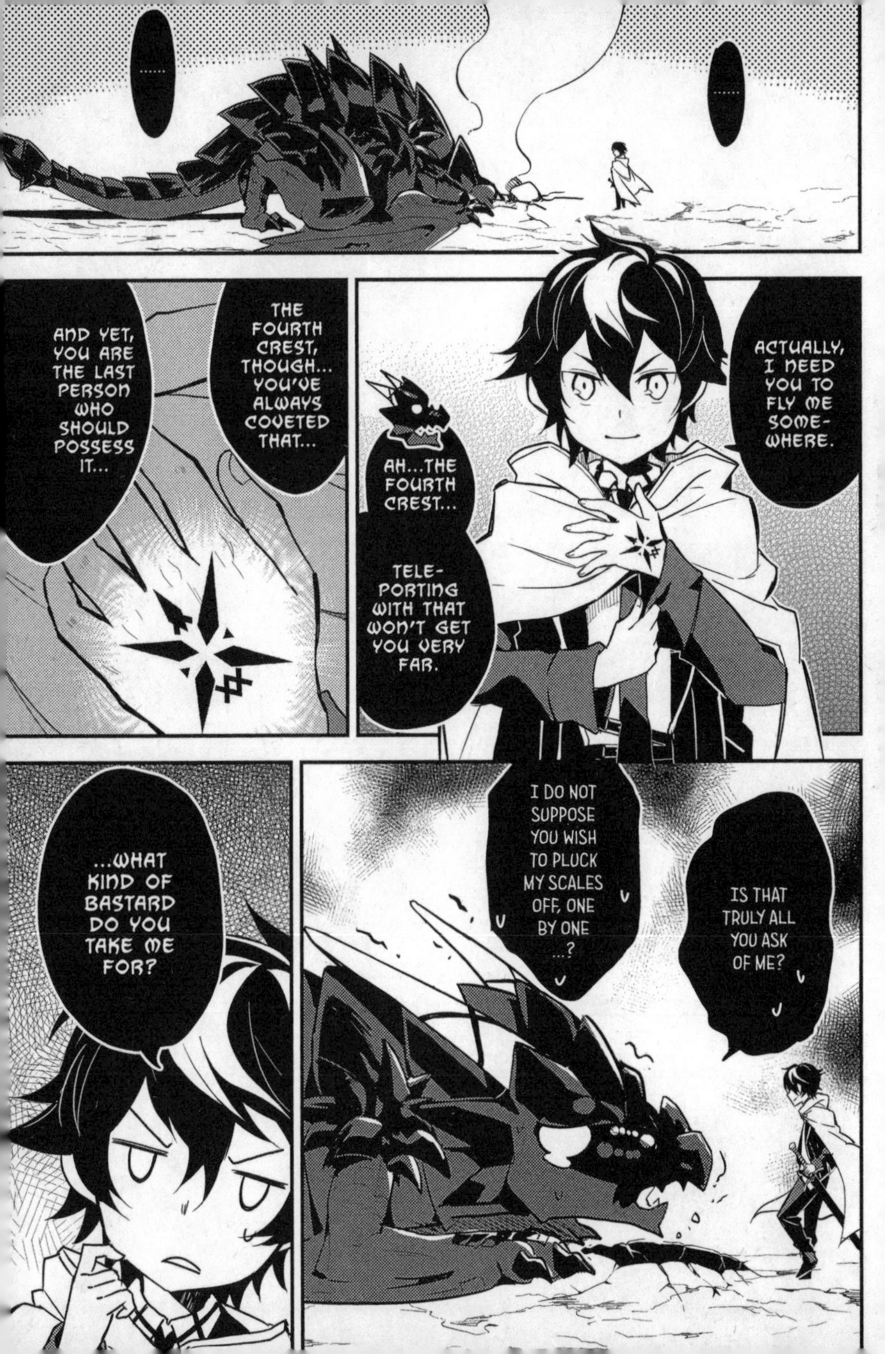
......
......
ACTUALLY, I NEED YOU TO FLY ME SOME-WHERE.
AH...THE FOURTH CREST...
TELE-PORTING WITH THAT WON'T GET YOU VERY FAR.
THE FOURTH CREST, THOUGH... YOU'VE ALWAYS COVETED THAT...
AND YET, YOU ARE THE LAST PERSON WHO SHOULD POSSESS IT...
IS THAT TRULY ALL YOU ASK OF ME?
I DO NOT SUPPOSE YOU WISH TO PLUCK MY SCALES OFF, ONE BY ONE ...?
...WHAT KIND OF BASTARD DO YOU TAKE ME FOR?

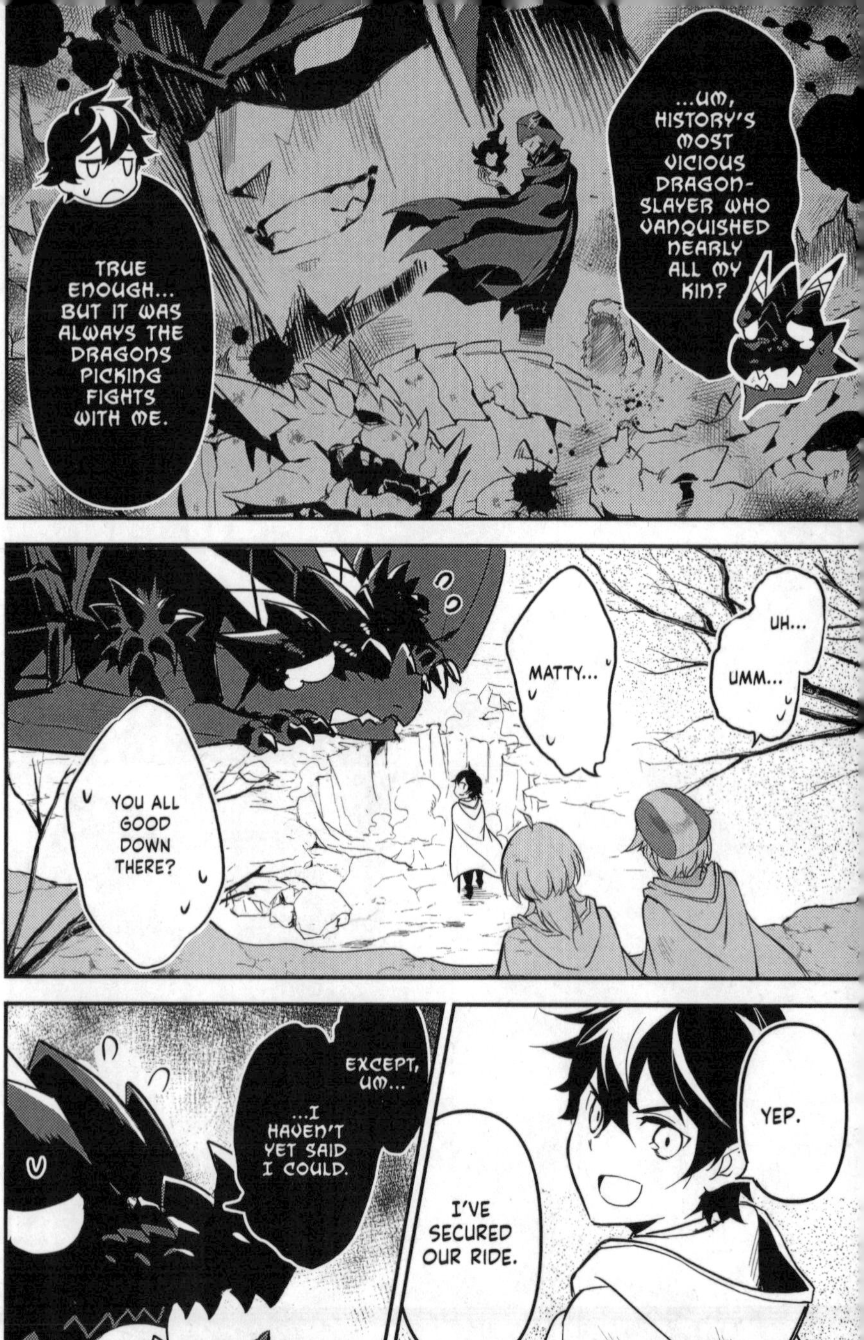
...UM, HISTORY'S MOST VICIOUS DRAGON-SLAYER WHO VANQUISHED NEARLY ALL MY KIN?
TRUE ENOUGH... BUT IT WAS ALWAYS THE DRAGONS PICKING FIGHTS WITH ME.
UH...
UMM...
MATTY...
YOU ALL GOOD DOWN THERE?
YEP.
I'VE SECURED OUR RIDE.
EXCEPT, UM...
...I HAVEN'T YET SAID I COULD.

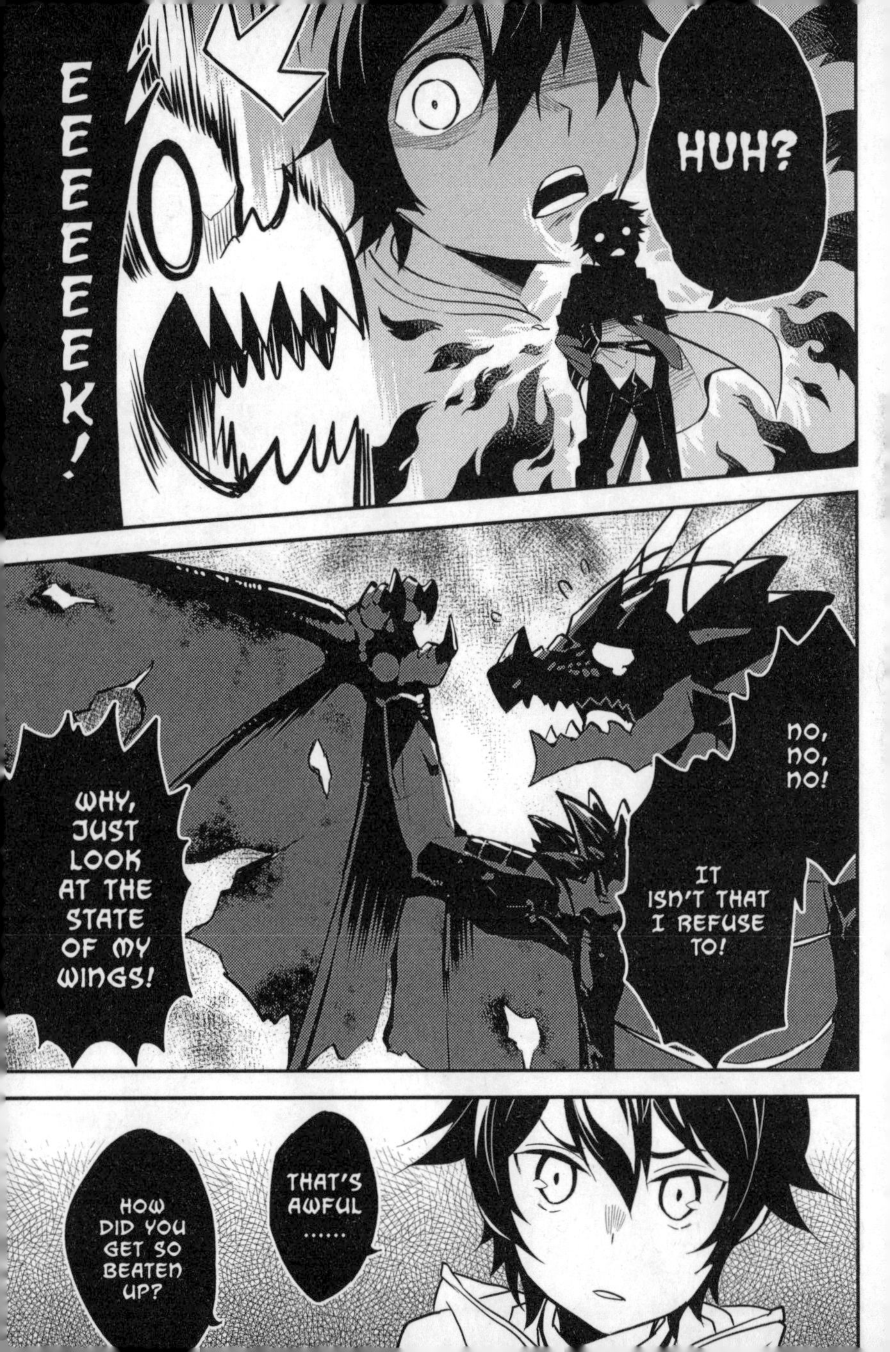
HUH?
EEEEEEEEK!
NO, NO, NO!
IT ISN'T THAT I REFUSE TO!
WHY, JUST LOOK AT THE STATE OF MY WINGS!
THAT'S AWFUL……
HOW DID YOU GET SO BEATEN UP?

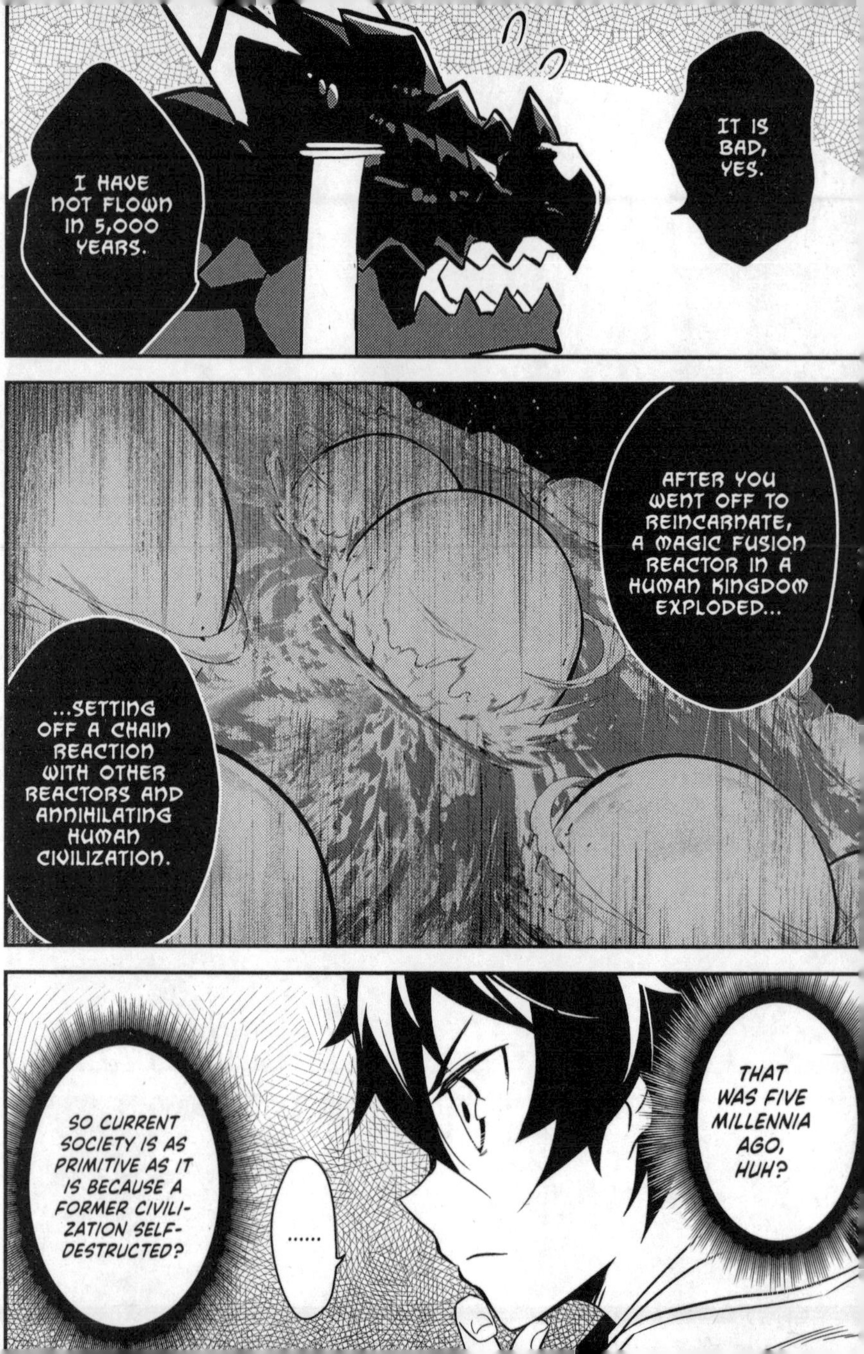
IT IS BAD, YES.
I HAVE NOT FLOWN IN 5,000 YEARS.
AFTER YOU WENT OFF TO REINCARNATE, A MAGIC FUSION REACTOR IN A HUMAN KINGDOM EXPLODED...
...SETTING OFF A CHAIN REACTION WITH OTHER REACTORS AND ANNIHILATING HUMAN CIVILIZATION.
THAT WAS FIVE MILLENNIA AGO, HUH?
......
SO CURRENT SOCIETY IS AS PRIMITIVE AS IT IS BECAUSE A FORMER CIVILI-ZATION SELF-DESTRUCTED?

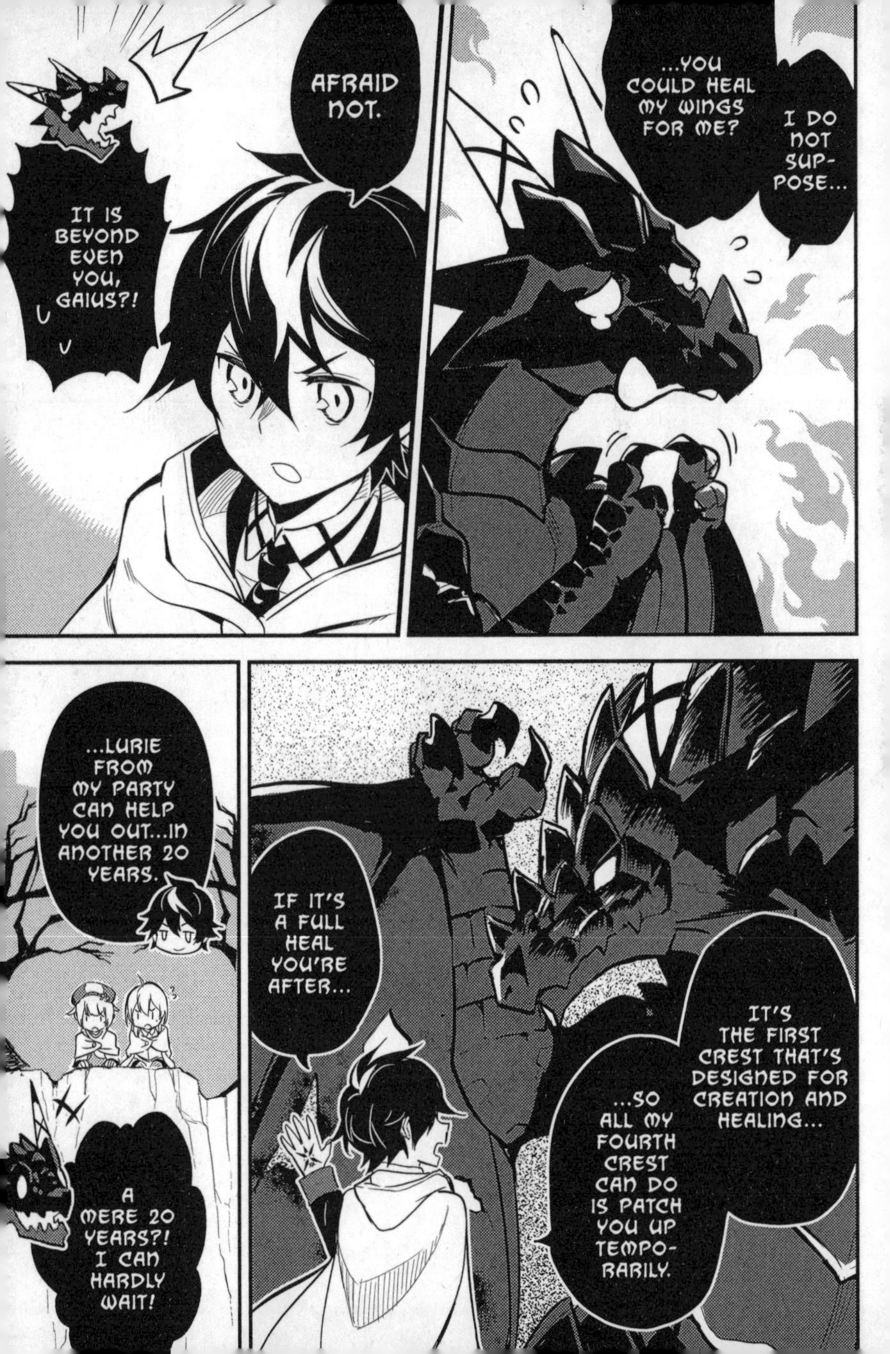
I DO NOT SUP-POSE...
...YOU COULD HEAL MY WINGS FOR ME?
AFRAID NOT.
IT IS BEYOND EVEN YOU, GAIUS?!
IF IT'S A FULL HEAL YOU'RE AFTER...
IT'S THE FIRST CREST THAT'S DESIGNED FOR CREATION AND HEALING...
...SO ALL MY FOURTH CREST CAN DO IS PATCH YOU UP TEMPO-RARILY.
...LURIE FROM MY PARTY CAN HELP YOU OUT...IN ANOTHER 20 YEARS.
A MERE 20 YEARS?! I CAN HARDLY WAIT!

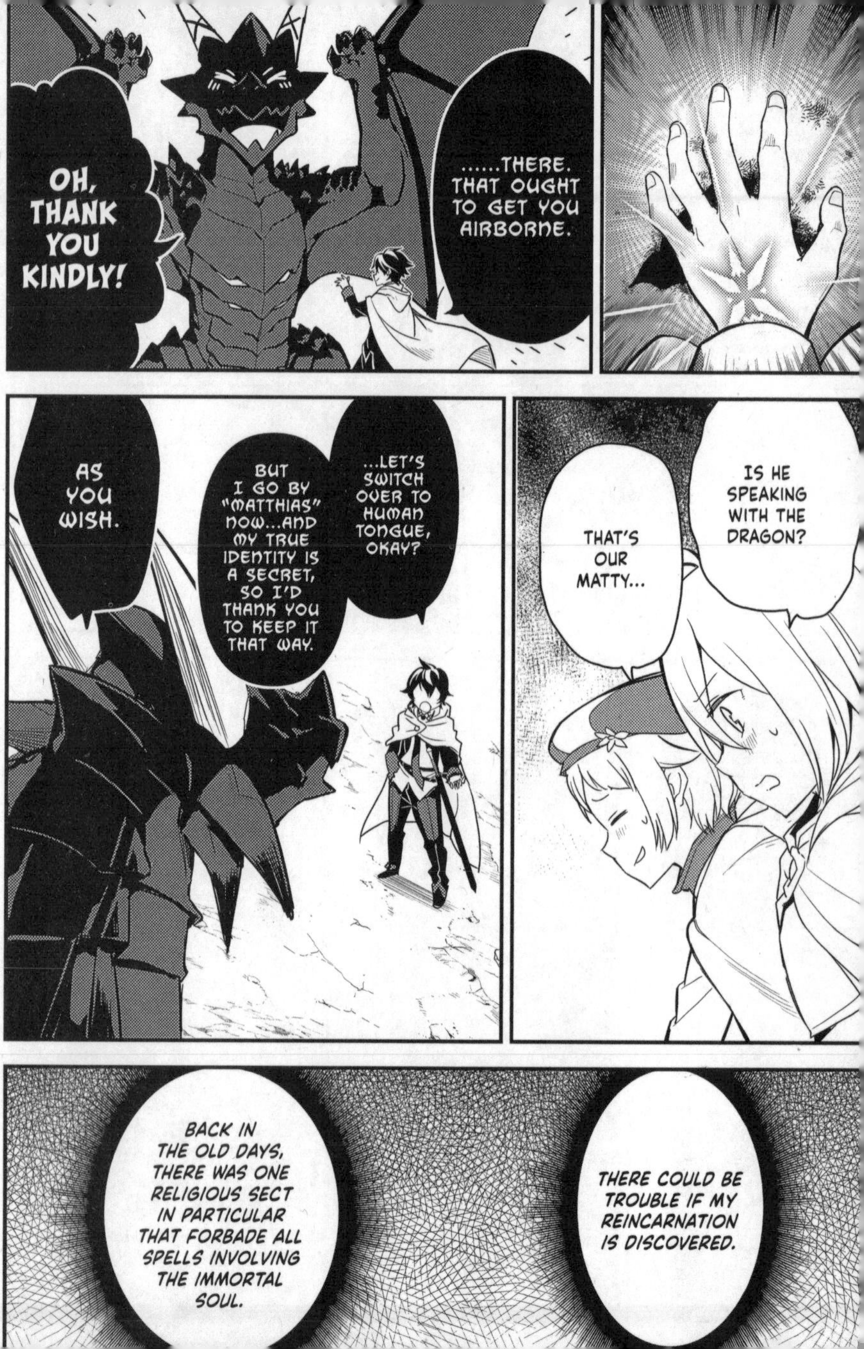

......THERE. THAT OUGHT TO GET YOU AIRBORNE.
OH, THANK YOU KINDLY!
IS HE SPEAKING WITH THE DRAGON?
THAT'S OUR MATTY...
...LET'S SWITCH OVER TO HUMAN TONGUE, OKAY?
BUT I GO BY "MATTHIAS" NOW...AND MY TRUE IDENTITY IS A SECRET, SO I'D THANK YOU TO KEEP IT THAT WAY.
AS YOU WISH.
THERE COULD BE TROUBLE IF MY REINCARNATION IS DISCOVERED.
BACK IN THE OLD DAYS, THERE WAS ONE RELIGIOUS SECT IN PARTICULAR THAT FORBADE ALL SPELLS INVOLVING THE IMMORTAL SOUL.

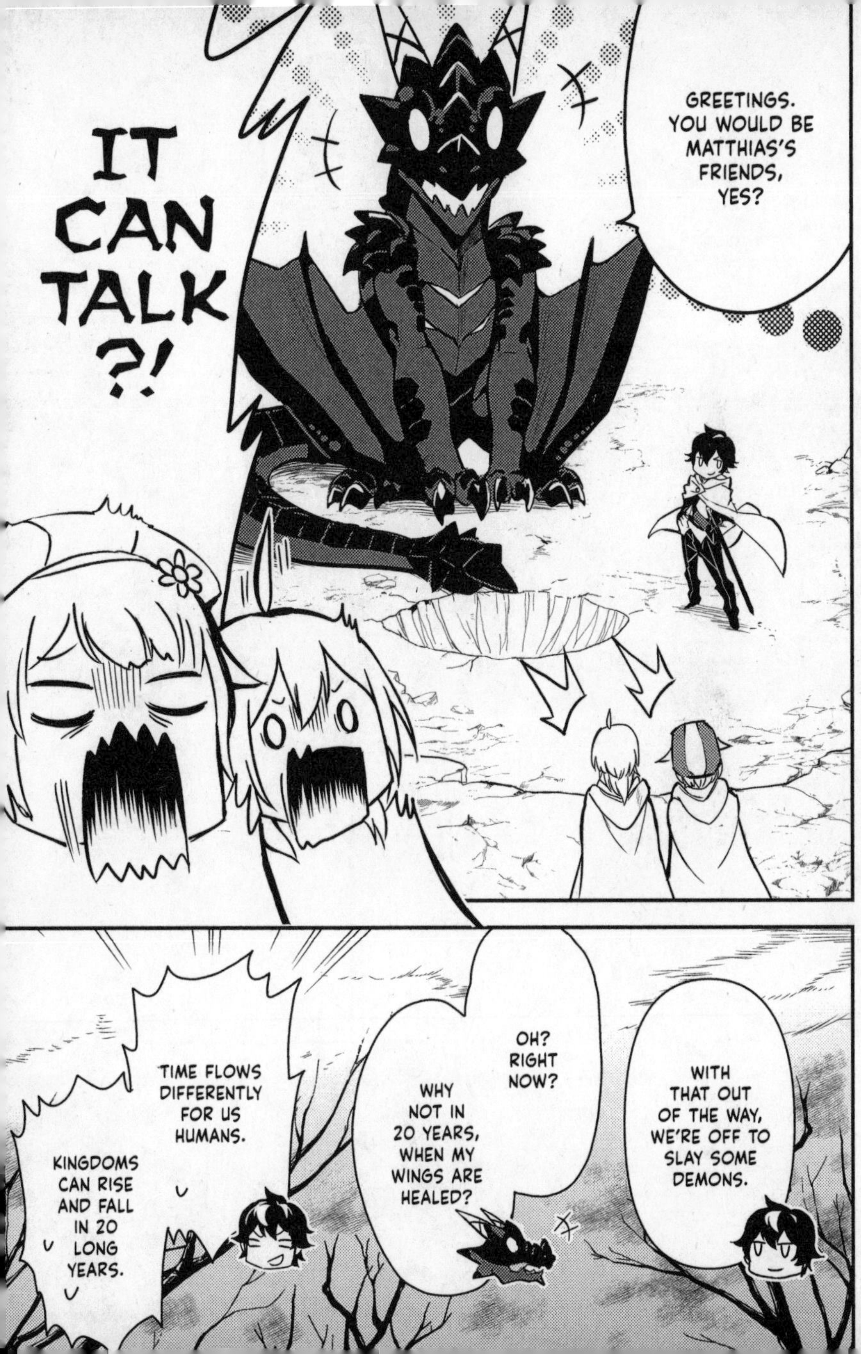
GREETINGS. YOU WOULD BE MATTHIAS'S FRIENDS, YES?
IT CAN TALK?!
WITH THAT OUT OF THE WAY, WE'RE OFF TO SLAY SOME DEMONS.
OH? RIGHT NOW?
WHY NOT IN 20 YEARS, WHEN MY WINGS ARE HEALED?
TIME FLOWS DIFFERENTLY FOR US HUMANS.
KINGDOMS CAN RISE AND FALL IN 20 LONG YEARS.

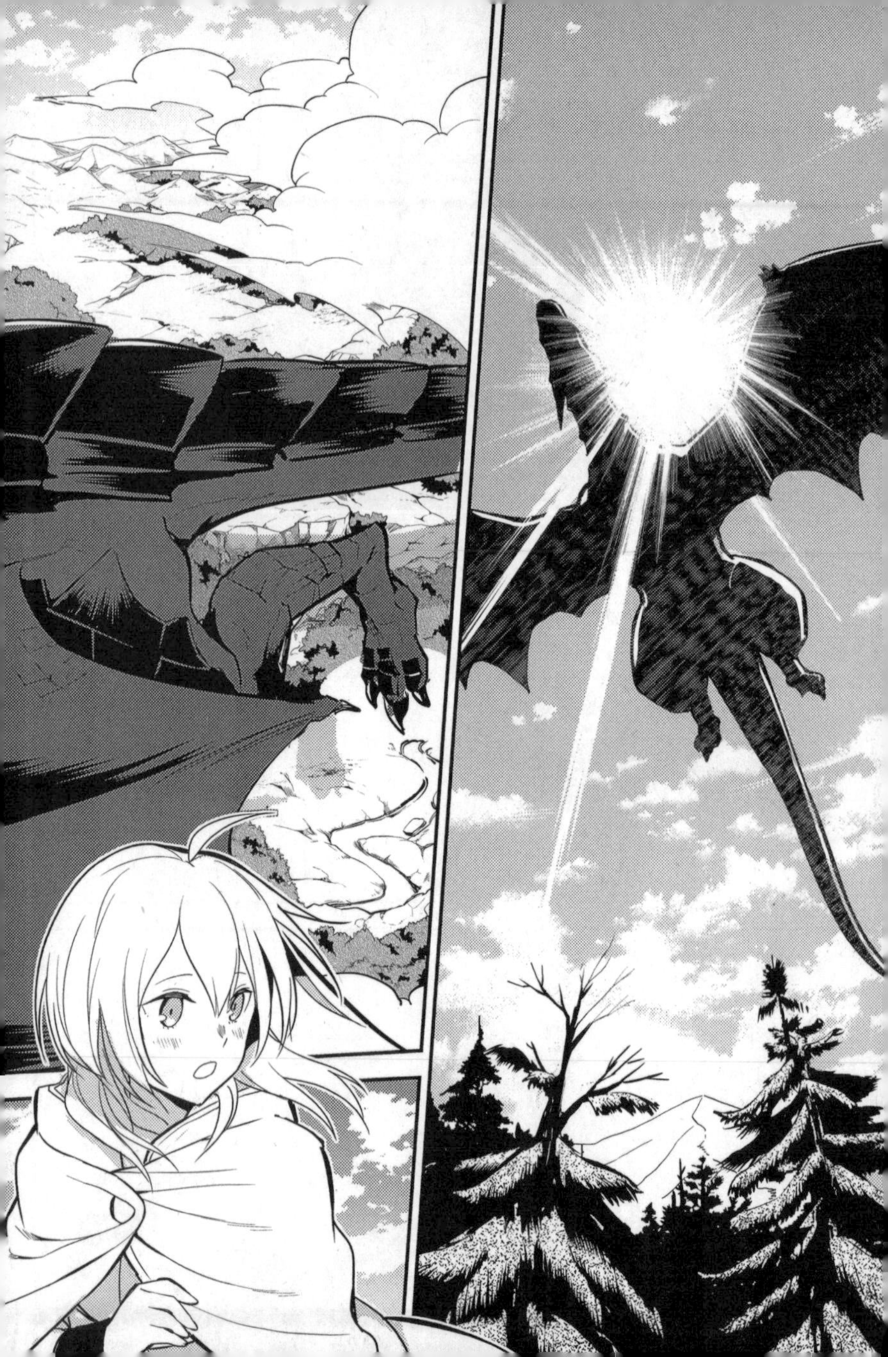

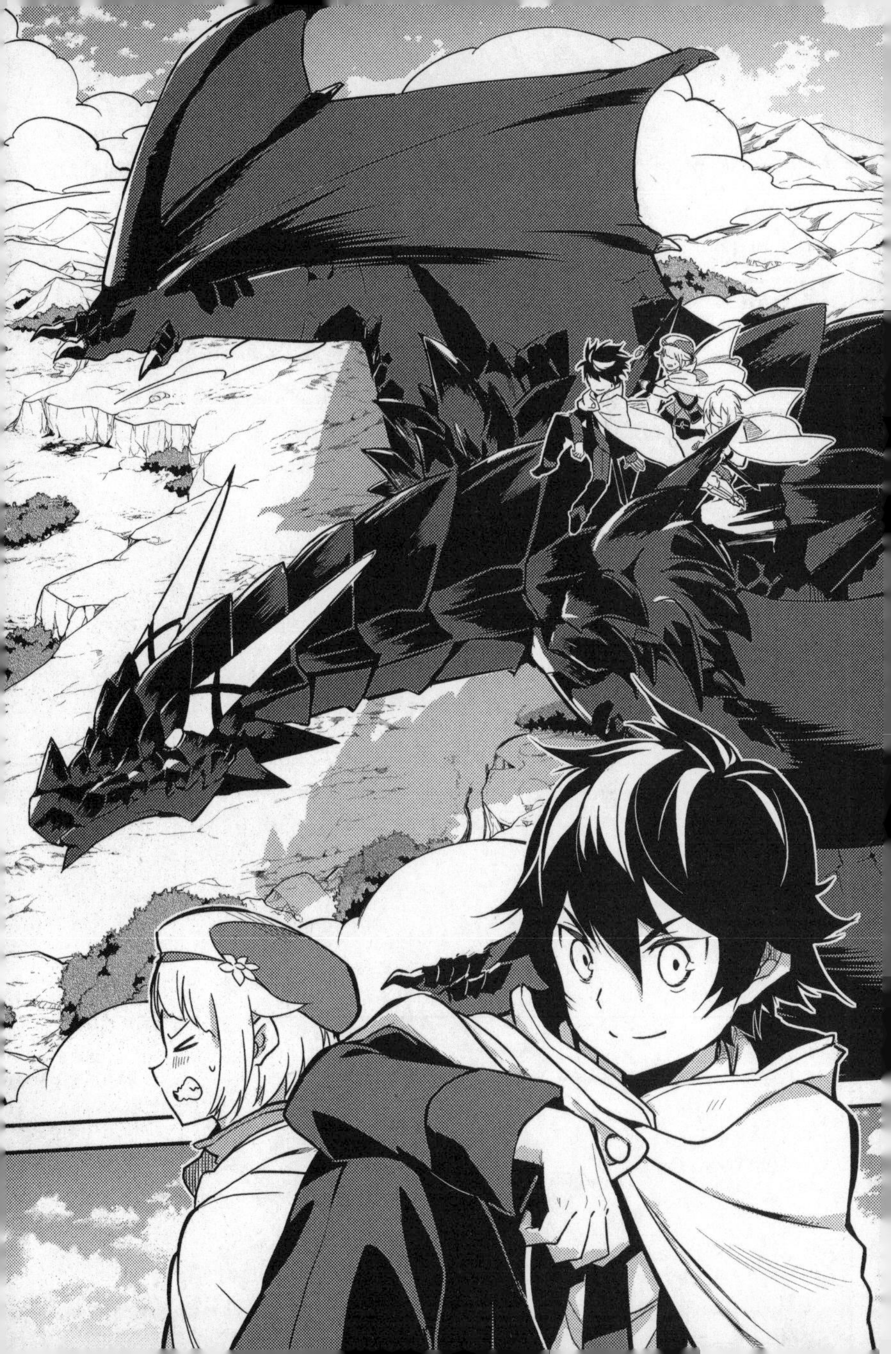

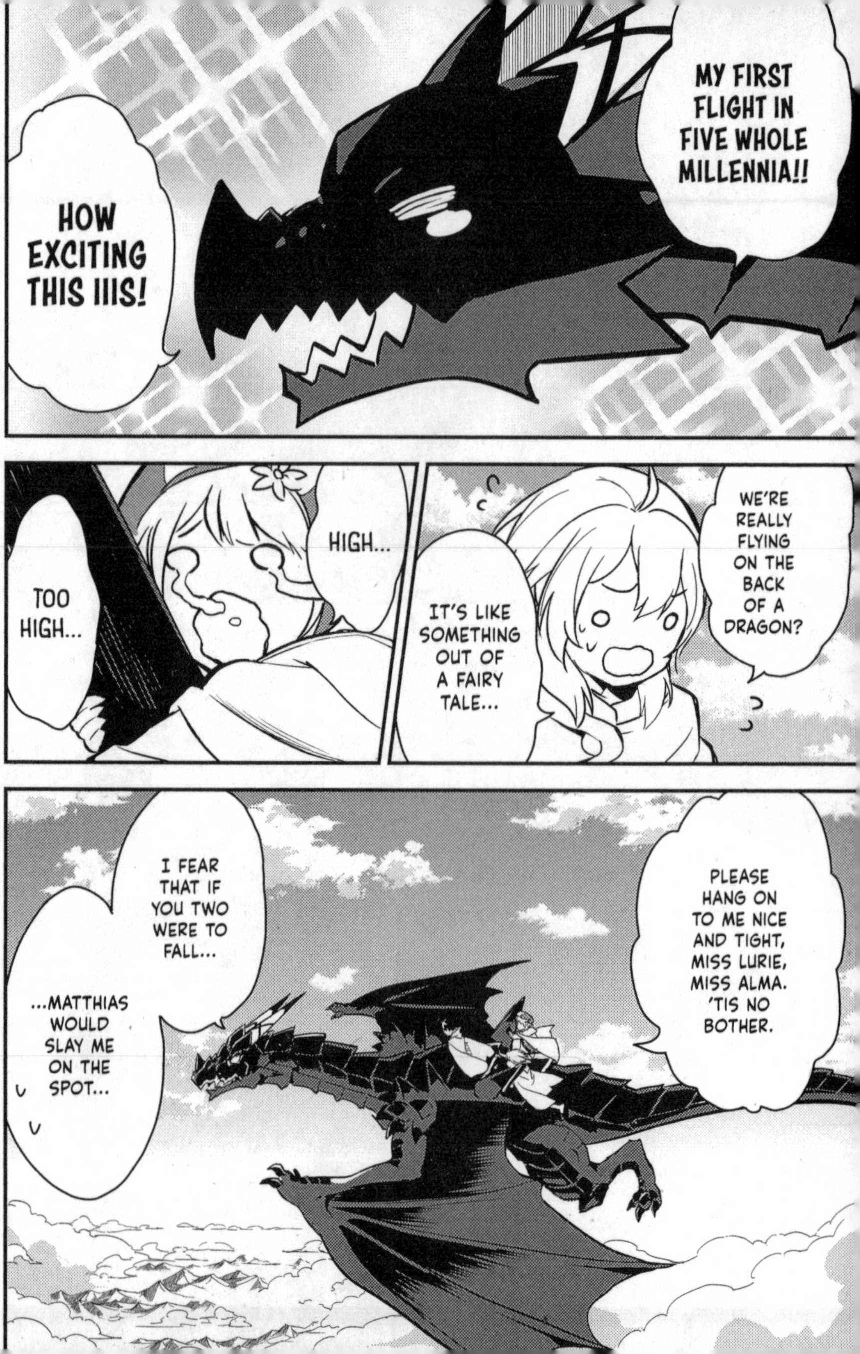
MY FIRST FLIGHT IN FIVE WHOLE MILLENNIA!!
HOW EXCITING THIS IIIS!
WE'RE REALLY FLYING ON THE BACK OF A DRAGON?
IT'S LIKE SOMETHING OUT OF A FAIRY TALE...
HIGH...
TOO HIGH...
PLEASE HANG ON TO ME NICE AND TIGHT, MISS LURIE, MISS ALMA. 'TIS NO BOTHER.
I FEAR THAT IF YOU TWO WERE TO FALL...
...MATTHIAS WOULD SLAY ME ON THE SPOT...

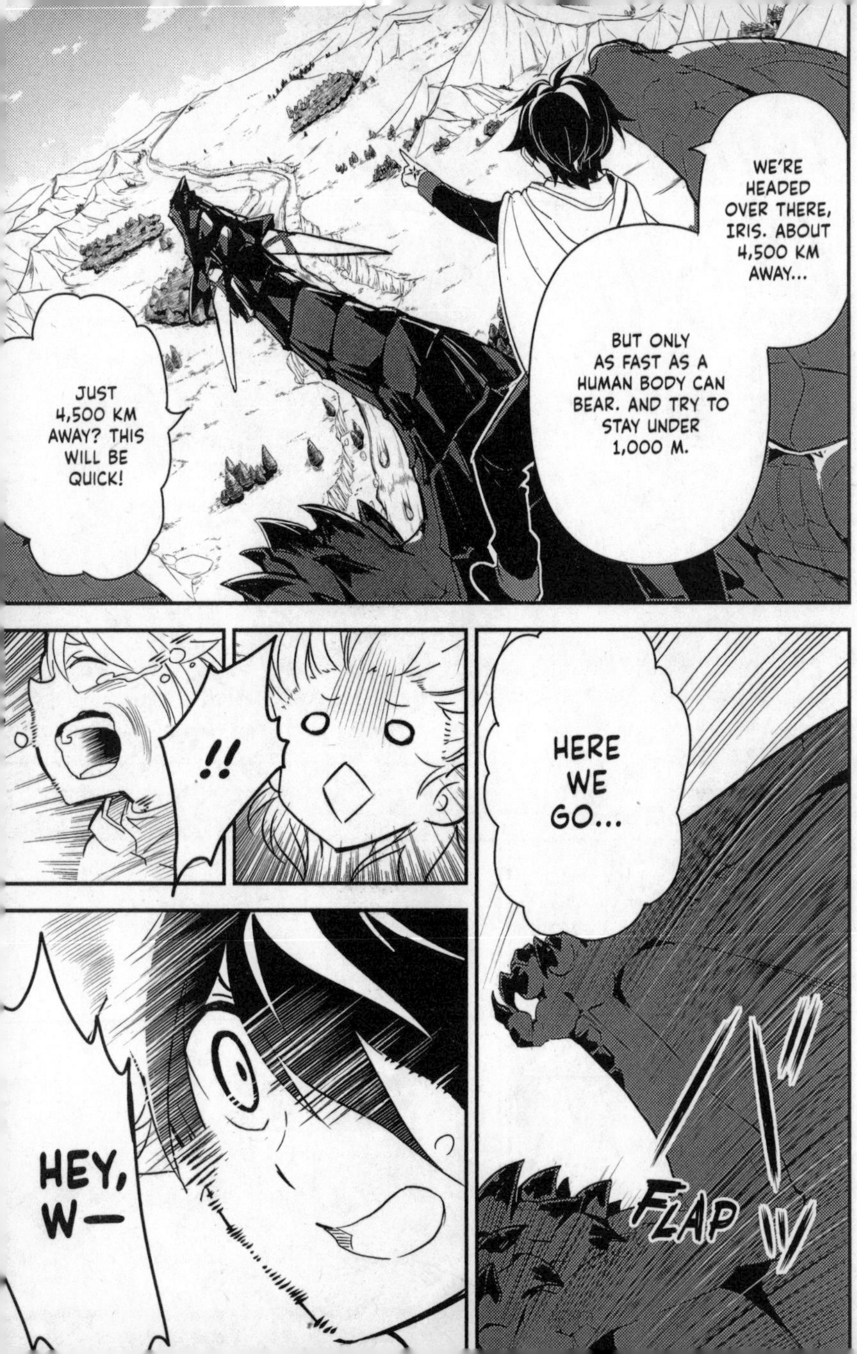
WE'RE HEADED OVER THERE, IRIS. ABOUT 4,500 KM AWAY...
BUT ONLY AS FAST AS A HUMAN BODY CAN BEAR. AND TRY TO STAY UNDER 1,000 M.
JUST 4,500 KM AWAY? THIS WILL BE QUICK!
HERE WE GO...
FLAP
!!
HEY, W—

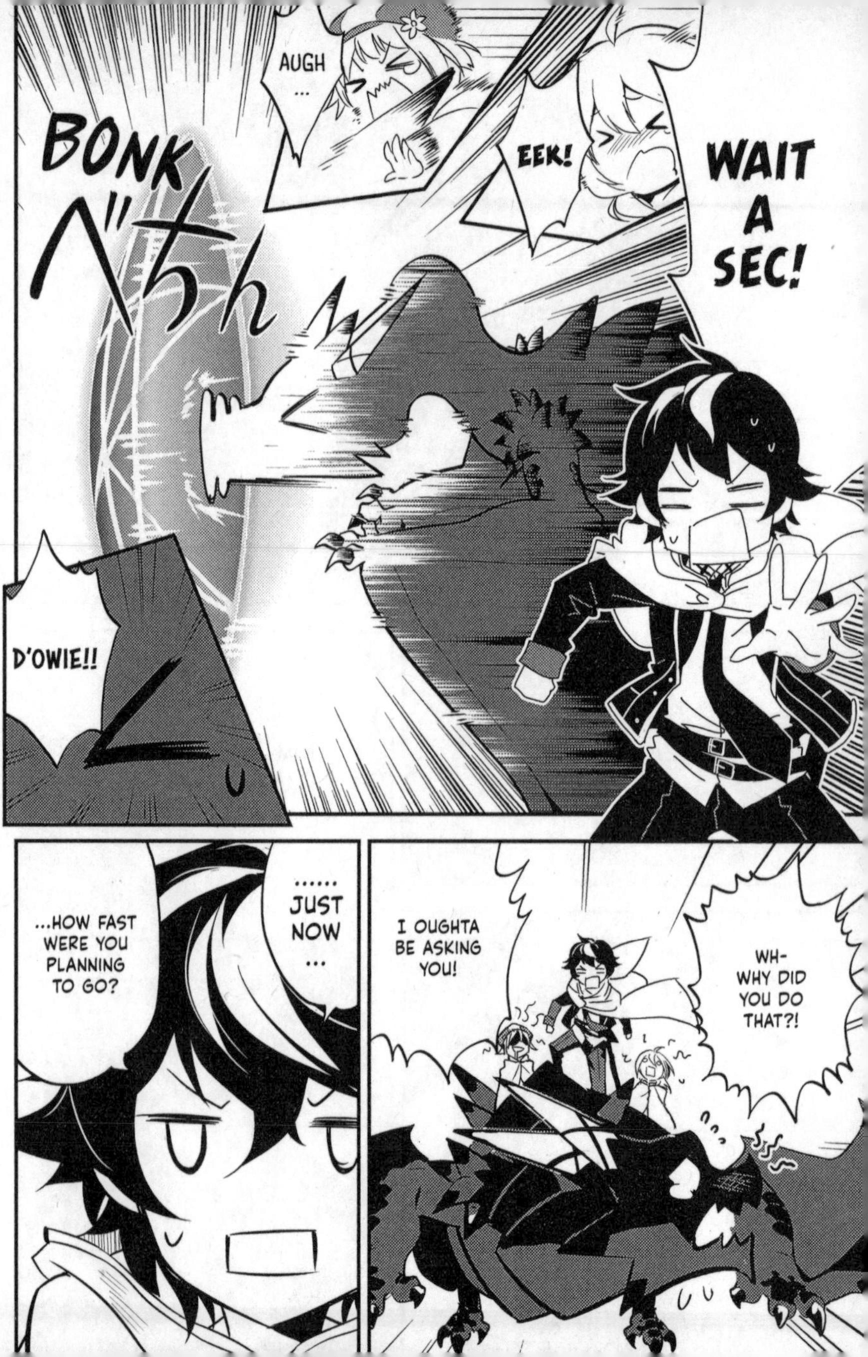
WAIT A SEC!
EEK!
AUGH ...
BONK
べちん
D'OWIE!!
WH- WHY DID YOU DO THAT?!
I OUGHTA BE ASKING YOU!
...... JUST NOW ...
...HOW FAST WERE YOU PLANNING TO GO?

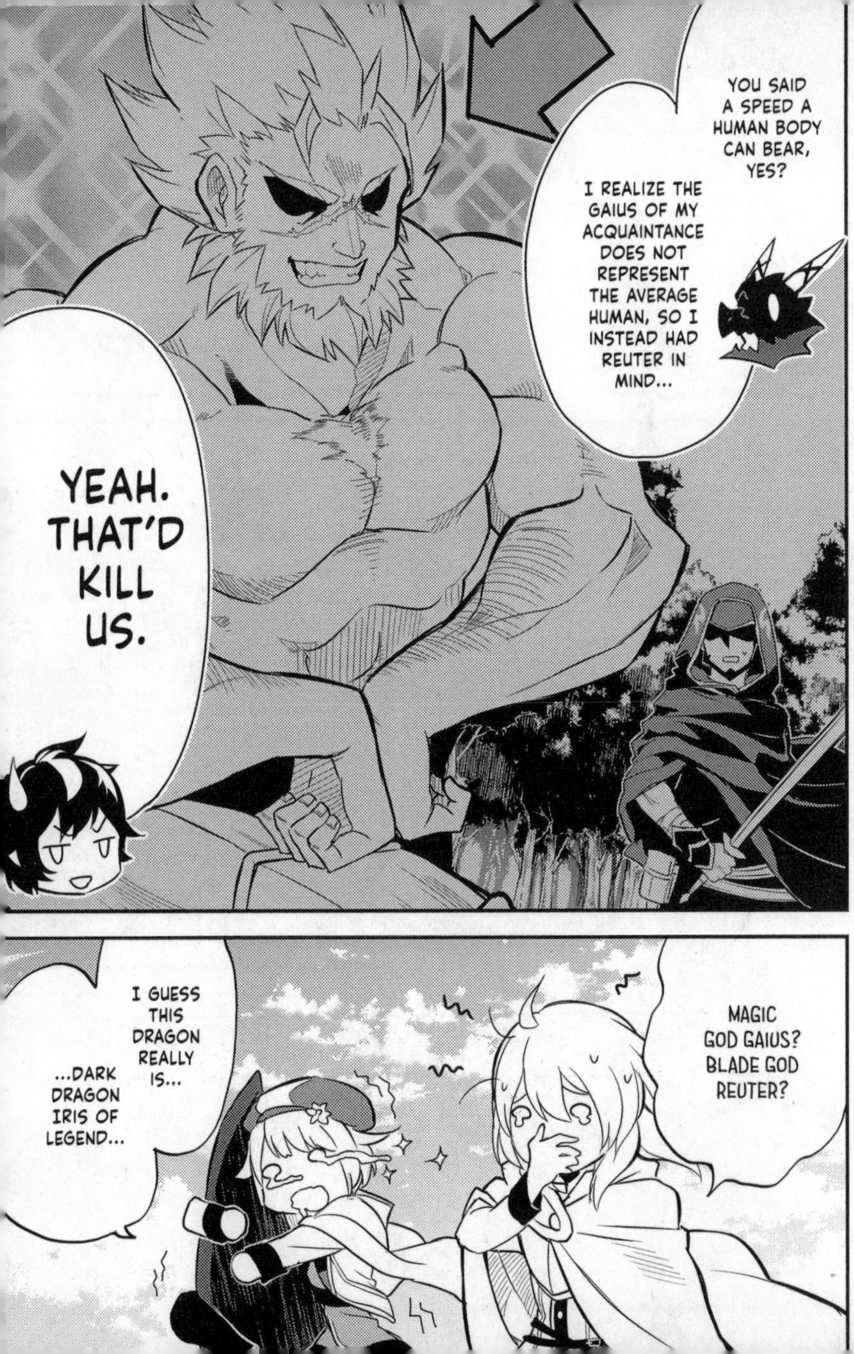
YOU SAID A SPEED A HUMAN BODY CAN BEAR, YES?
I REALIZE THE GAIUS OF MY ACQUAINTANCE DOES NOT REPRESENT THE AVERAGE HUMAN, SO I INSTEAD HAD REUTER IN MIND...
YEAH. THAT'D KILL US.
MAGIC GOD GAIUS? BLADE GOD REUTER?
I GUESS THIS DRAGON REALLY IS...
...DARK DRAGON IRIS OF LEGEND...

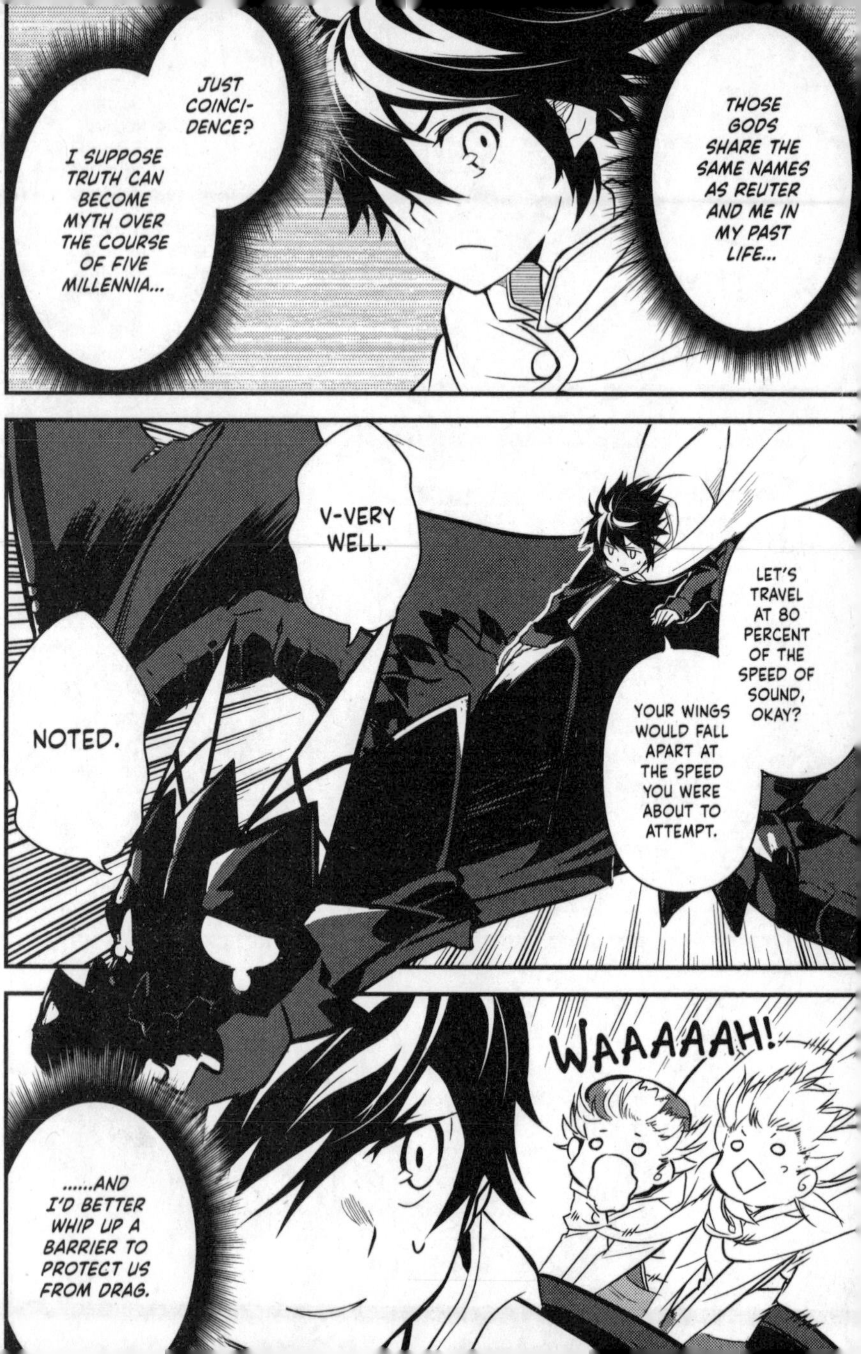
THOSE GODS SHARE THE SAME NAMES AS REUTER AND ME IN MY PAST LIFE...
JUST COINCIDENCE?
I SUPPOSE TRUTH CAN BECOME MYTH OVER THE COURSE OF FIVE MILLENNIA...
LET'S TRAVEL AT 80 PERCENT OF THE SPEED OF SOUND, OKAY?
YOUR WINGS WOULD FALL APART AT THE SPEED YOU WERE ABOUT TO ATTEMPT.
V-VERY WELL.
NOTED.
WAAAAAH!
......AND I'D BETTER WHIP UP A BARRIER TO PROTECT US FROM DRAG.

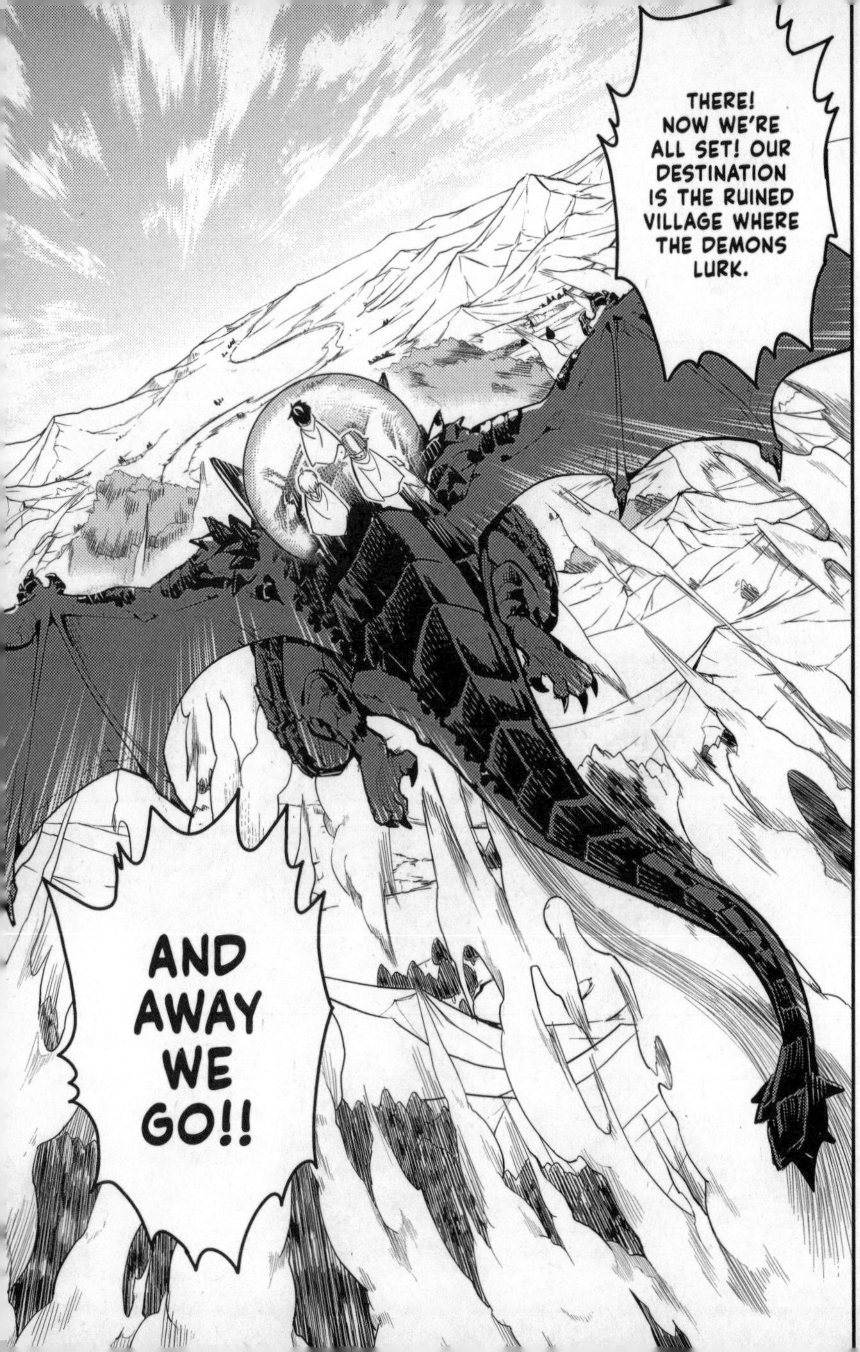
THERE! NOW WE'RE ALL SET! OUR DESTINATION IS THE RUINED VILLAGE WHERE THE DEMONS LURK.
AND AWAY WE GO!!

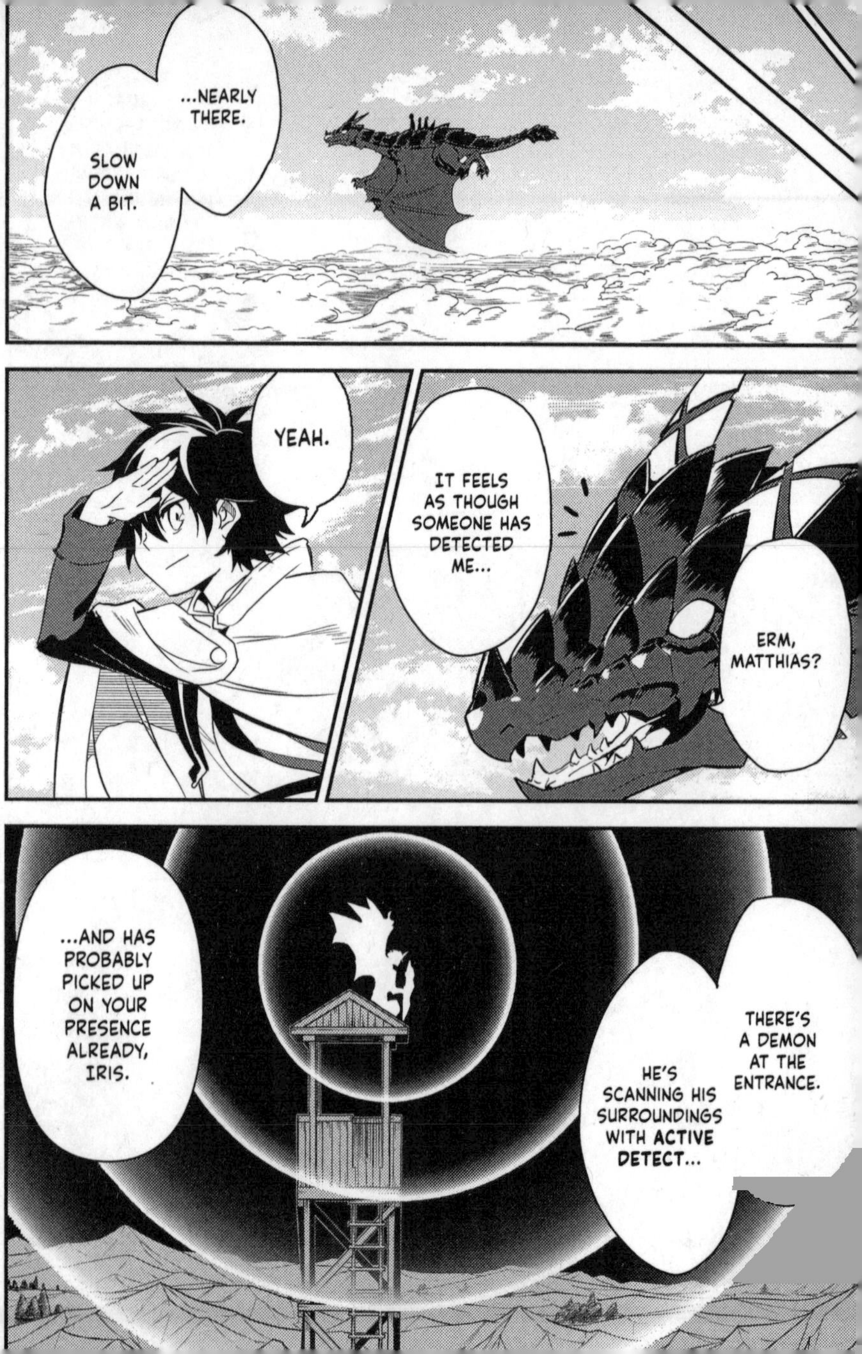

...NEARLY THERE.
SLOW DOWN A BIT.
ERM, MATTHIAS?
IT FEELS AS THOUGH SOMEONE HAS DETECTED ME...
YEAH.
THERE'S A DEMON AT THE ENTRANCE.
HE'S SCANNING HIS SURROUNDINGS WITH ACTIVE DETECT...
...AND HAS PROBABLY PICKED UP ON YOUR PRESENCE ALREADY, IRIS.

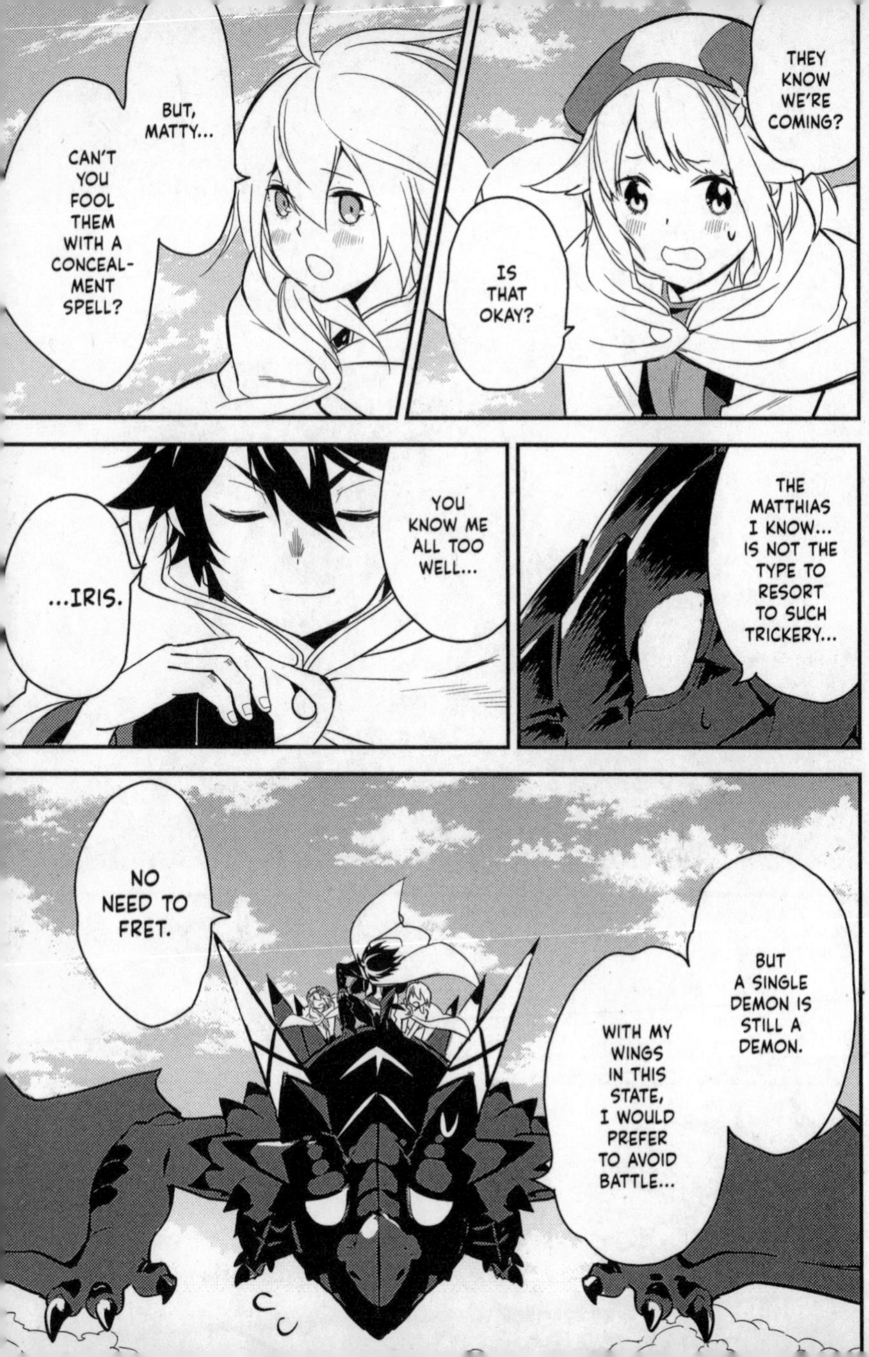
THEY KNOW WE'RE COMING?
IS THAT OKAY?
BUT, MATTY...
CAN'T YOU FOOL THEM WITH A CONCEAL-MENT SPELL?
THE MATTHIAS I KNOW... IS NOT THE TYPE TO RESORT TO SUCH TRICKERY...
YOU KNOW ME ALL TOO WELL...
...IRIS.
BUT A SINGLE DEMON IS STILL A DEMON.
WITH MY WINGS IN THIS STATE, I WOULD PREFER TO AVOID BATTLE...
NO NEED TO FRET.

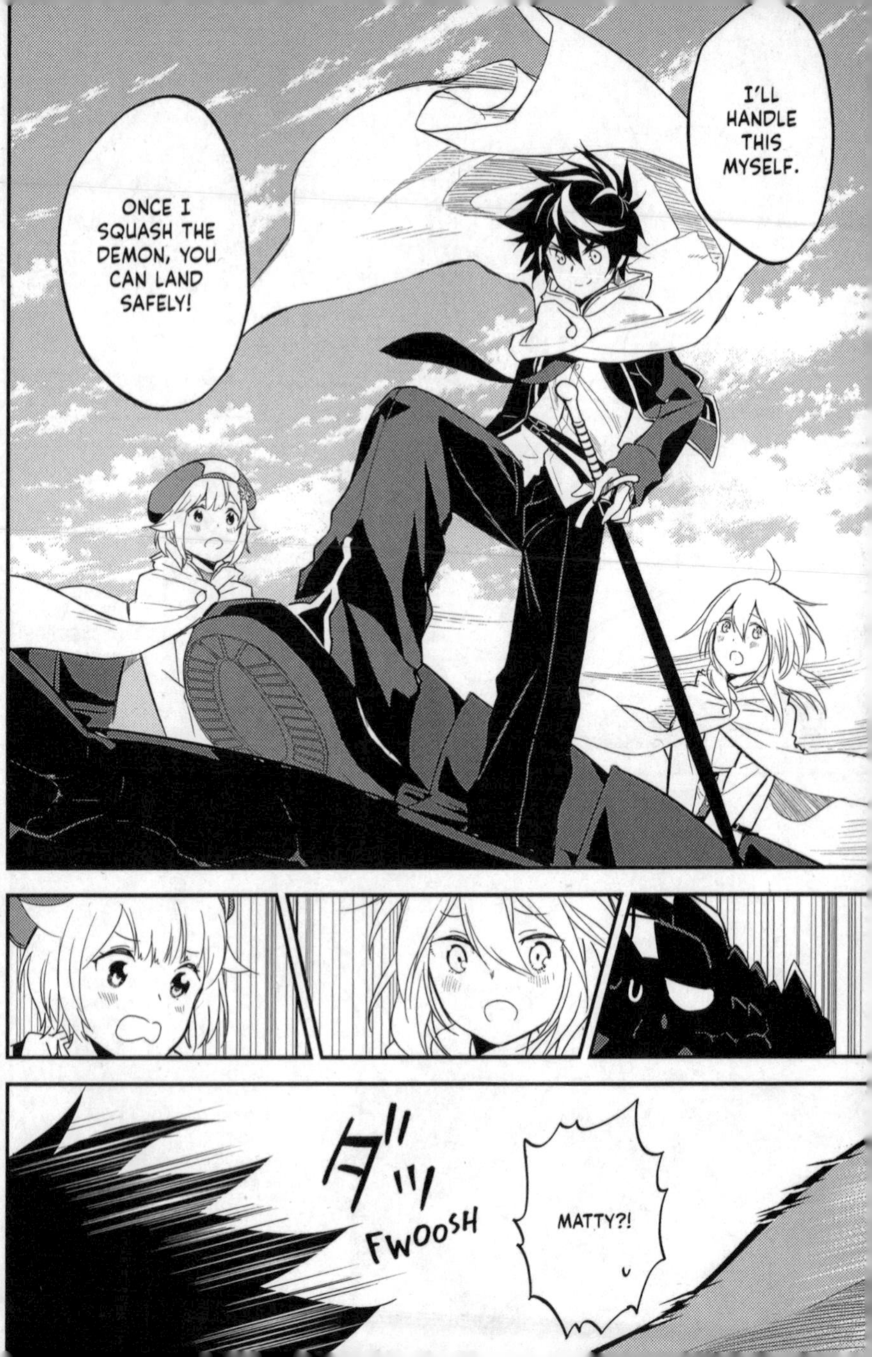
I'LL HANDLE THIS MYSELF.
ONCE I SQUASH THE DEMON, YOU CAN LAND SAFELY!
MATTY?!
ダッ
FWOOSH

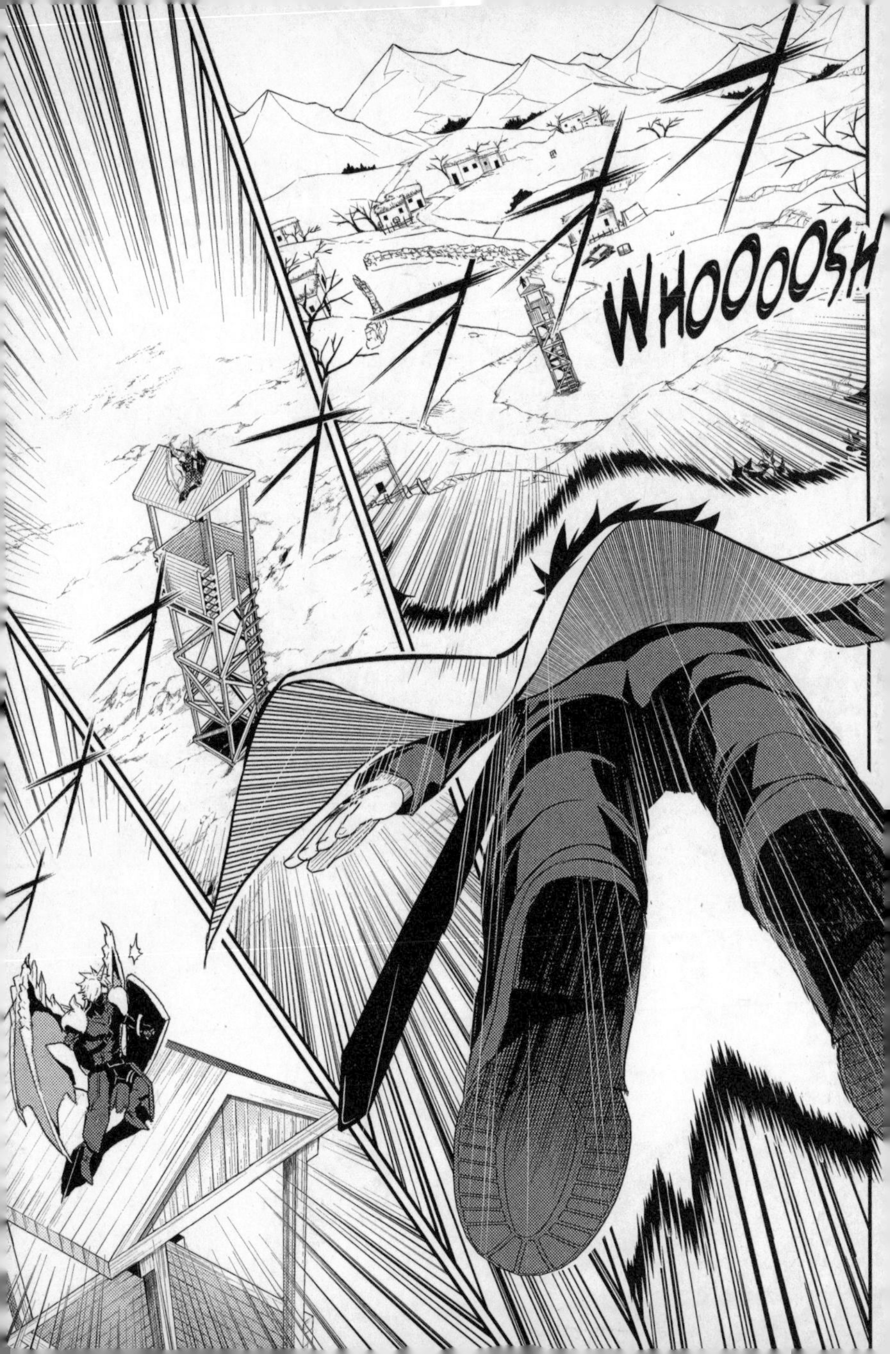
WHOOOOSH

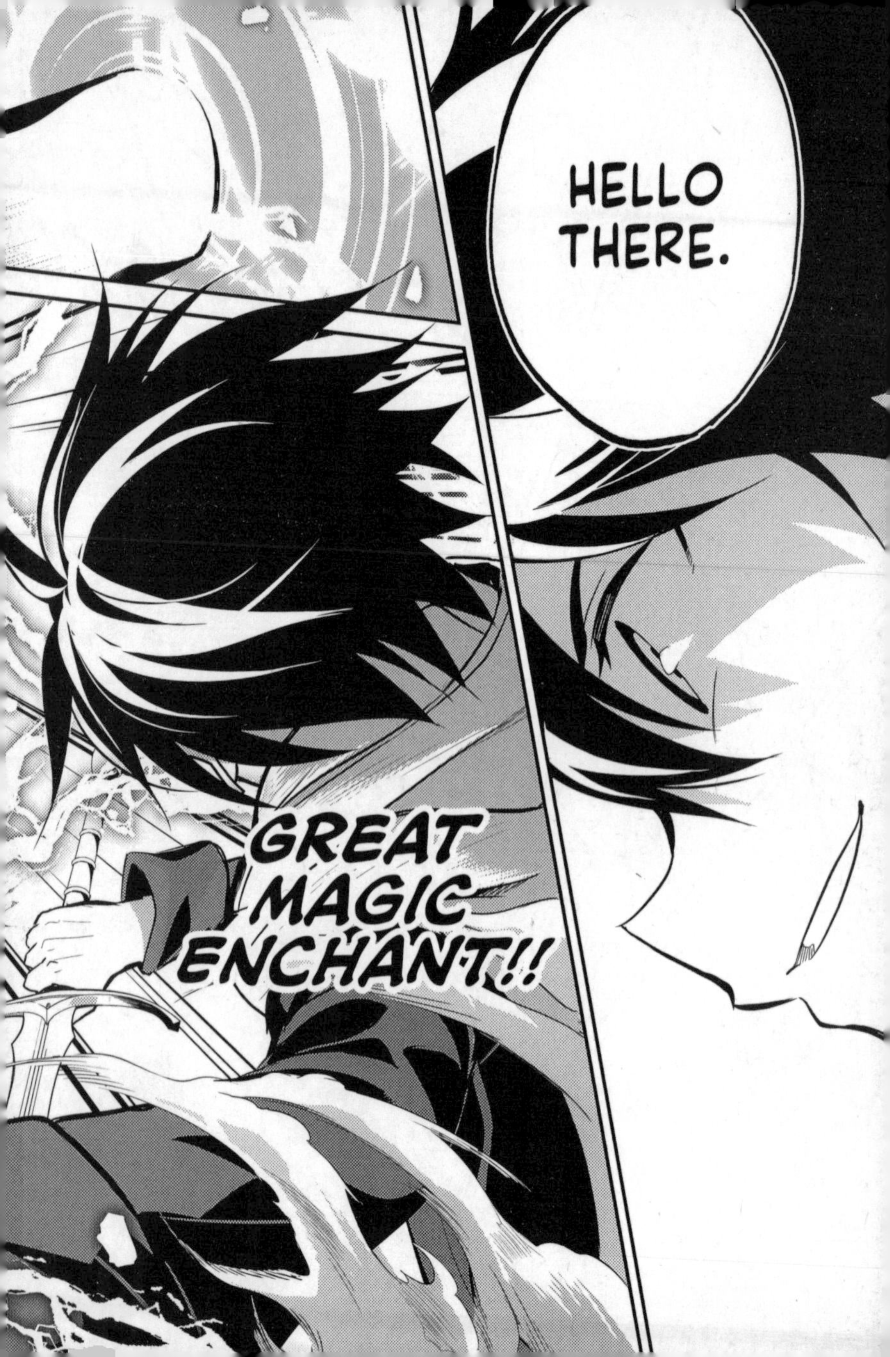
HELLO THERE.
GREAT MAGIC ENCHANT!!

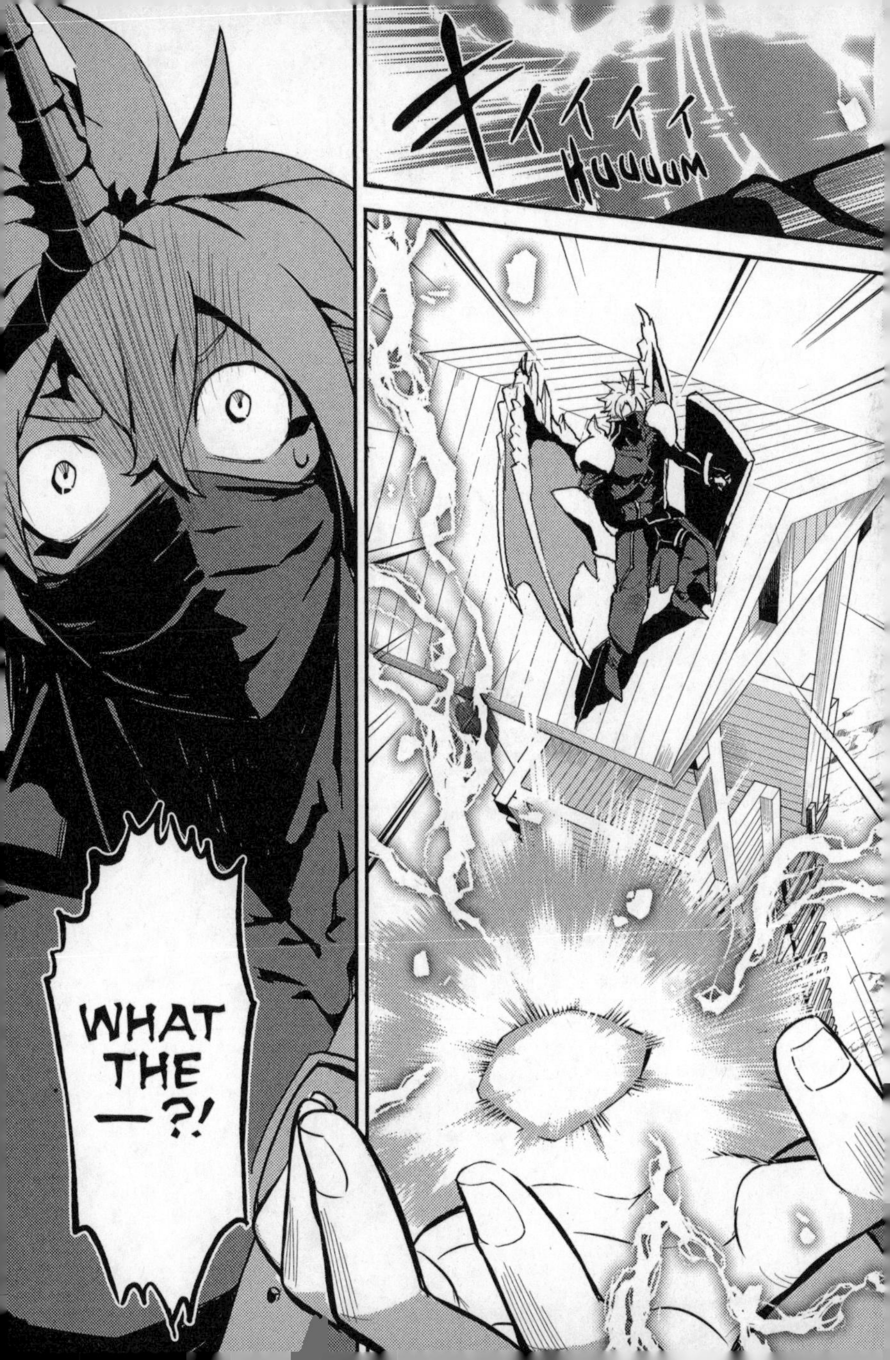
キイイイイ
HUUUUM
WHAT THE—?!

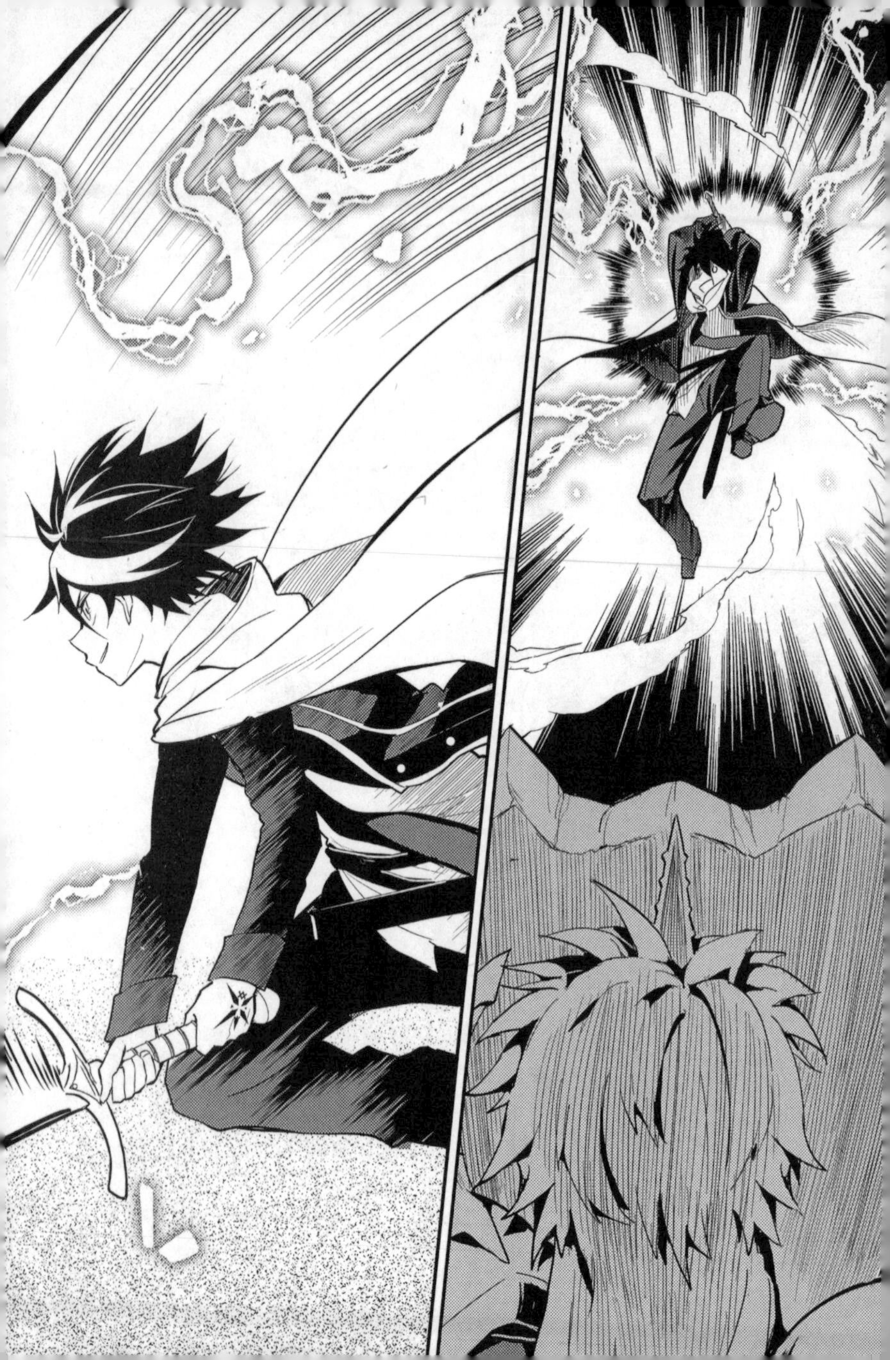

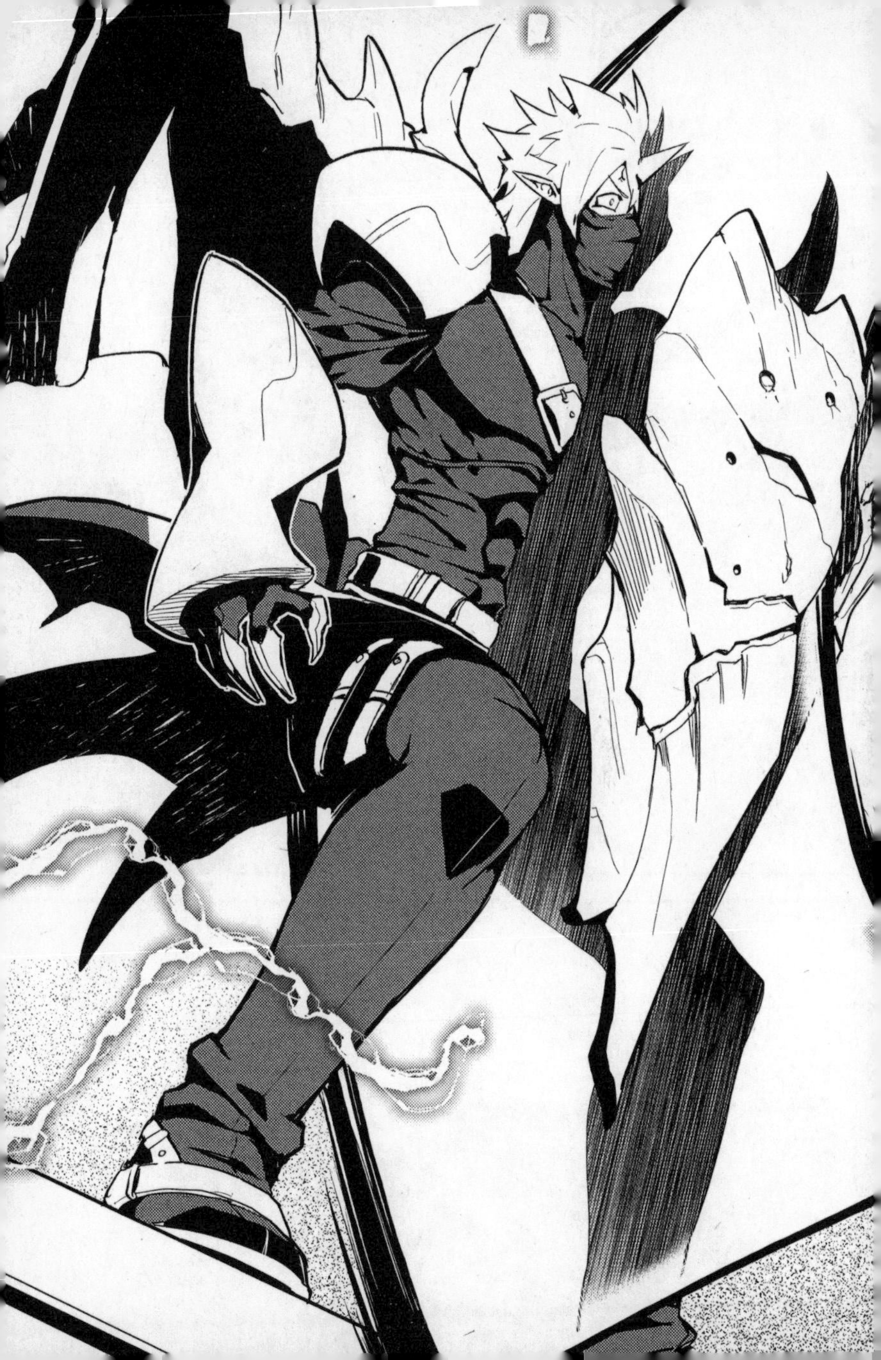

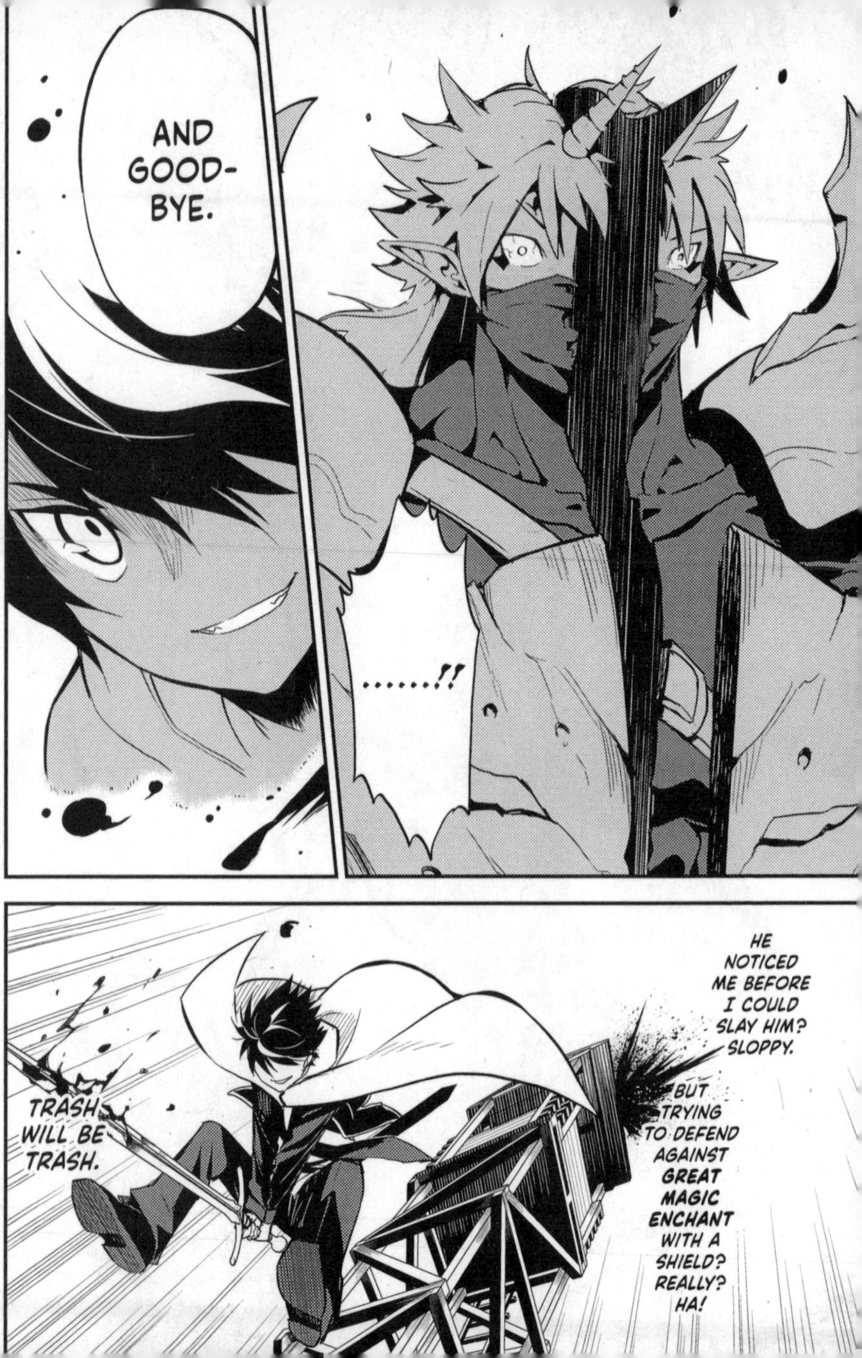
......!!
AND GOOD-BYE.
HE NOTICED ME BEFORE I COULD SLAY HIM? SLOPPY.
BUT TRYING TO DEFEND AGAINST GREAT MAGIC ENCHANT WITH A SHIELD? REALLY? HA!
TRASH WILL BE TRASH.

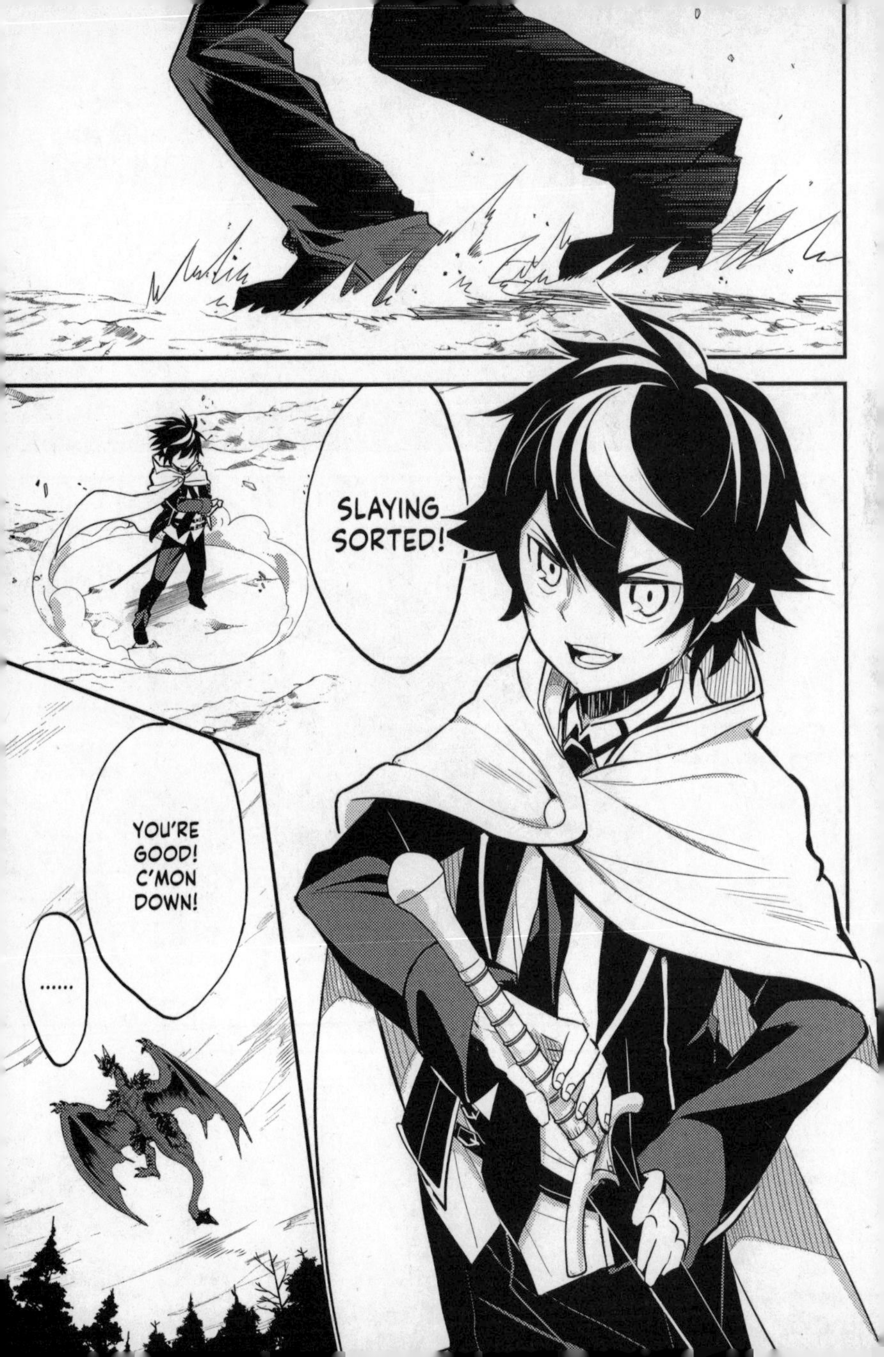
SLAYING SORTED!
YOU'RE GOOD! C'MON DOWN!
......

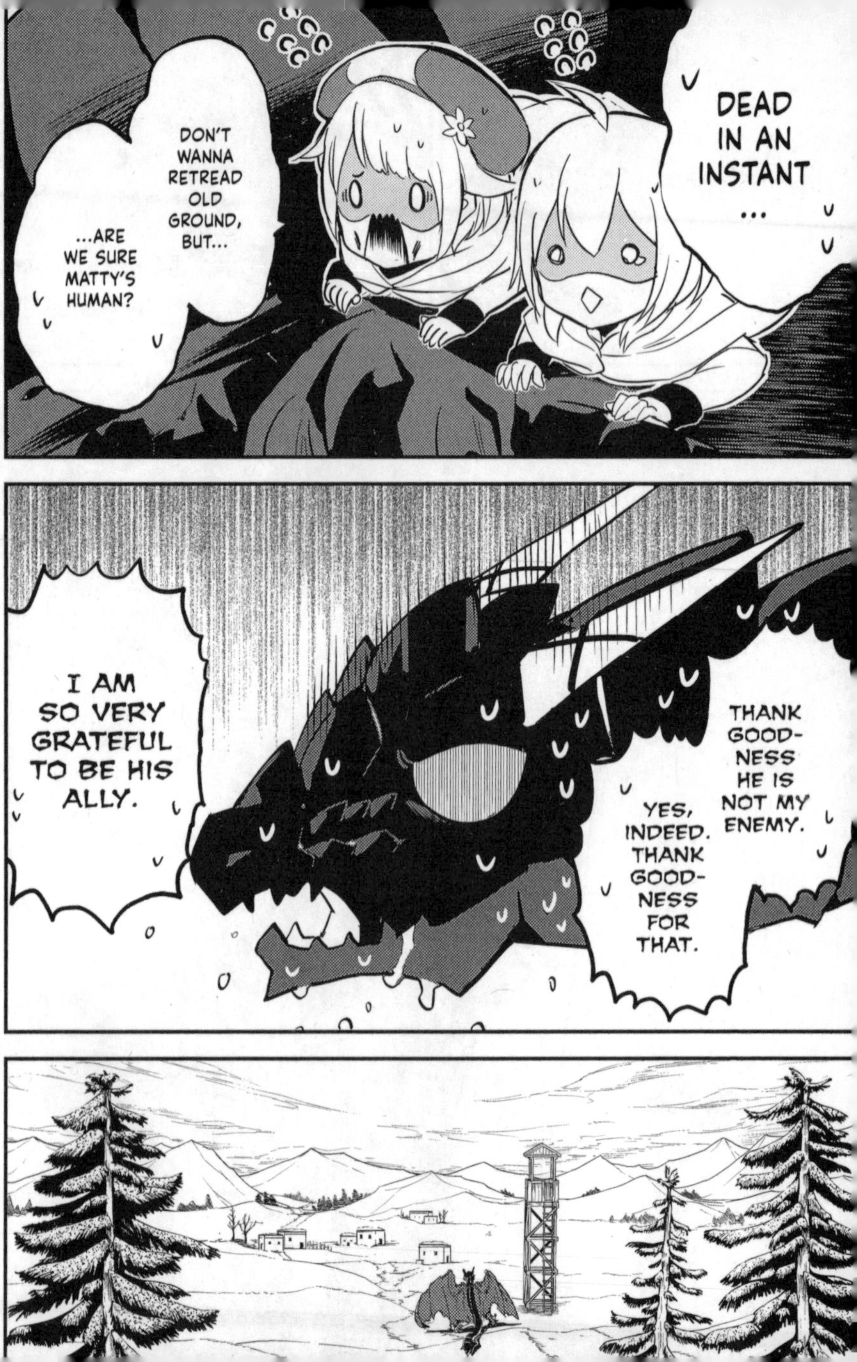
DEAD IN AN INSTANT...
DON'T WANNA RETREAD OLD GROUND, BUT...
...ARE WE SURE MATTY'S HUMAN?
THANK GOODNESS HE IS NOT MY ENEMY.
YES, INDEED. THANK GOODNESS FOR THAT.
I AM SO VERY GRATEFUL TO BE HIS ALLY.

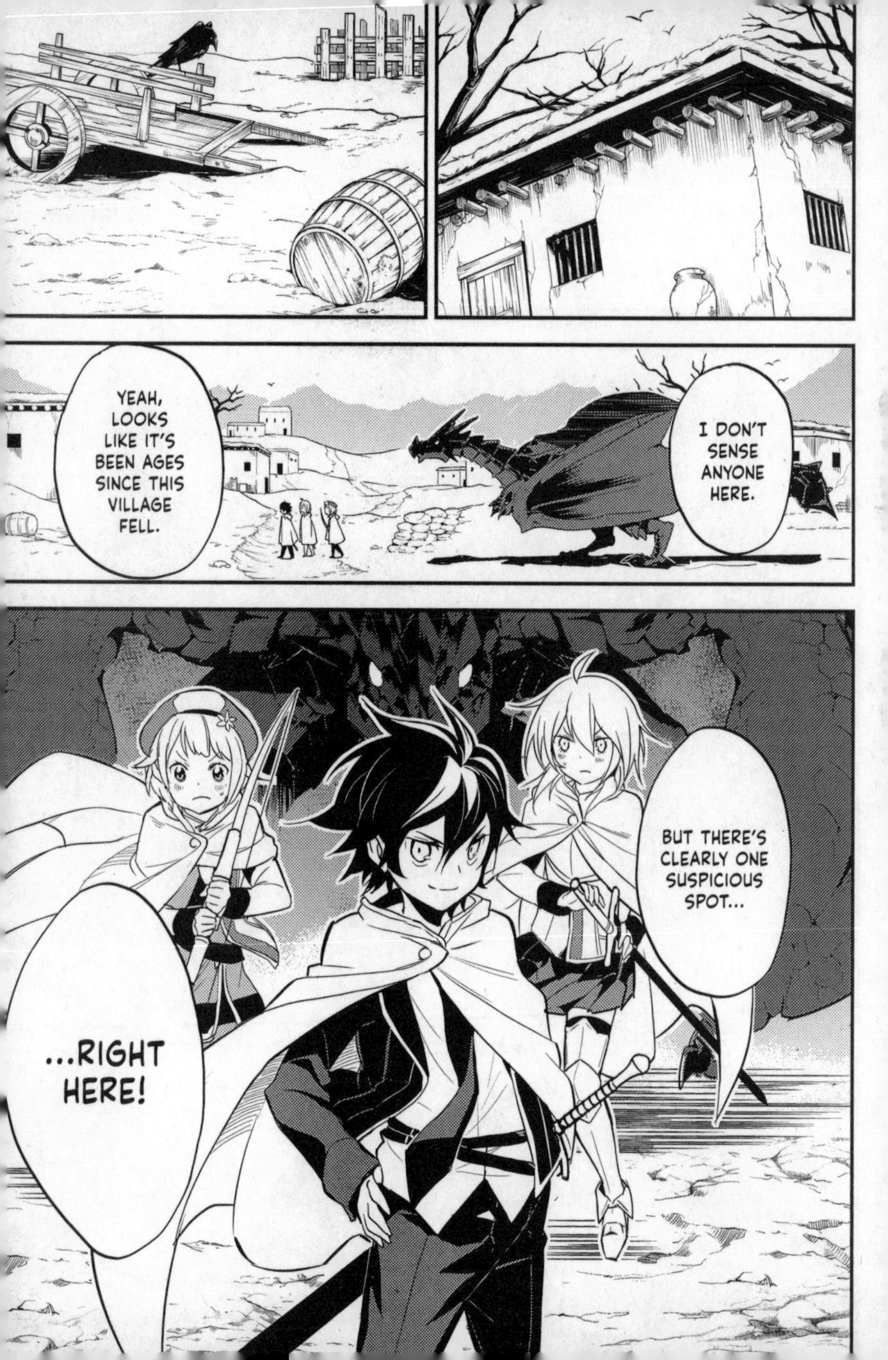
I DON'T SENSE ANYONE HERE.
YEAH, LOOKS LIKE IT'S BEEN AGES SINCE THIS VILLAGE FELL.
BUT THERE'S CLEARLY ONE SUSPICIOUS SPOT...
...RIGHT HERE!

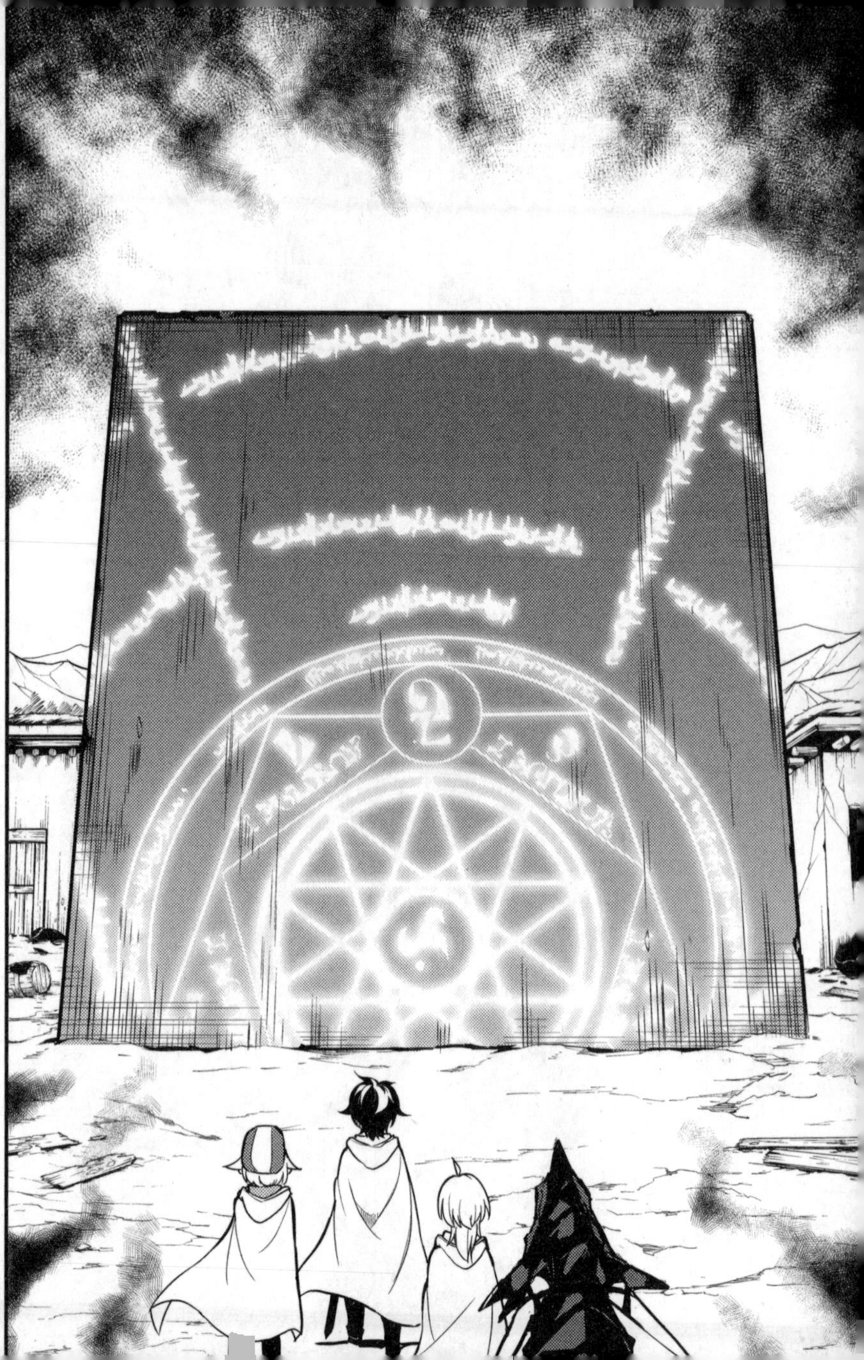

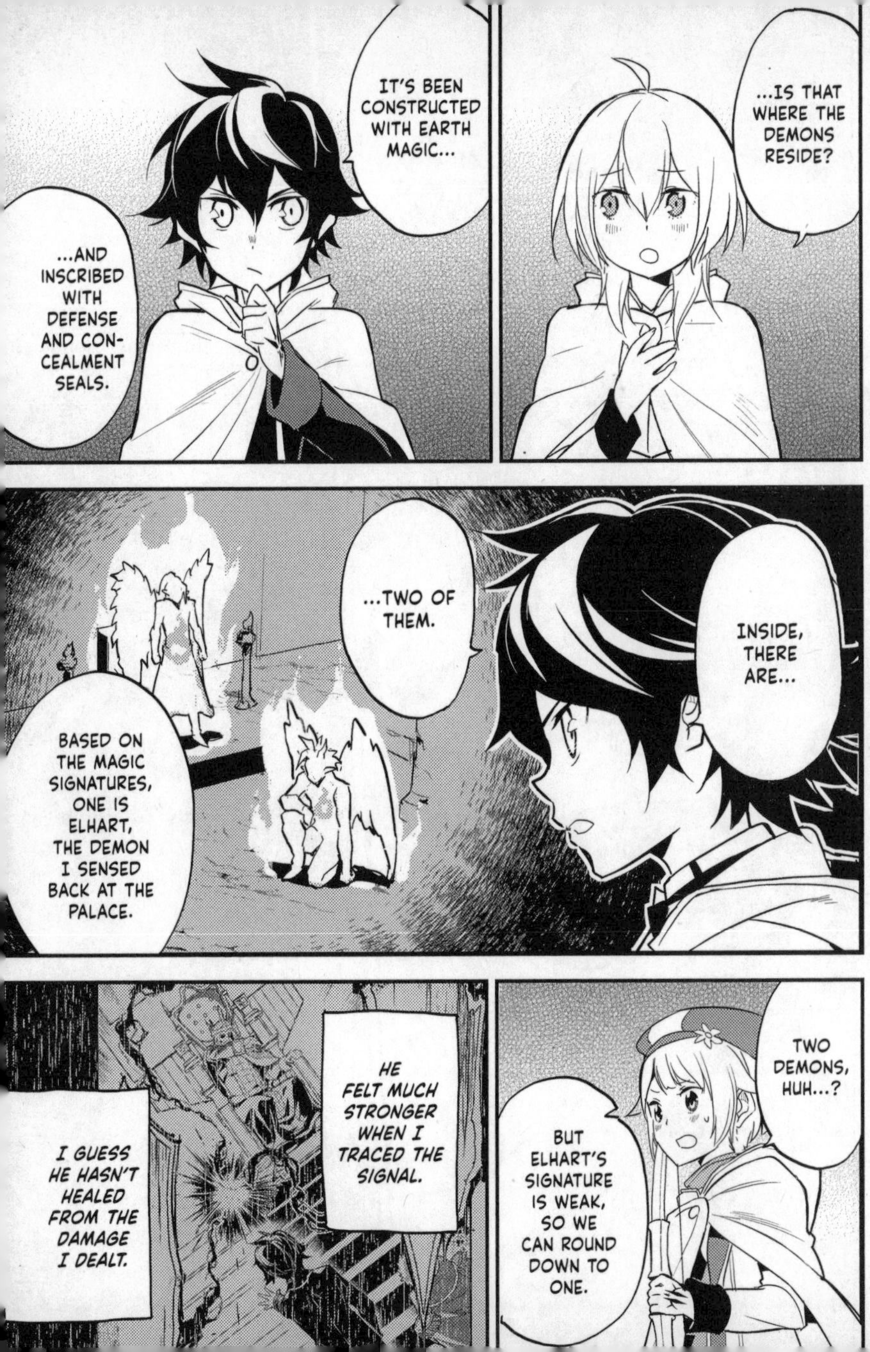
...IS THAT WHERE THE DEMONS RESIDE?
IT'S BEEN CONSTRUCTED WITH EARTH MAGIC...
...AND INSCRIBED WITH DEFENSE AND CON-CEALMENT SEALS.
INSIDE, THERE ARE...
...TWO OF THEM.
BASED ON THE MAGIC SIGNATURES, ONE IS ELHART, THE DEMON I SENSED BACK AT THE PALACE.
TWO DEMONS, HUH...?
BUT ELHART'S SIGNATURE IS WEAK, SO WE CAN ROUND DOWN TO ONE.
HE FELT MUCH STRONGER WHEN I TRACED THE SIGNAL.
I GUESS HE HASN'T HEALED FROM THE DAMAGE I DEALT.

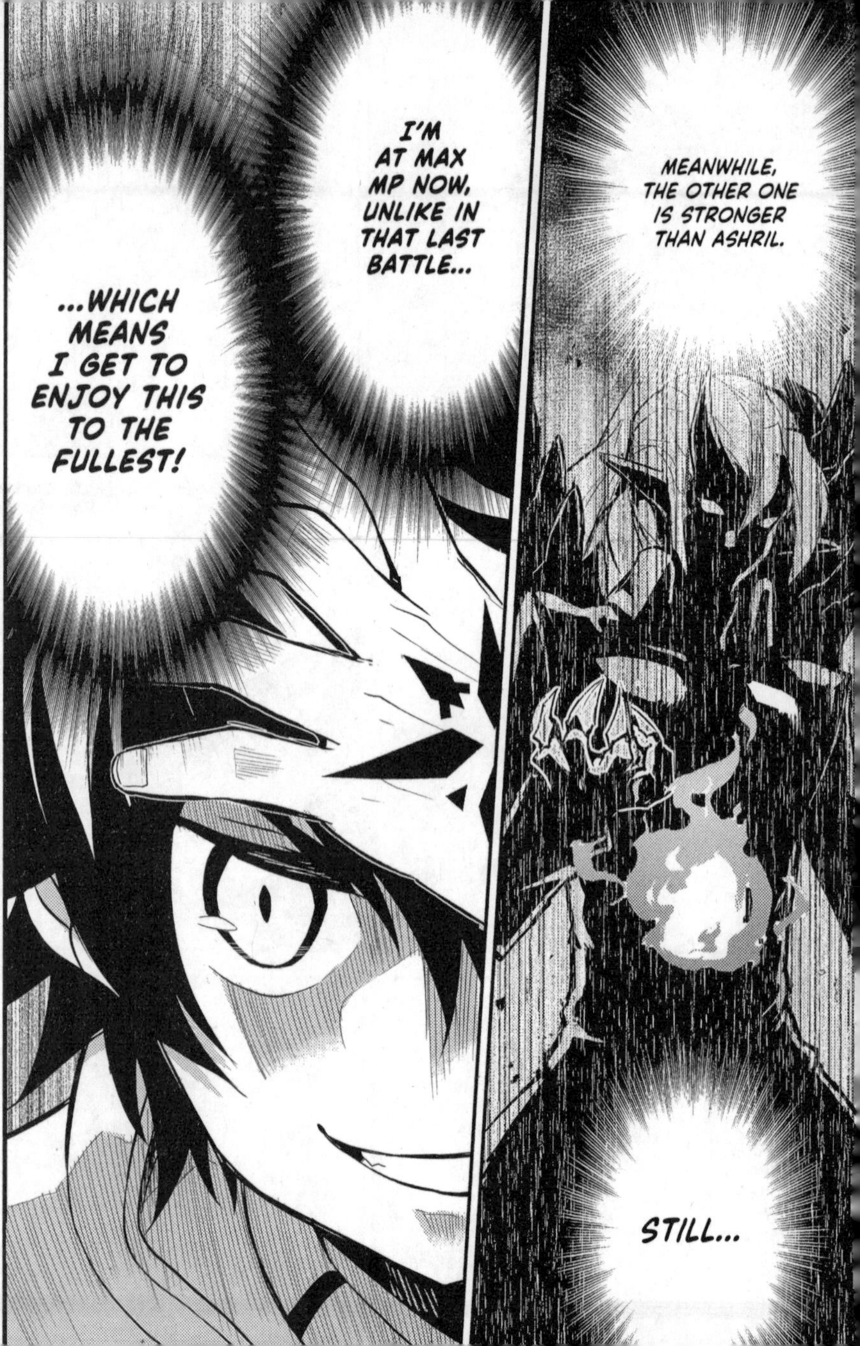
MEANWHILE, THE OTHER ONE IS STRONGER THAN ASHRIL.
STILL...
I'M AT MAX MP NOW, UNLIKE IN THAT LAST BATTLE...
...WHICH MEANS I GET TO ENJOY THIS TO THE FULLEST!

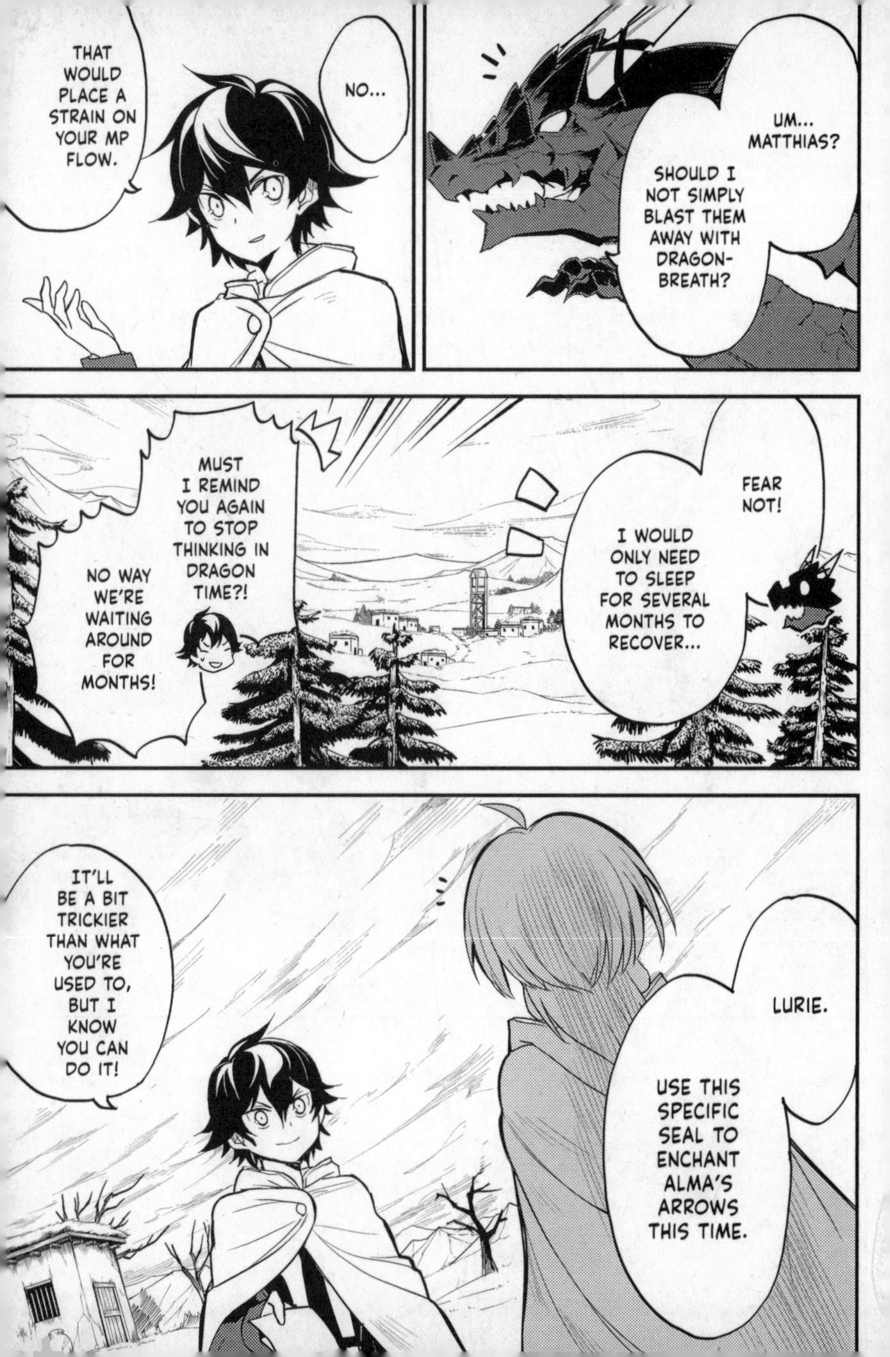
UM... MATTHIAS?
SHOULD I NOT SIMPLY BLAST THEM AWAY WITH DRAGON-BREATH?
NO...
THAT WOULD PLACE A STRAIN ON YOUR MP FLOW.
FEAR NOT!
I WOULD ONLY NEED TO SLEEP FOR SEVERAL MONTHS TO RECOVER...
MUST I REMIND YOU AGAIN TO STOP THINKING IN DRAGON TIME?!
NO WAY WE'RE WAITING AROUND FOR MONTHS!
LURIE.
USE THIS SPECIFIC SEAL TO ENCHANT ALMA'S ARROWS THIS TIME.
IT'LL BE A BIT TRICKIER THAN WHAT YOU'RE USED TO, BUT I KNOW YOU CAN DO IT!

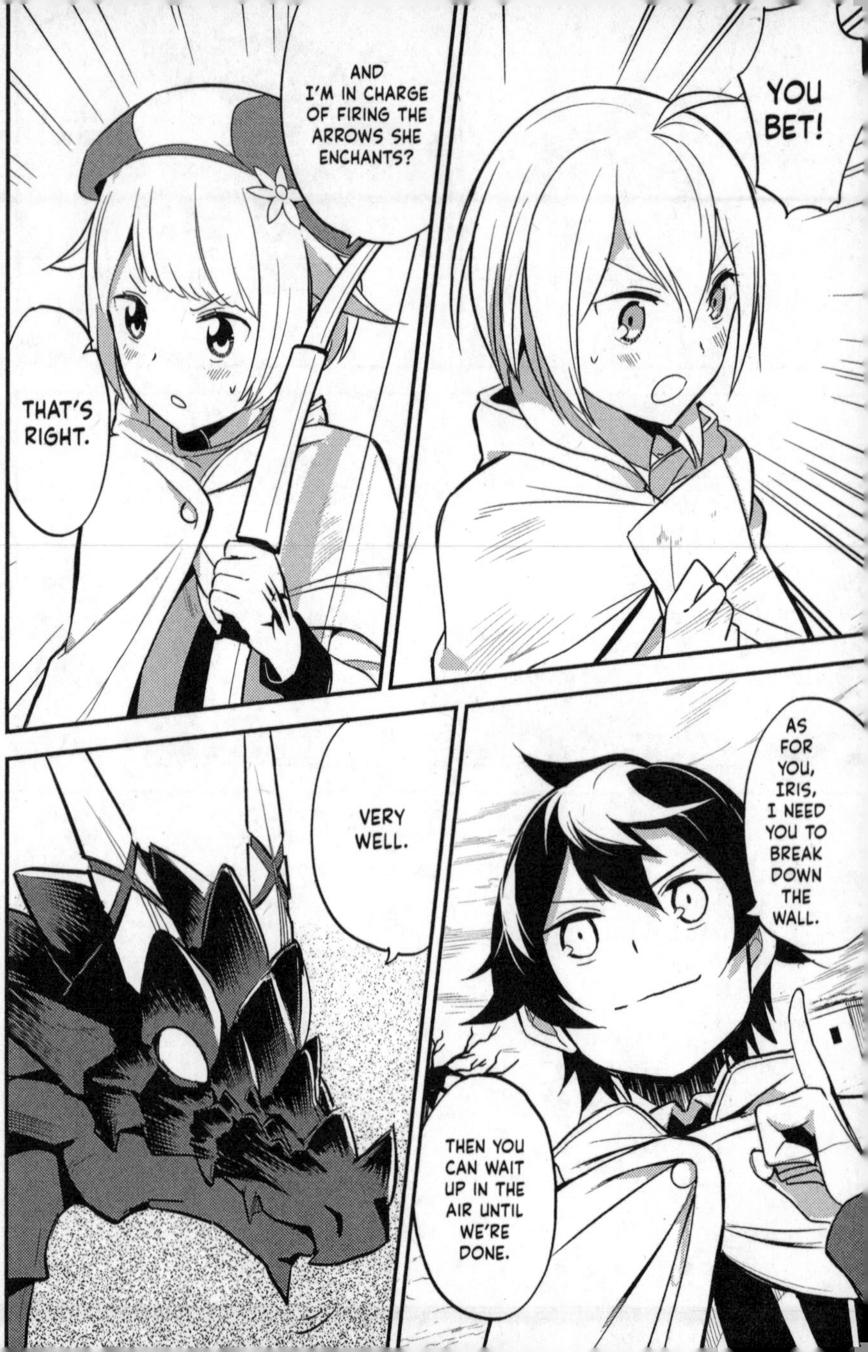
YOU BET!
AND I'M IN CHARGE OF FIRING THE ARROWS SHE ENCHANTS?
THAT'S RIGHT.
AS FOR YOU, IRIS, I NEED YOU TO BREAK DOWN THE WALL.
THEN YOU CAN WAIT UP IN THE AIR UNTIL WE'RE DONE.
VERY WELL.

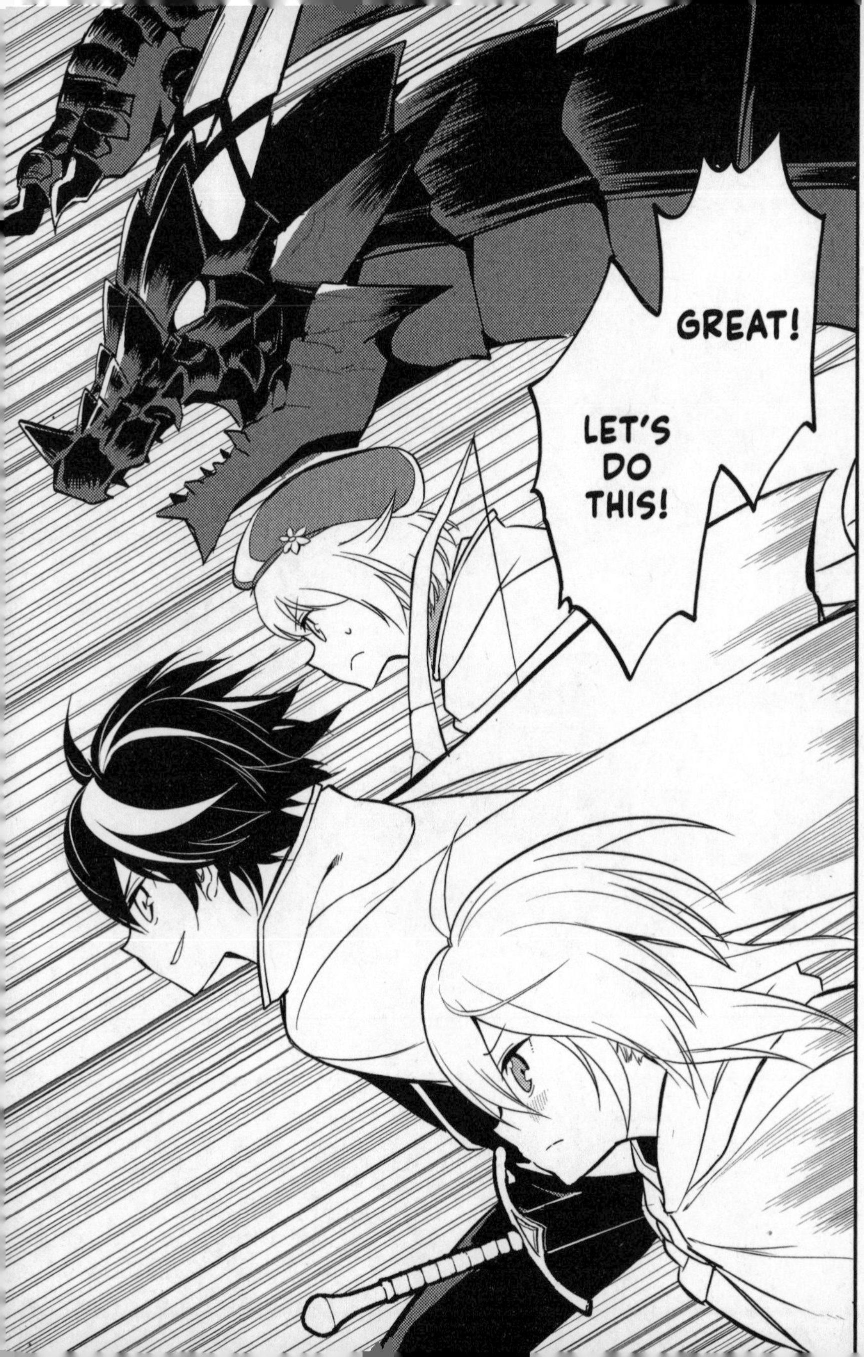
GREAT!
LET'S DO THIS!

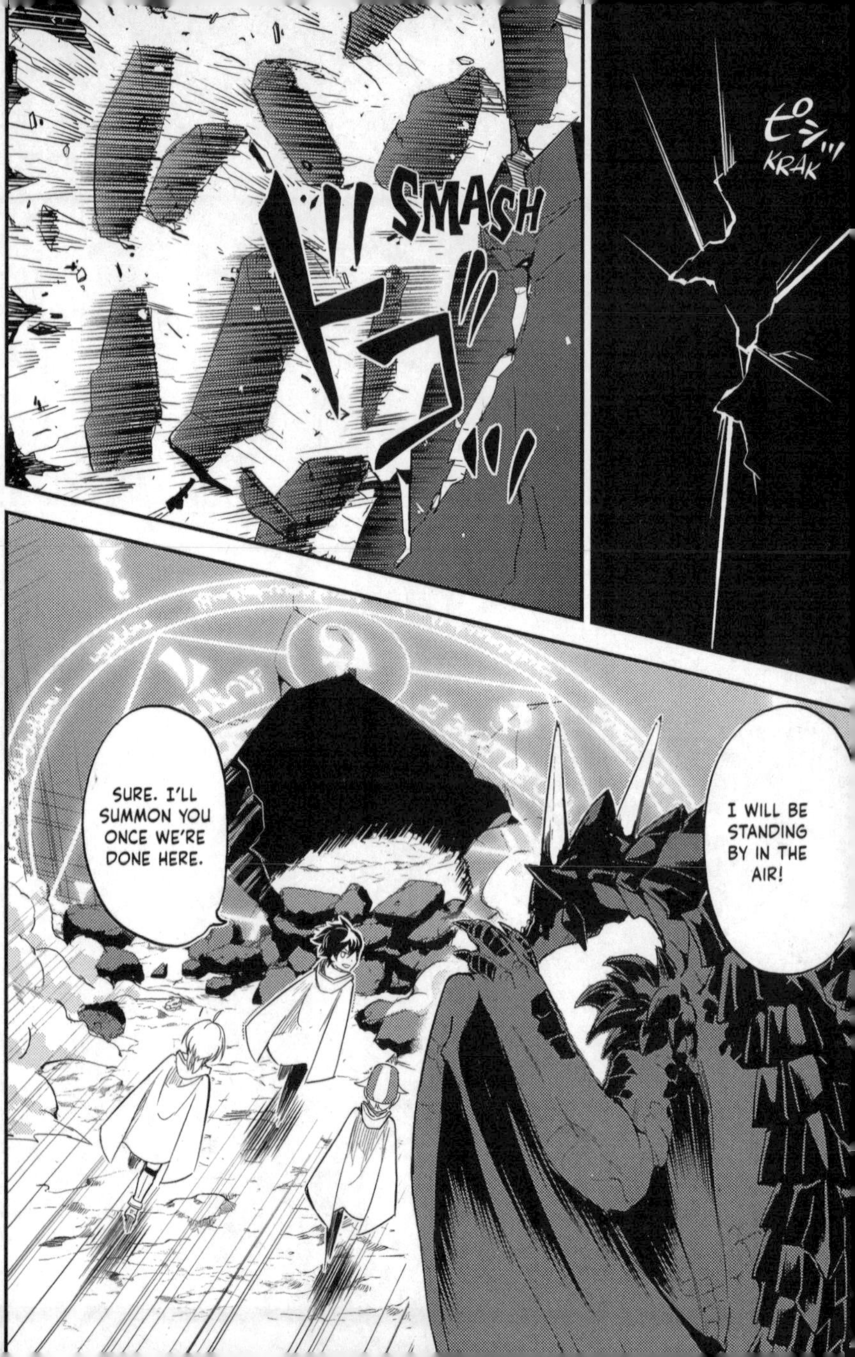
KRAK
SMASH
I WILL BE STANDING BY IN THE AIR!
SURE. I'LL SUMMON YOU ONCE WE'RE DONE HERE.

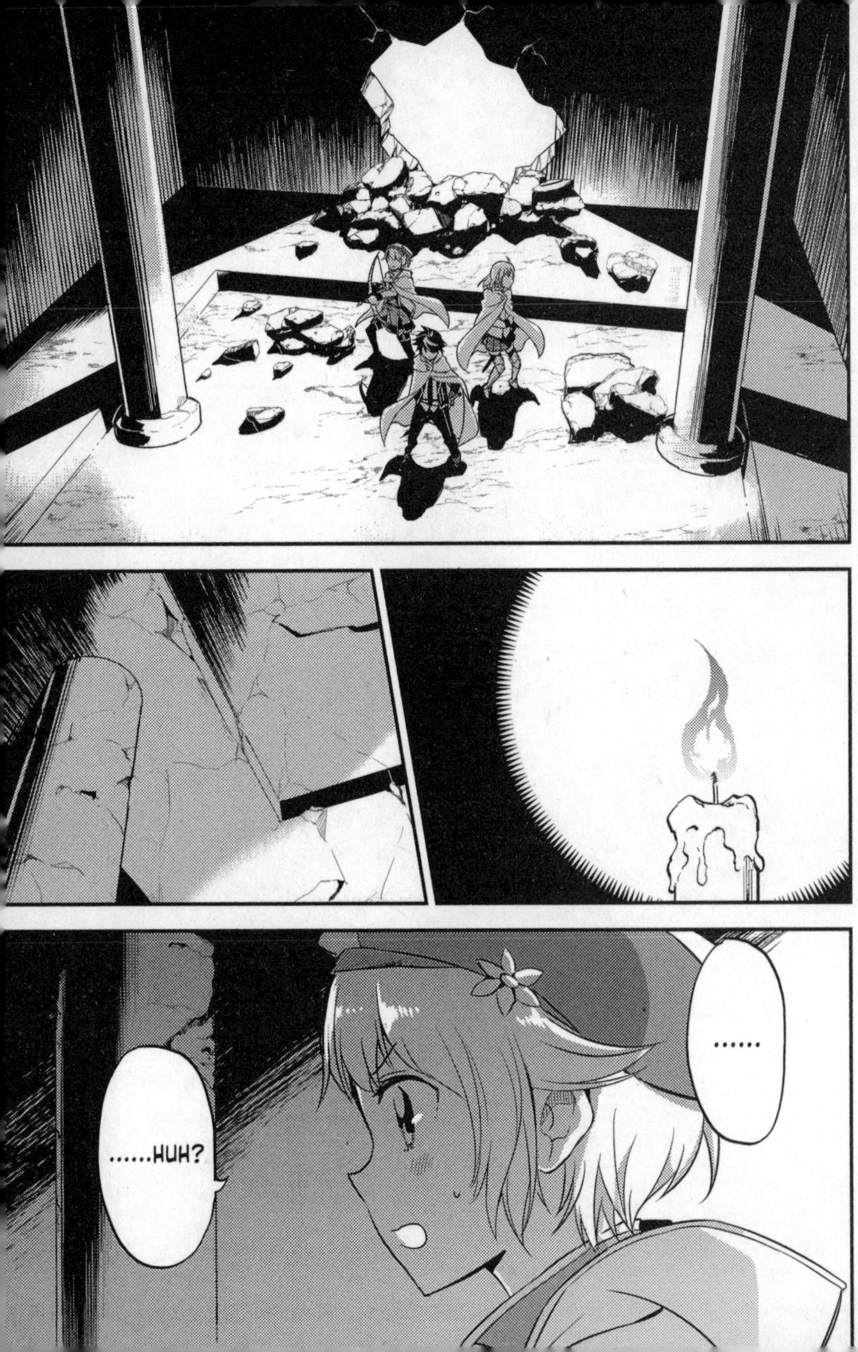
......
......HUH?

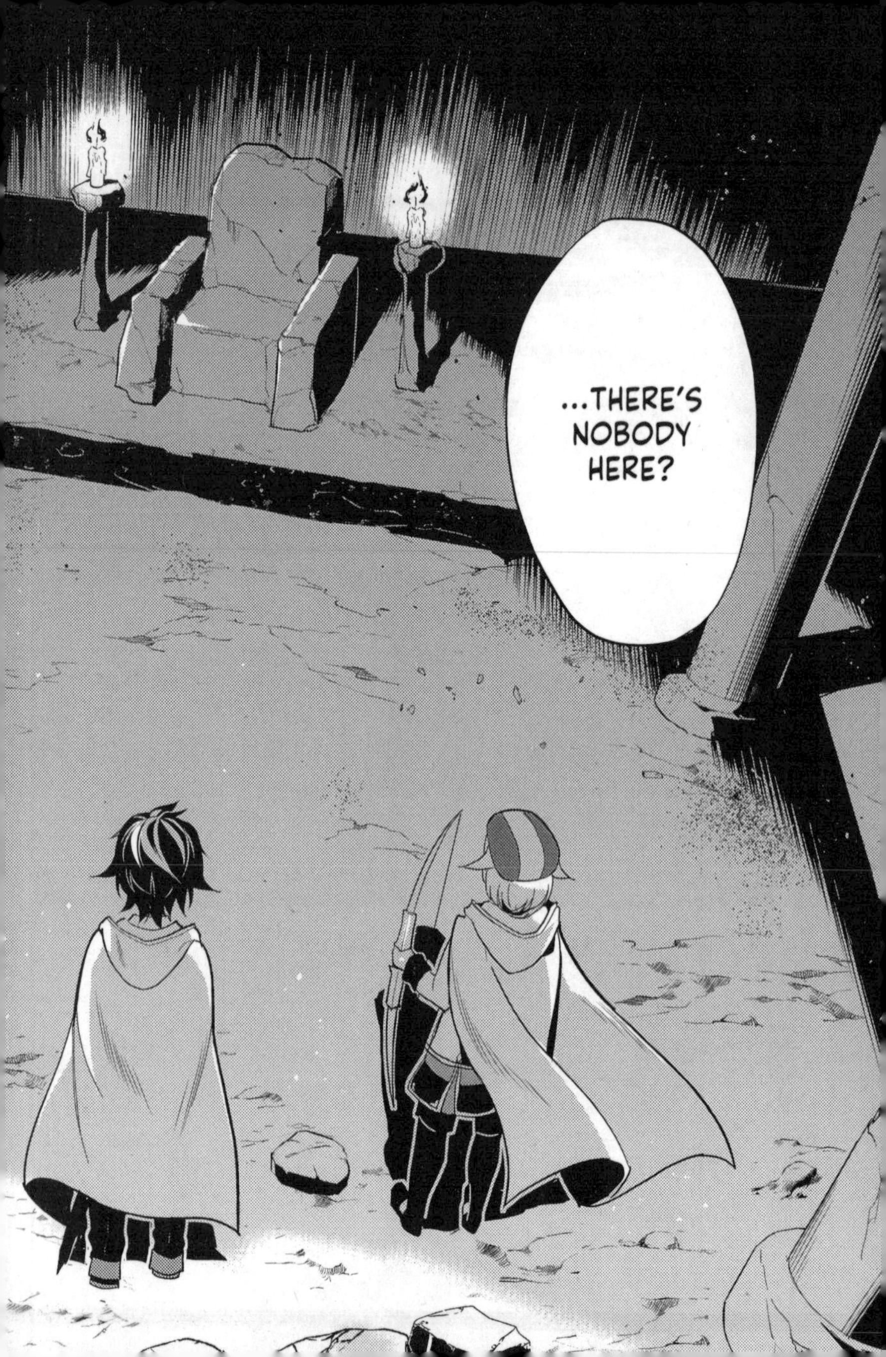
...THERE'S NOBODY HERE?

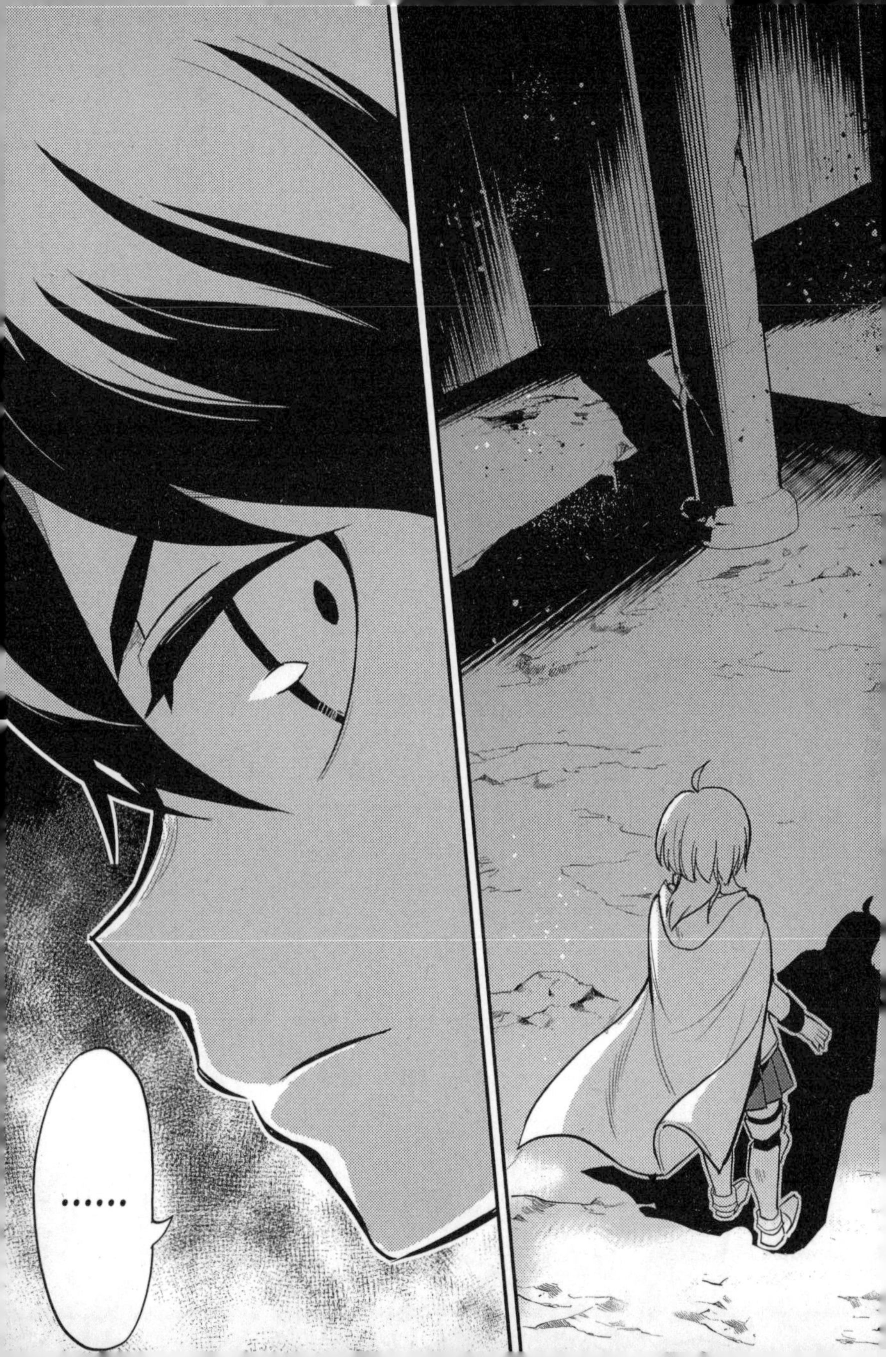
......

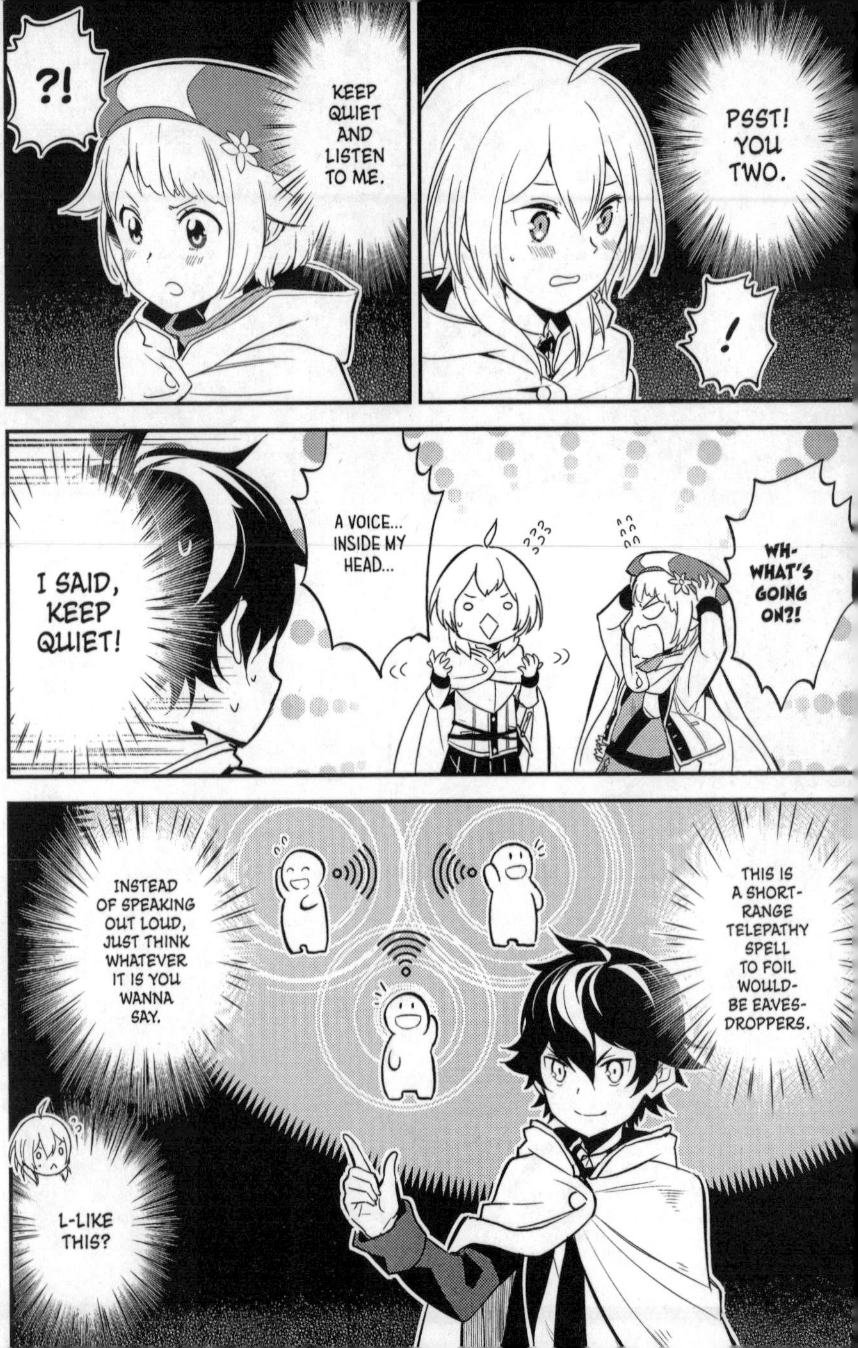
PSST! YOU TWO.
!
KEEP QUIET AND LISTEN TO ME.
?!
WH-WHAT'S GOING ON?!
A VOICE... INSIDE MY HEAD...
I SAID, KEEP QUIET!
THIS IS A SHORT-RANGE TELEPATHY SPELL TO FOIL WOULD-BE EAVES-DROPPERS.
INSTEAD OF SPEAKING OUT LOUD, JUST THINK WHATEVER IT IS YOU WANNA SAY.
L-LIKE THIS?

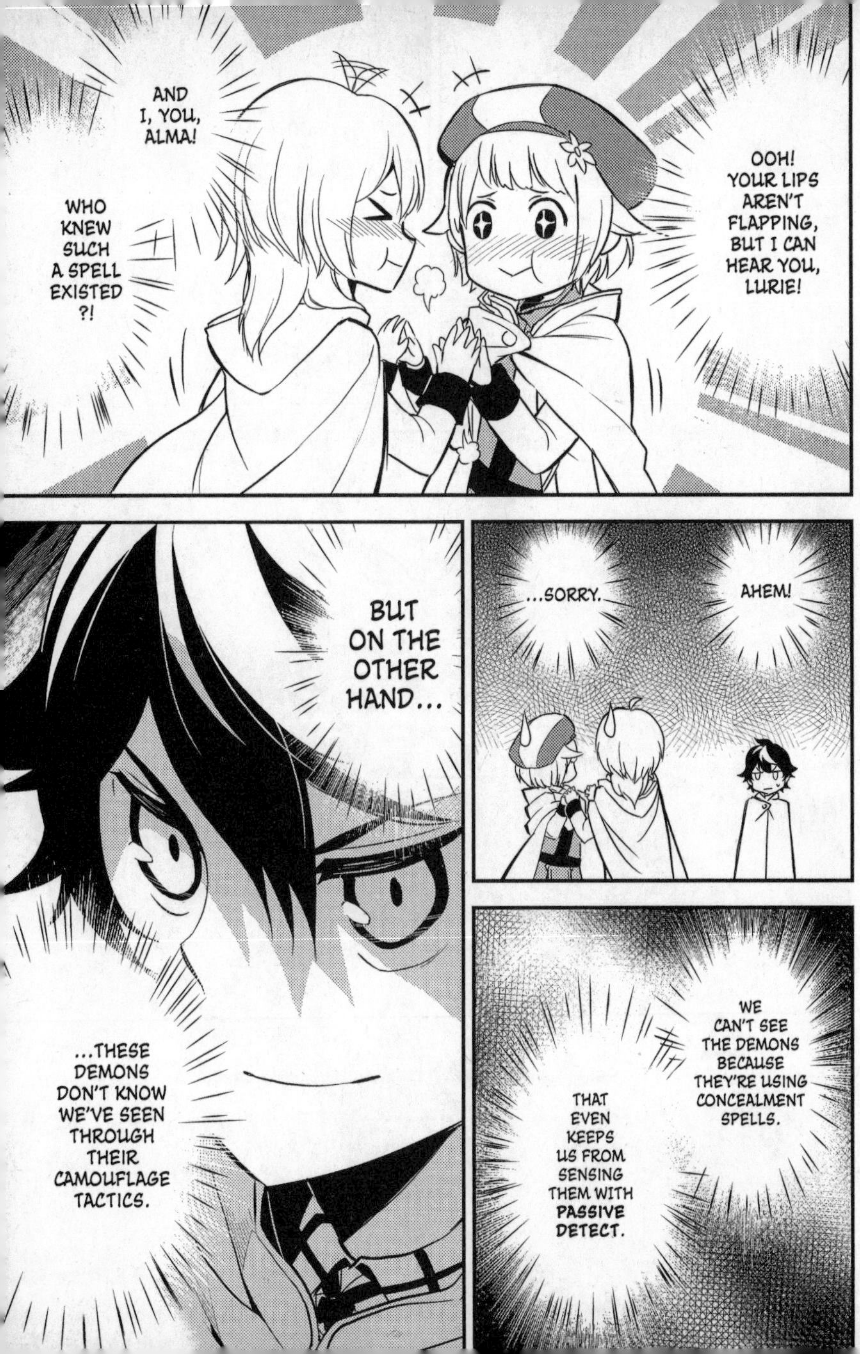
OOH! YOUR LIPS AREN'T FLAPPING, BUT I CAN HEAR YOU, LURIE!
AND I, YOU, ALMA!
WHO KNEW SUCH A SPELL EXISTED?!
AHEM!
...SORRY.
WE CAN'T SEE THE DEMONS BECAUSE THEY'RE USING CONCEALMENT SPELLS.
THAT EVEN KEEPS US FROM SENSING THEM WITH PASSIVE DETECT.
BUT ON THE OTHER HAND...
...THESE DEMONS DON'T KNOW WE'VE SEEN THROUGH THEIR CAMOUFLAGE TACTICS.

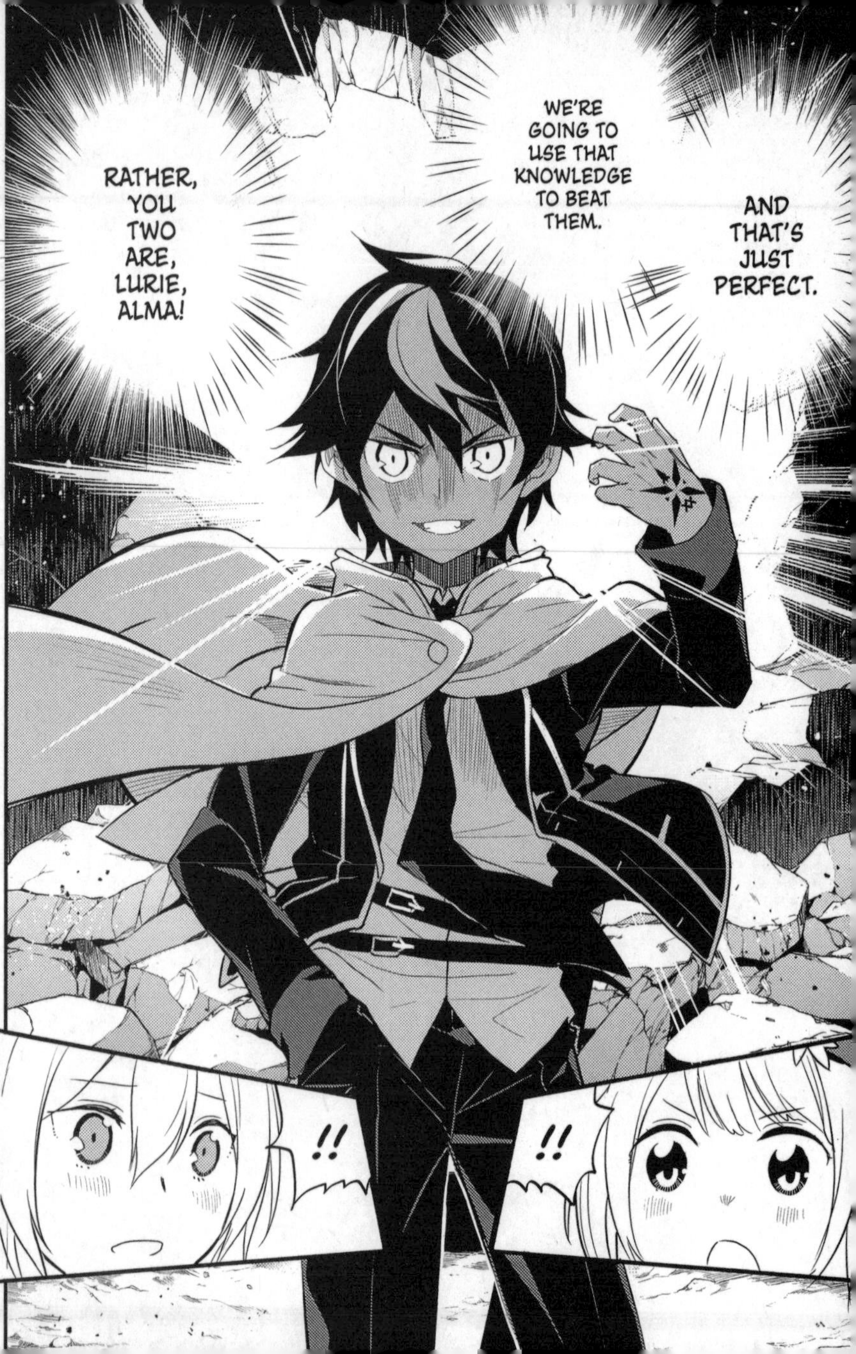
AND THAT'S JUST PERFECT.
WE'RE GOING TO USE THAT KNOWLEDGE TO BEAT THEM.
RATHER, YOU TWO ARE, LURIE, ALMA!
!!
!!

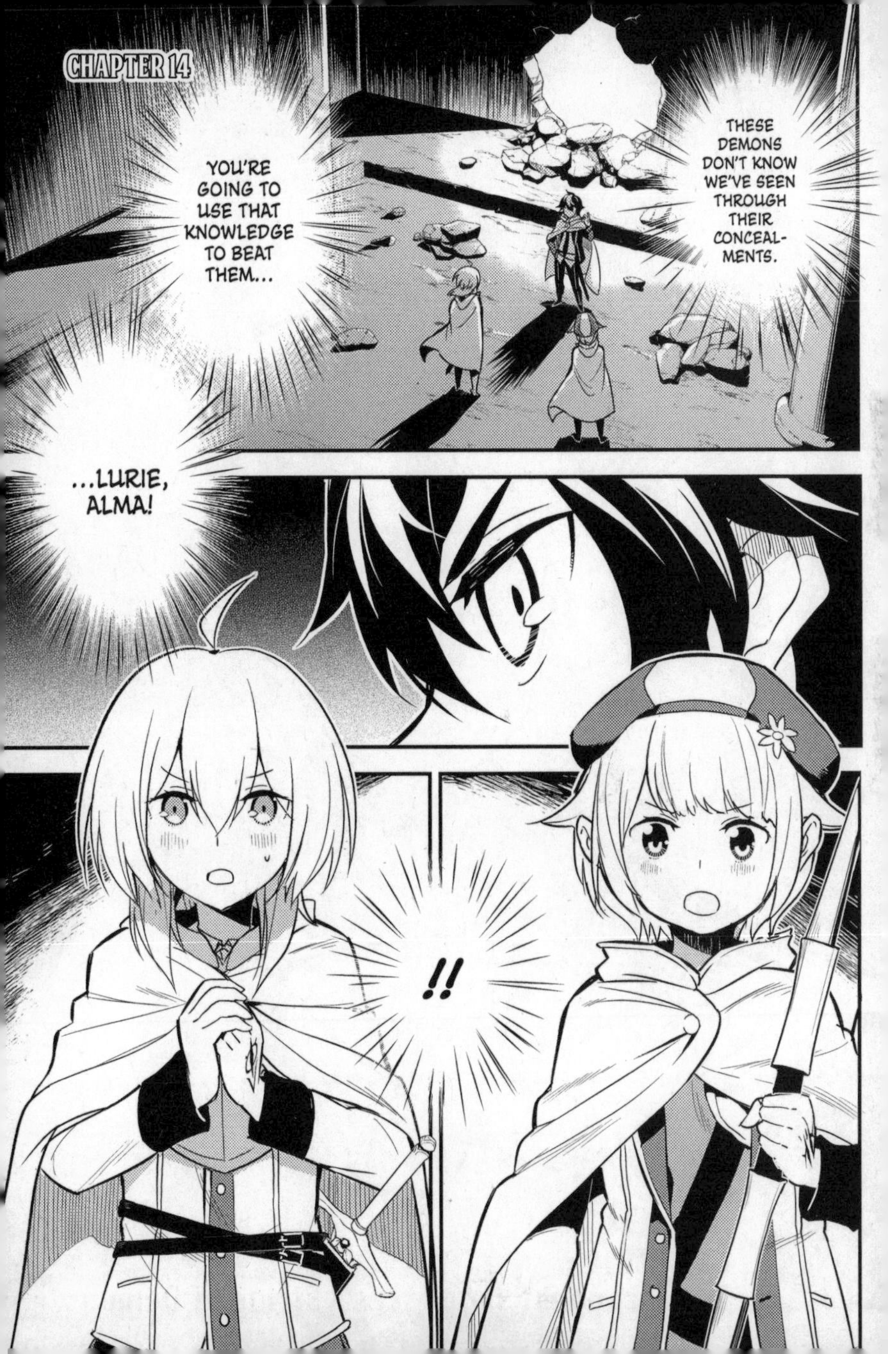
CHAPTER 14
THESE DEMONS DON'T KNOW WE'VE SEEN THROUGH THEIR CONCEAL-MENTS.
YOU'RE GOING TO USE THAT KNOWLEDGE TO BEAT THEM...
...LURIE, ALMA!
!!

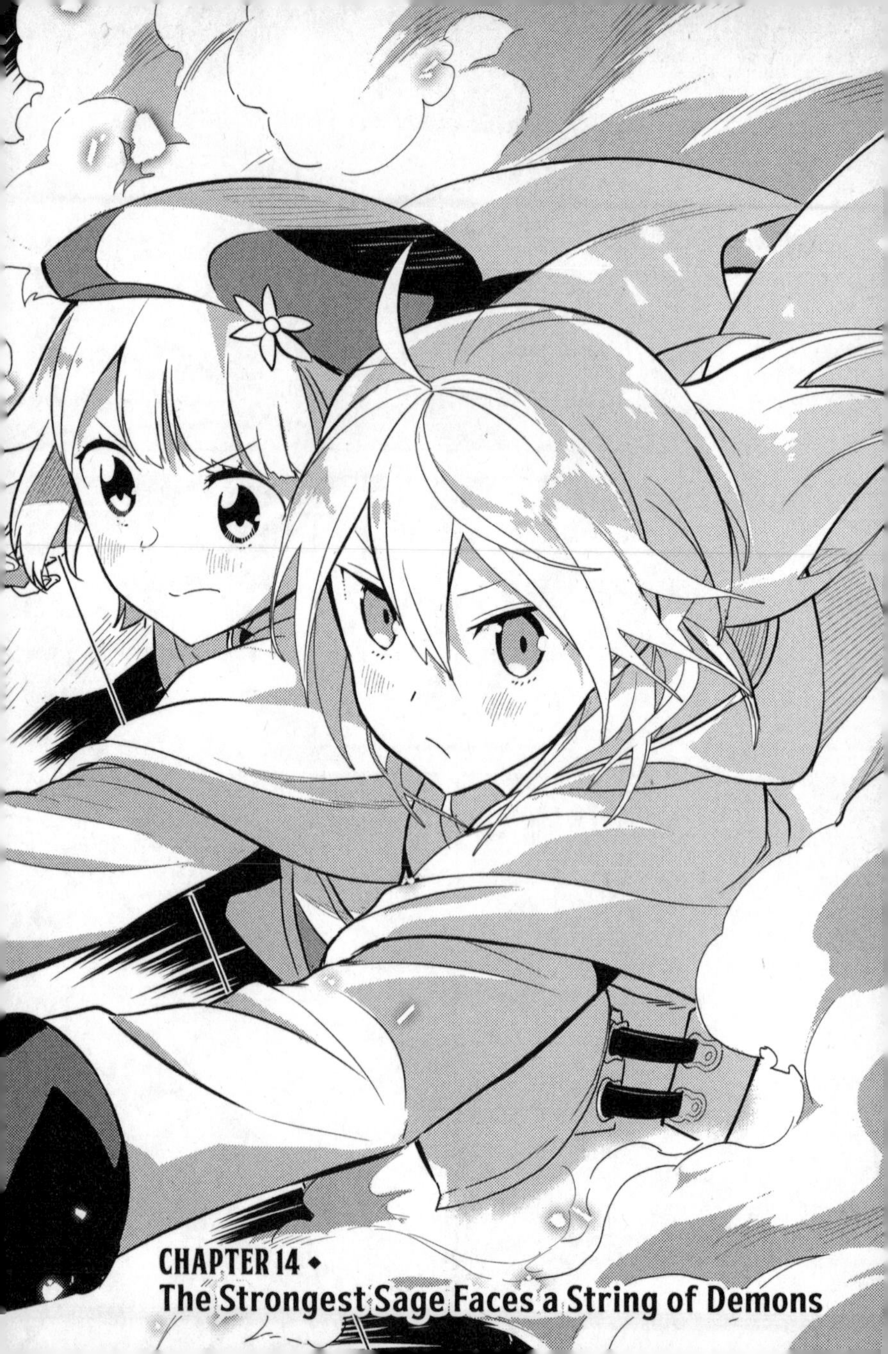

CHAPTER 14 ◆ The Strongest Sage Faces a String of Demons

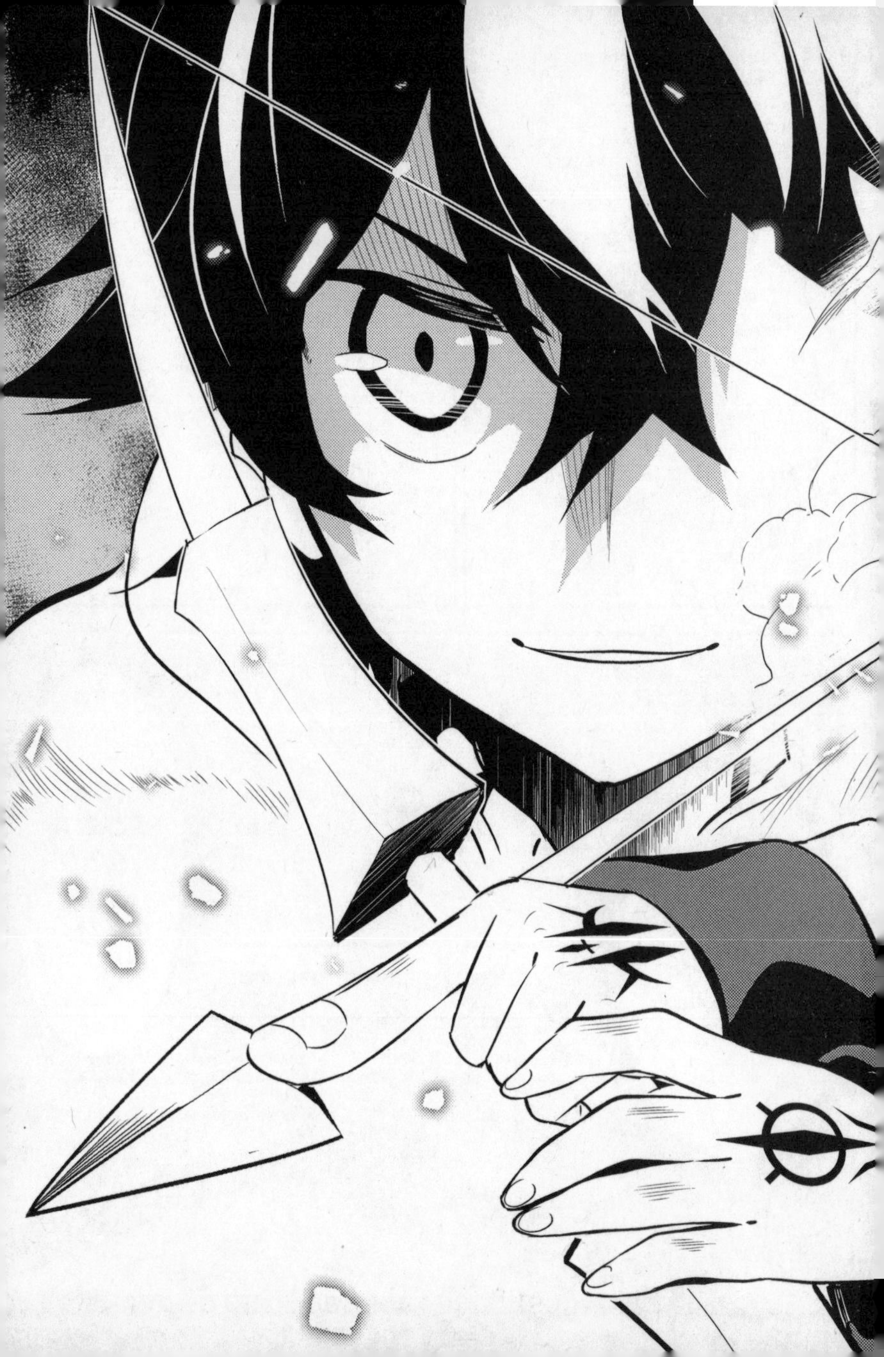

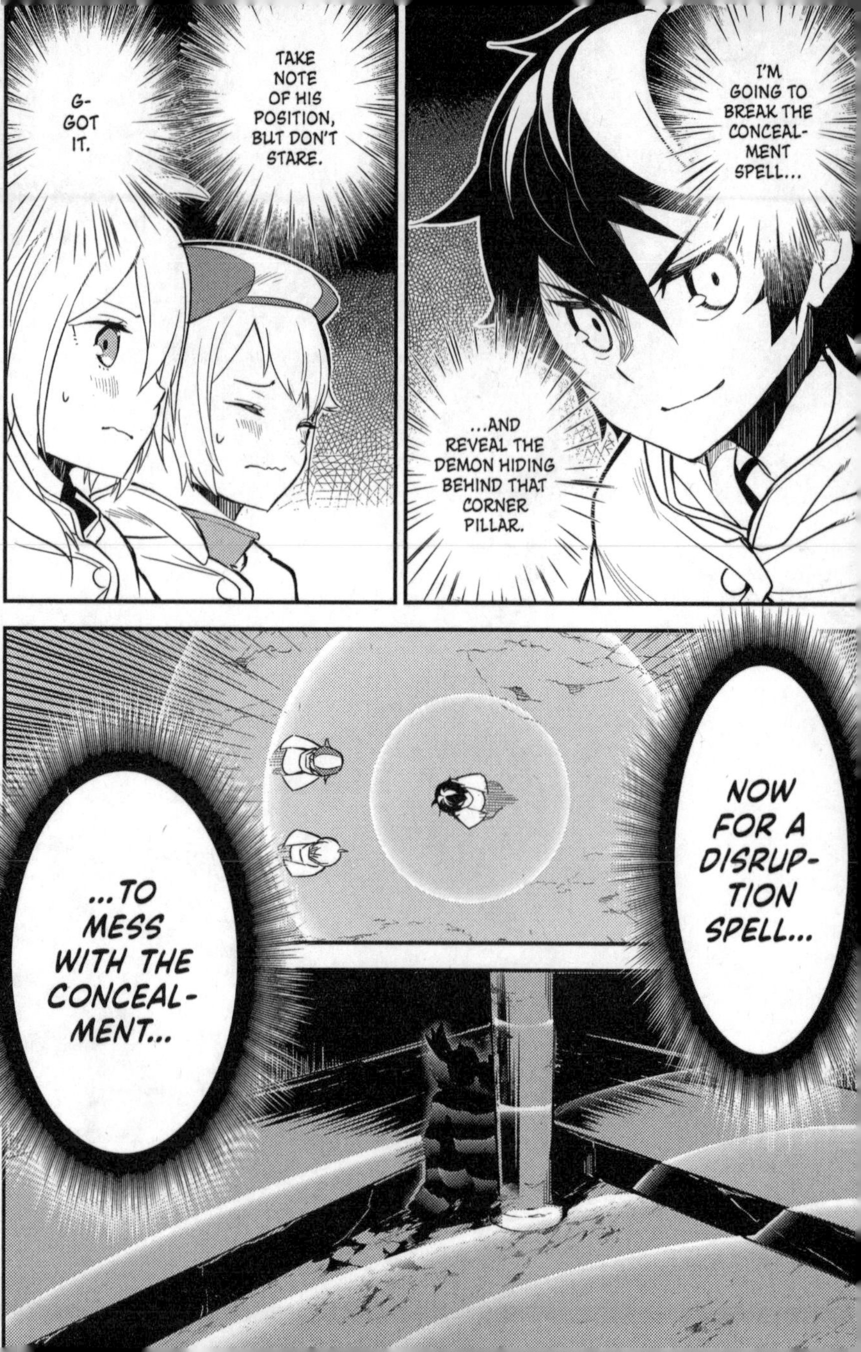
I'M GOING TO BREAK THE CONCEAL-MENT SPELL...
...AND REVEAL THE DEMON HIDING BEHIND THAT CORNER PILLAR.
TAKE NOTE OF HIS POSITION, BUT DON'T STARE.
G-GOT IT.
NOW FOR A DISRUP-TION SPELL...
...TO MESS WITH THE CONCEAL-MENT...

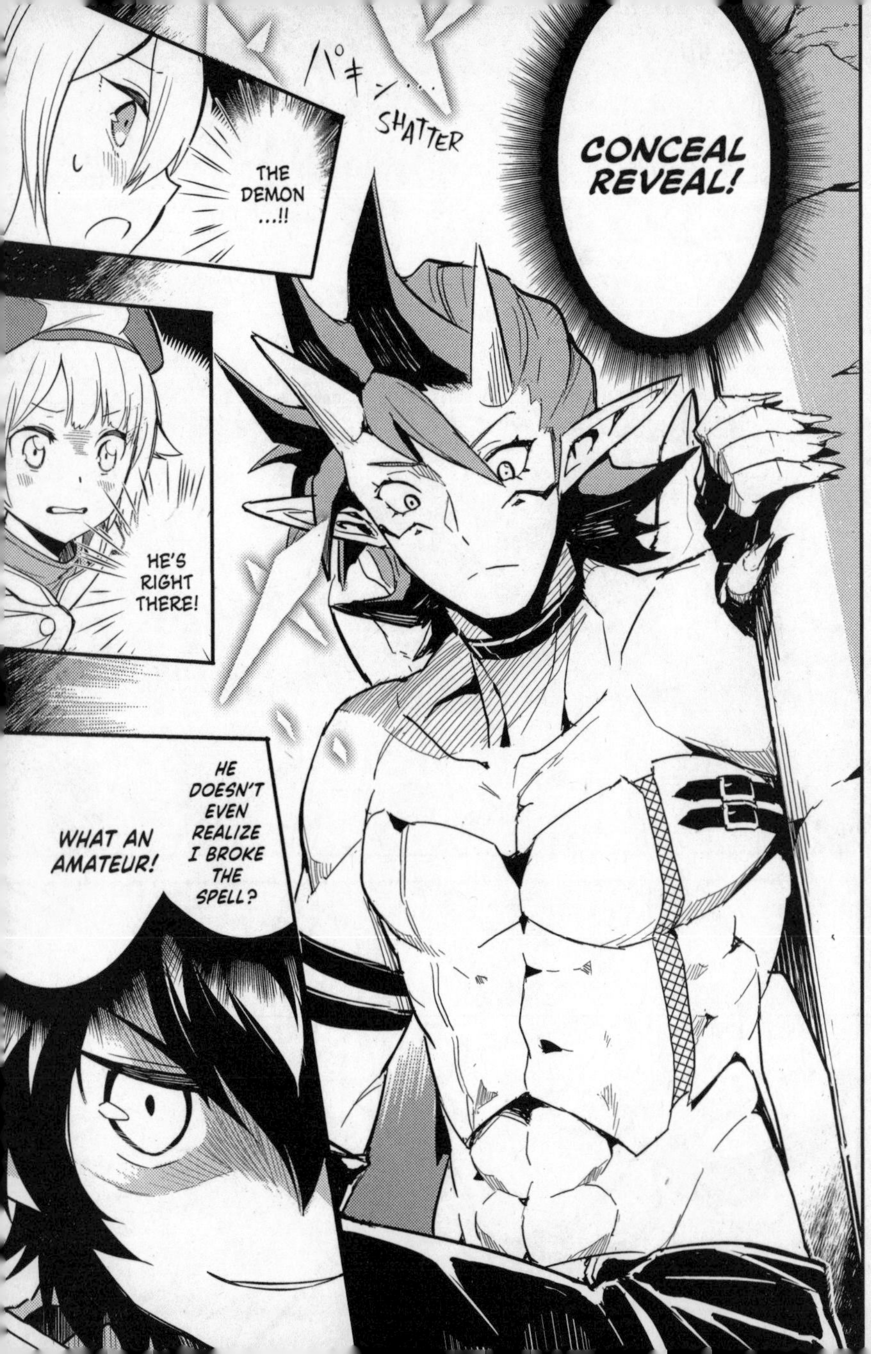
CONCEAL REVEAL!
パキン…
SHATTER
THE DEMON ...!!
HE'S RIGHT THERE!
HE DOESN'T EVEN REALIZE I BROKE THE SPELL?
WHAT AN AMATEUR!

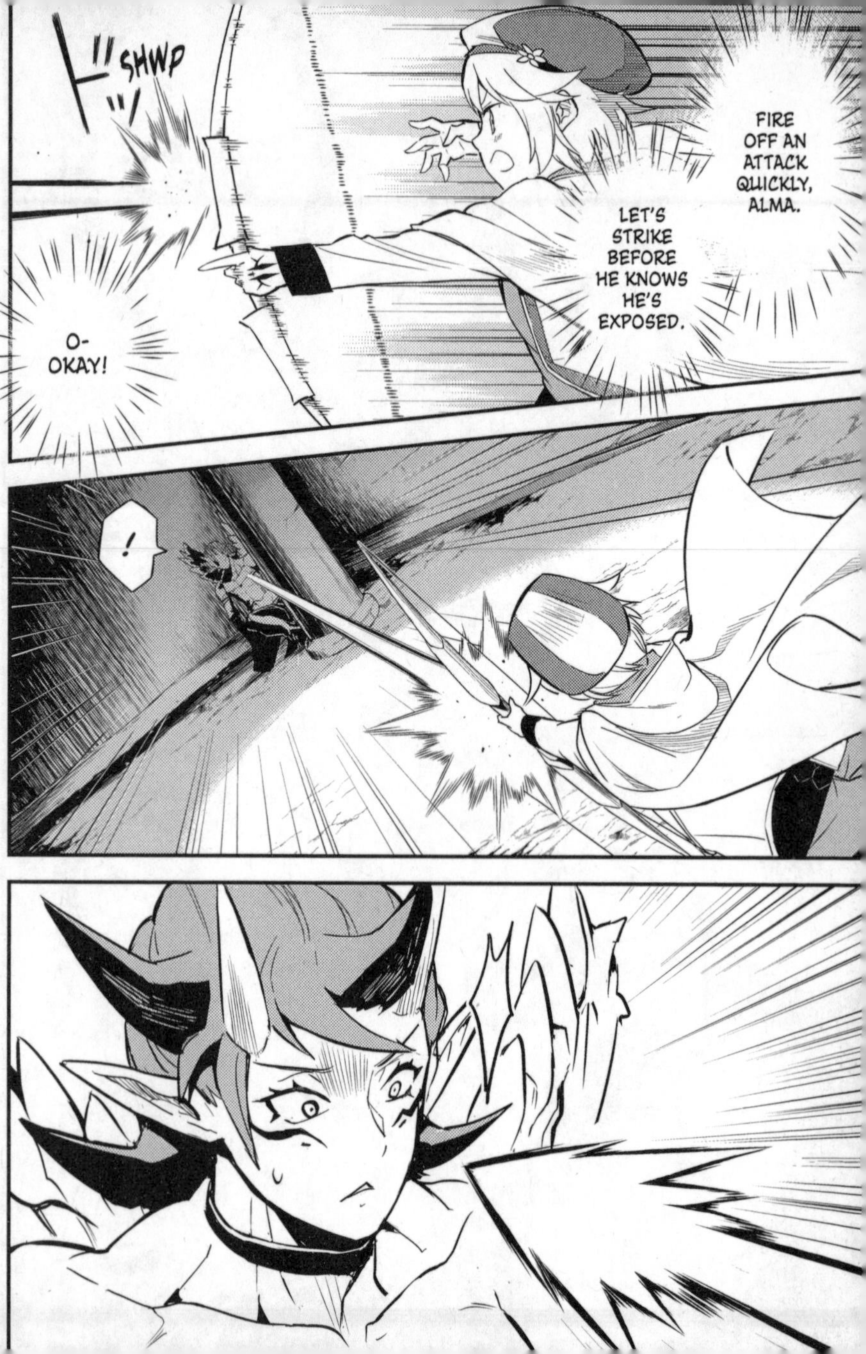
FIRE OFF AN ATTACK QUICKLY, ALMA.
LET'S STRIKE BEFORE HE KNOWS HE'S EXPOSED.
O-OKAY!
SHWP
!

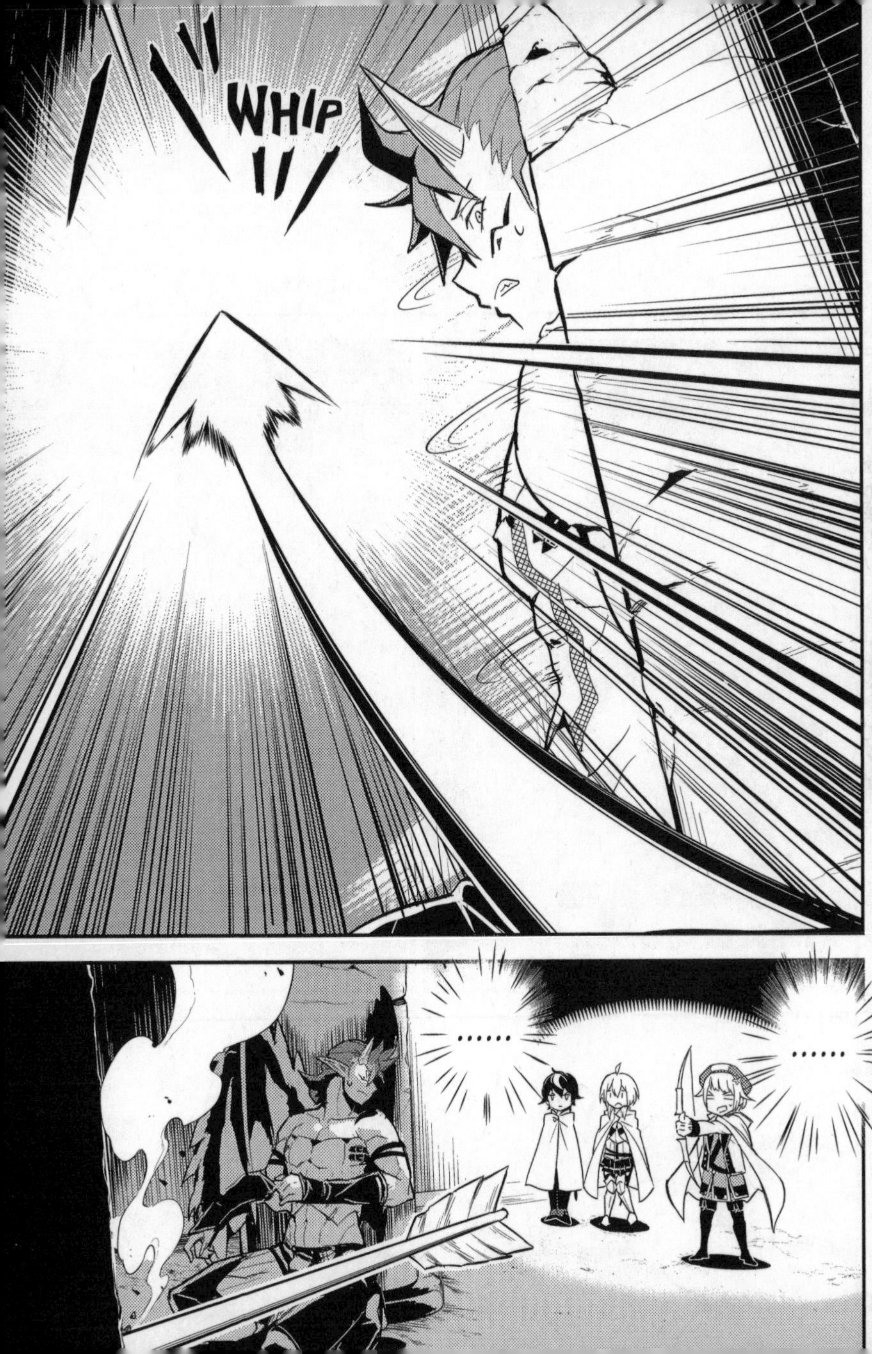
WHIP
......
......

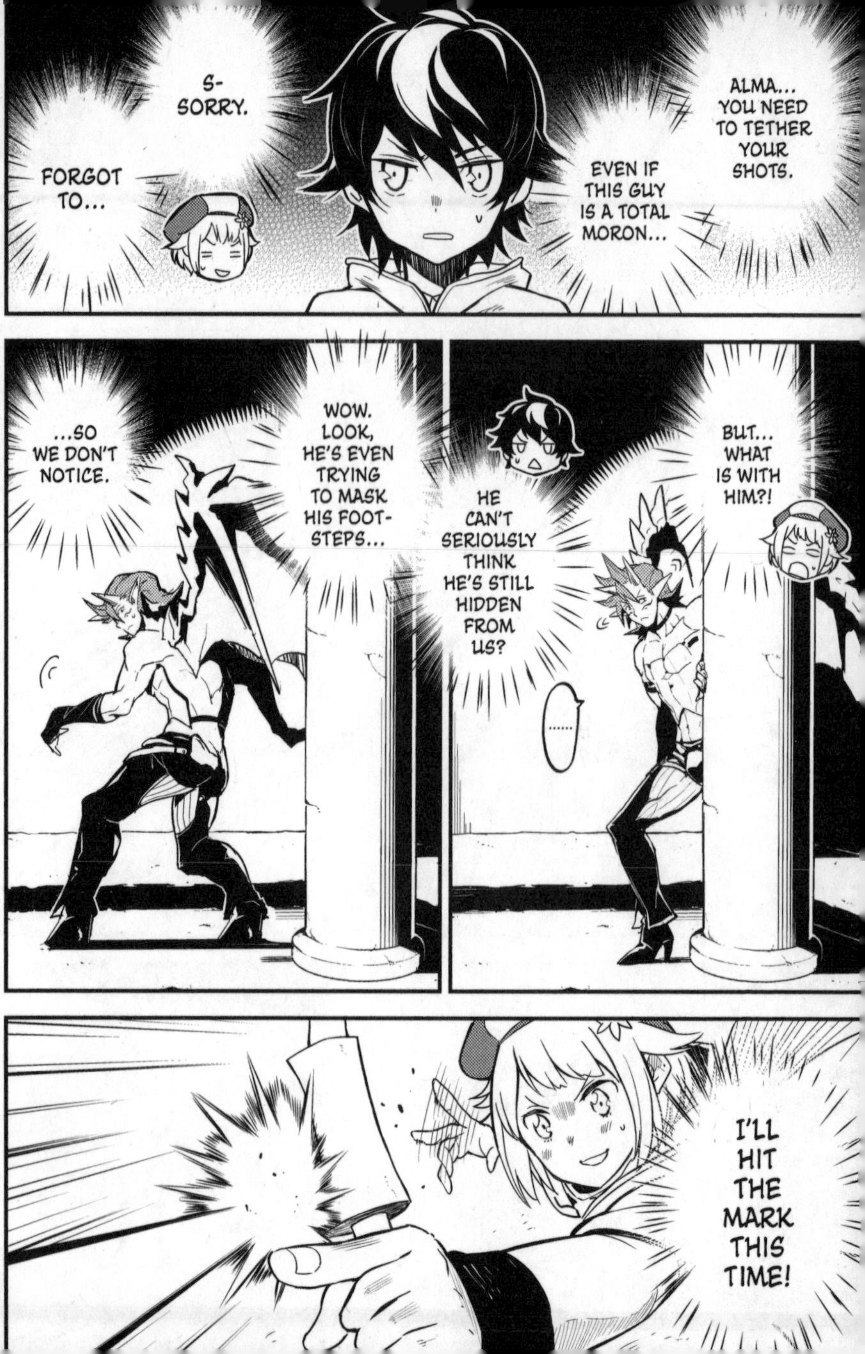
ALMA... YOU NEED TO TETHER YOUR SHOTS.
EVEN IF THIS GUY IS A TOTAL MORON...
S- SORRY.
FORGOT TO...
BUT... WHAT IS WITH HIM?!
HE CAN'T SERIOUSLY THINK HE'S STILL HIDDEN FROM US?
......
WOW. LOOK, HE'S EVEN TRYING TO MASK HIS FOOT- STEPS...
...SO WE DON'T NOTICE.
I'LL HIT THE MARK THIS TIME!

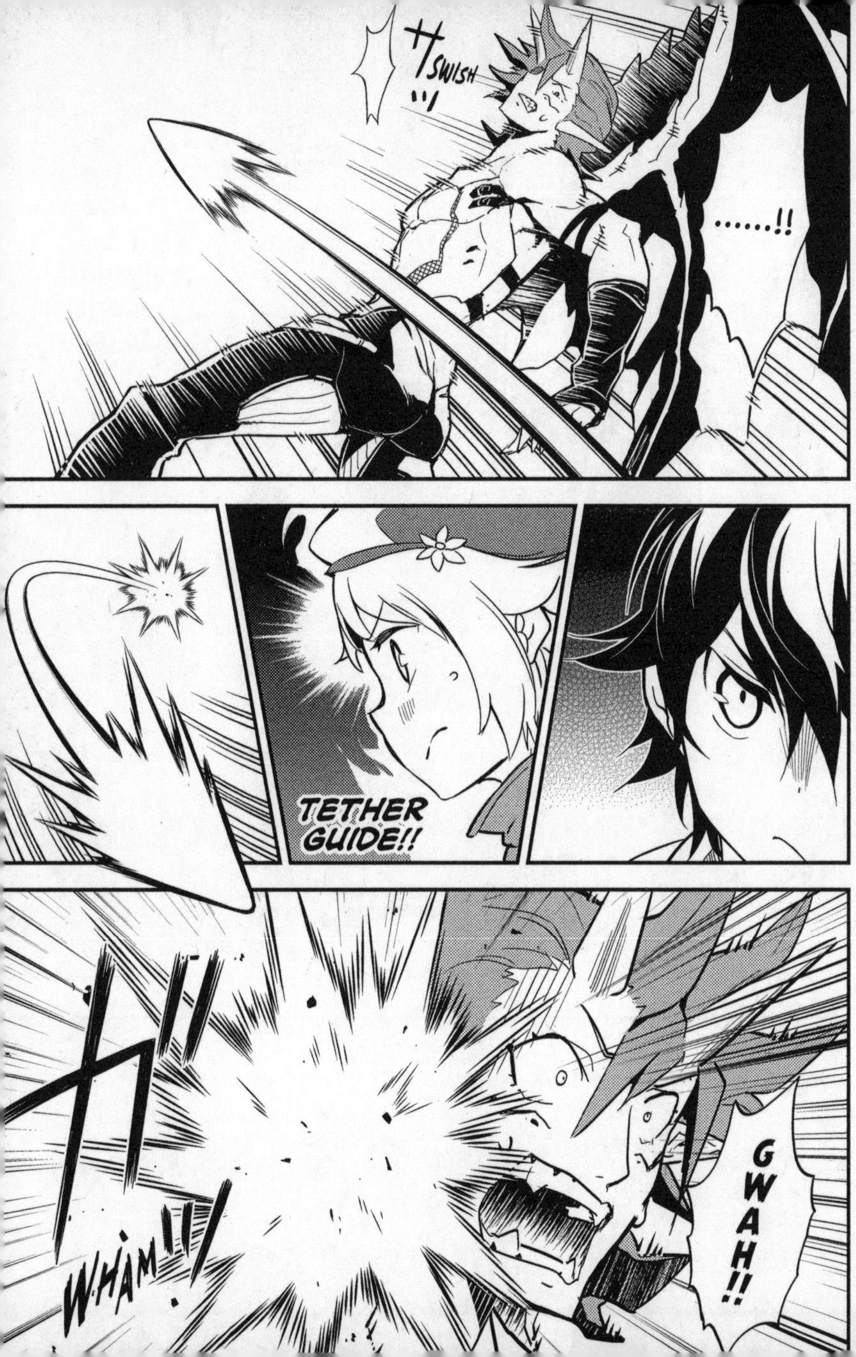
SWISH
......!!
TETHER GUIDE!!
GWAH!!
WHAM!!

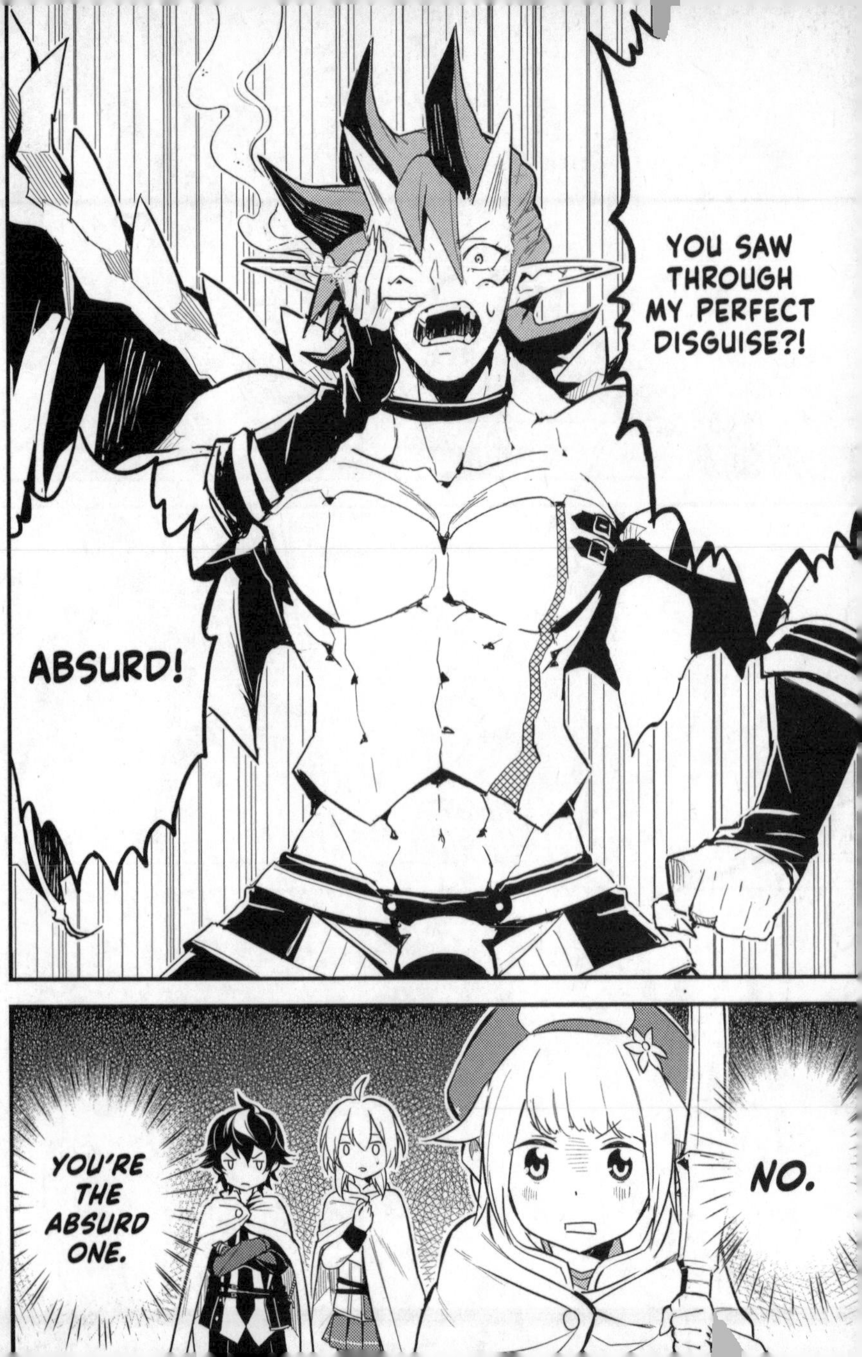
YOU SAW THROUGH MY PERFECT DISGUISE?!
ABSURD!
NO.
YOU'RE THE ABSURD ONE.

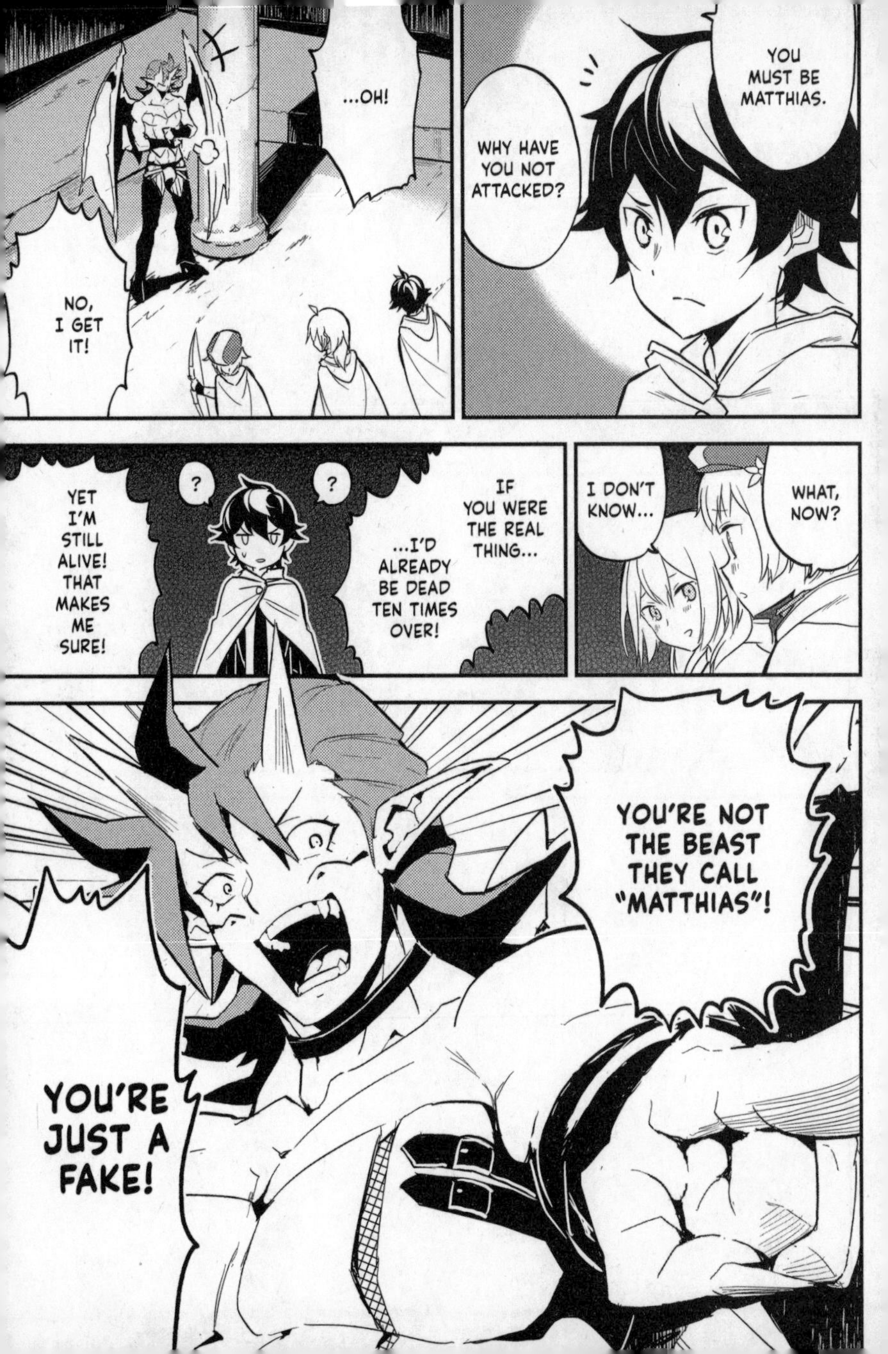
YOU MUST BE MATTHIAS.
WHY HAVE YOU NOT ATTACKED?
...OH!
NO, I GET IT!
WHAT, NOW?
I DON'T KNOW...
IF YOU WERE THE REAL THING...
...I'D ALREADY BE DEAD TEN TIMES OVER!
?
?
YET I'M STILL ALIVE! THAT MAKES ME SURE!
YOU'RE NOT THE BEAST THEY CALL "MATTHIAS"!
YOU'RE JUST A FAKE!

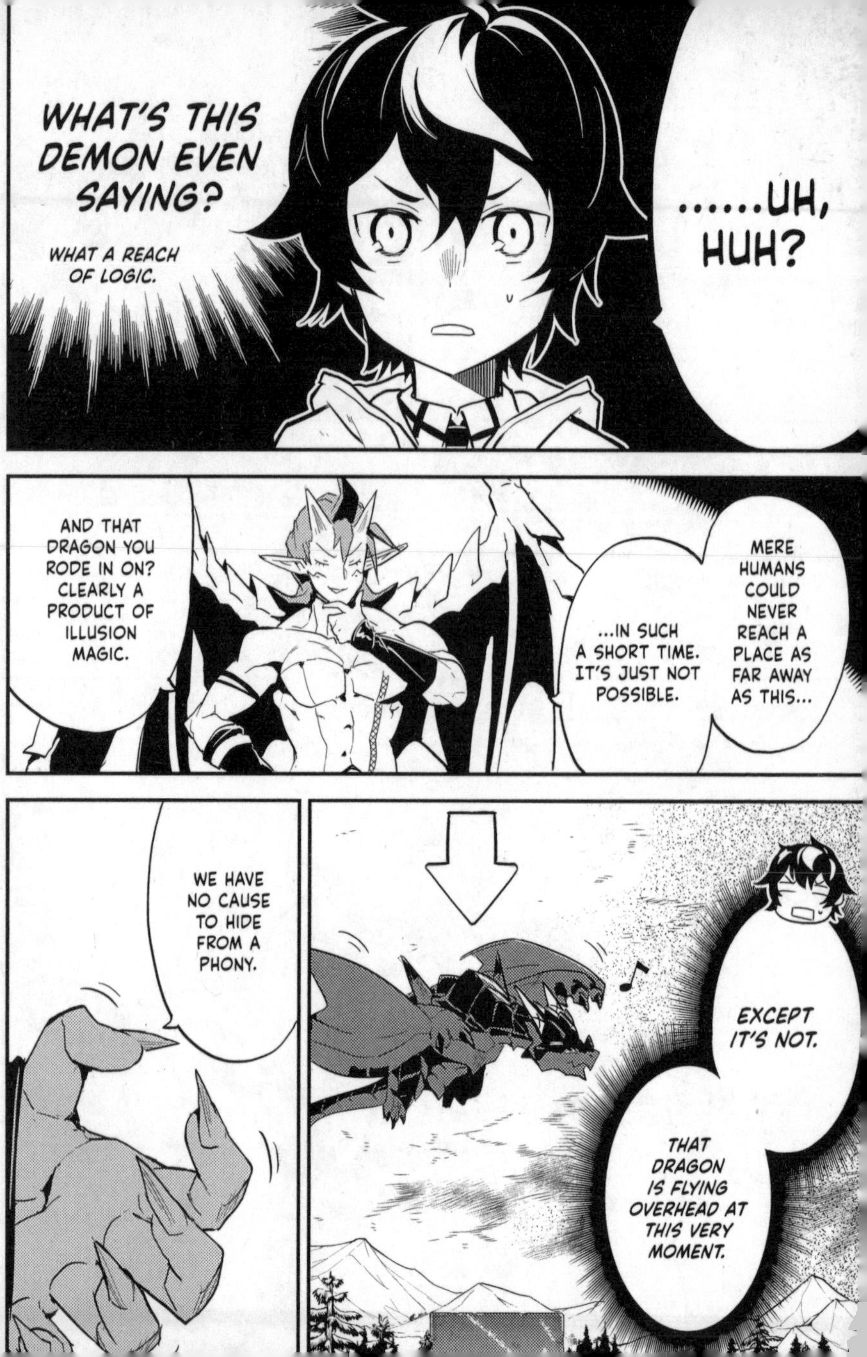

......UH, HUH?
WHAT'S THIS DEMON EVEN SAYING?
WHAT A REACH OF LOGIC.
MERE HUMANS COULD NEVER REACH A PLACE AS FAR AWAY AS THIS...
...IN SUCH A SHORT TIME. IT'S JUST NOT POSSIBLE.
AND THAT DRAGON YOU RODE IN ON? CLEARLY A PRODUCT OF ILLUSION MAGIC.
EXCEPT IT'S NOT.
THAT DRAGON IS FLYING OVERHEAD AT THIS VERY MOMENT.
WE HAVE NO CAUSE TO HIDE FROM A PHONY.

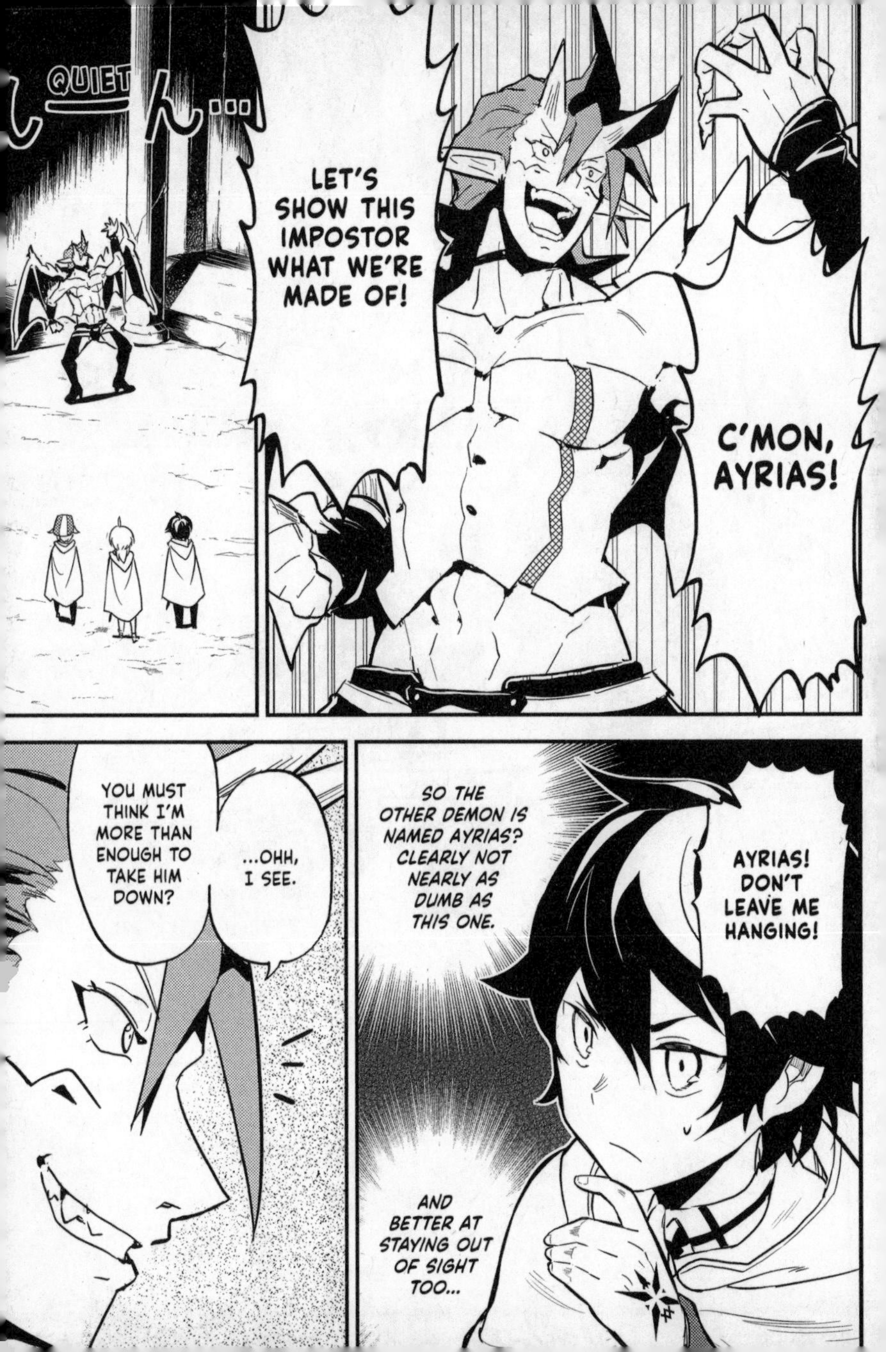
LET'S SHOW THIS IMPOSTOR WHAT WE'RE MADE OF!
C'MON, AYRIAS!
QUIET
AYRIAS! DON'T LEAVE ME HANGING!
SO THE OTHER DEMON IS NAMED AYRIAS? CLEARLY NOT NEARLY AS DUMB AS THIS ONE.
AND BETTER AT STAYING OUT OF SIGHT TOO...
...OHH, I SEE.
YOU MUST THINK I'M MORE THAN ENOUGH TO TAKE HIM DOWN?

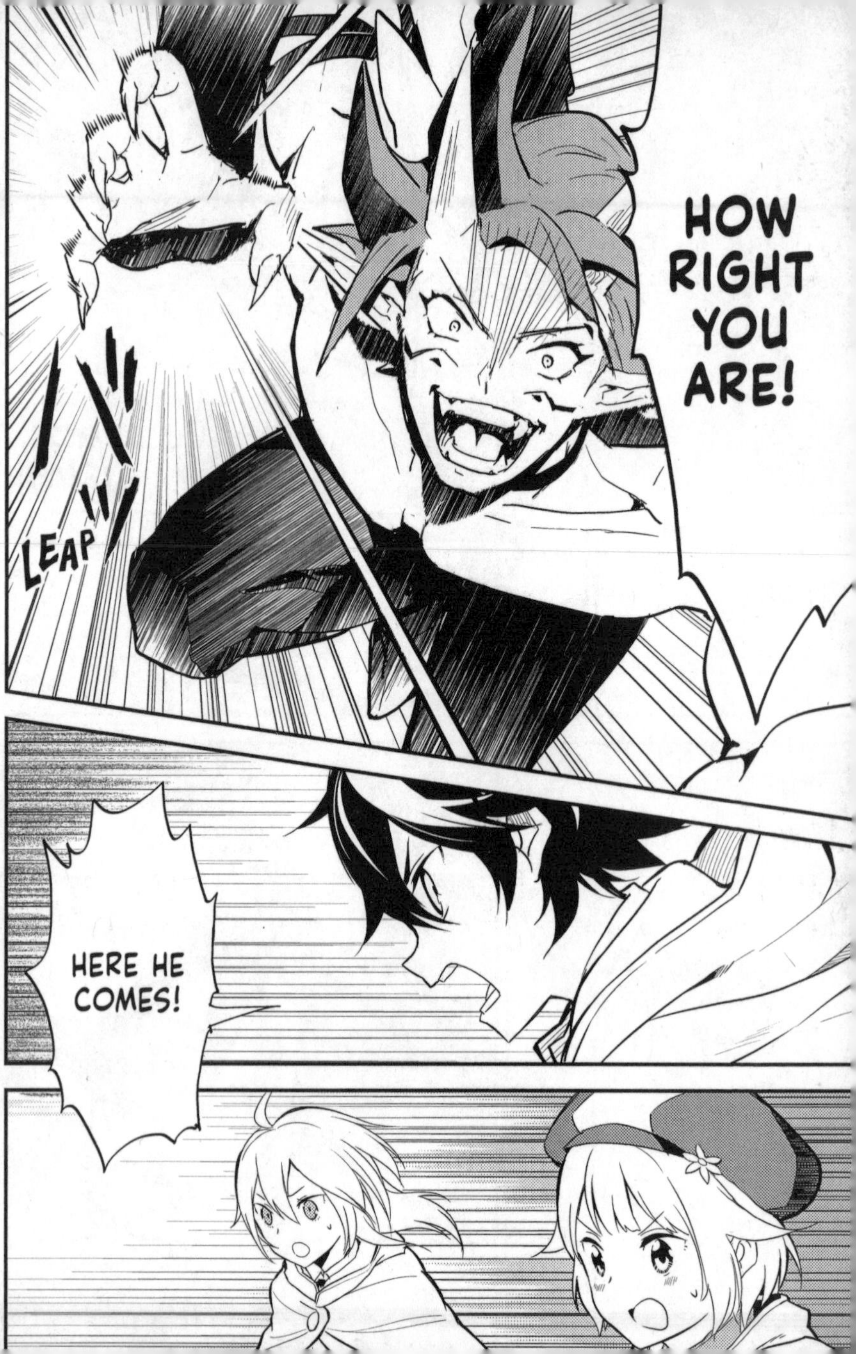
HOW RIGHT YOU ARE!
LEAP
HERE HE COMES!

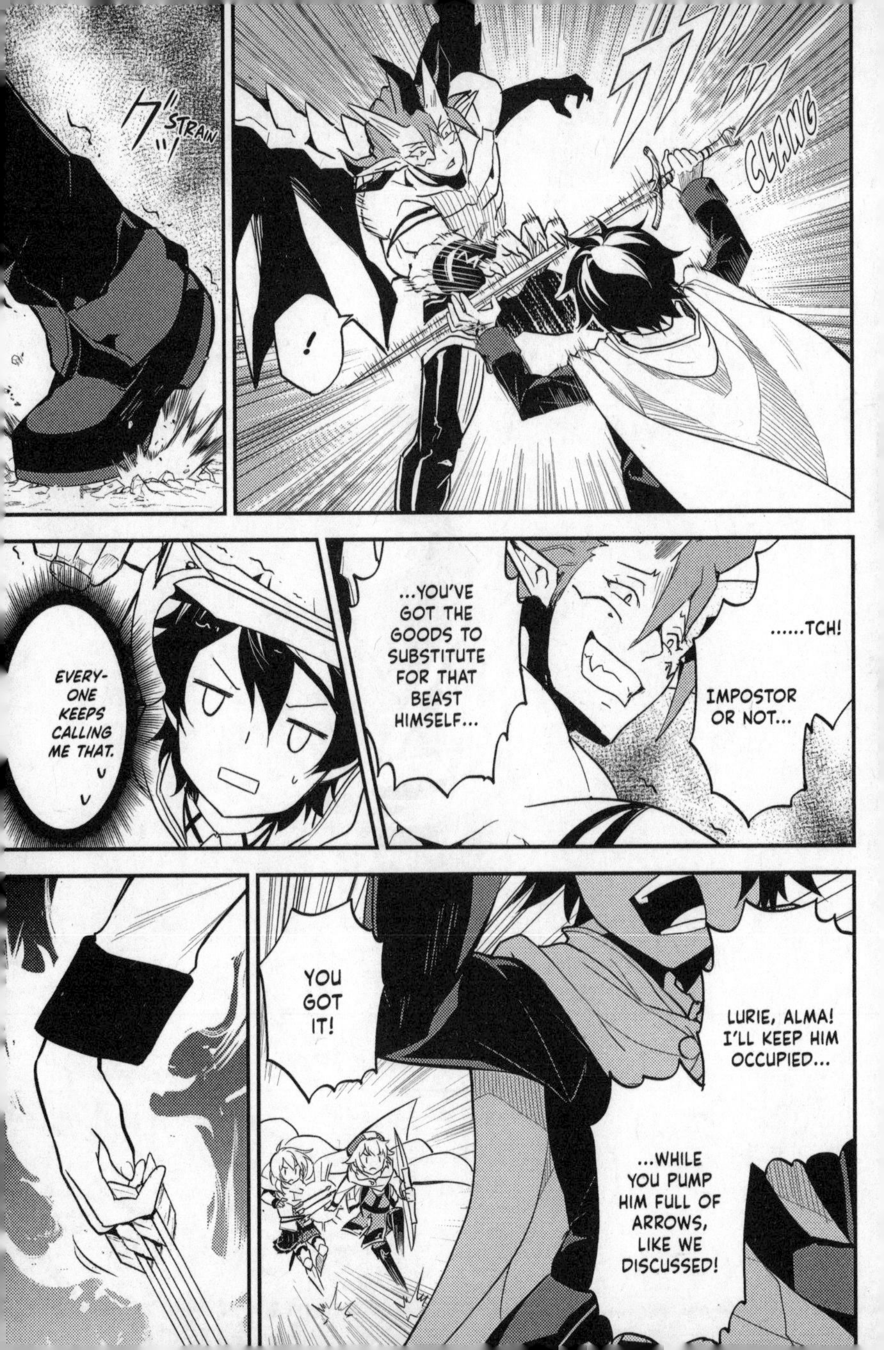
CLANG
!
STRAIN
......TCH!
IMPOSTOR OR NOT...
...YOU'VE GOT THE GOODS TO SUBSTITUTE FOR THAT BEAST HIMSELF...
EVERY-ONE KEEPS CALLING ME THAT.
LURIE, ALMA! I'LL KEEP HIM OCCUPIED...
...WHILE YOU PUMP HIM FULL OF ARROWS, LIKE WE DISCUSSED!
YOU GOT IT!

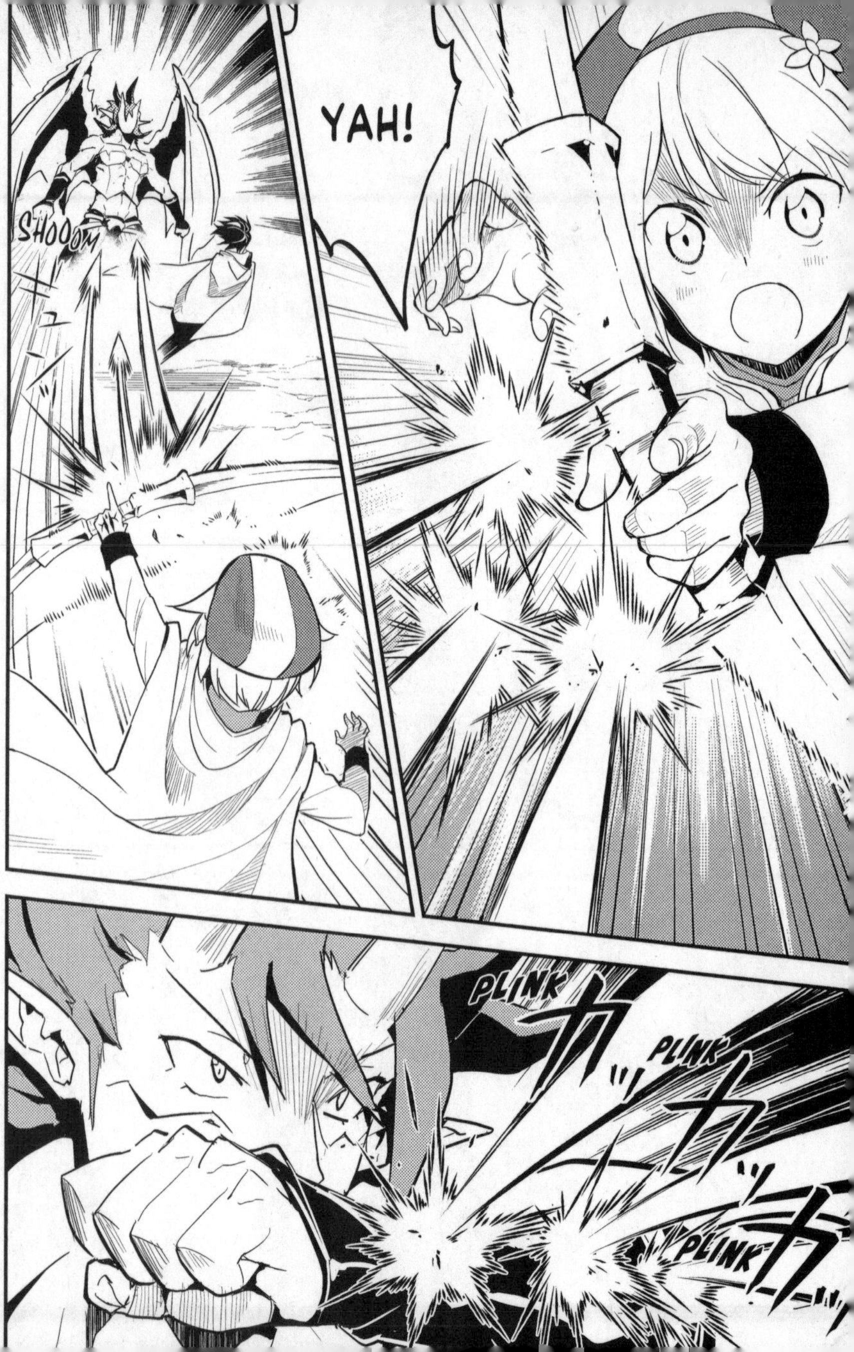
YAH!
SHOOOM
PLINK
PLINK
PLINK

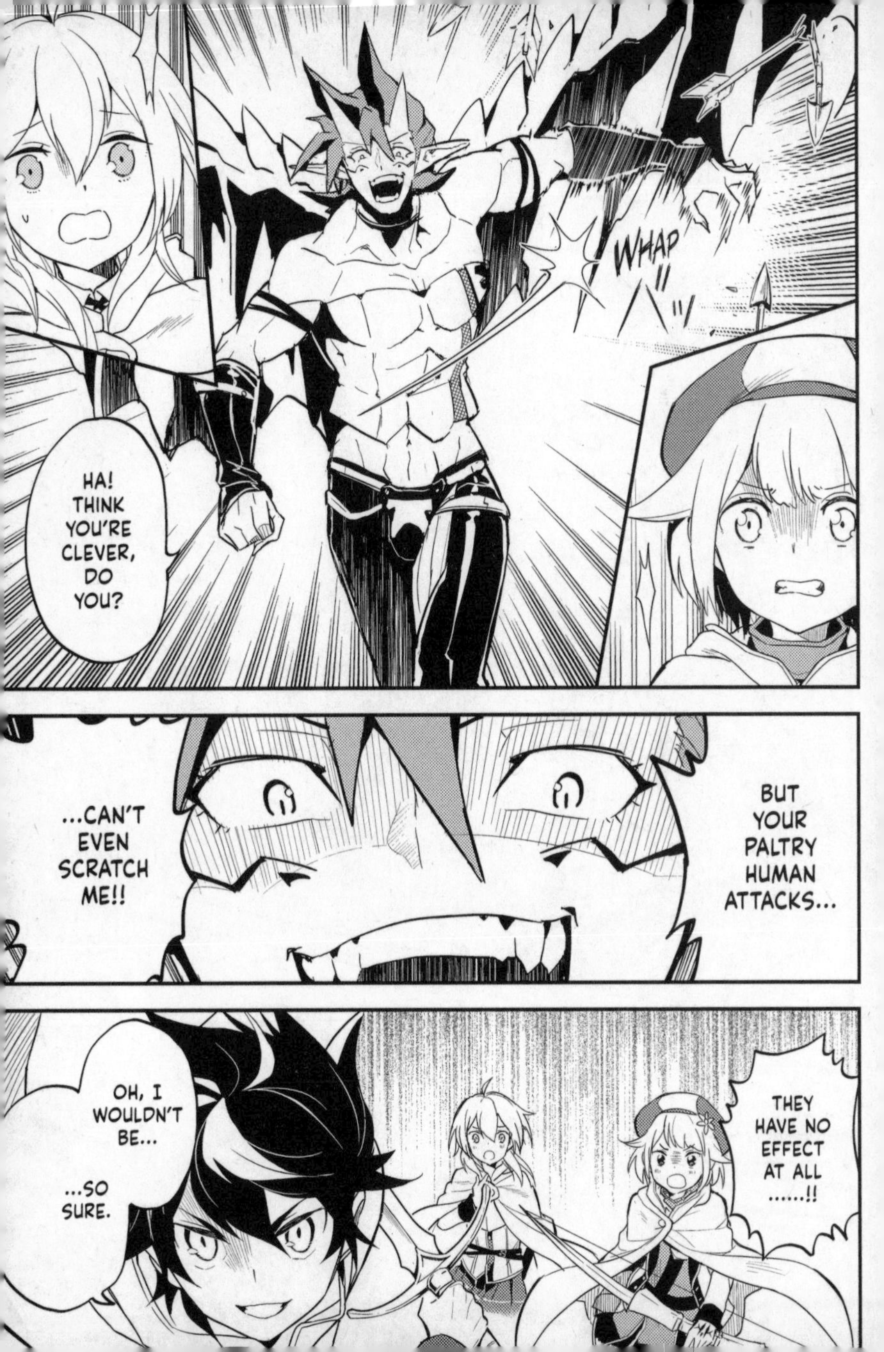
WHAP
HA! THINK YOU'RE CLEVER, DO YOU?
BUT YOUR PALTRY HUMAN ATTACKS...
...CAN'T EVEN SCRATCH ME!!
THEY HAVE NO EFFECT AT ALL ......!!
OH, I WOULDN'T BE...
...SO SURE.

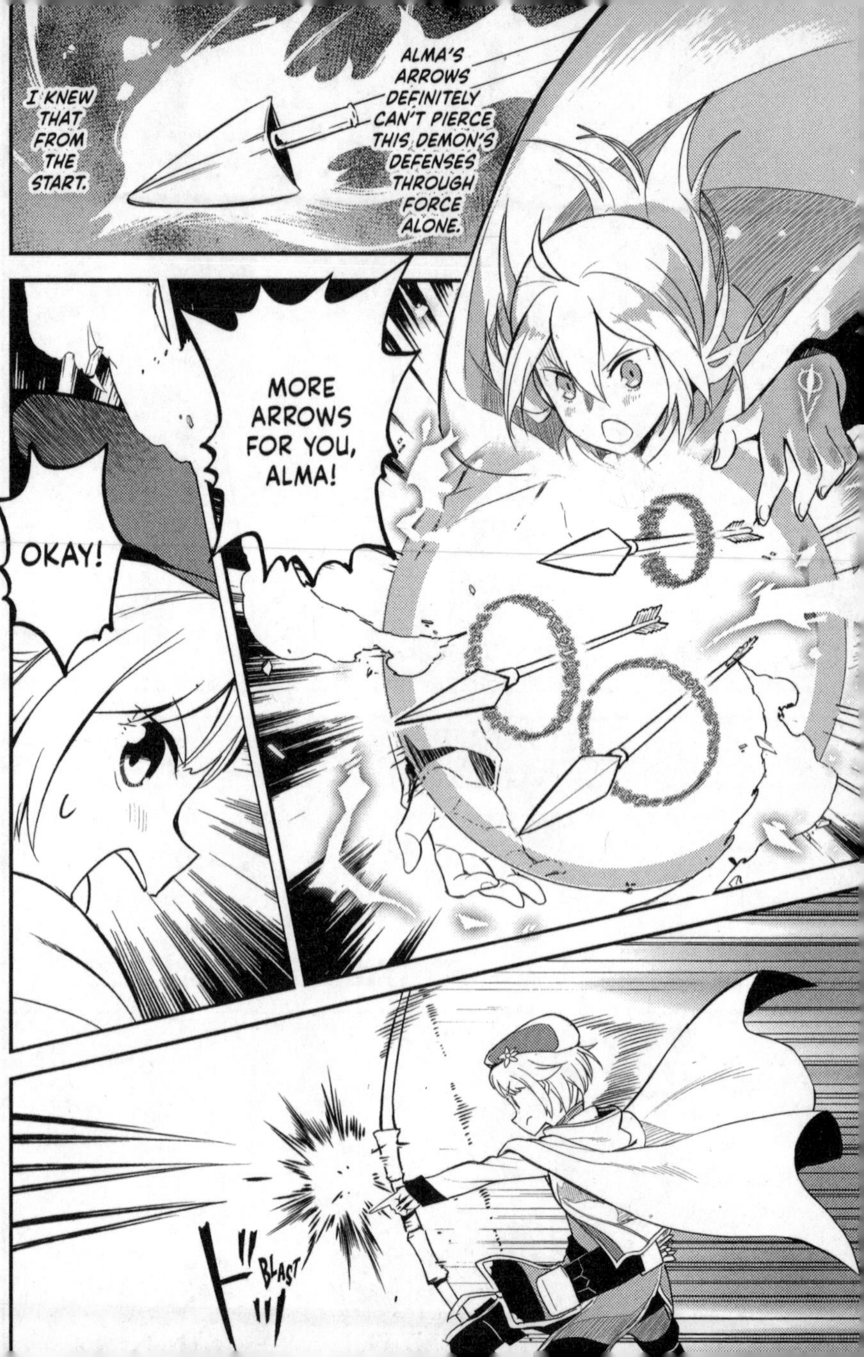
ALMA'S ARROWS DEFINITELY CAN'T PIERCE THIS DEMON'S DEFENSES THROUGH FORCE ALONE.
I KNEW THAT FROM THE START.
MORE ARROWS FOR YOU, ALMA!
OKAY!
BLAST

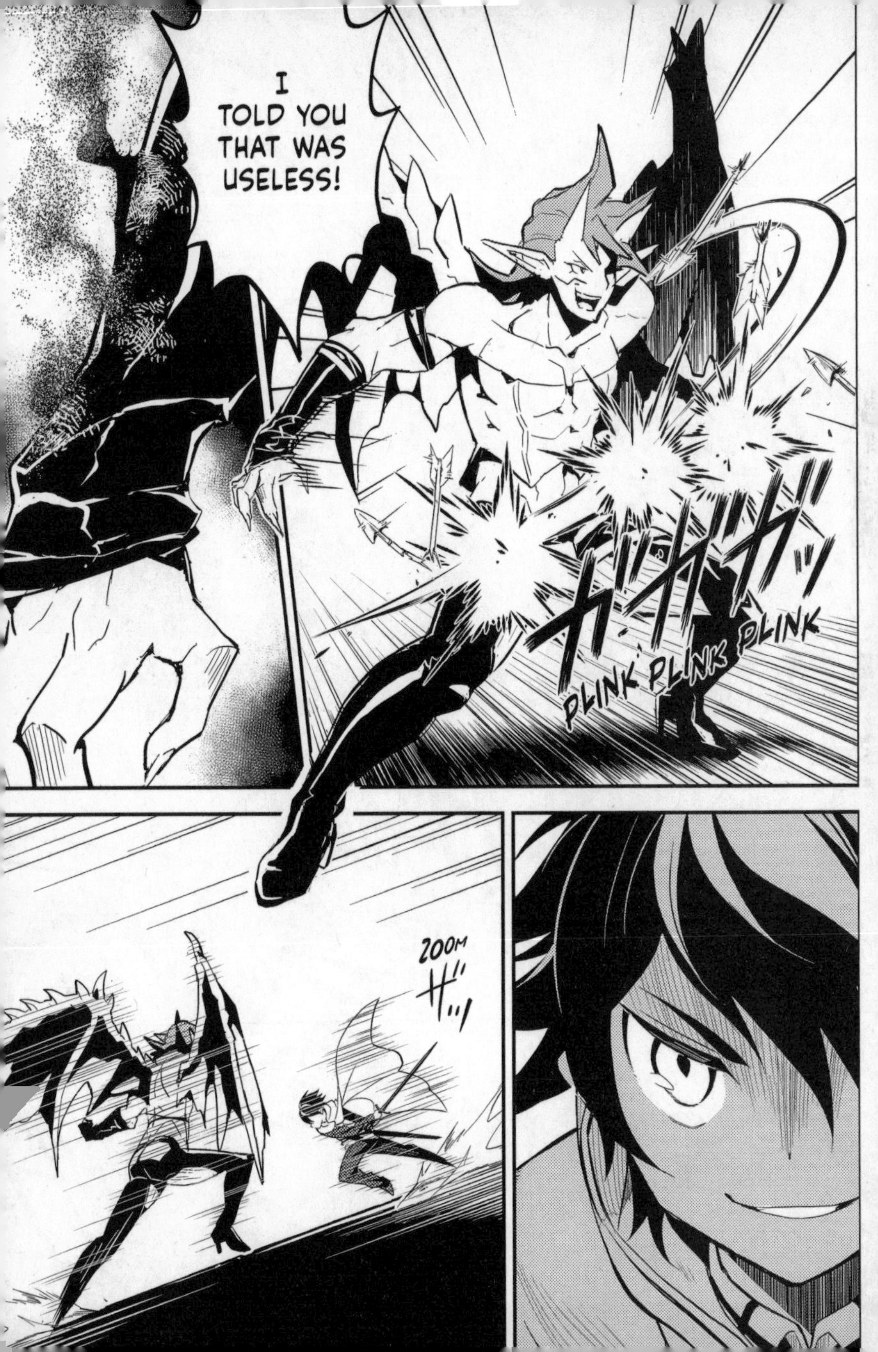
I TOLD YOU THAT WAS USELESS!
PLINK PLINK PLINK
ZOOM

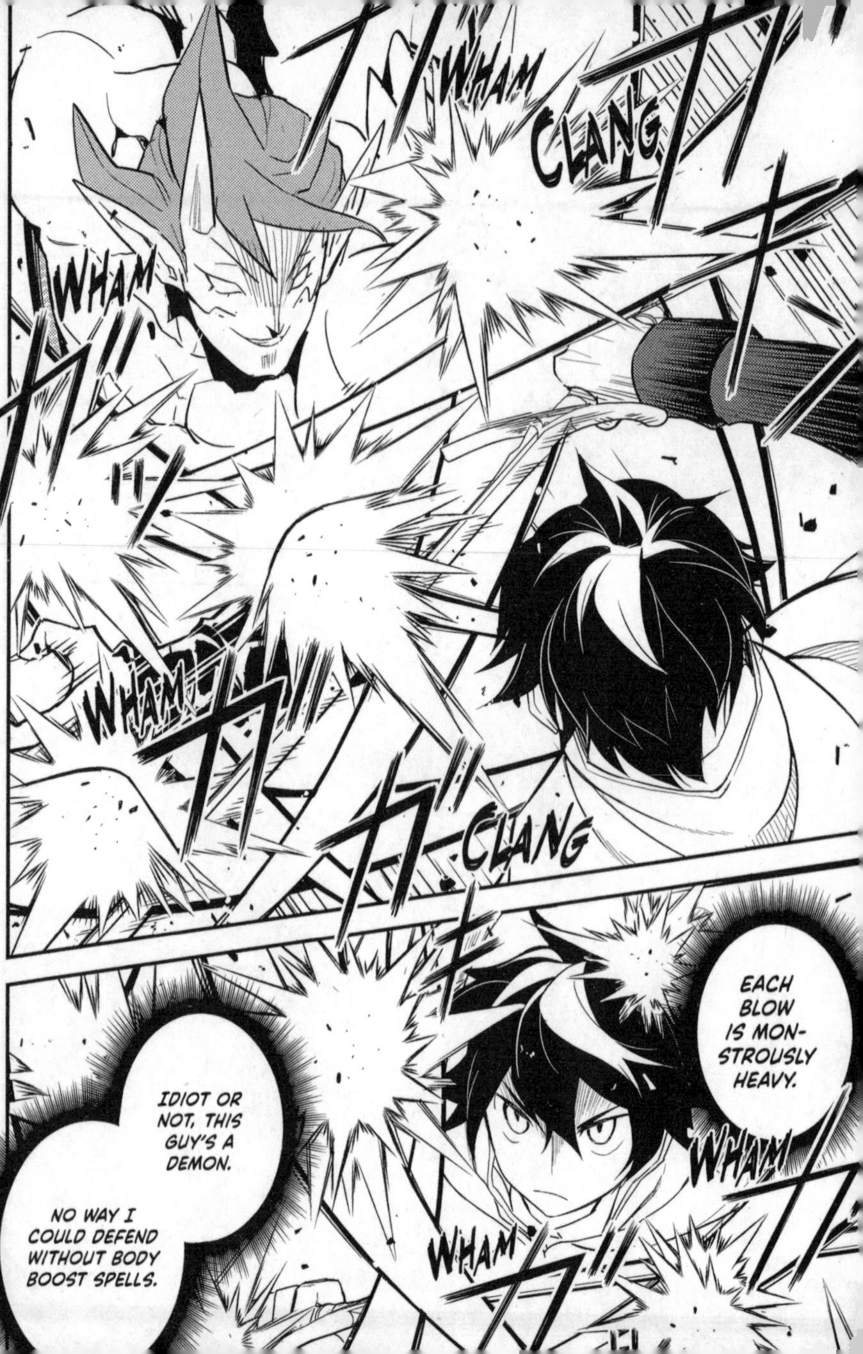
CLANG
WHAM
WHAM
WHAM
CLANG
EACH BLOW IS MON-STROUSLY HEAVY.
IDIOT OR NOT, THIS GUY'S A DEMON.
NO WAY I COULD DEFEND WITHOUT BODY BOOST SPELLS.
WHAM
WHAM

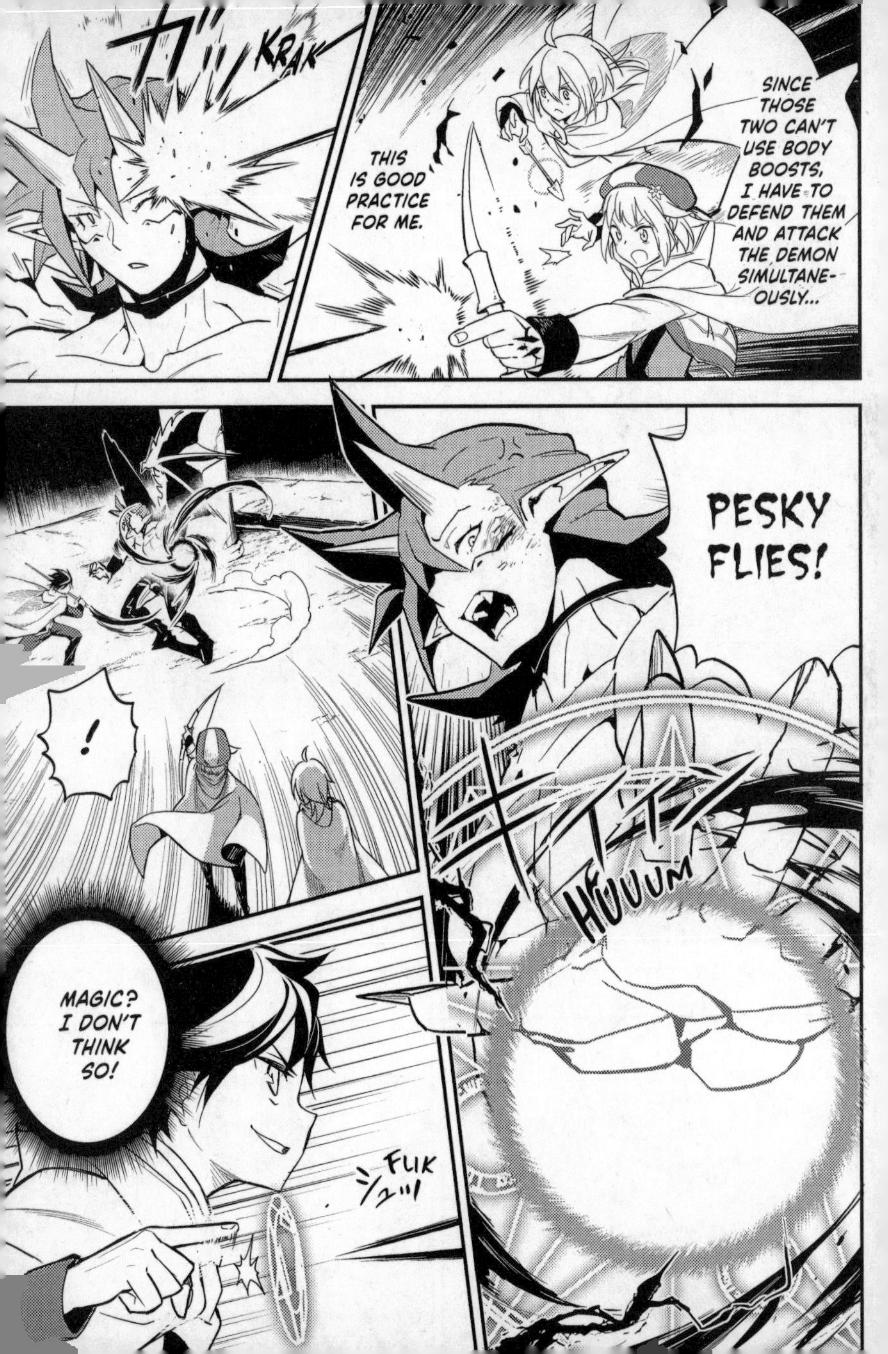
SINCE THOSE TWO CAN'T USE BODY BOOSTS, I HAVE TO DEFEND THEM AND ATTACK THE DEMON SIMULTANE-OUSLY...
THIS IS GOOD PRACTICE FOR ME.
KRAK
PESKY FLIES!
HUUUM
!
MAGIC? I DON'T THINK SO!
FLIK

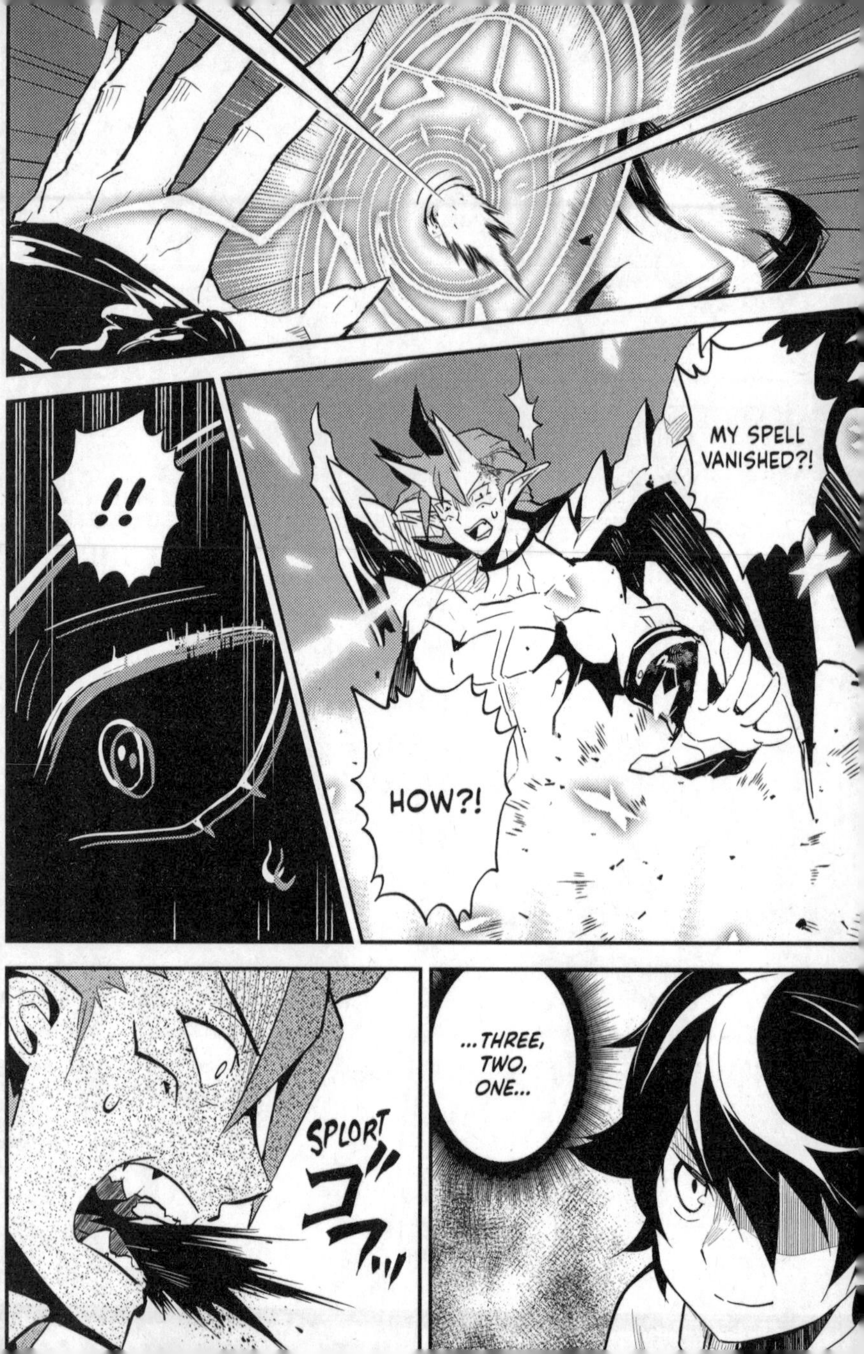
MY SPELL VANISHED?!
HOW?!
!!
...THREE, TWO, ONE...
SPLORT
ゴフッ

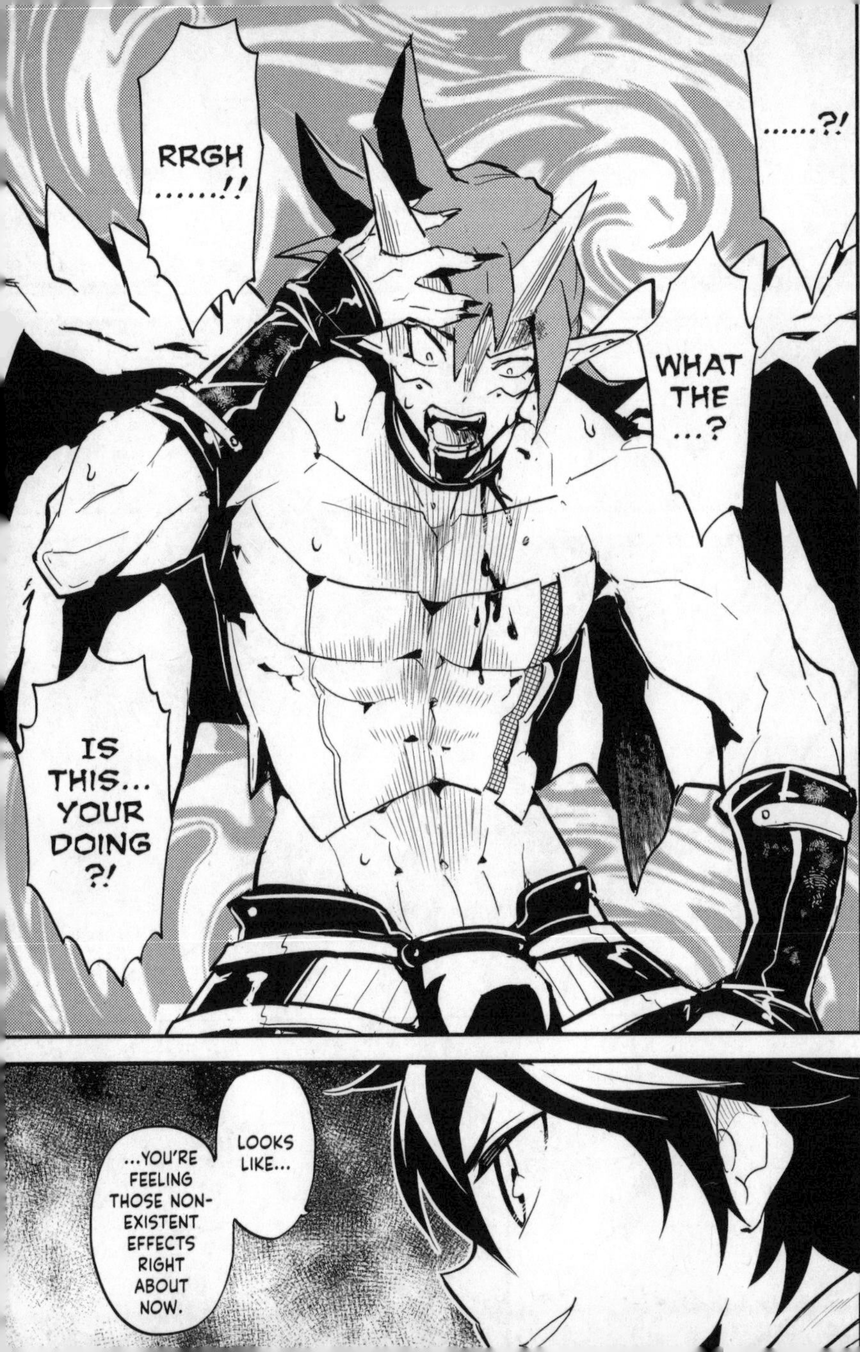
......?!
RRGH ......!!
WHAT THE ...?
IS THIS... YOUR DOING ?!
LOOKS LIKE...
...YOU'RE FEELING THOSE NON-EXISTENT EFFECTS RIGHT ABOUT NOW.

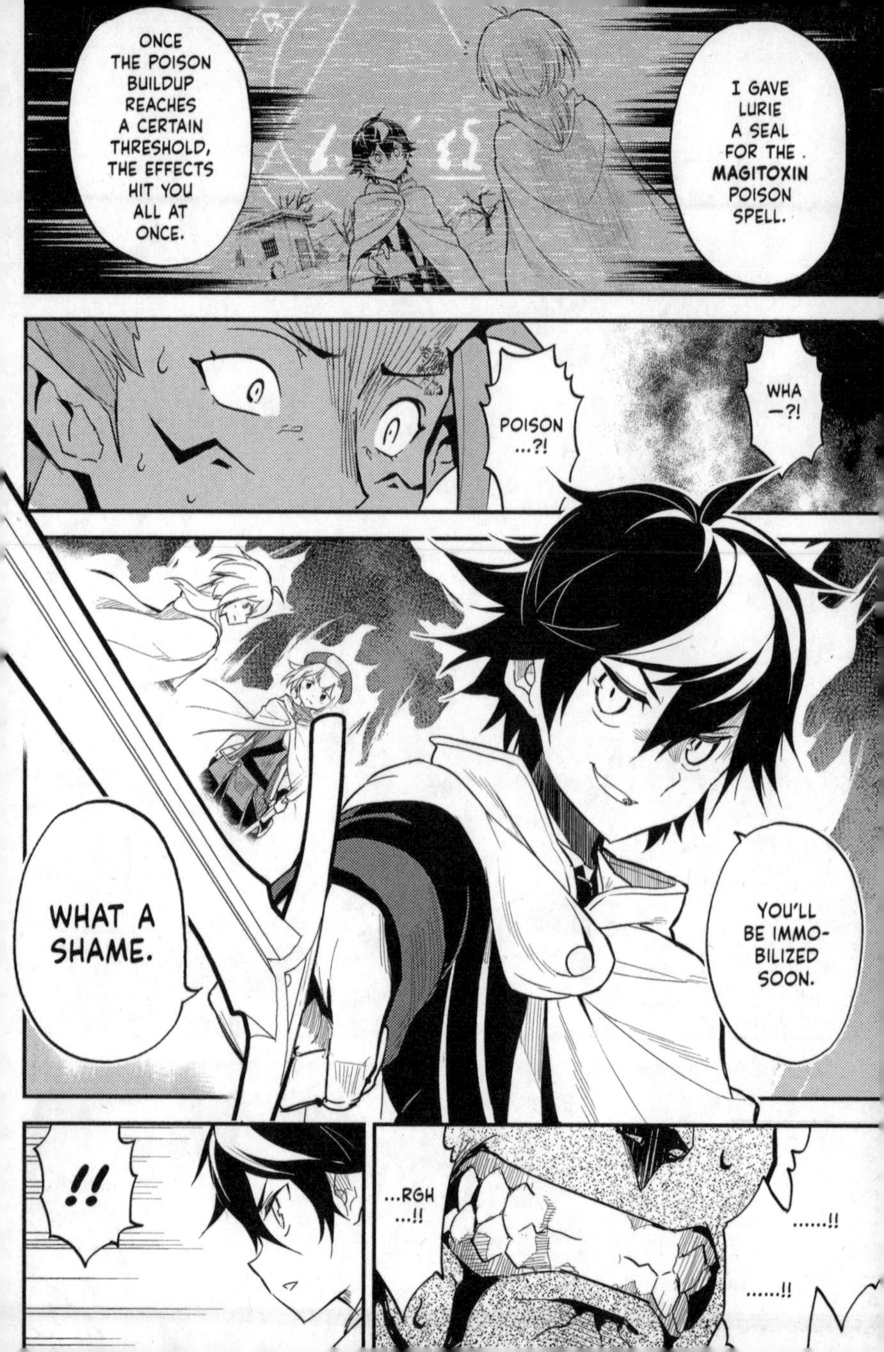
I GAVE LURIE A SEAL FOR THE MAGITOXIN POISON SPELL.
ONCE THE POISON BUILDUP REACHES A CERTAIN THRESHOLD, THE EFFECTS HIT YOU ALL AT ONCE.
WHA—?!
POISON...?!
YOU'LL BE IMMOBILIZED SOON.
WHAT A SHAME.
......!!
......!!
...RGH ...!!
!!

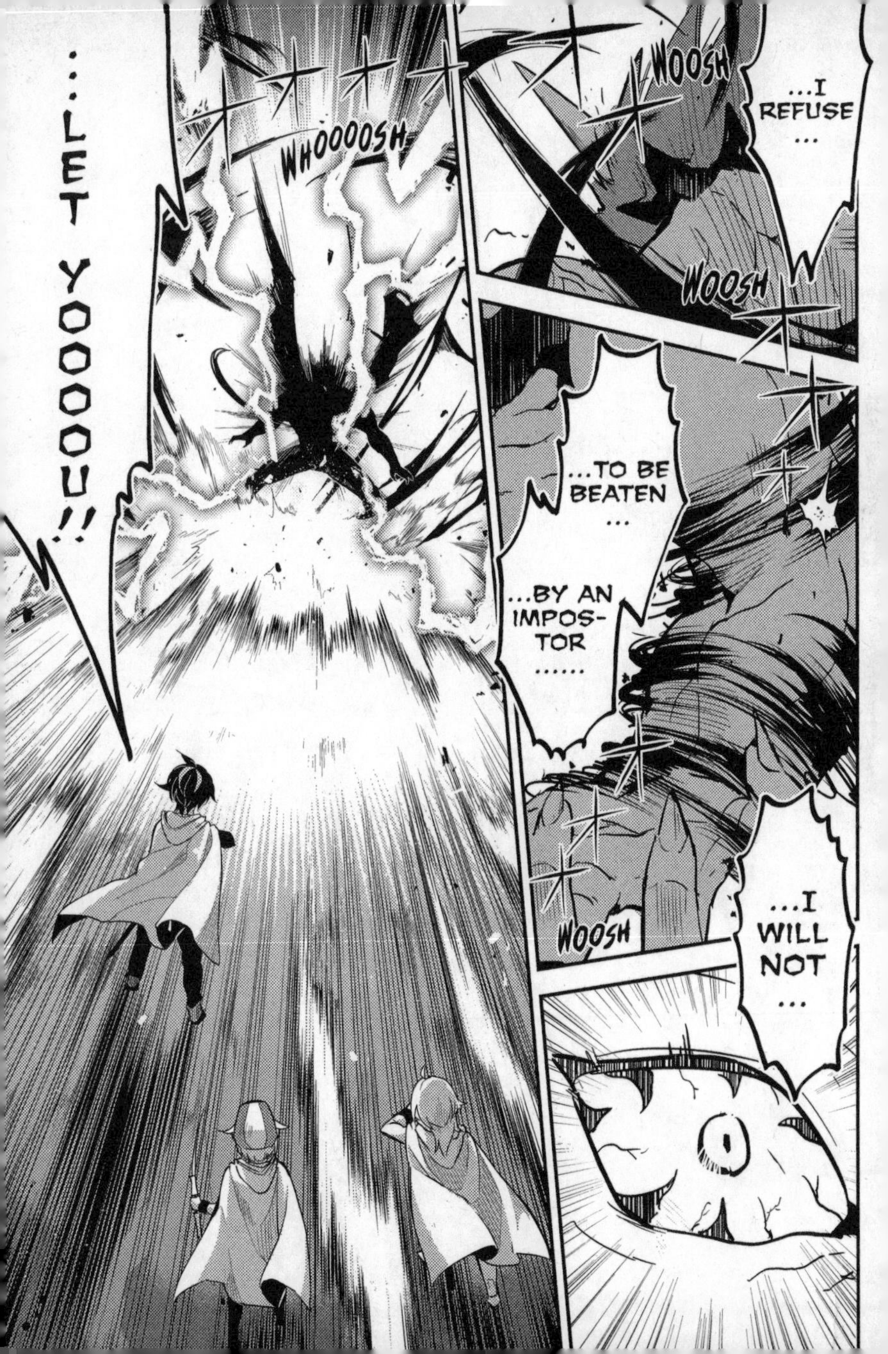
WOOSH
...I REFUSE ...
WOOSH
...TO BE BEATEN ...
...BY AN IMPOSTOR ......
WOOSH
...I WILL NOT ...
WHOOOOSH
...LET YOOOOOU!!

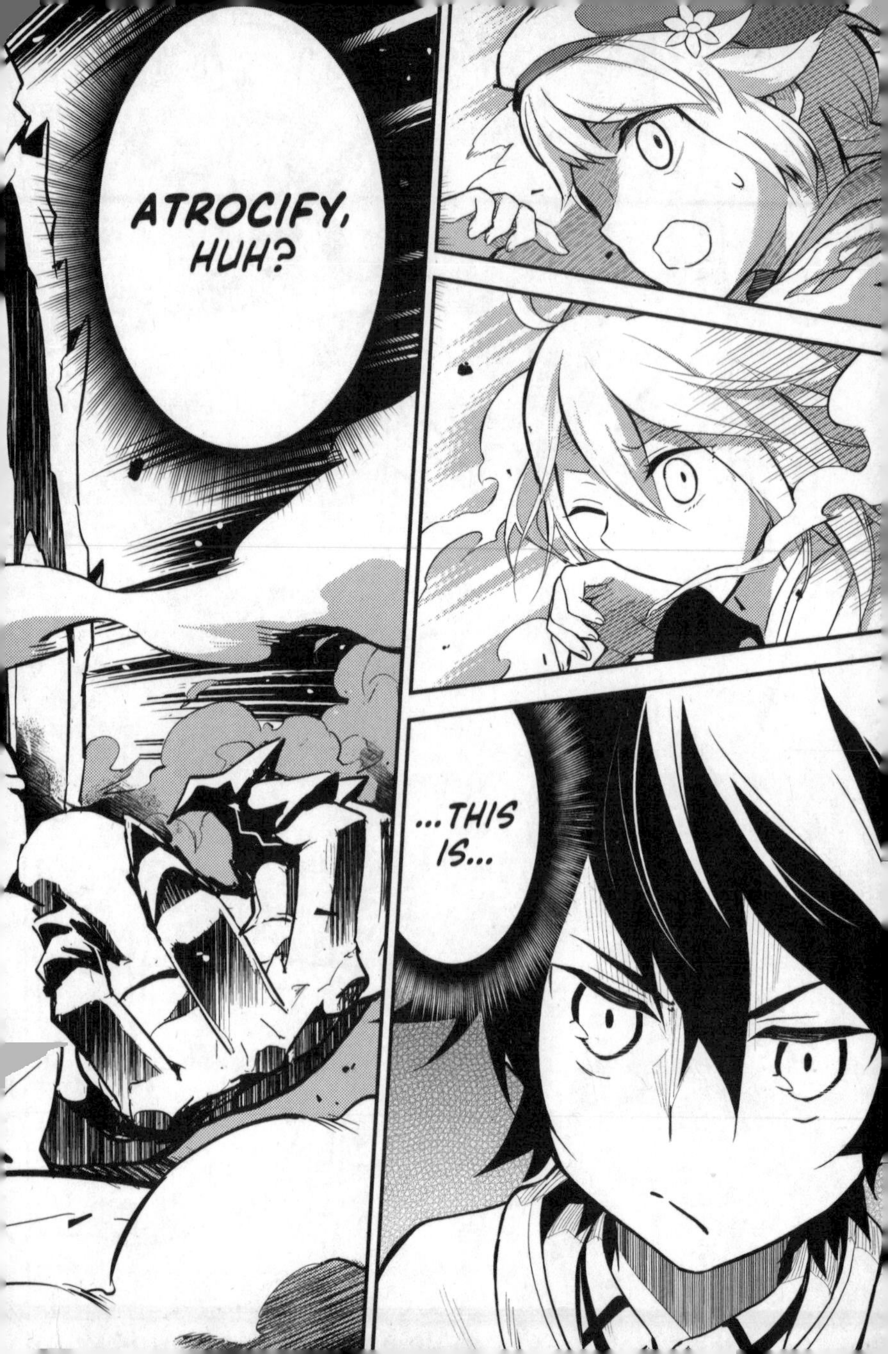
...THIS IS...
ATROCIFY, HUH?

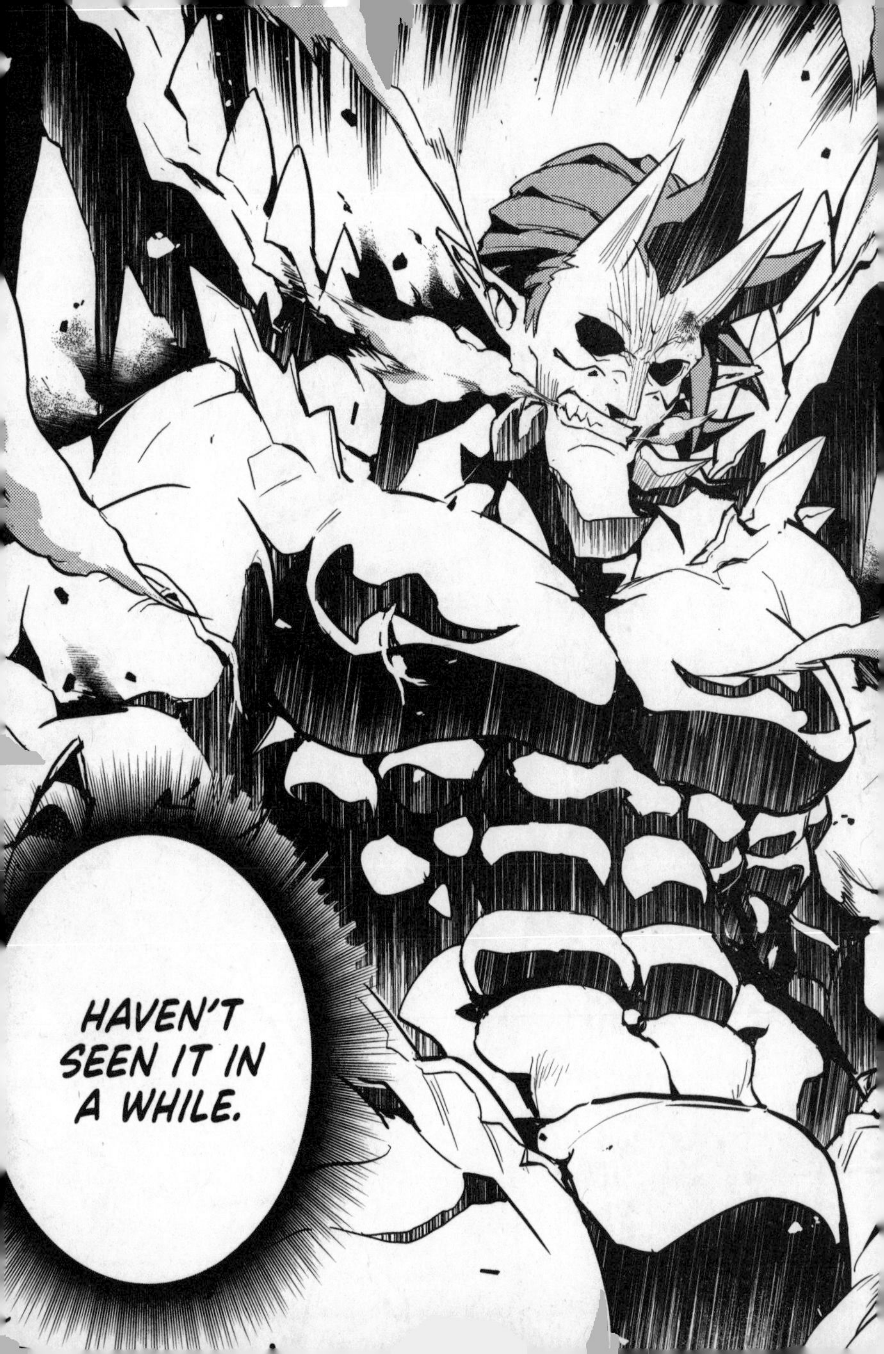
HAVEN'T SEEN IT IN A WHILE.

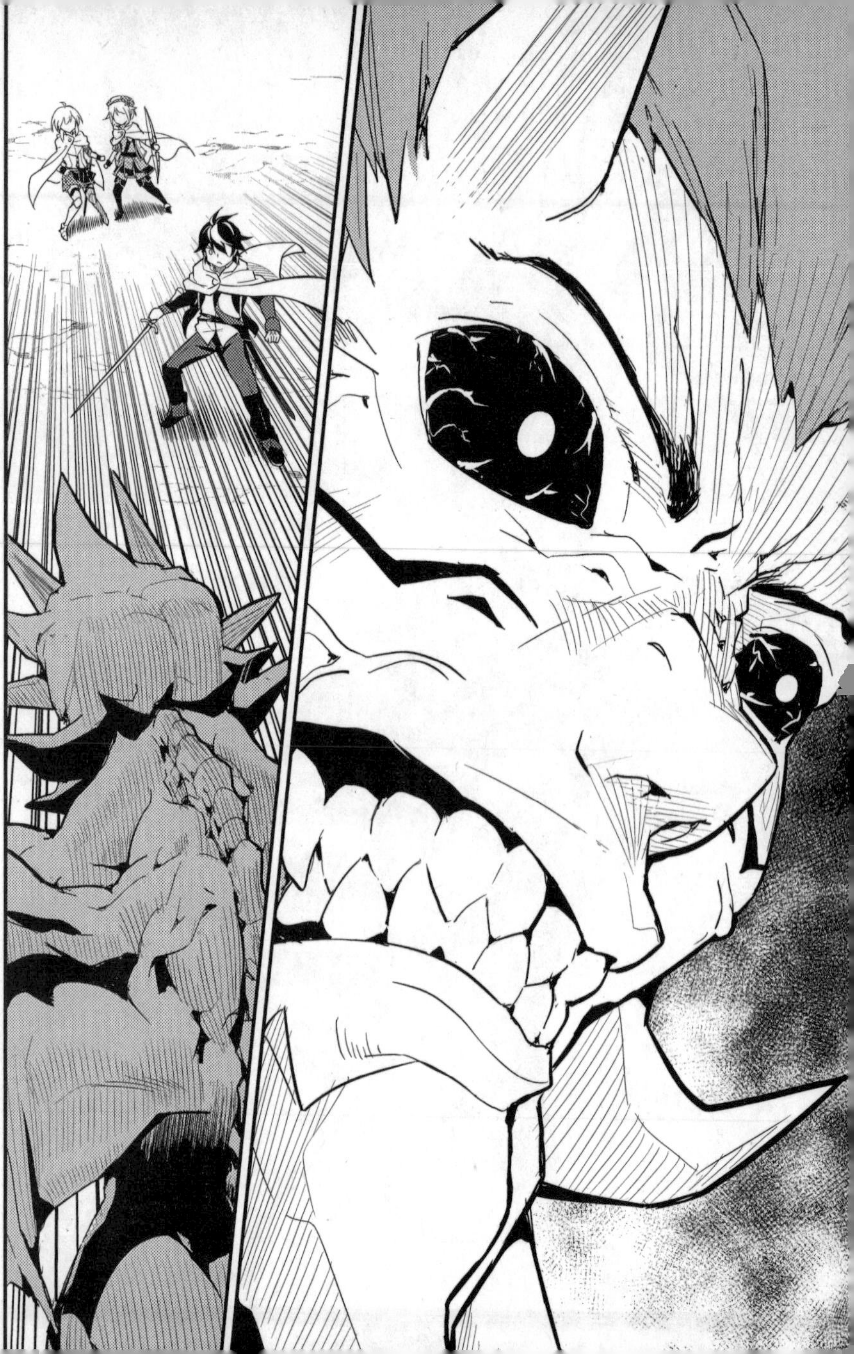

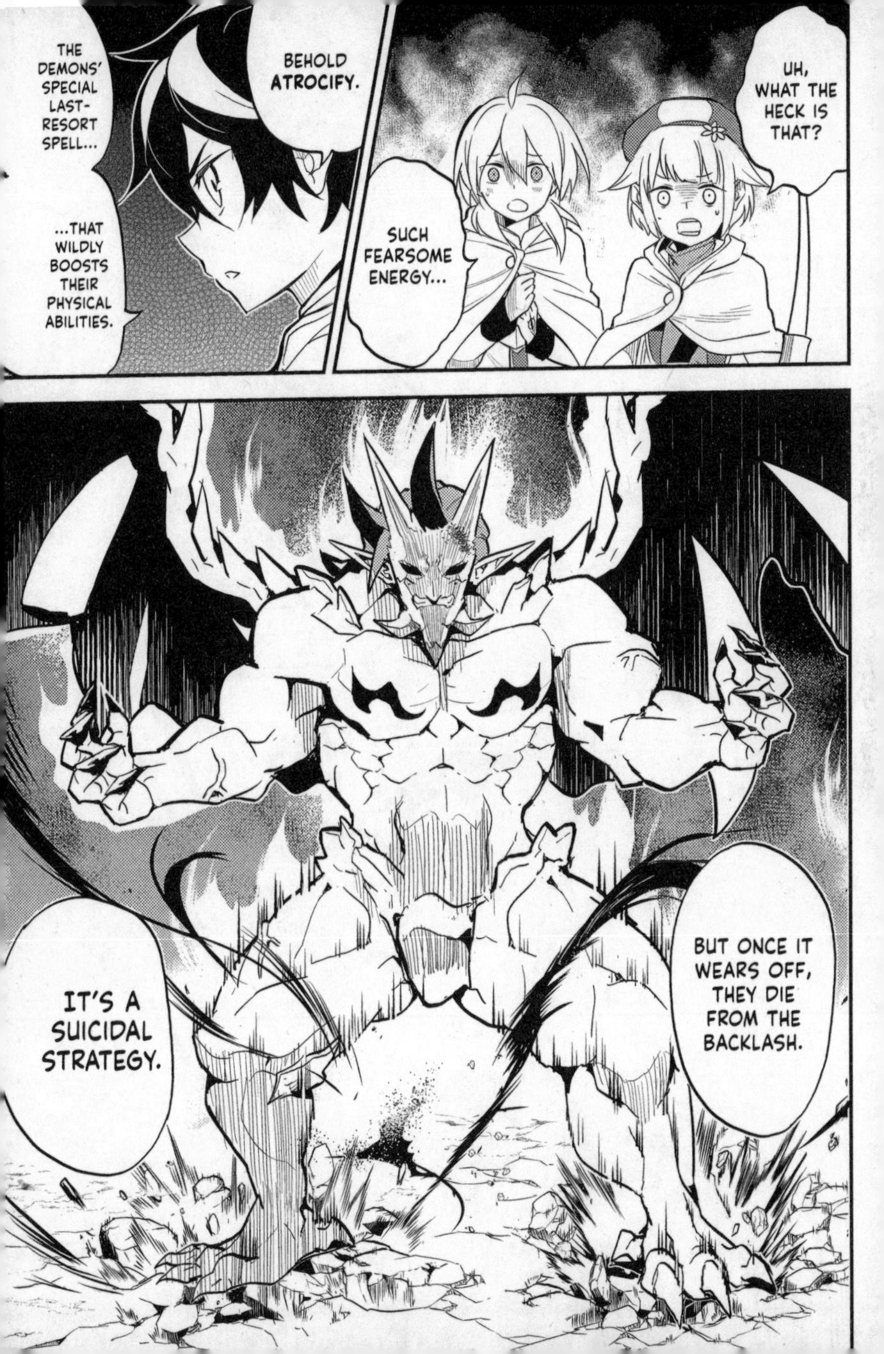
UH, WHAT THE HECK IS THAT?
SUCH FEARSOME ENERGY...
BEHOLD ATROCIFY.
THE DEMONS' SPECIAL LAST-RESORT SPELL...
...THAT WILDLY BOOSTS THEIR PHYSICAL ABILITIES.
BUT ONCE IT WEARS OFF, THEY DIE FROM THE BACKLASH.
IT'S A SUICIDAL STRATEGY.

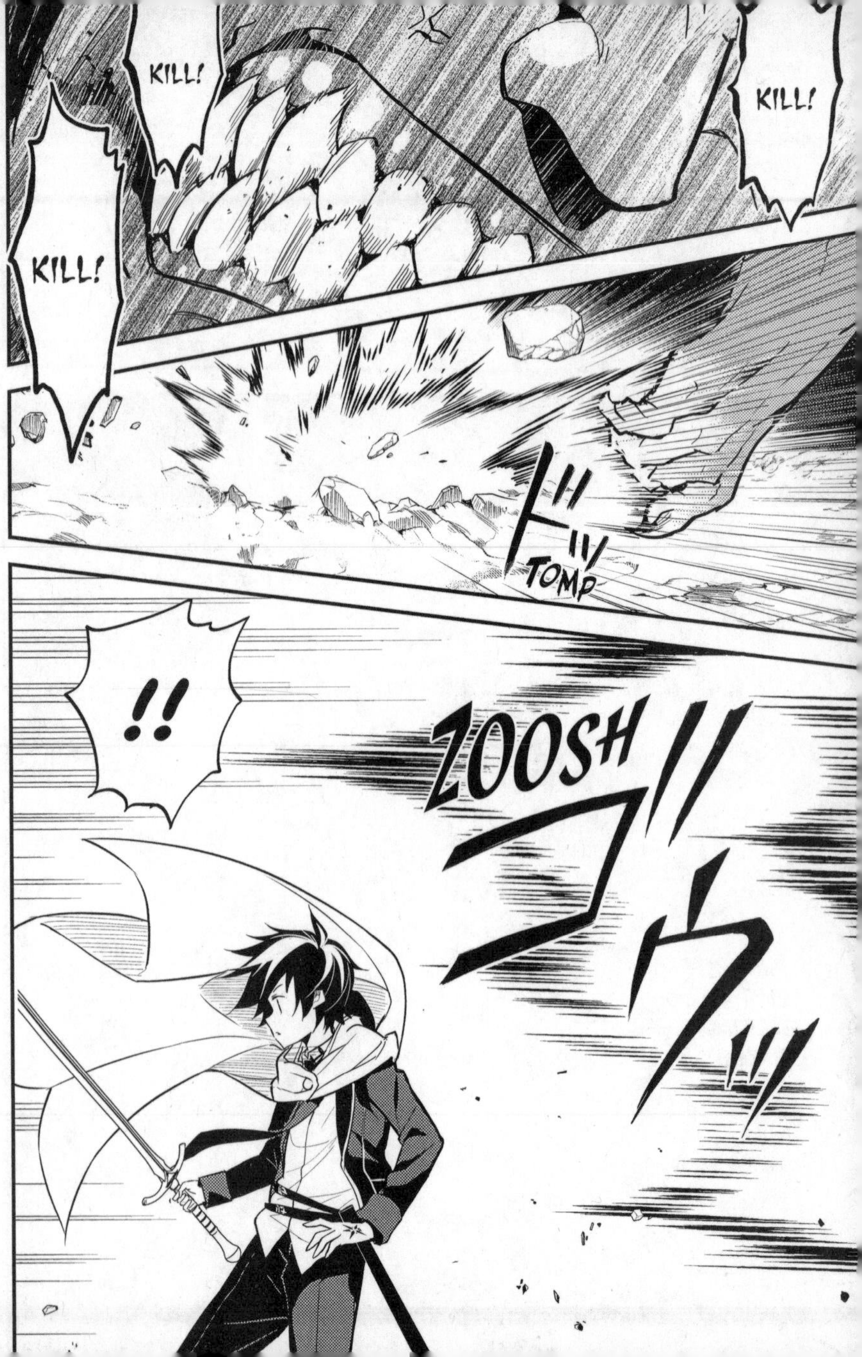
KILL!
KILL!
KILL!
TOMP
!!
ZOOSH

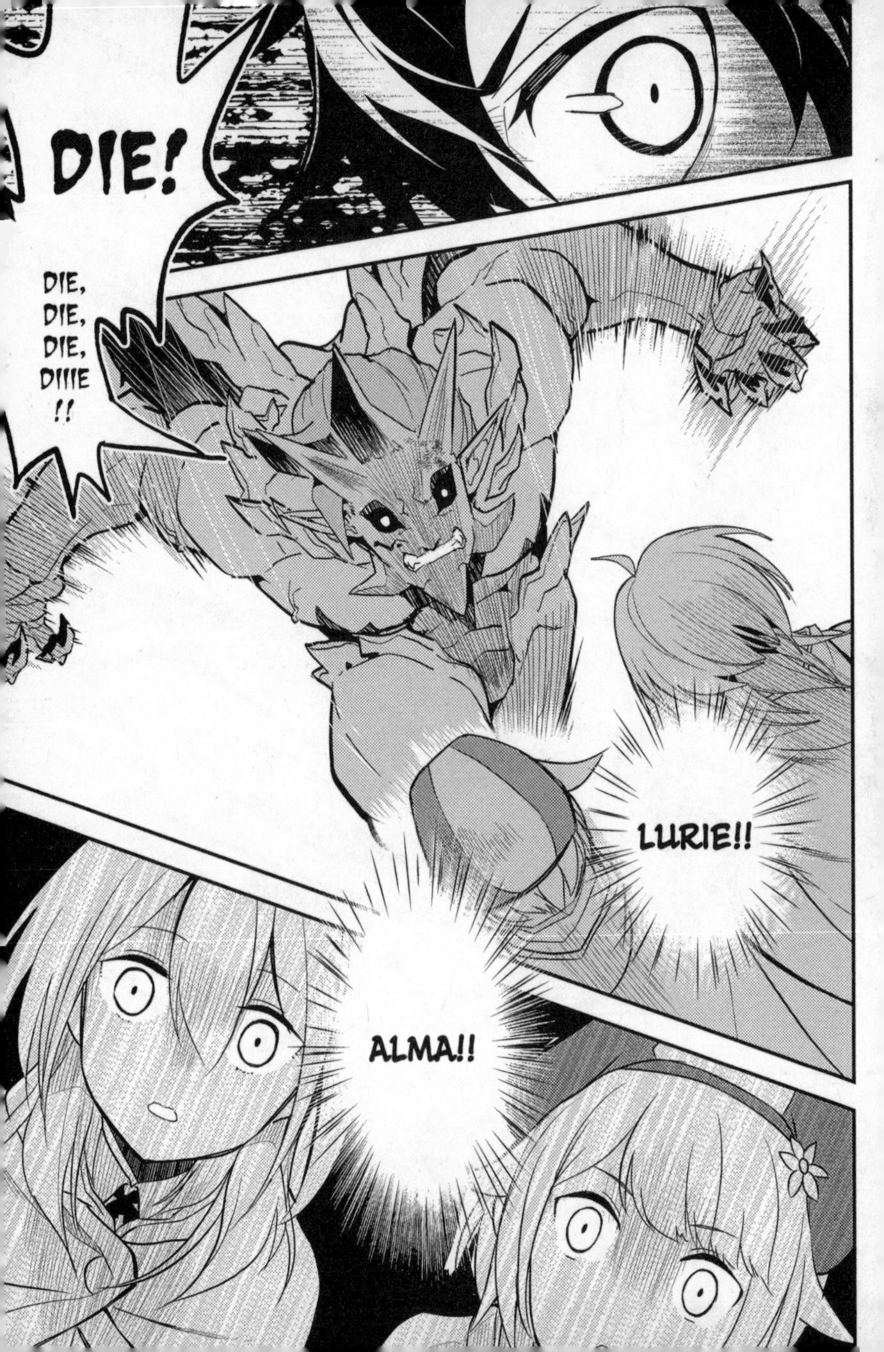
DIE!
DIE, DIE, DIE, DIIIE!!
LURIE!!
ALMA!!

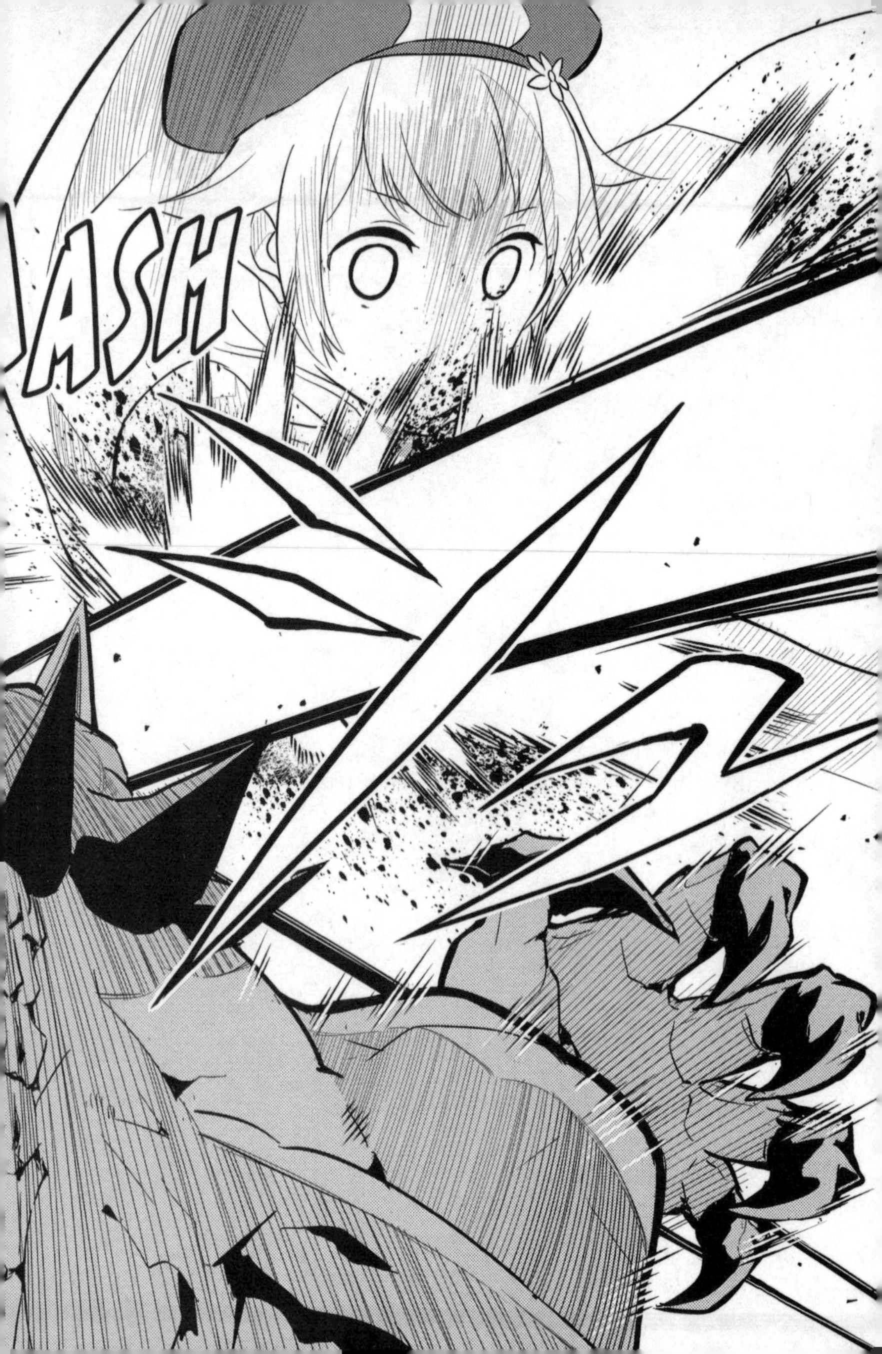
ASH

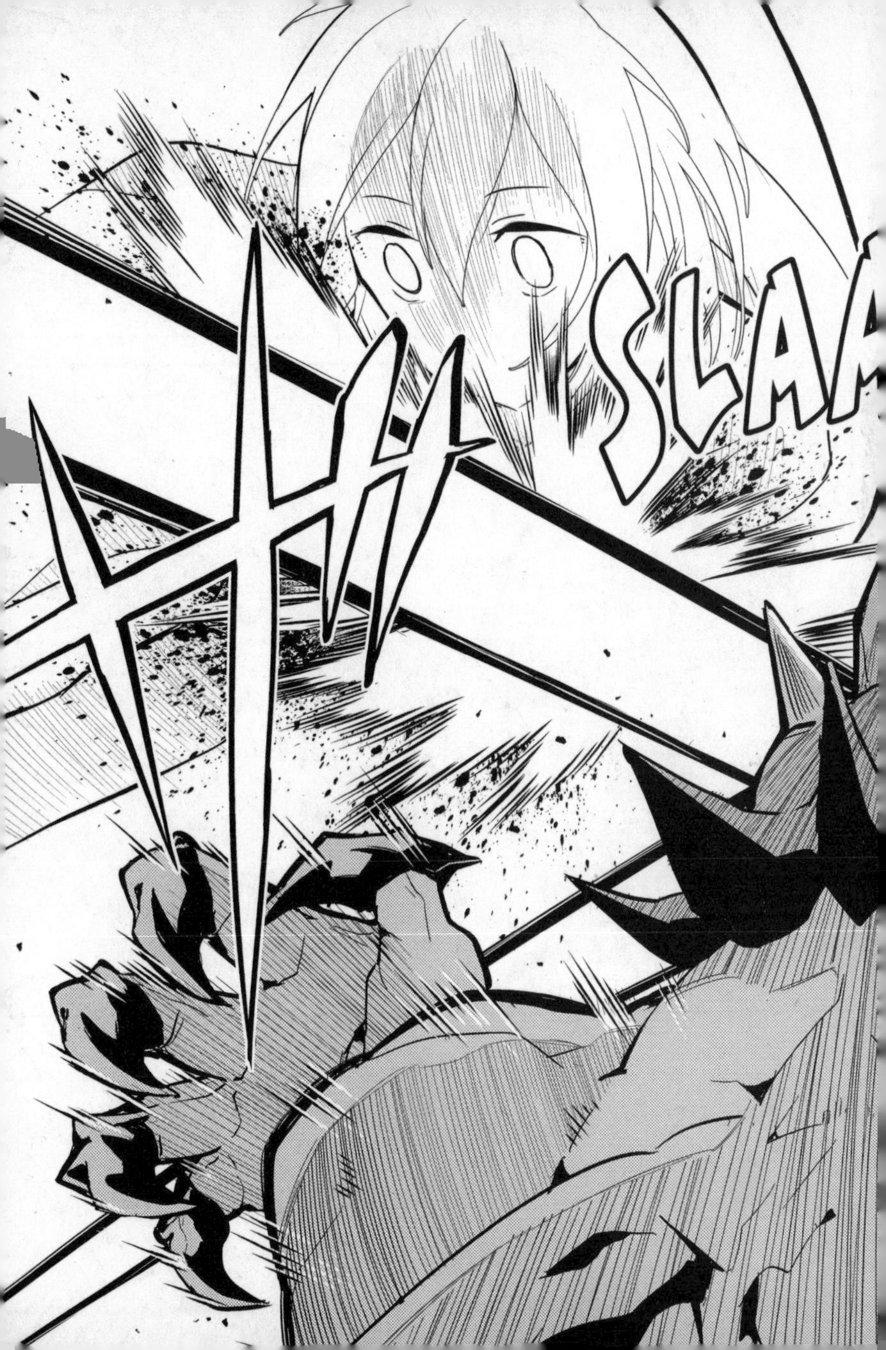
SLAA

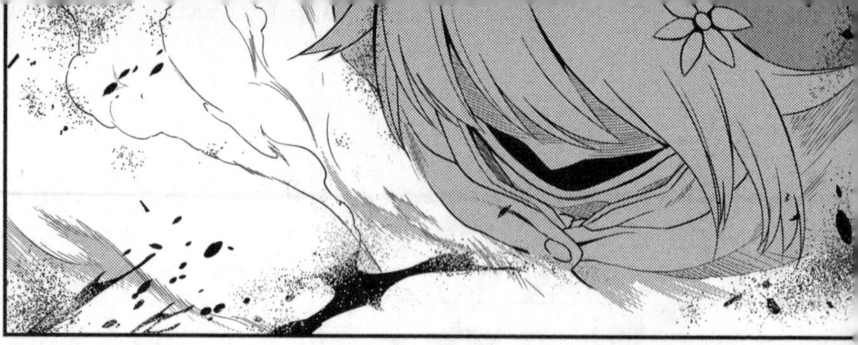
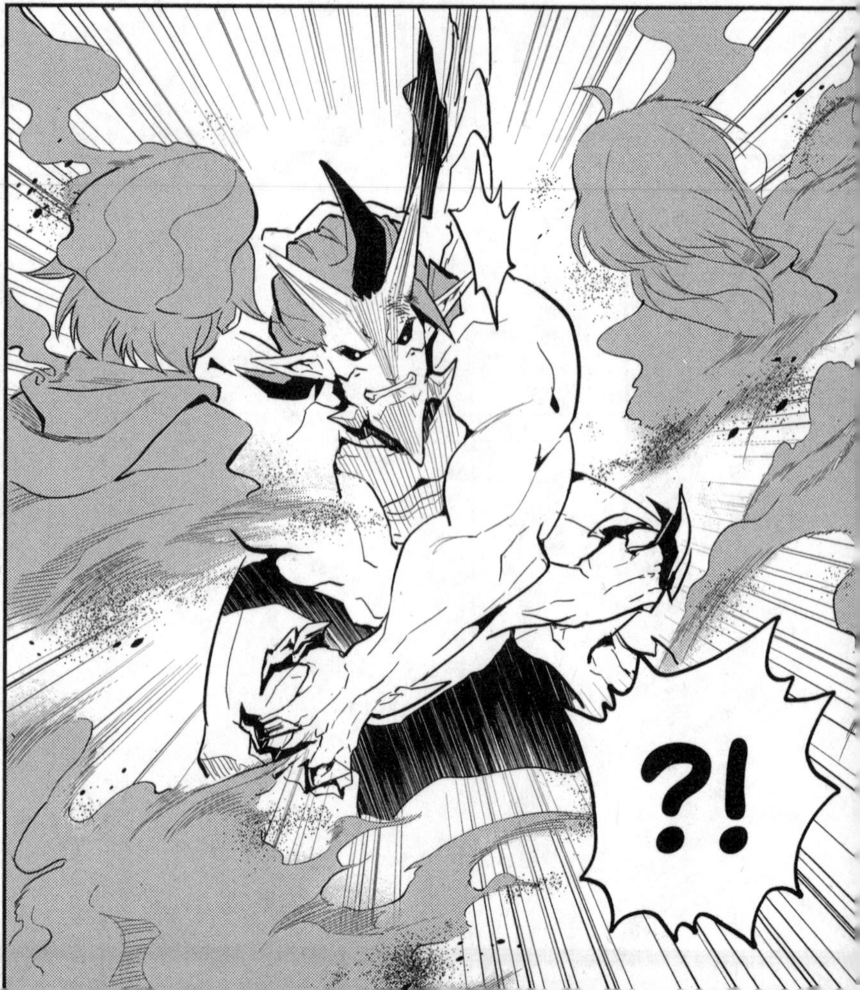
?!

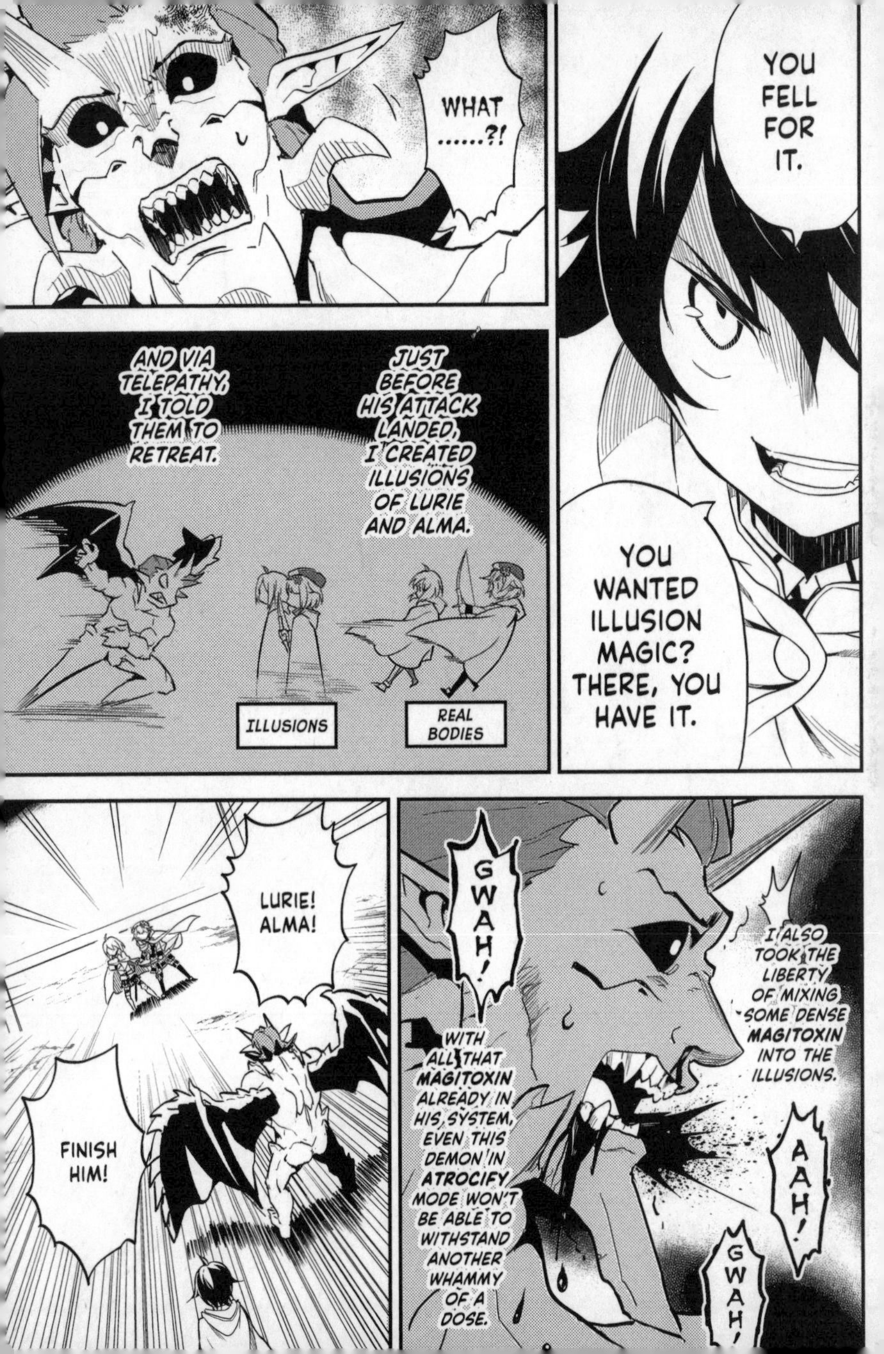
YOU FELL FOR IT.
YOU WANTED ILLUSION MAGIC? THERE, YOU HAVE IT.
WHAT ......?!
JUST BEFORE HIS ATTACK LANDED, I CREATED ILLUSIONS OF LURIE AND ALMA.
AND VIA TELEPATHY, I TOLD THEM TO RETREAT.
REAL BODIES
ILLUSIONS
I ALSO TOOK THE LIBERTY OF MIXING SOME DENSE MAGITOXIN INTO THE ILLUSIONS.
GWAH!
AAH!
WITH ALL THAT MAGITOXIN ALREADY IN HIS SYSTEM, EVEN THIS DEMON IN ATROCIFY MODE WON'T BE ABLE TO WITHSTAND ANOTHER WHAMMY OF A DOSE.
GWAH!
LURIE! ALMA!
FINISH HIM!

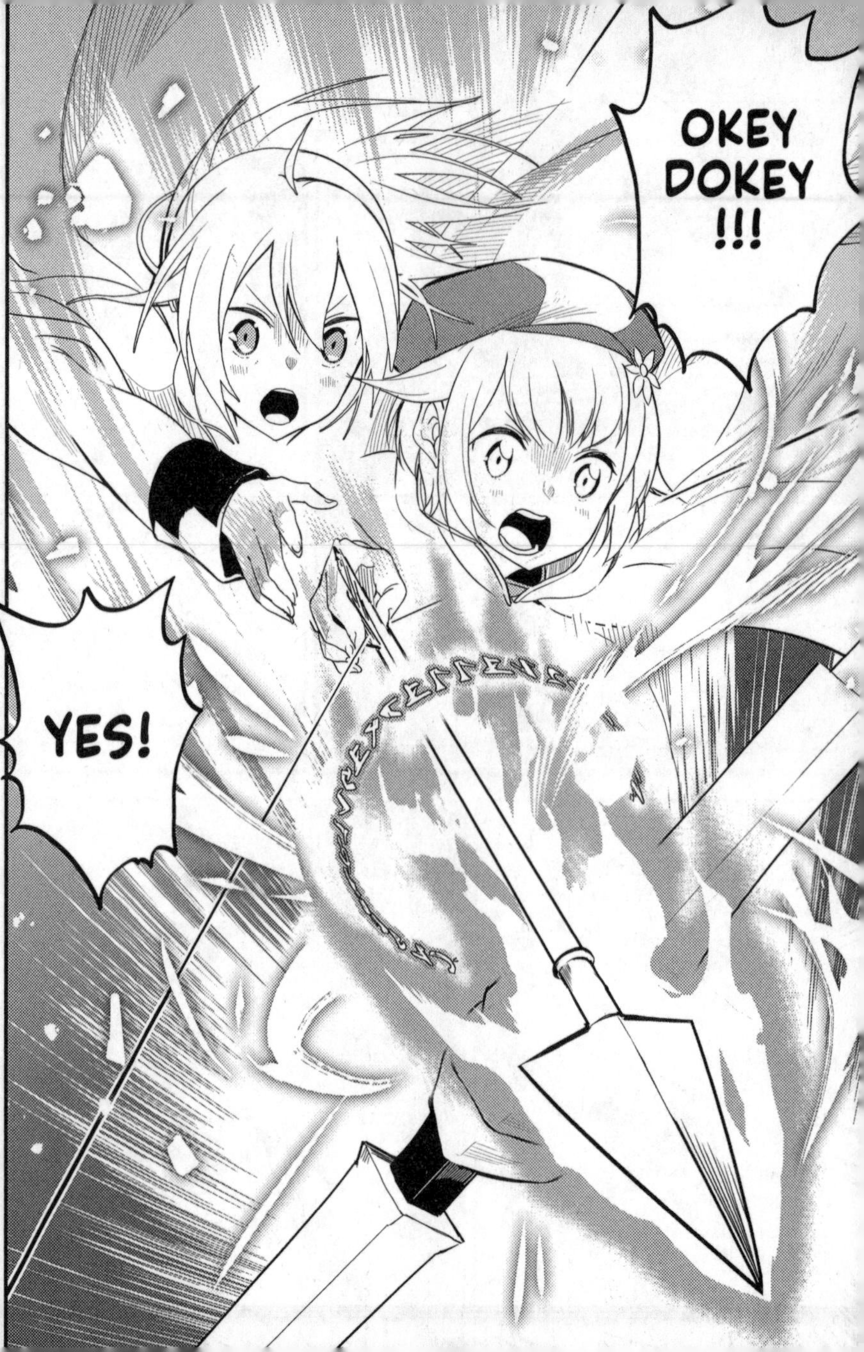
OKEY DOKEY !!!
YES!

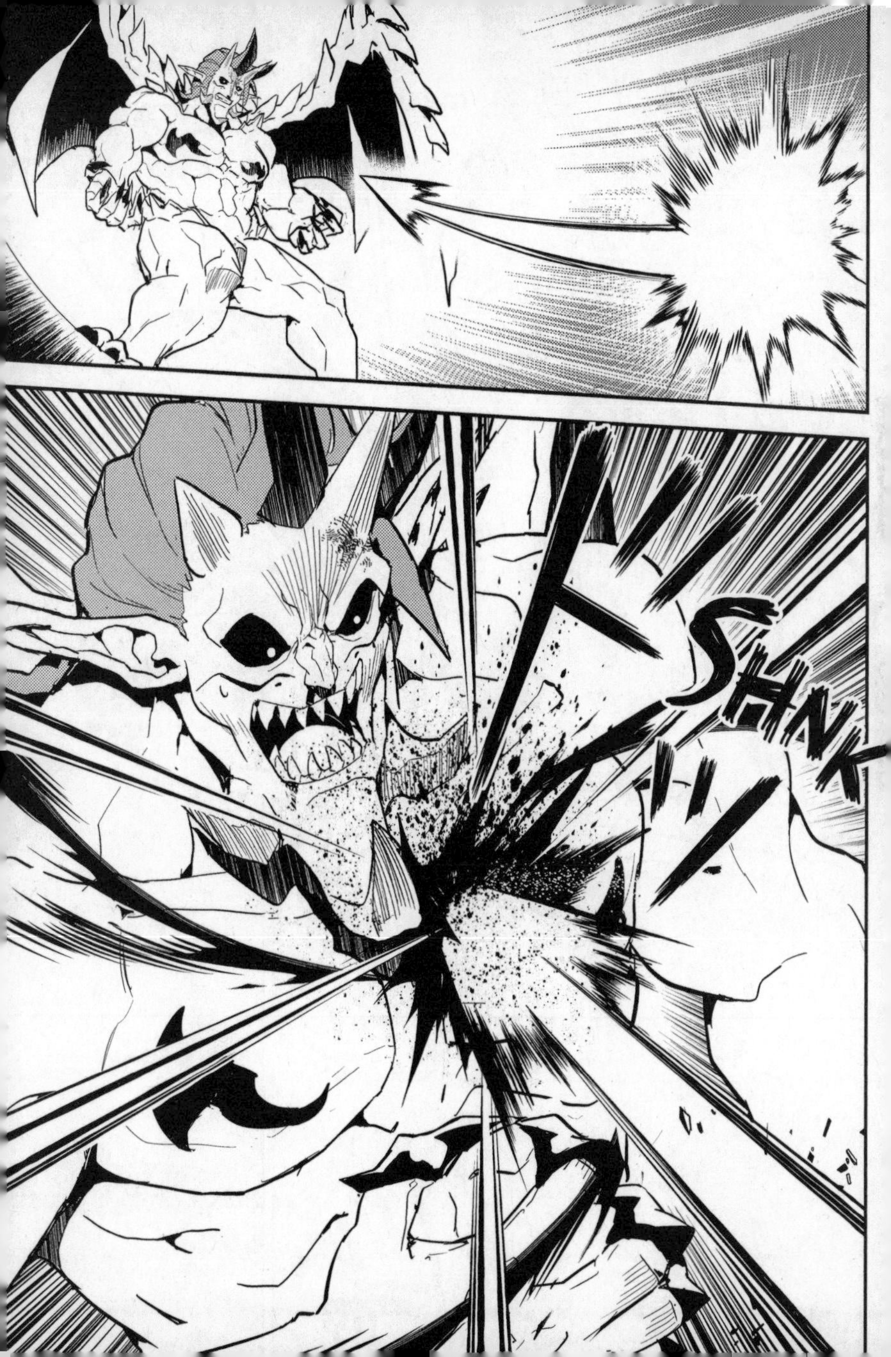
SHNK

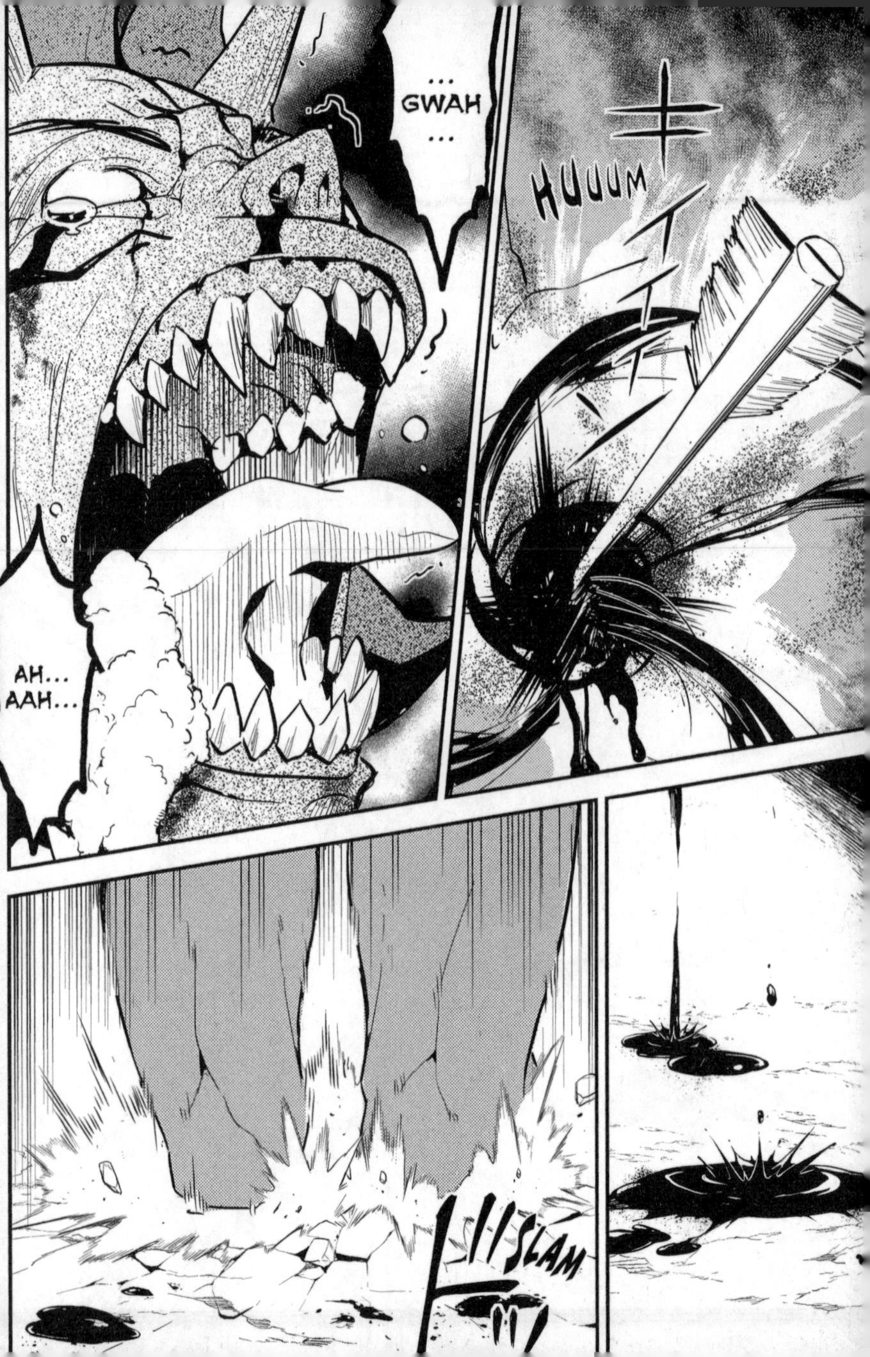
HUUUM
... GWAH ...
AH... AAH...
SLAM

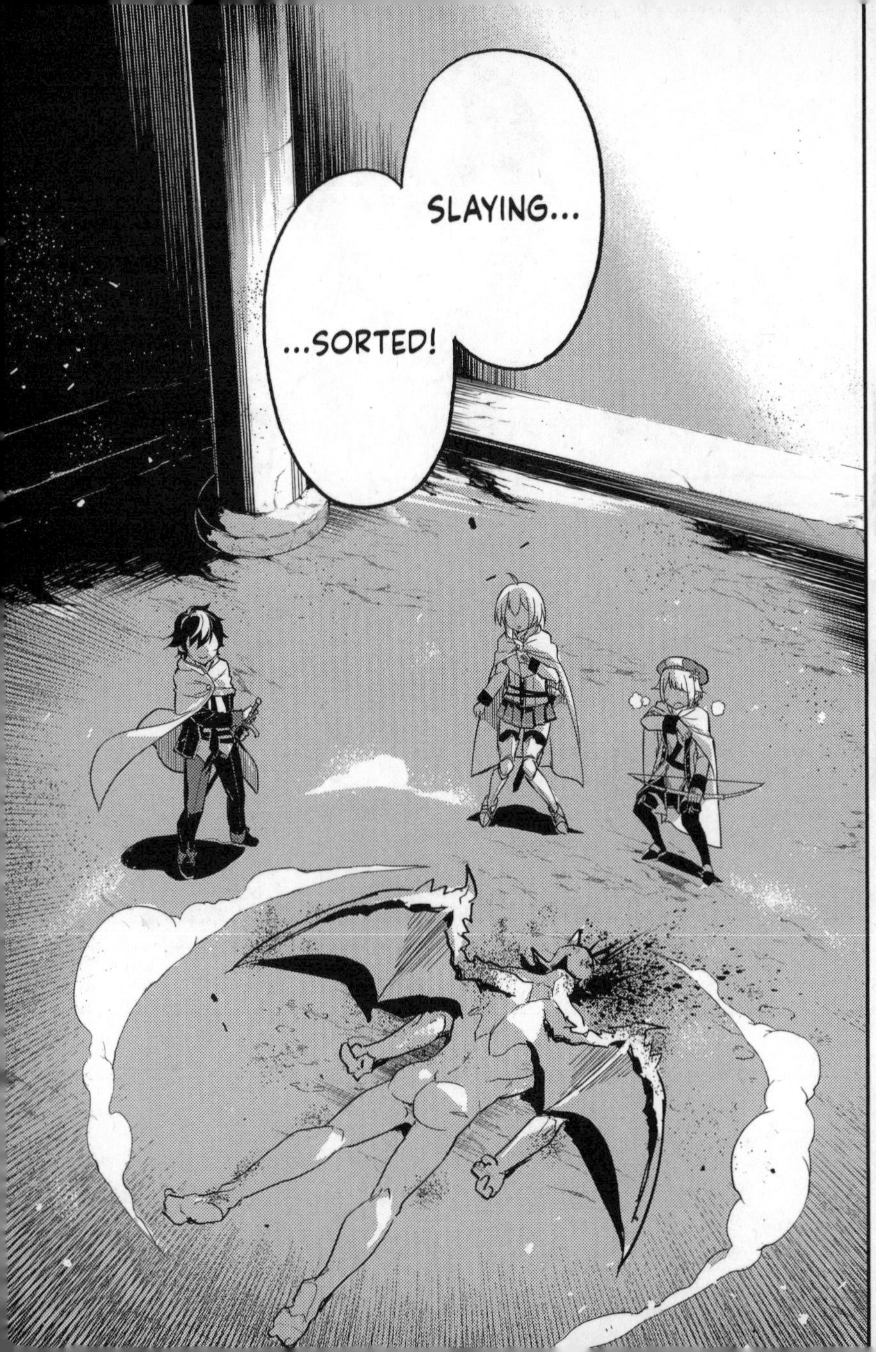
SLAYING...
...SORTED!

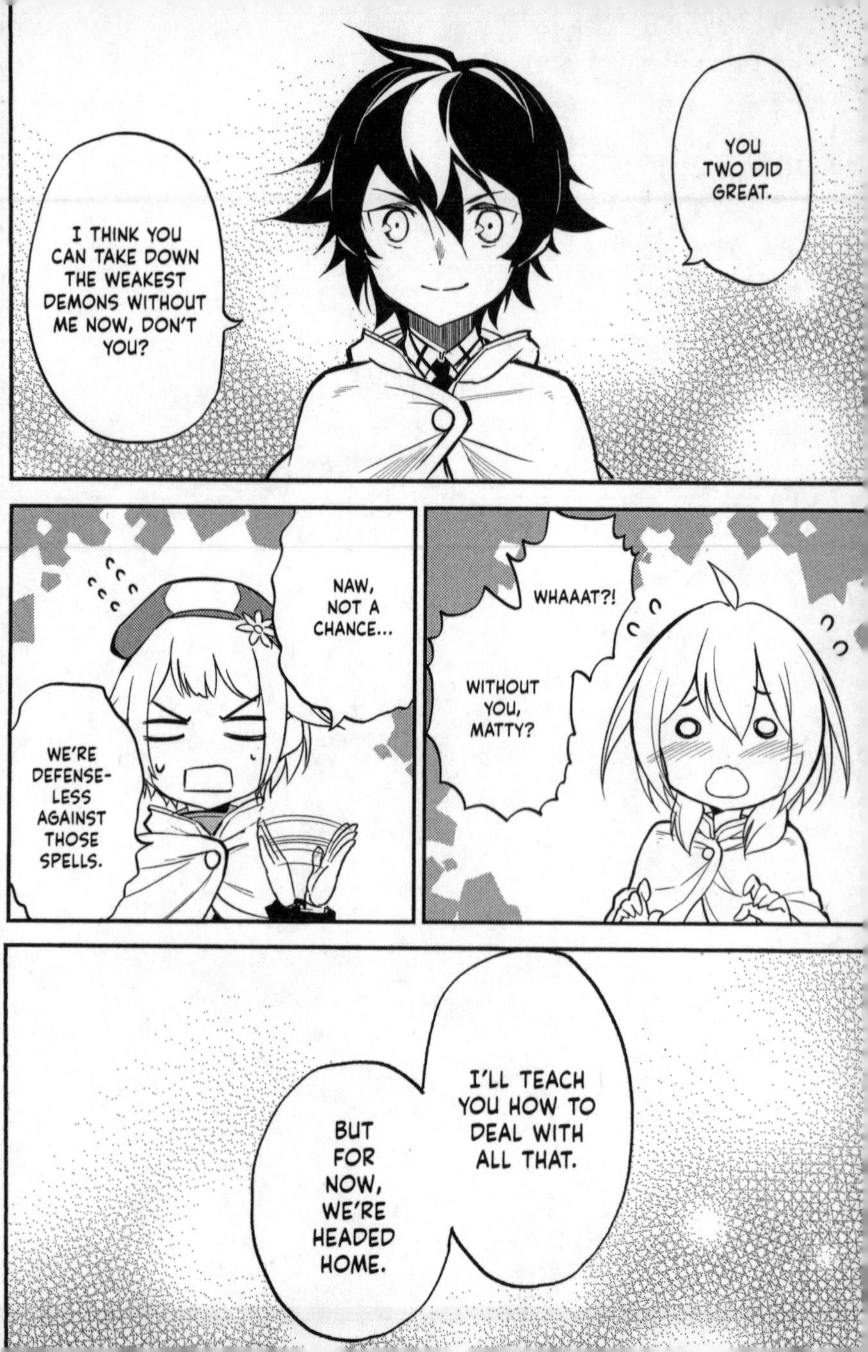
YOU TWO DID GREAT.
I THINK YOU CAN TAKE DOWN THE WEAKEST DEMONS WITHOUT ME NOW, DON'T YOU?
WHAAAT?!
WITHOUT YOU, MATTY?
NAW, NOT A CHANCE...
WE'RE DEFENSE-LESS AGAINST THOSE SPELLS.
I'LL TEACH YOU HOW TO DEAL WITH ALL THAT.
BUT FOR NOW, WE'RE HEADED HOME.

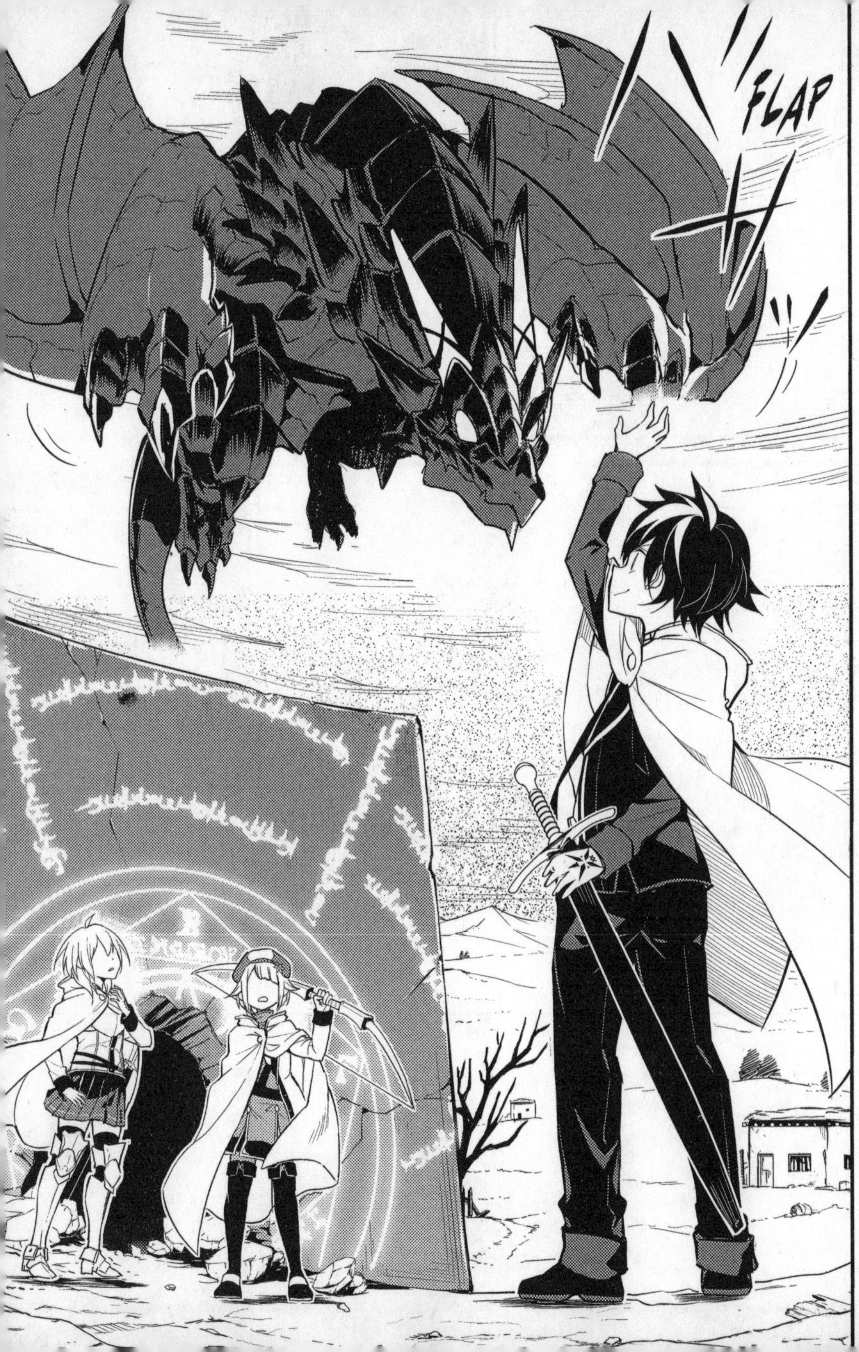
FLAP

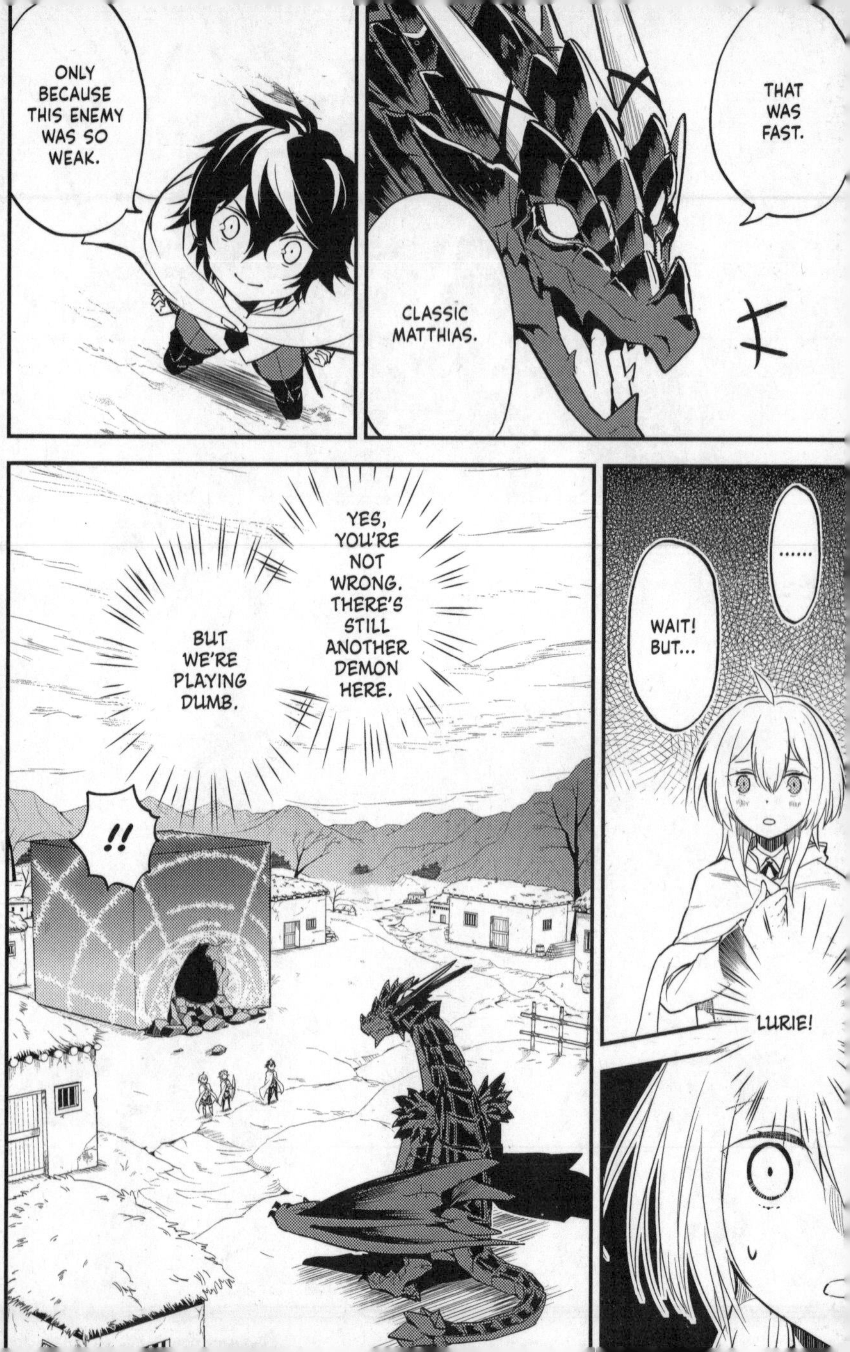
THAT WAS FAST.
CLASSIC MATTHIAS.
ONLY BECAUSE THIS ENEMY WAS SO WEAK.
......
WAIT! BUT...
LURIE!
YES, YOU'RE NOT WRONG. THERE'S STILL ANOTHER DEMON HERE.
BUT WE'RE PLAYING DUMB.
!!

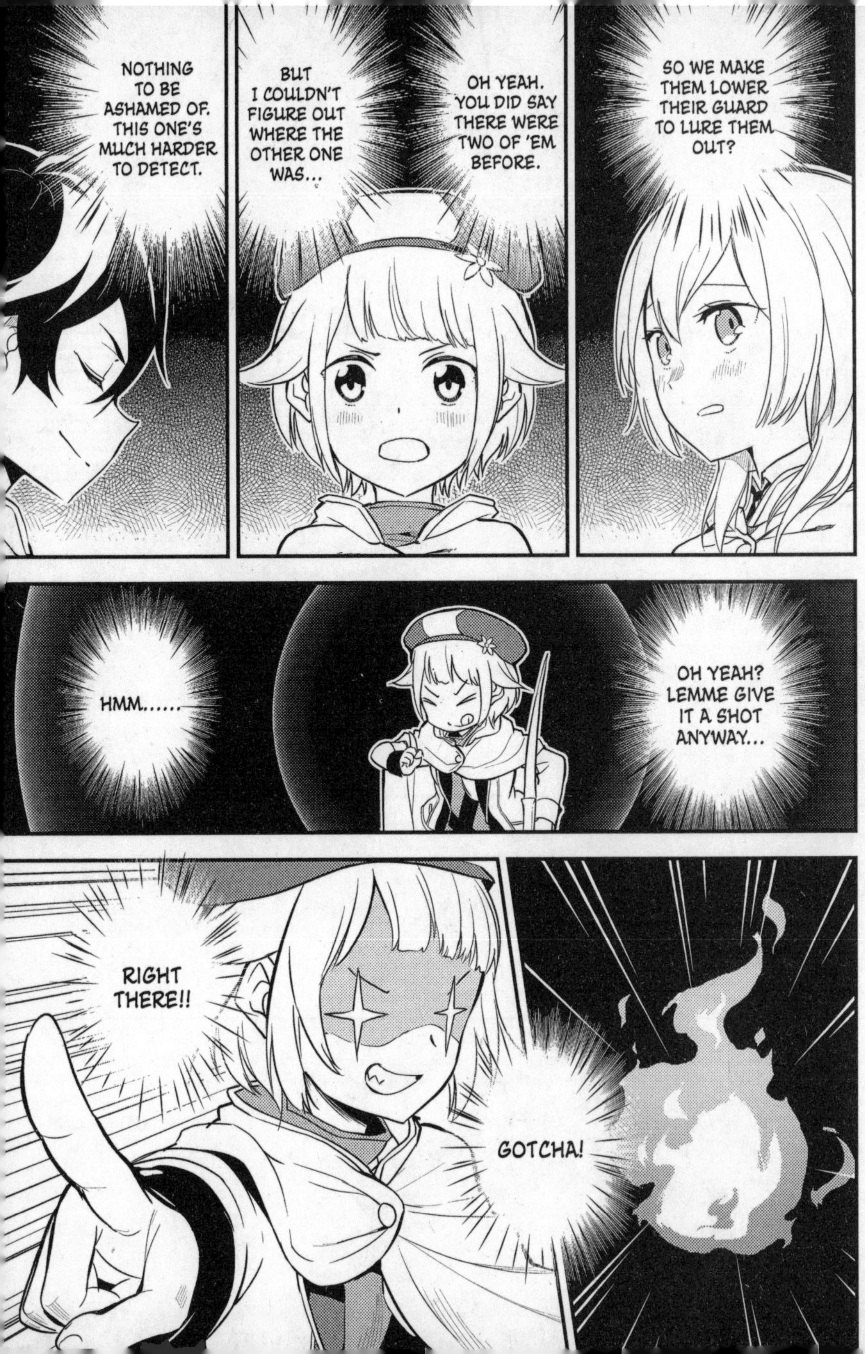

SO WE MAKE THEM LOWER THEIR GUARD TO LURE THEM OUT?
OH YEAH. YOU DID SAY THERE WERE TWO OF 'EM BEFORE.
BUT I COULDN'T FIGURE OUT WHERE THE OTHER ONE WAS...
NOTHING TO BE ASHAMED OF. THIS ONE'S MUCH HARDER TO DETECT.
OH YEAH? LEMME GIVE IT A SHOT ANYWAY...
HMM......
RIGHT THERE!!
GOTCHA!

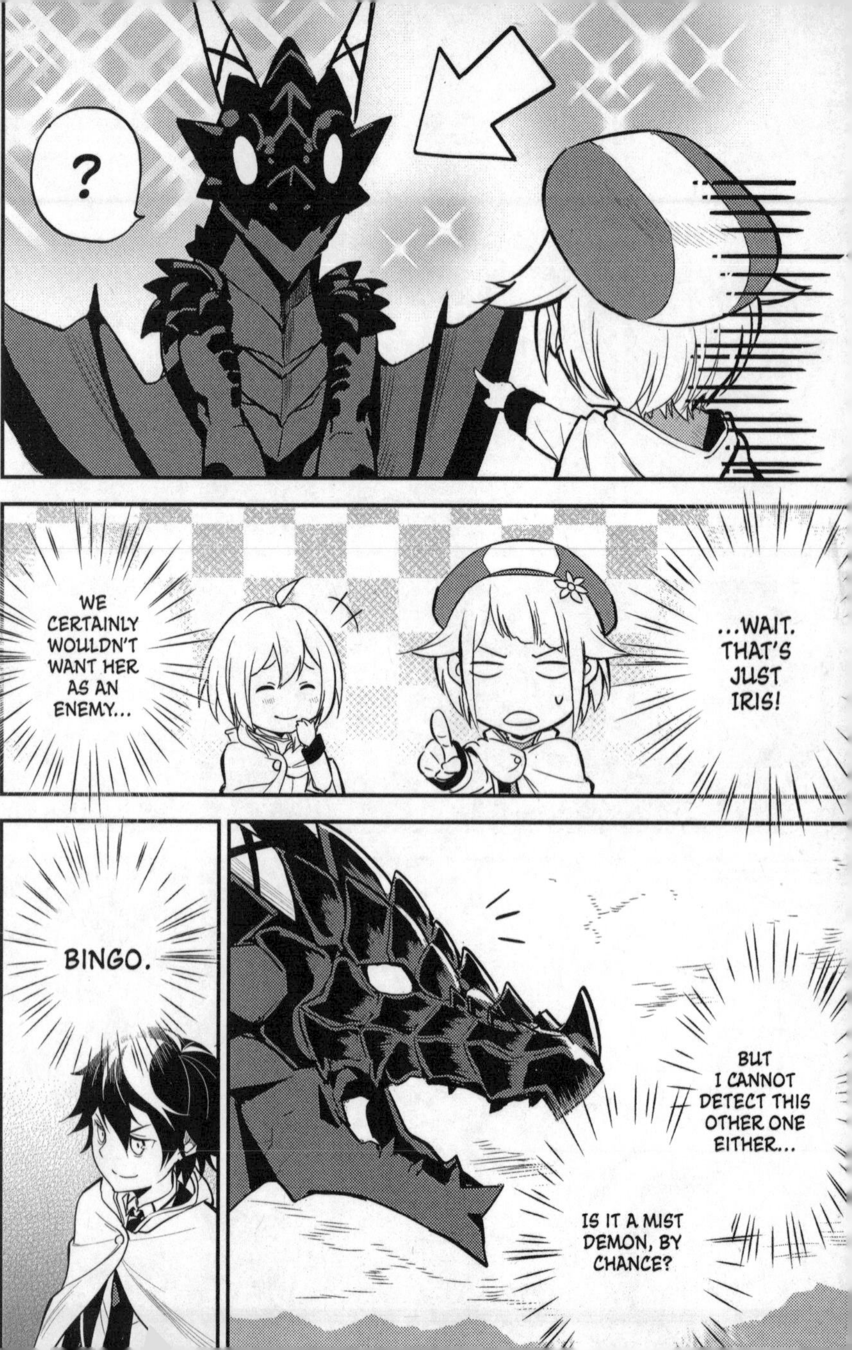
?
...WAIT. THAT'S JUST IRIS!
WE CERTAINLY WOULDN'T WANT HER AS AN ENEMY...
BUT I CANNOT DETECT THIS OTHER ONE EITHER...
IS IT A MIST DEMON, BY CHANCE?
BINGO.

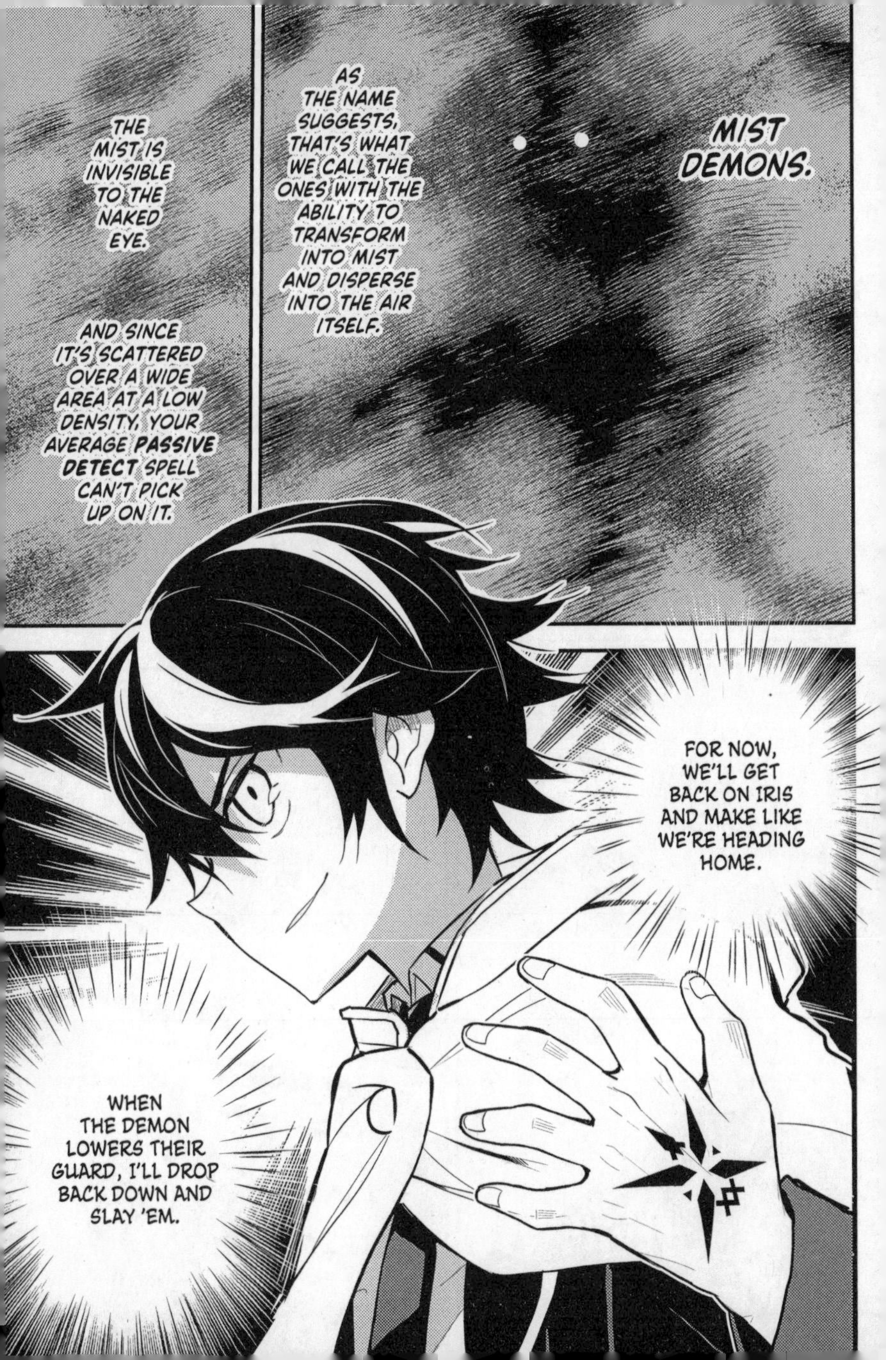
MIST DEMONS.
AS THE NAME SUGGESTS, THAT'S WHAT WE CALL THE ONES WITH THE ABILITY TO TRANSFORM INTO MIST AND DISPERSE INTO THE AIR ITSELF.
THE MIST IS INVISIBLE TO THE NAKED EYE.
AND SINCE IT'S SCATTERED OVER A WIDE AREA AT A LOW DENSITY, YOUR AVERAGE **PASSIVE DETECT** SPELL CAN'T PICK UP ON IT.
FOR NOW, WE'LL GET BACK ON IRIS AND MAKE LIKE WE'RE HEADING HOME.
WHEN THE DEMON LOWERS THEIR GUARD, I'LL DROP BACK DOWN AND SLAY 'EM.

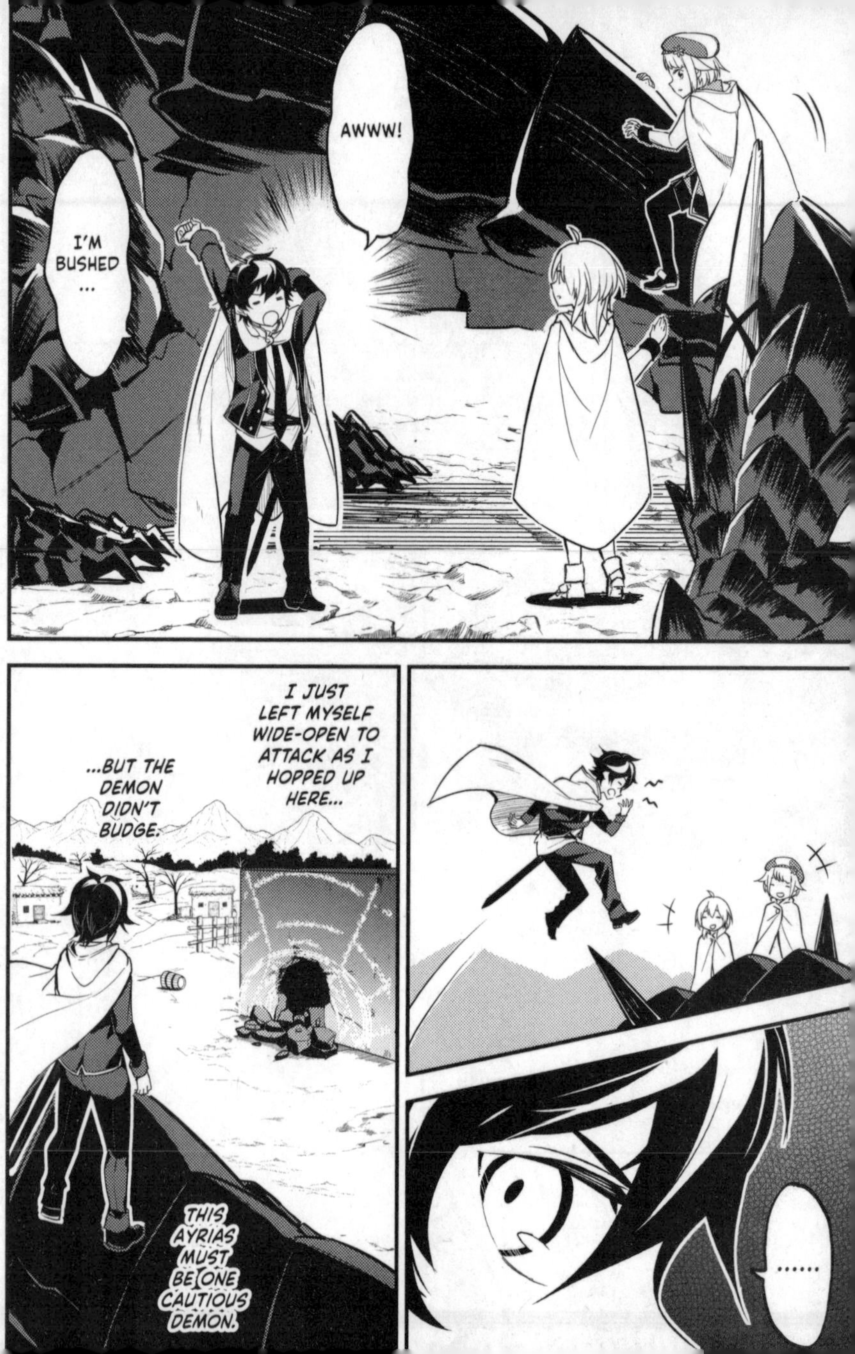
AWWW!
I'M BUSHED ...
......
I JUST LEFT MYSELF WIDE-OPEN TO ATTACK AS I HOPPED UP HERE...
...BUT THE DEMON DIDN'T BUDGE.
THIS AYRIAS MUST BE ONE CAUTIOUS DEMON.

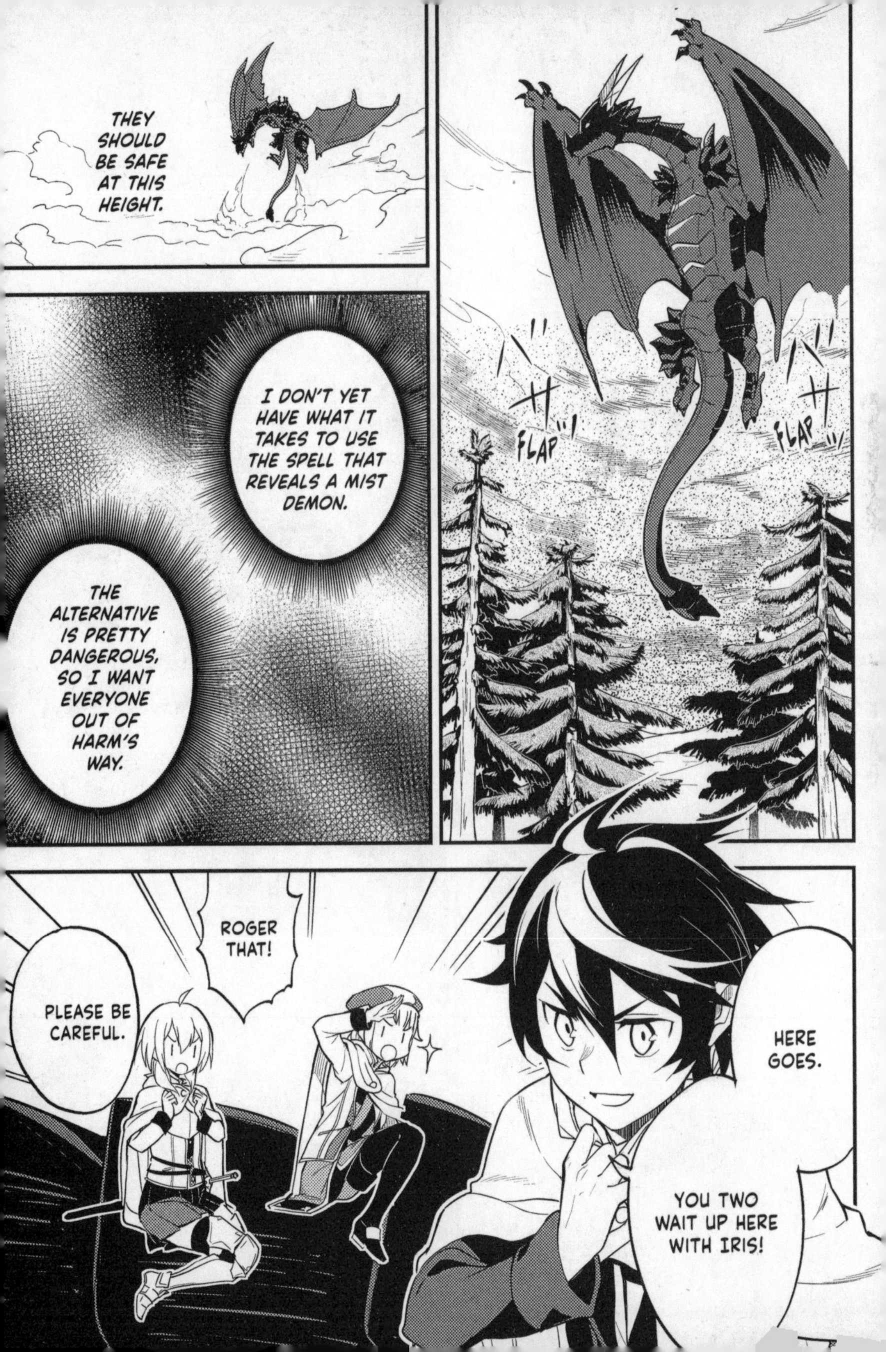
FLAP
FLAP
THEY SHOULD BE SAFE AT THIS HEIGHT.
I DON'T YET HAVE WHAT IT TAKES TO USE THE SPELL THAT REVEALS A MIST DEMON.
THE ALTERNATIVE IS PRETTY DANGEROUS, SO I WANT EVERYONE OUT OF HARM'S WAY.
HERE GOES.
YOU TWO WAIT UP HERE WITH IRIS!
ROGER THAT!
PLEASE BE CAREFUL.

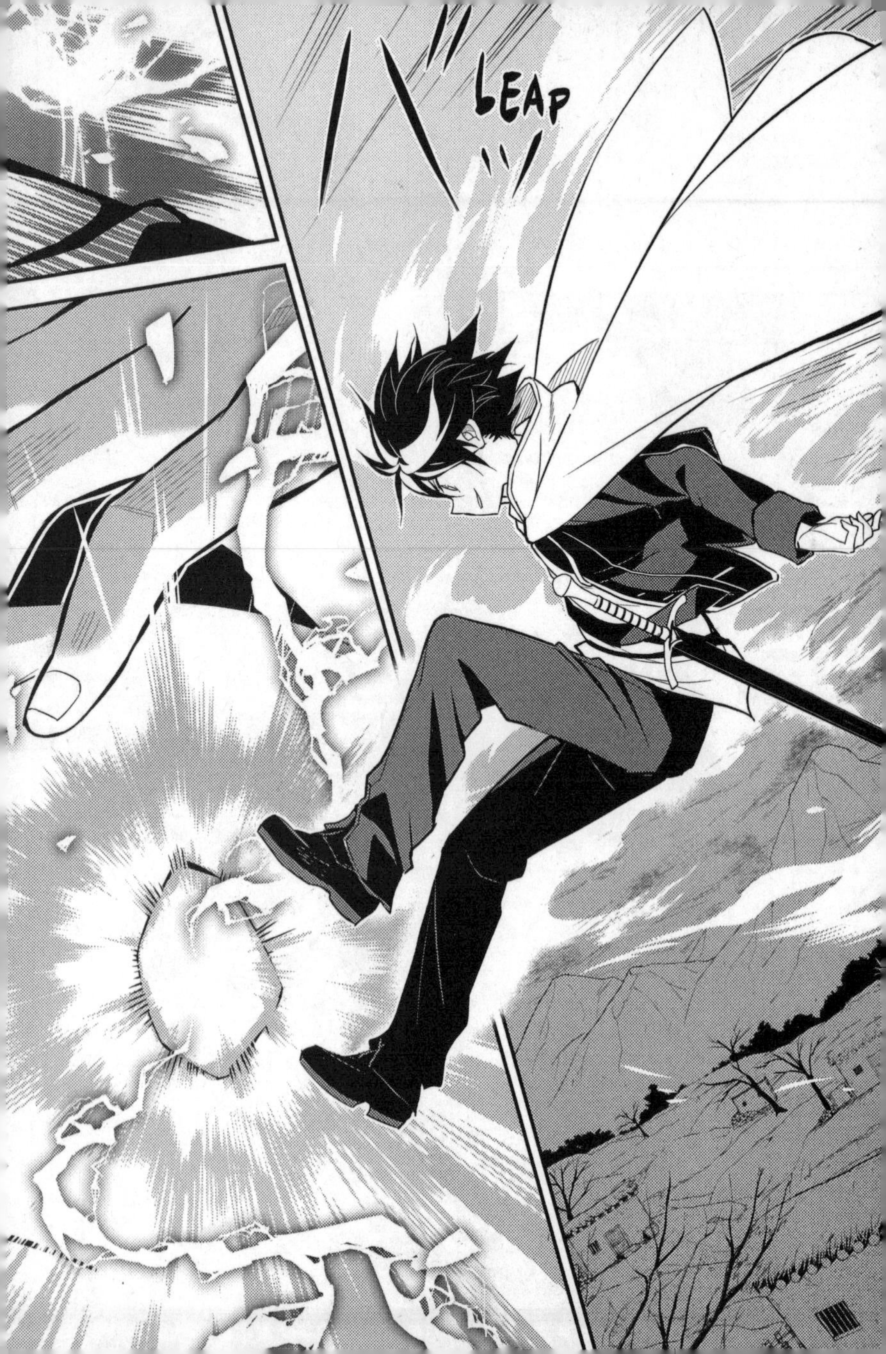
LEAP

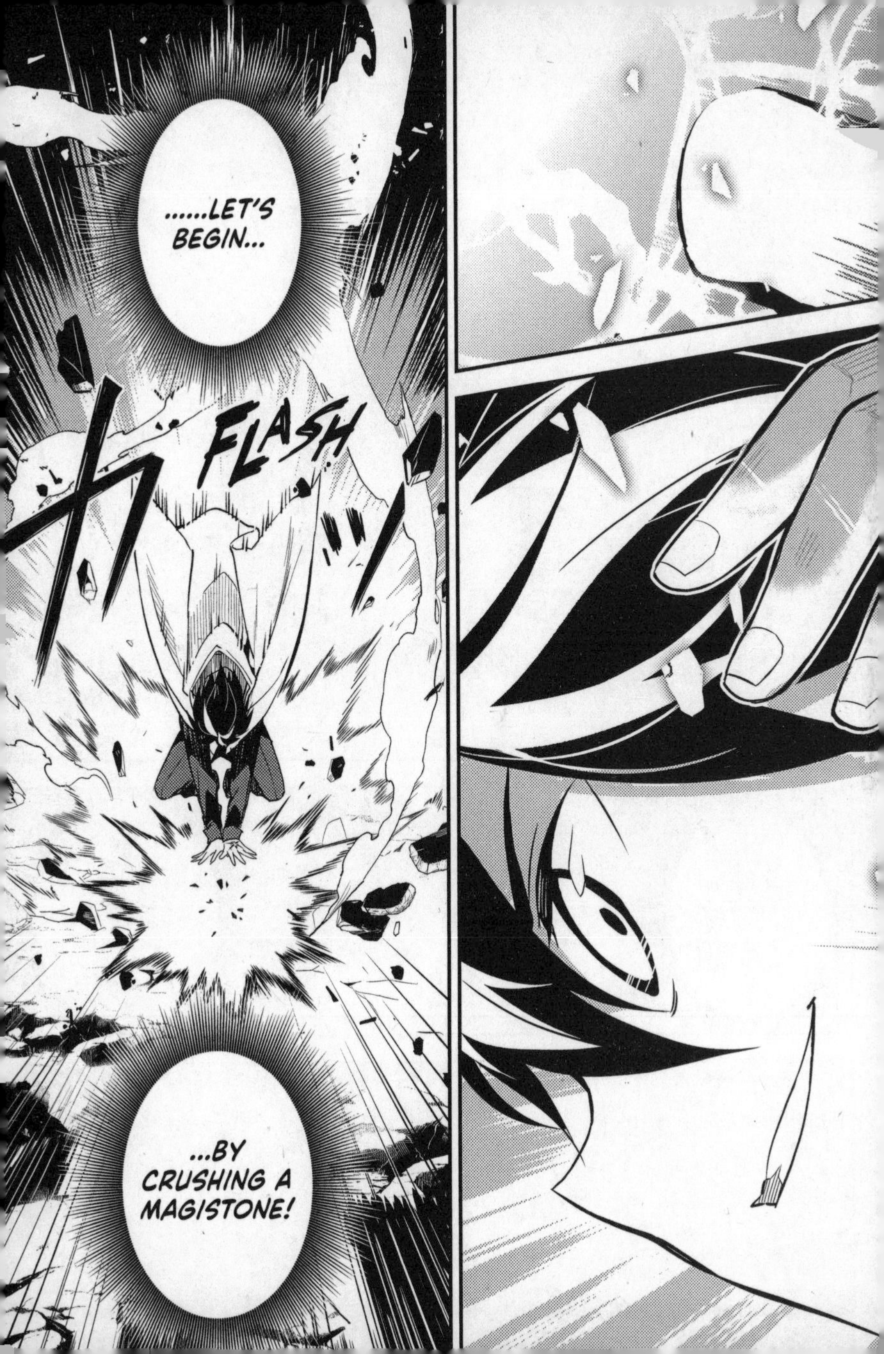
......LET'S BEGIN...
FLASH
...BY CRUSHING A MAGISTONE!

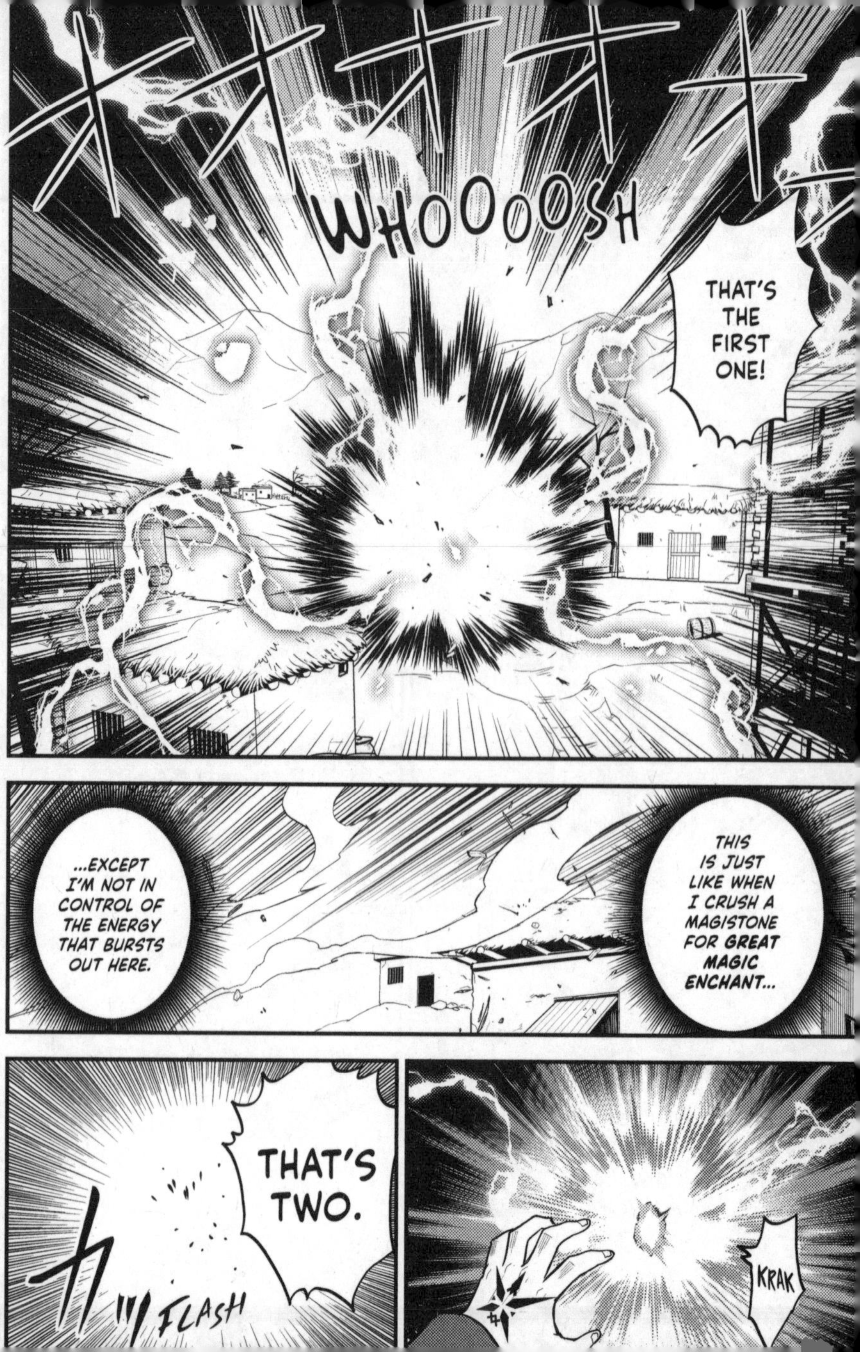
WHOOOOSH
THAT'S THE FIRST ONE!
THIS IS JUST LIKE WHEN I CRUSH A MAGISTONE FOR GREAT MAGIC ENCHANT...
...EXCEPT I'M NOT IN CONTROL OF THE ENERGY THAT BURSTS OUT HERE.
KRAK
THAT'S TWO.
FLASH

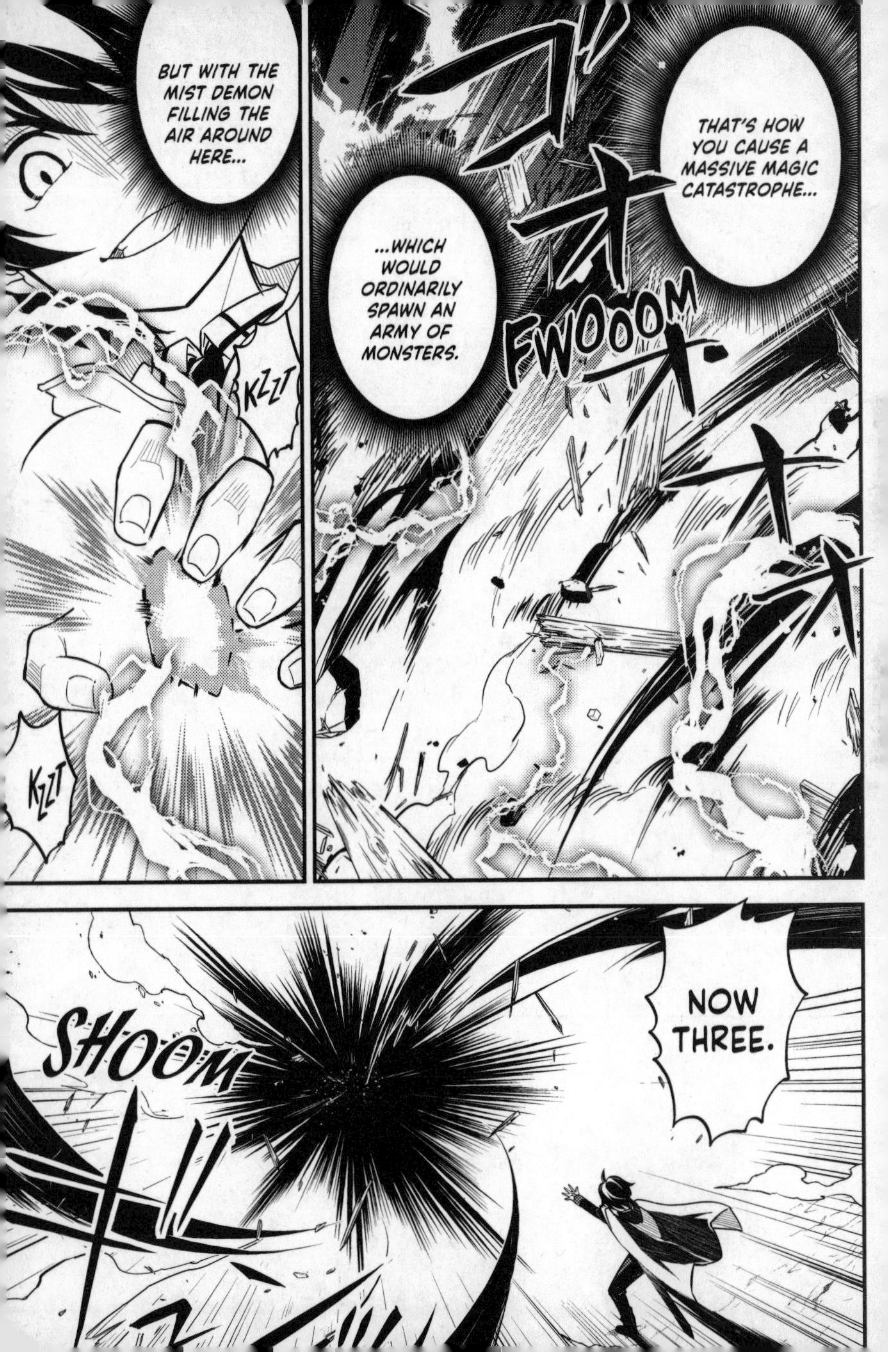
THAT'S HOW YOU CAUSE A MASSIVE MAGIC CATASTROPHE...
...WHICH WOULD ORDINARILY SPAWN AN ARMY OF MONSTERS.
FWOOOM
BUT WITH THE MIST DEMON FILLING THE AIR AROUND HERE...
KZZT
KZZT
NOW THREE.
SHOOM

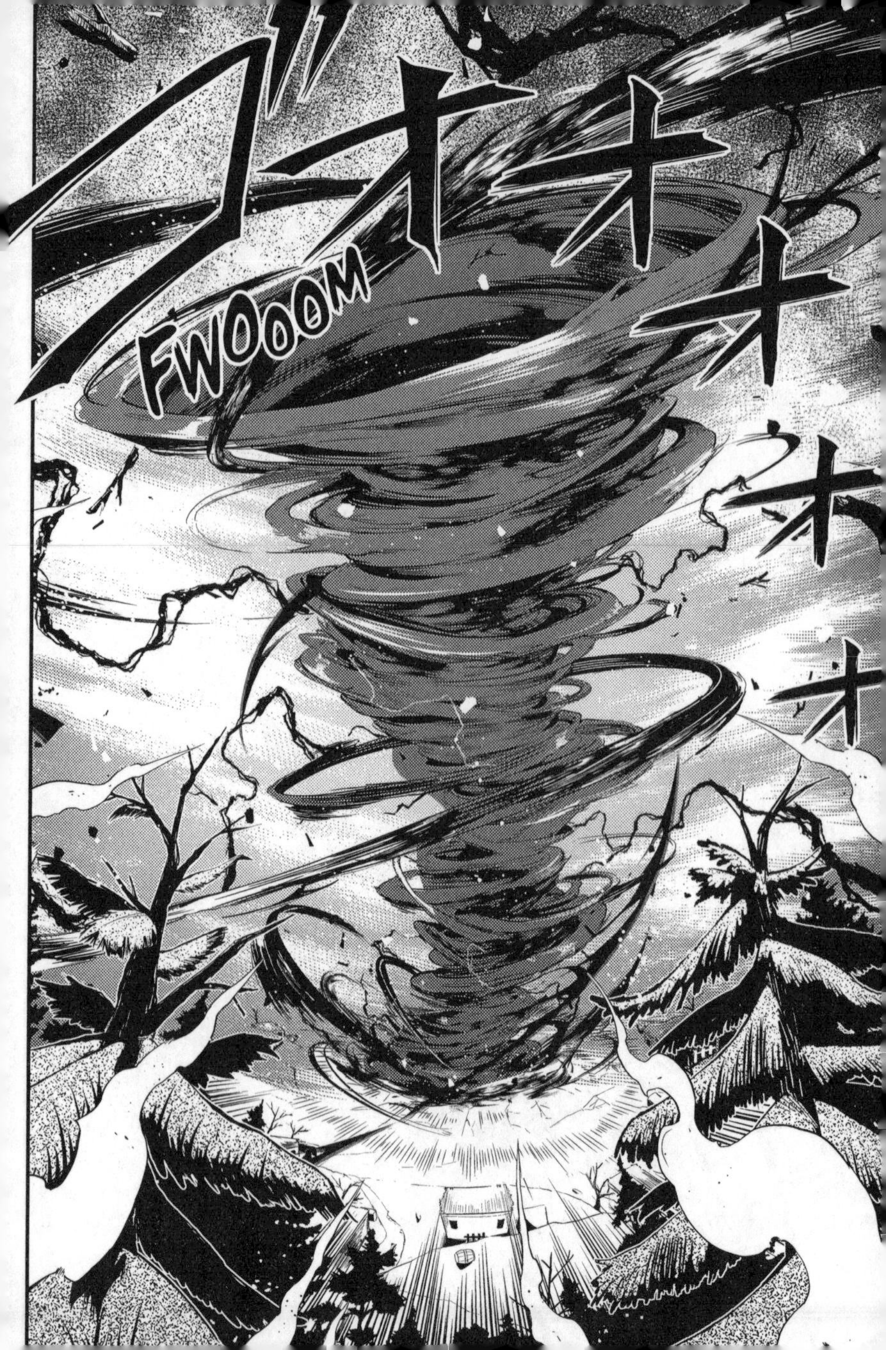
ゴオオオオオ
FWOOOM

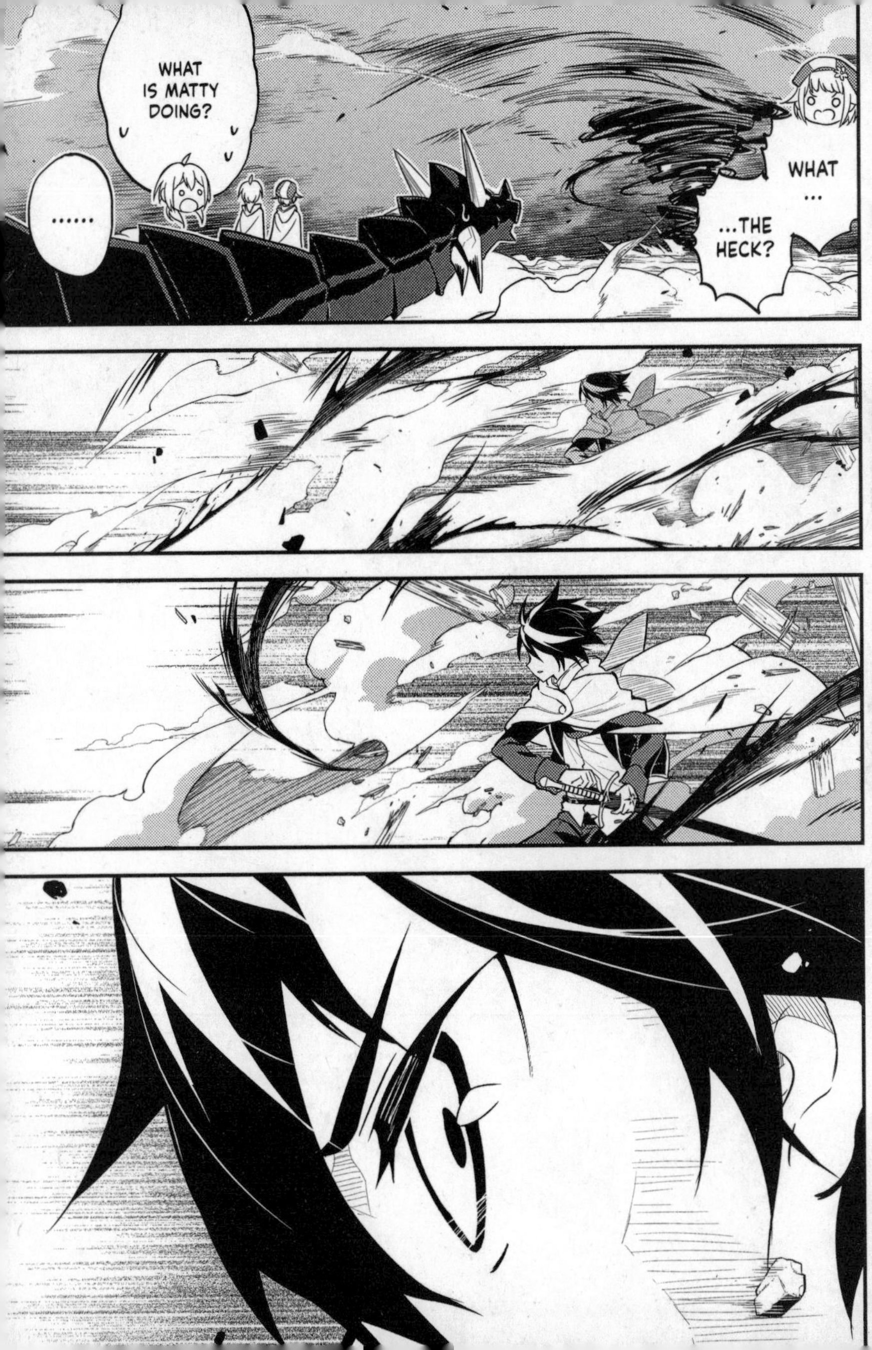
WHAT ...
...THE HECK?
WHAT IS MATTY DOING?
......

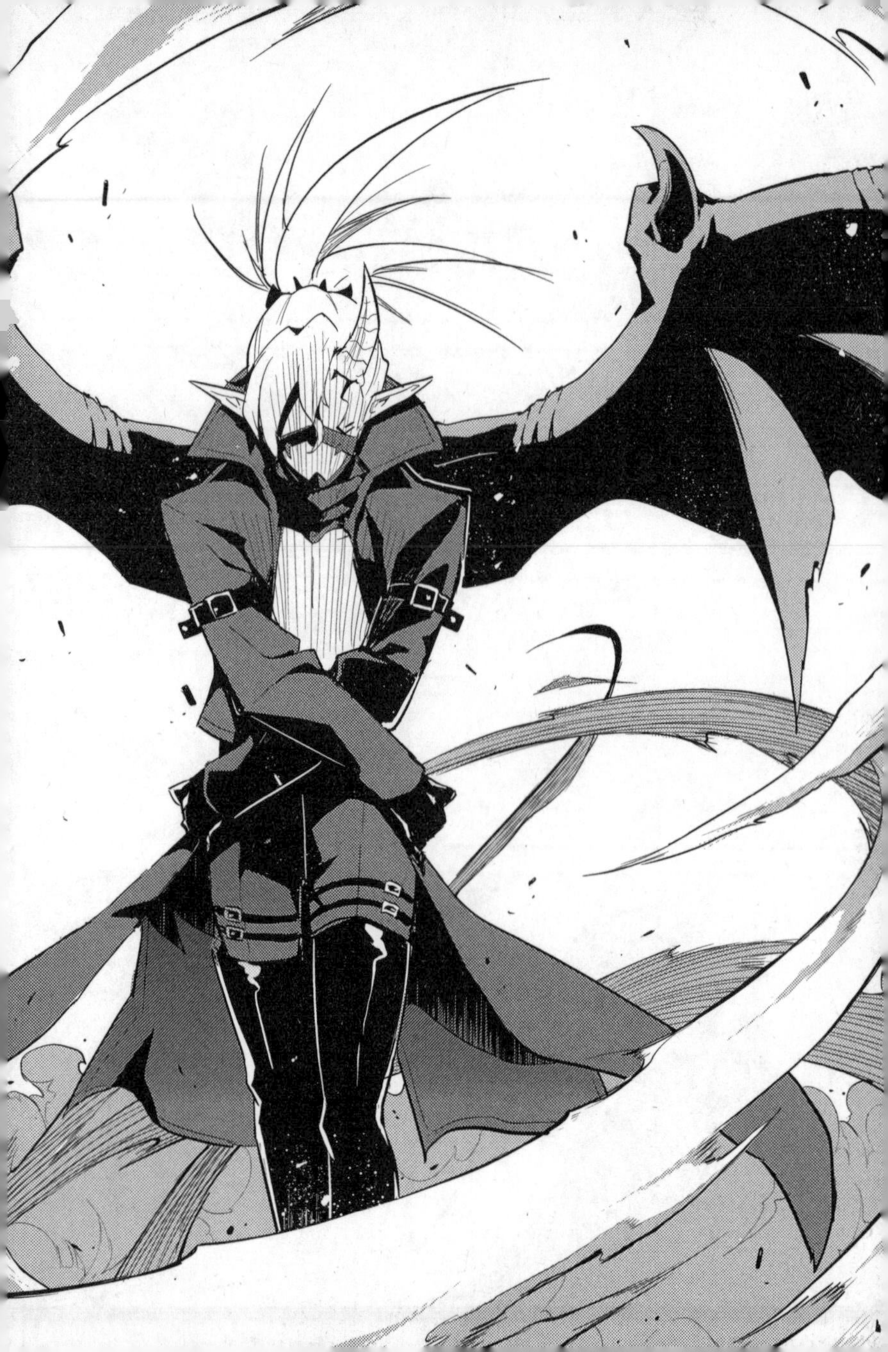

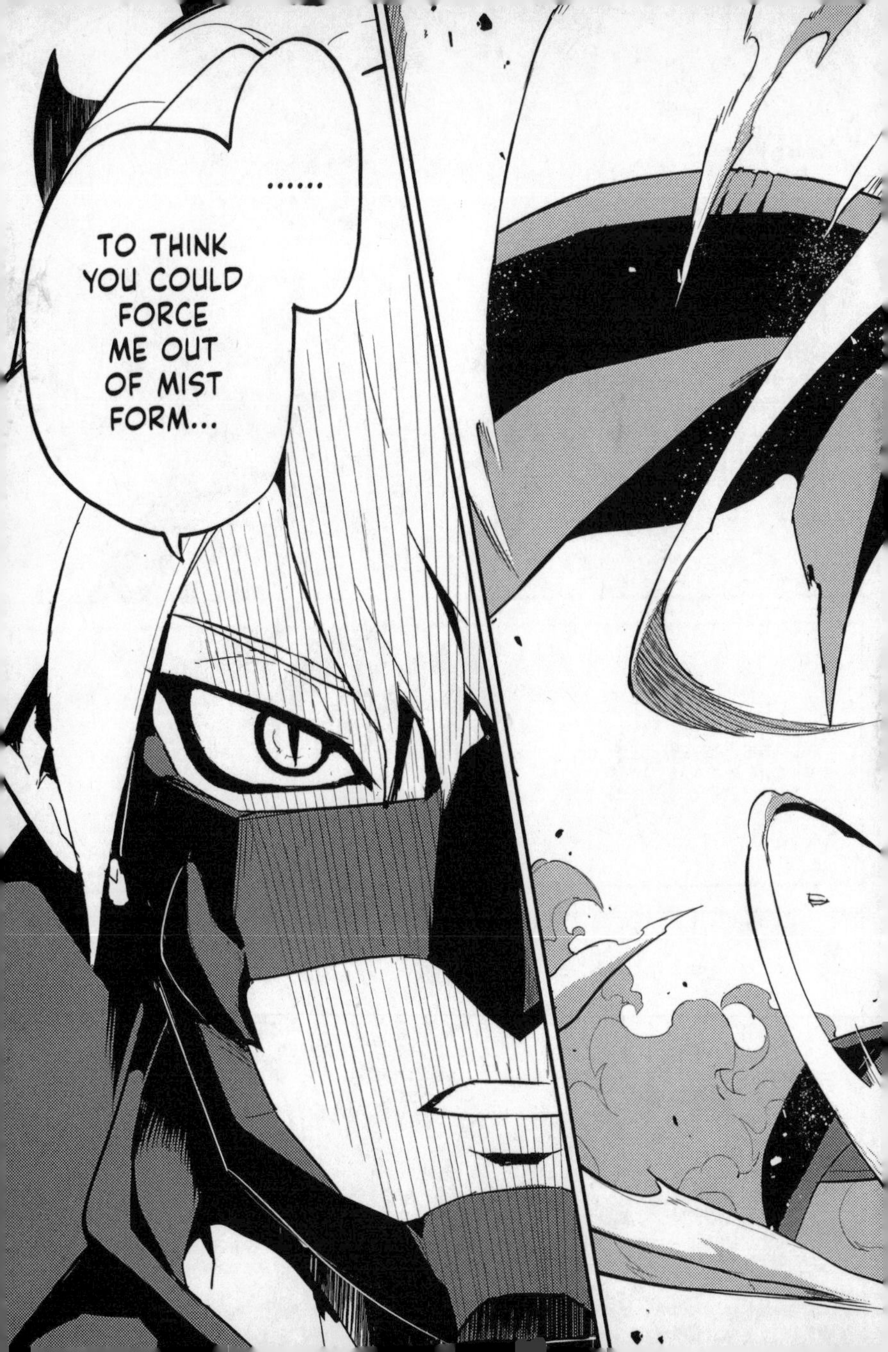
......
TO THINK YOU COULD FORCE ME OUT OF MIST FORM...

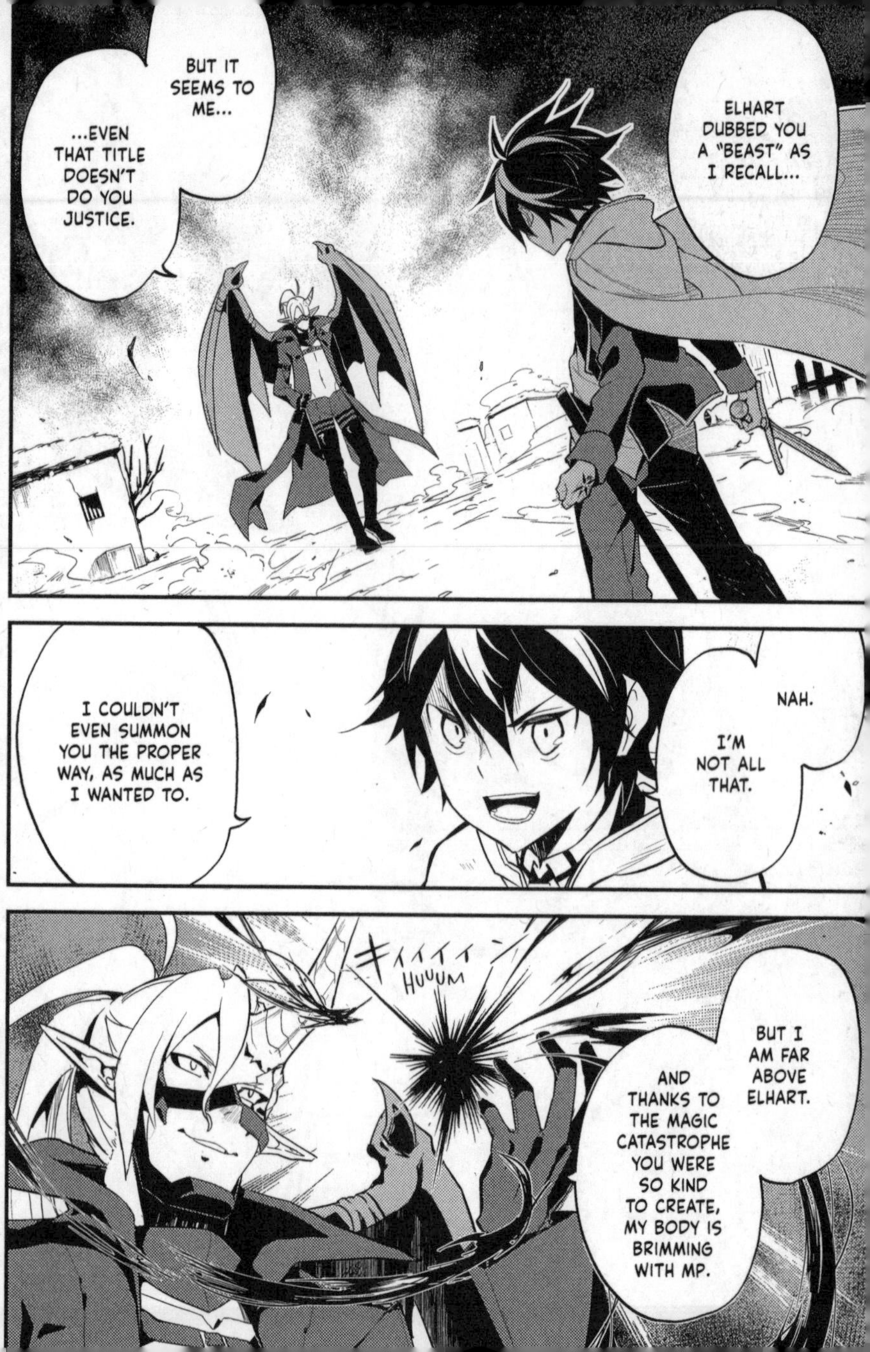
ELHART DUBBED YOU A "BEAST" AS I RECALL...
BUT IT SEEMS TO ME...
...EVEN THAT TITLE DOESN'T DO YOU JUSTICE.
NAH.
I'M NOT ALL THAT.
I COULDN'T EVEN SUMMON YOU THE PROPER WAY, AS MUCH AS I WANTED TO.
キイイイイン
HUUUM
BUT I AM FAR ABOVE ELHART.
AND THANKS TO THE MAGIC CATASTROPHE YOU WERE SO KIND TO CREATE, MY BODY IS BRIMMING WITH MP.

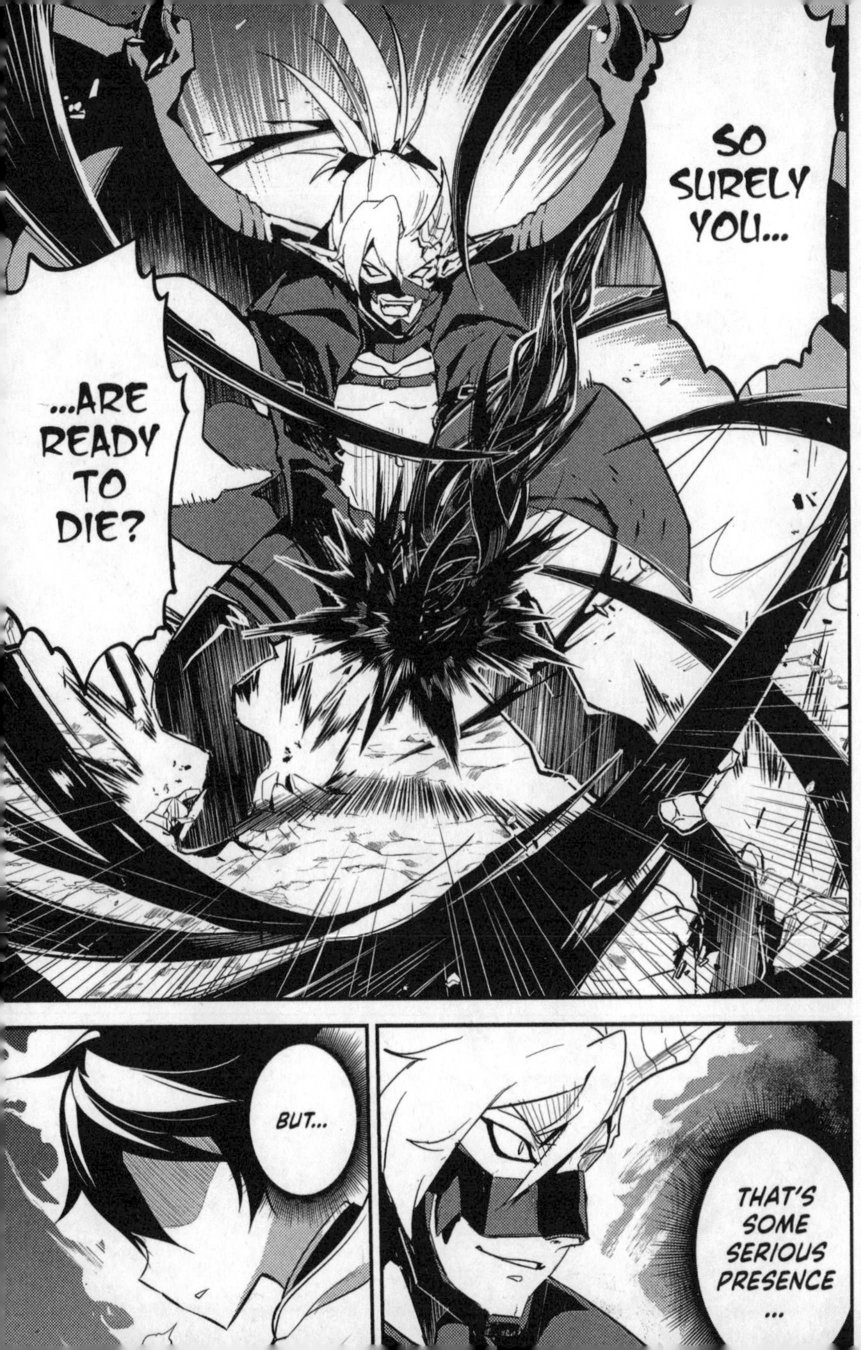
SO SURELY YOU...
...ARE READY TO DIE?
THAT'S SOME SERIOUS PRESENCE...
BUT...

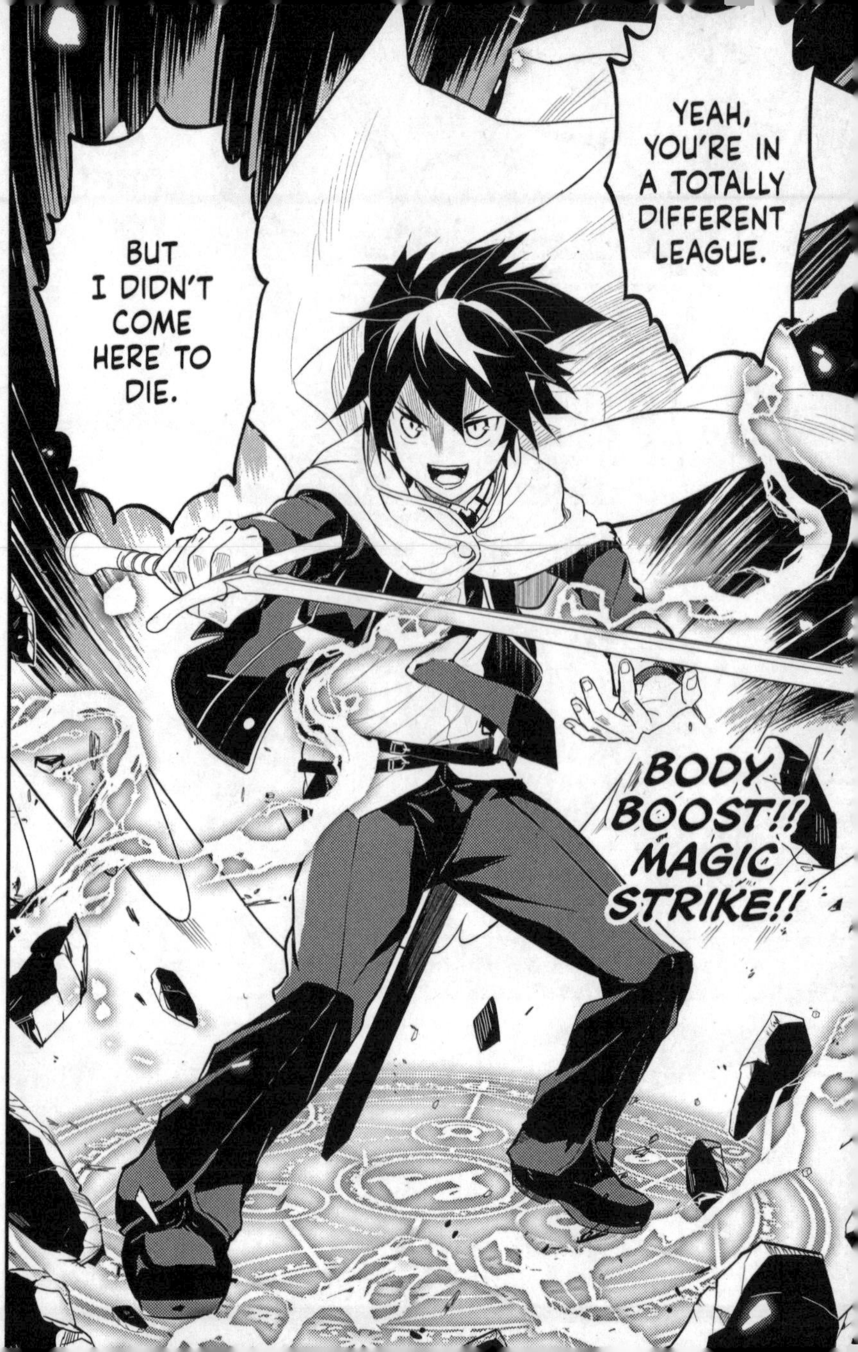
YEAH, YOU'RE IN A TOTALLY DIFFERENT LEAGUE.
BUT I DIDN'T COME HERE TO DIE.
BODY BOOST!! MAGIC STRIKE!!

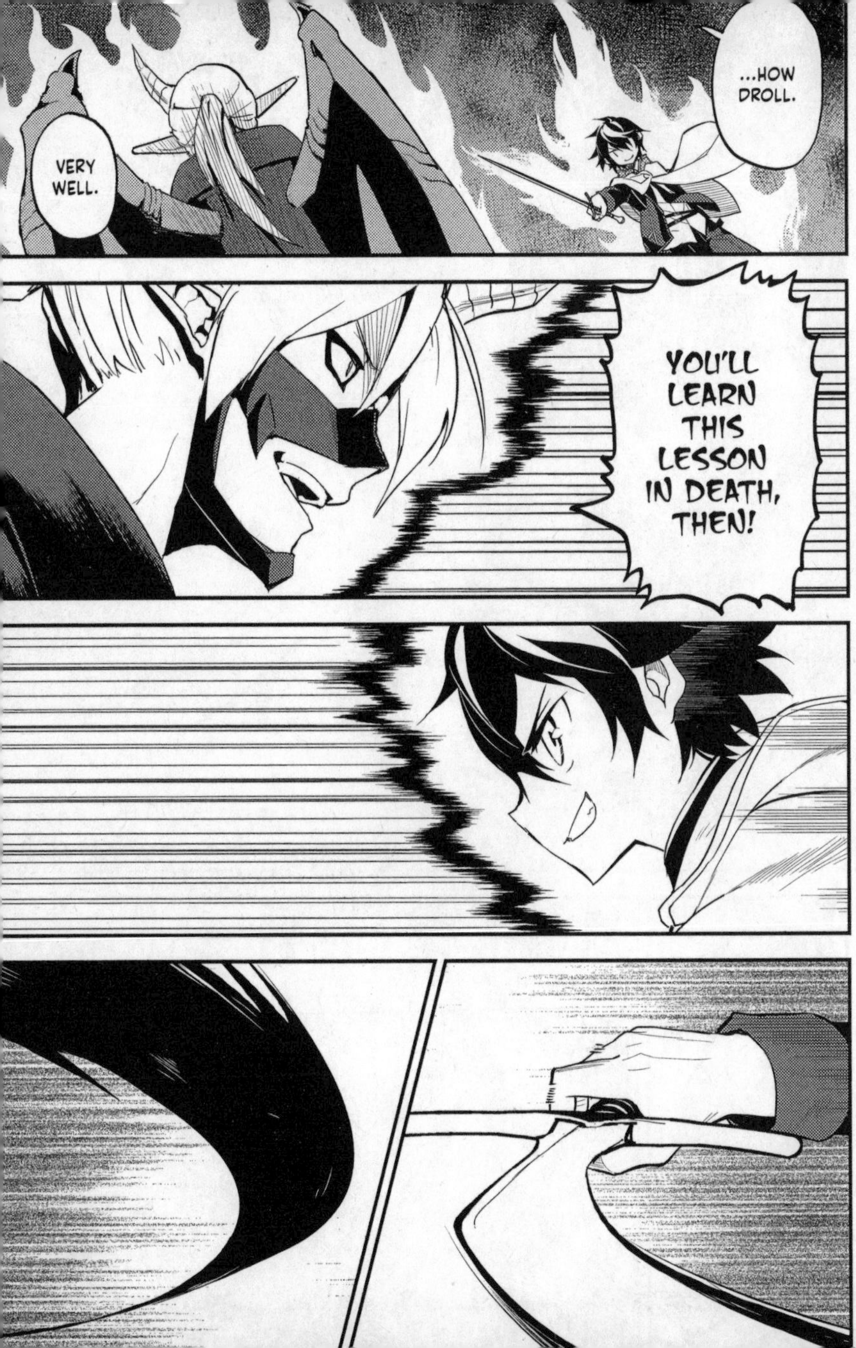
...HOW DROLL.
VERY WELL.
YOU'LL LEARN THIS LESSON IN DEATH, THEN!

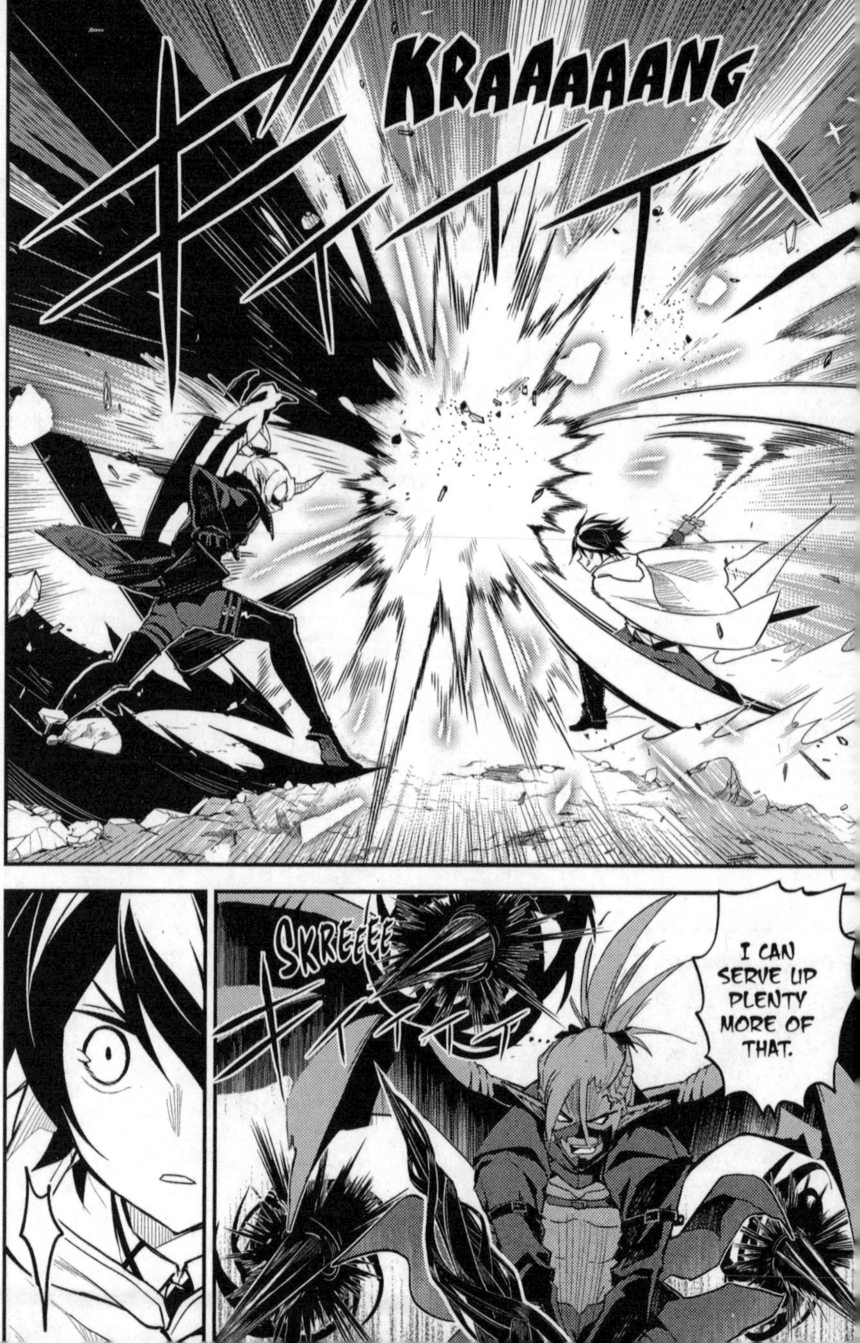
KRAAAAANG
SKREEEE
I CAN SERVE UP PLENTY MORE OF THAT.

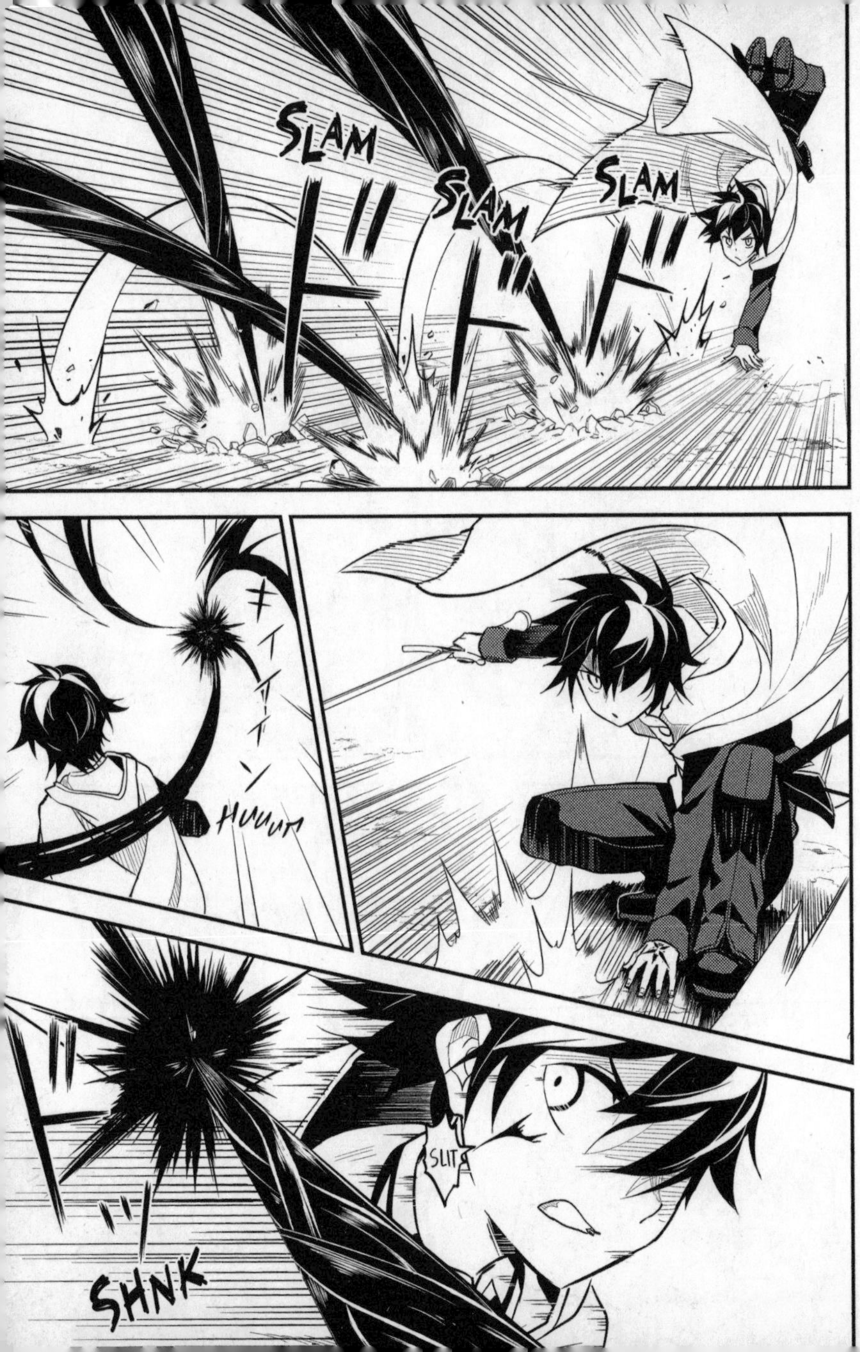
SLAM
SLAM
SLAM
キイイイン
HUUUM
SLIT
SHNK

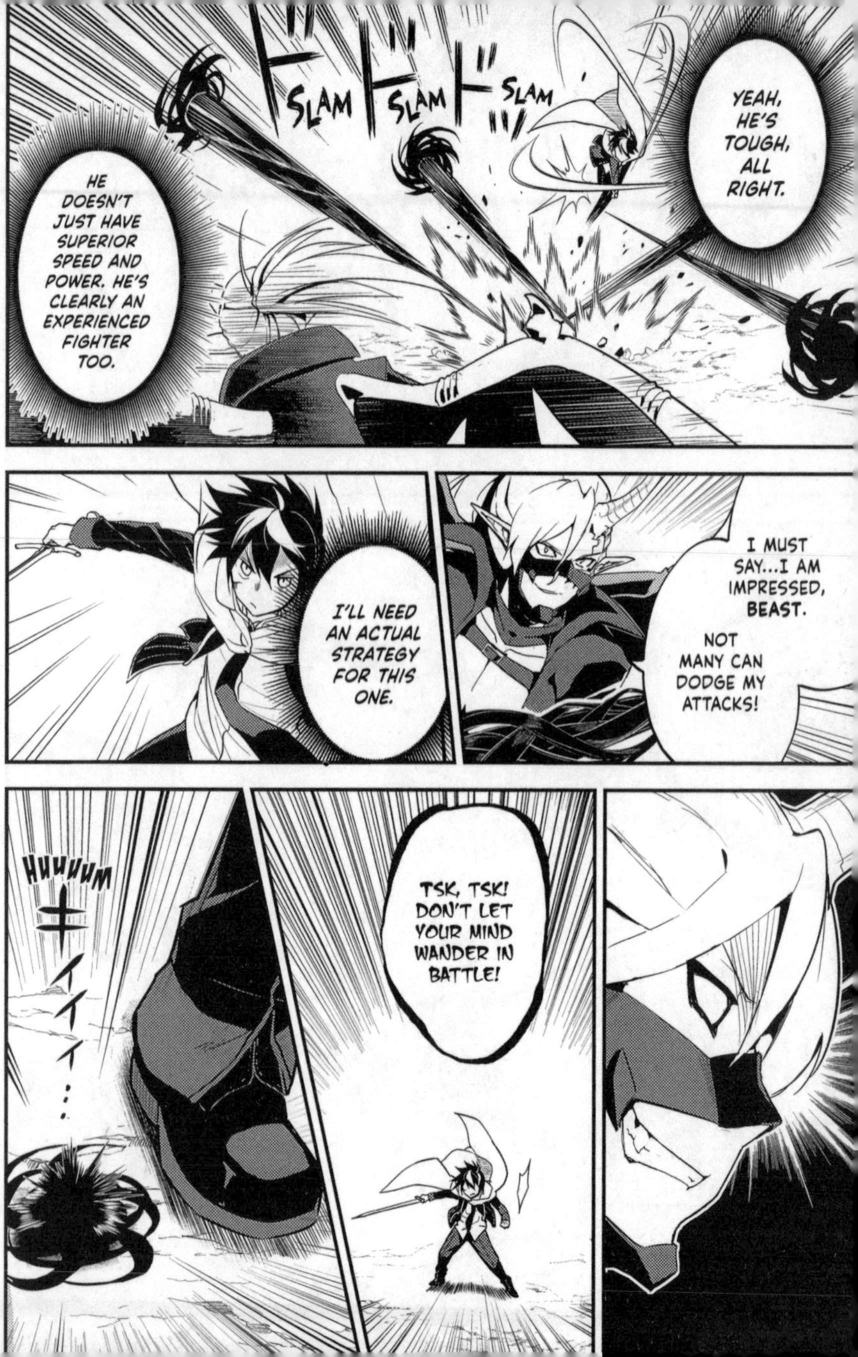
SLAM SLAM SLAM
YEAH, HE'S TOUGH, ALL RIGHT.
HE DOESN'T JUST HAVE SUPERIOR SPEED AND POWER. HE'S CLEARLY AN EXPERIENCED FIGHTER TOO.
I MUST SAY...I AM IMPRESSED, BEAST.
NOT MANY CAN DODGE MY ATTACKS!
I'LL NEED AN ACTUAL STRATEGY FOR THIS ONE.
TSK, TSK! DON'T LET YOUR MIND WANDER IN BATTLE!
HUUUUM

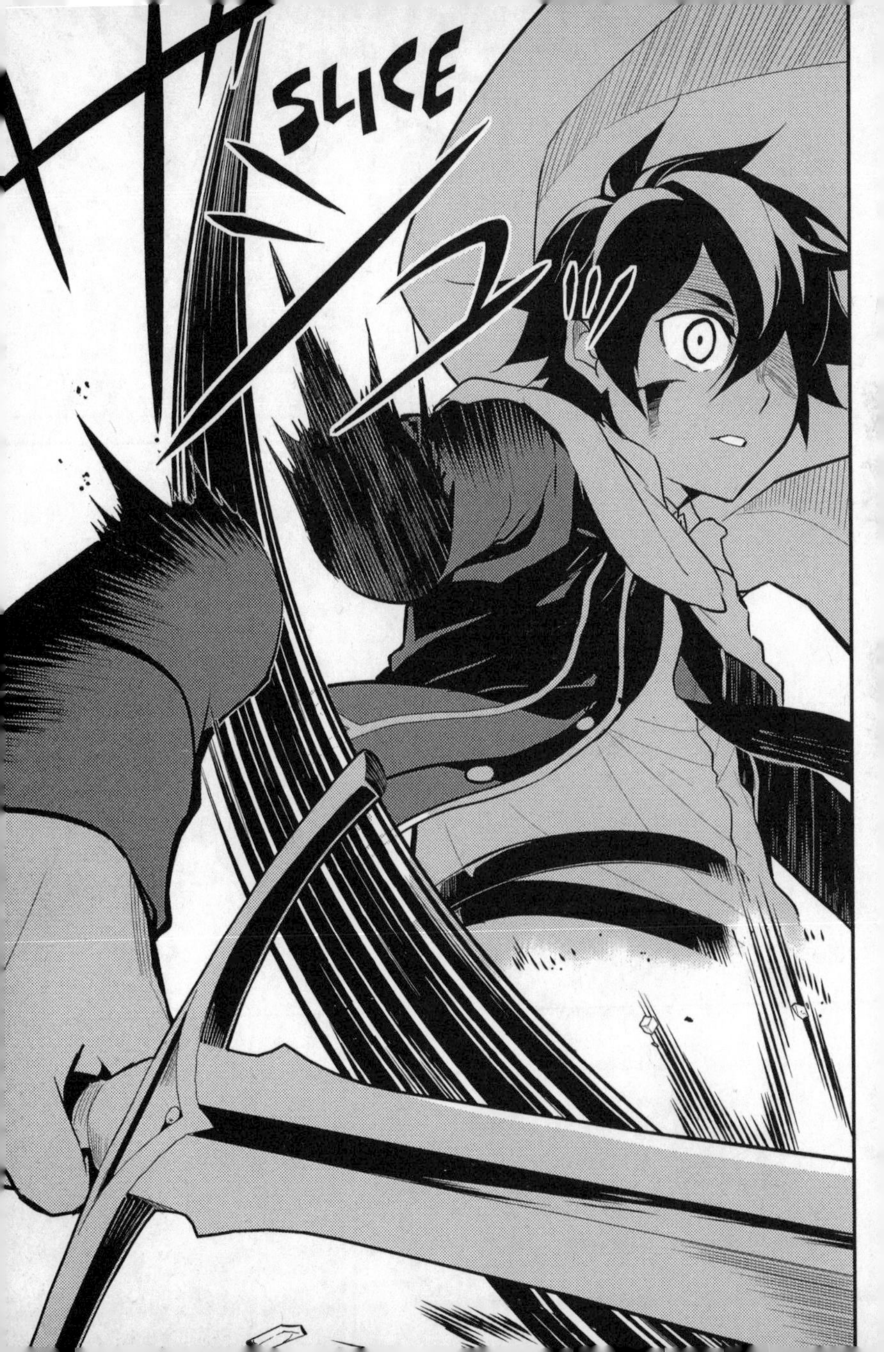
SLICE

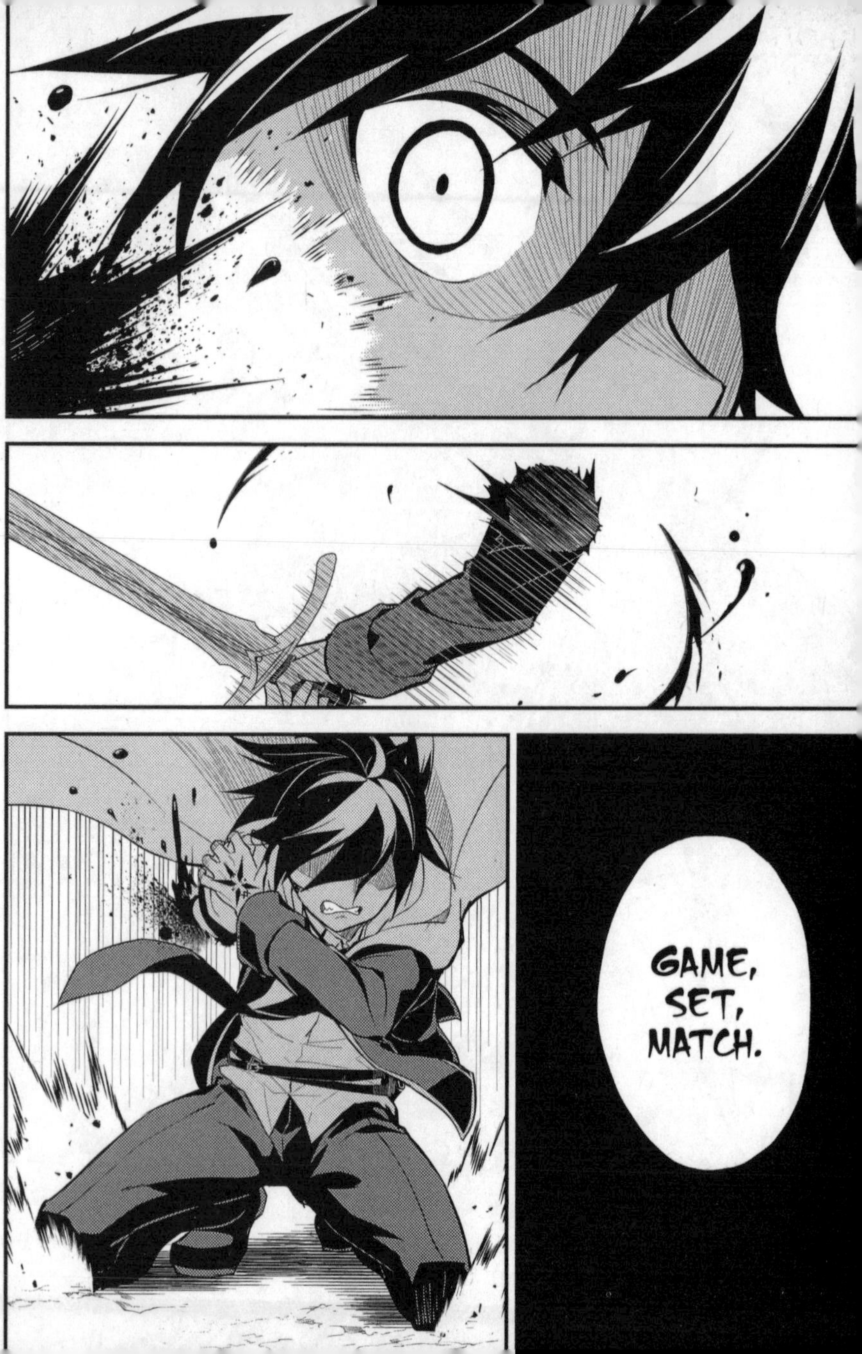
GAME, SET, MATCH.

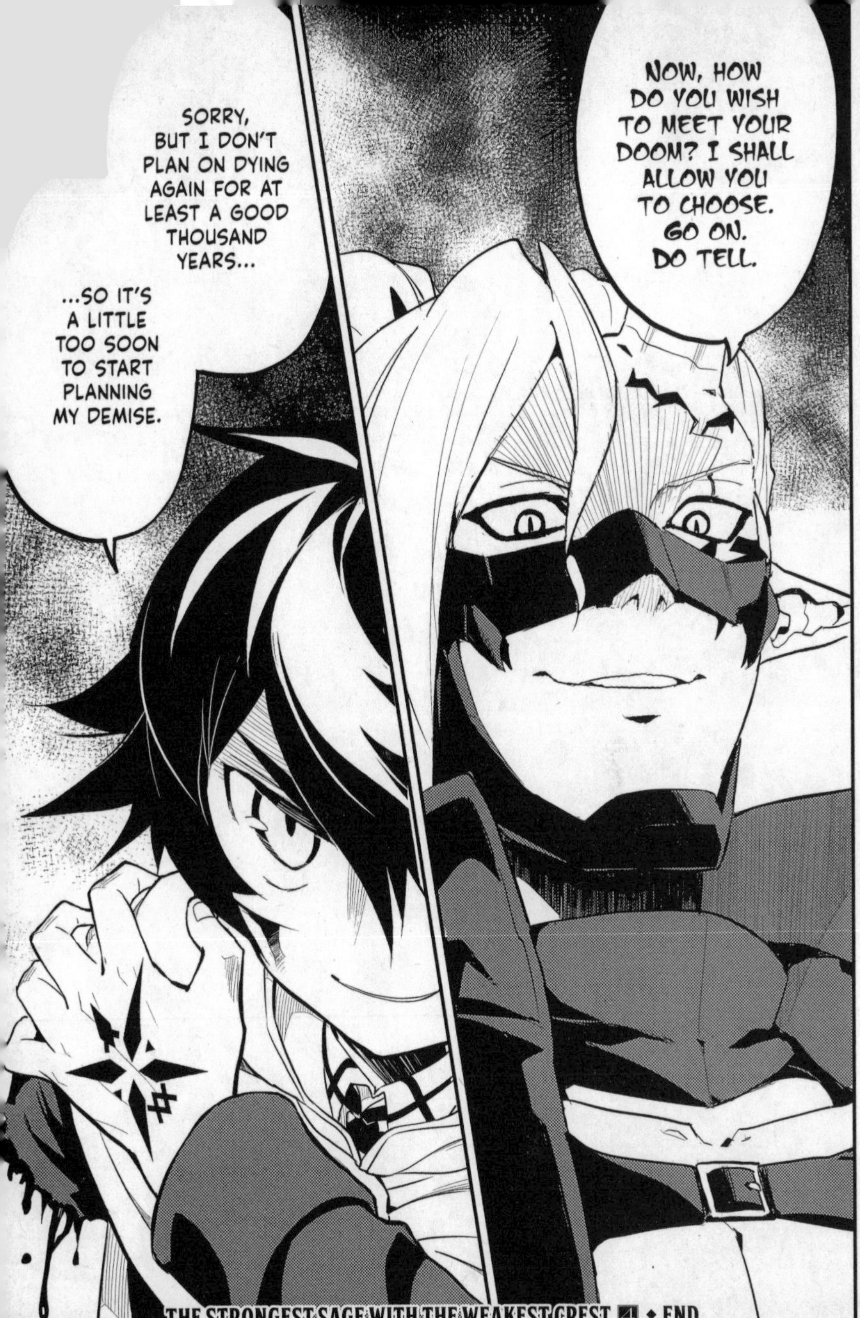
NOW, HOW DO YOU WISH TO MEET YOUR DOOM? I SHALL ALLOW YOU TO CHOOSE. GO ON. DO TELL.
SORRY, BUT I DON'T PLAN ON DYING AGAIN FOR AT LEAST A GOOD THOUSAND YEARS...
...SO IT'S A LITTLE TOO SOON TO START PLANNING MY DEMISE.

THE STRONGEST SAGE WITH THE WEAKEST CREST 4 ◆ END

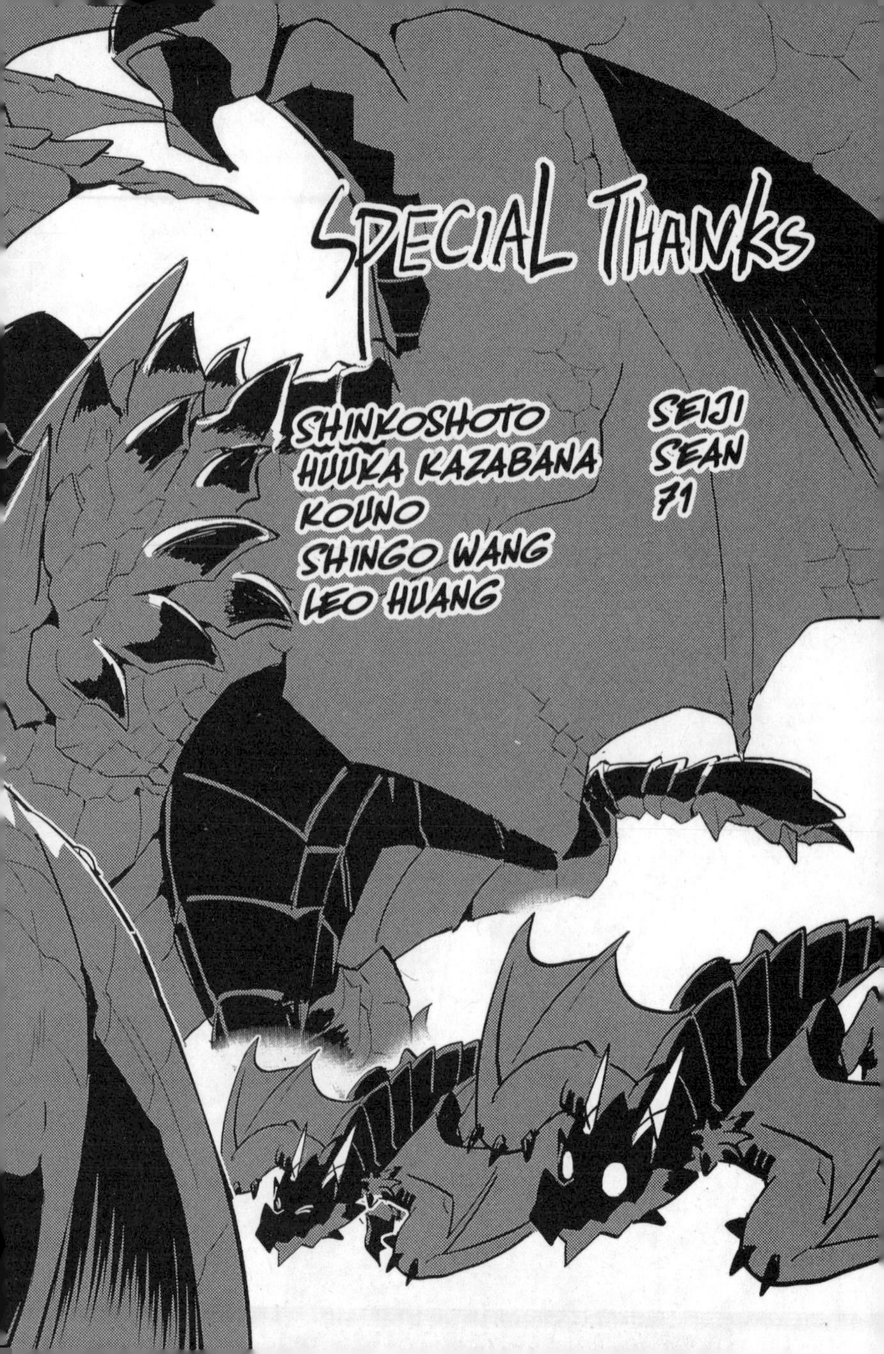
SPECIAL THANKS
SHINKOSHOTO
HUUKA KAZABANA
KOUNO
SHINGO WANG
LEO HUANG
SEIJI
SEAN
71

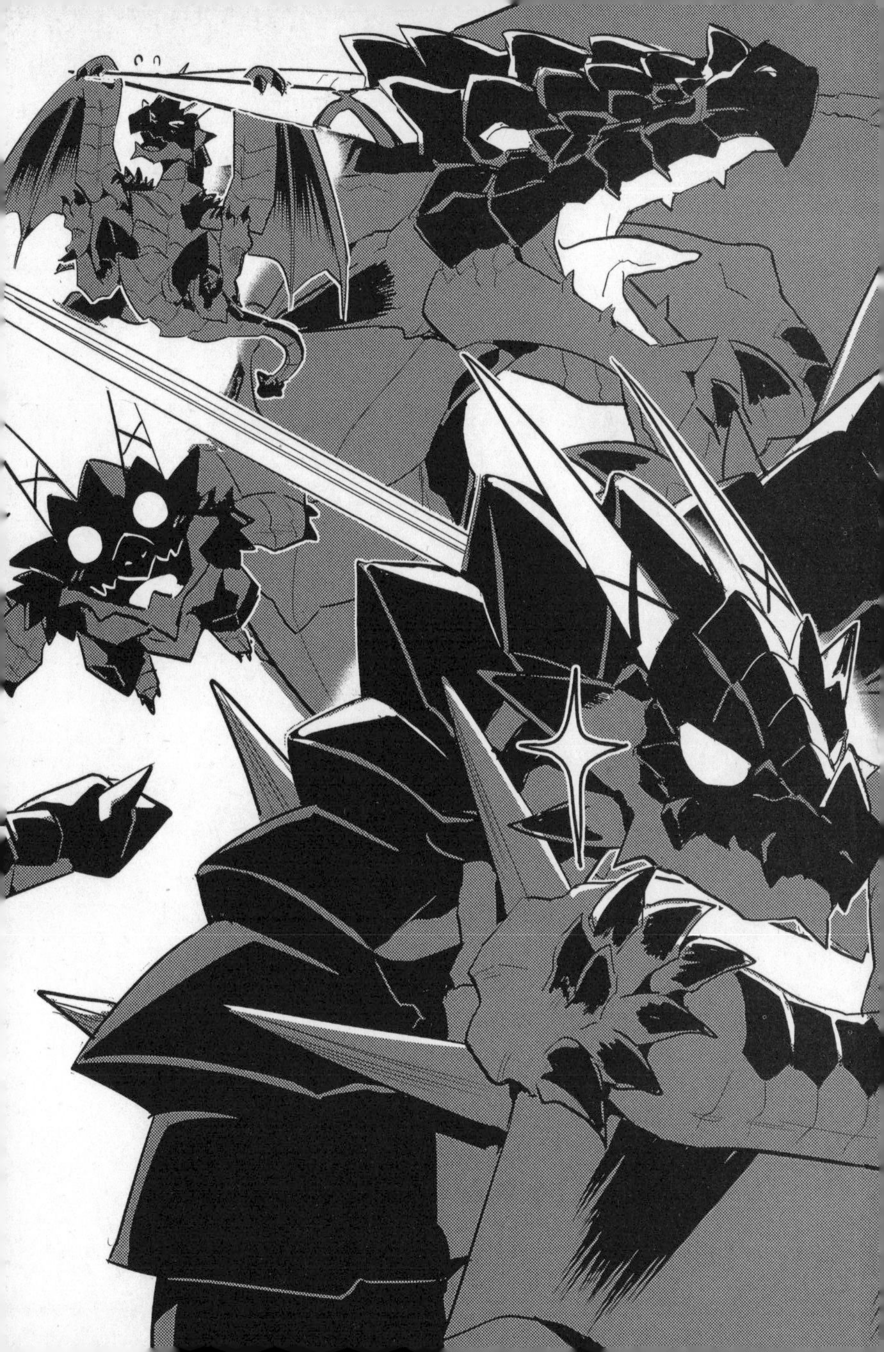

THE STRONGEST SAGE WITH THE WEAKEST CREST

To read a
brand-new
short story by
Shinkoshoto,
the author of
*The Strongest
Sage with the
Weakest Crest*,
please turn to
page 179 of this
book, where
you'll find the
story presented
in left-to-right
reading order!!

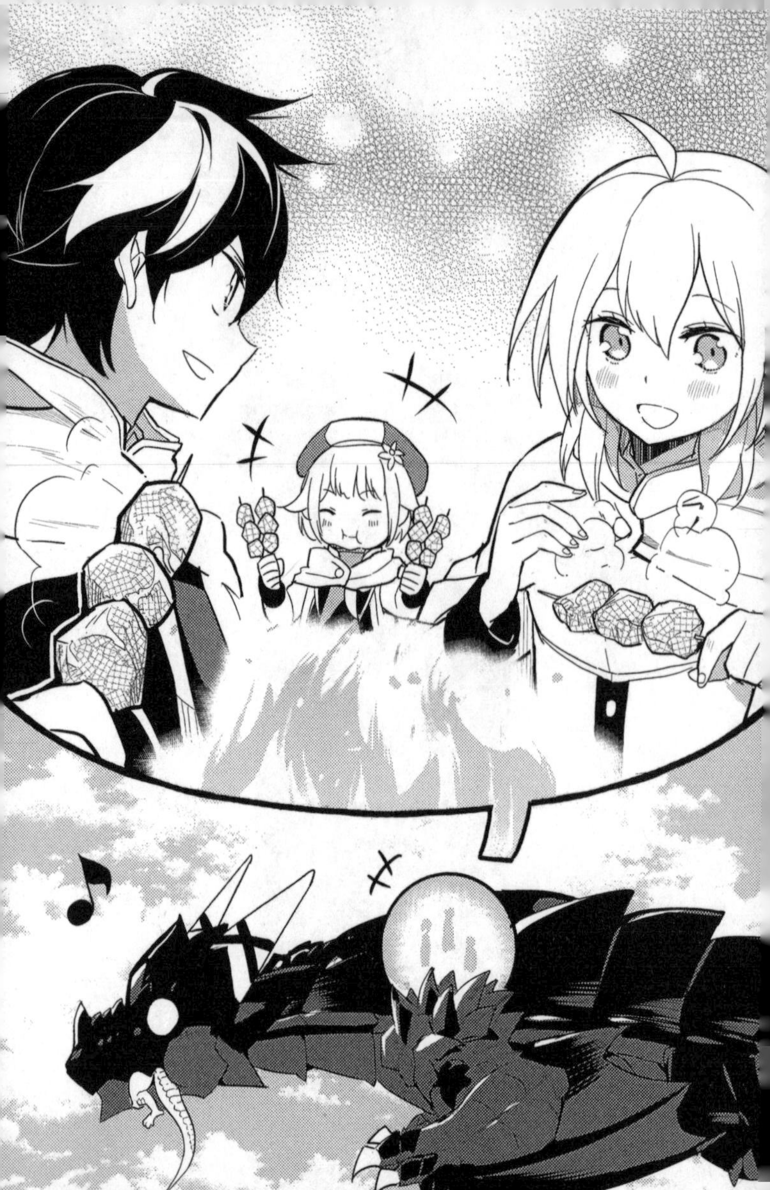

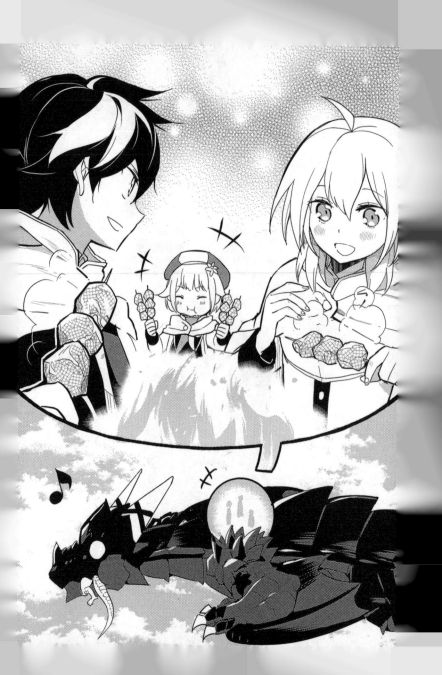

"Um... I'm wary of burning poor Iris with a cooking fire," said Lurie, glancing at the scales beneath our feet.

What an odd concern to have for the Dark Dragon.

"Ordinary fire will not hurt a bit, so please, cook away. Why, I used to call a pool of lava my home once upon a time, I'll have you know," explained Iris.

"L-lava, you say...? I guess we have nothing to worry about, then," said Lurie as she began to make our repast. Despite this, she asked Iris about the temperature several times throughout the process, even though Iris appeared wholly unconcerned about the fire on her back.

Before long, mealtime had arrived.

The lizard monster was far too much meat for our three human bellies, so Iris scarfed down the largest share of its body as if it were a small snack.

Still, the airborne hunting method was as dangerous as it was a pain in the butt, so I decided that we'd be better off stocking up on food before takeoff in future.

THE END

"E-even 200 meters is quite scary... One wrong move, and we may have a rough landing..." she gasped.

"This won't take long, so hang in there, okay?" I reassured her as I leapt from her back, rope still in hand. With Iris's flight speed skirting the speed of sound, the ground below whipped by in an alarming blur. One misplaced maneuver could see me splattered against an inconvenient tree. On the other hand, this meant I could deliver a sonic boom of a punch to any unlucky beast in my path. But since we wanted a whole monster ready for the pot and not a hard-to-cook, pulverized mess, such a move was inadvisable.

The simplest solution to this dilemma was to select a monster capable of withstanding a blow at the speed of sound. And lucky me, I spotted one right away—a giant lizard, about one kilometer dead ahead. I smacked it hard with some quick moves and yanked it right off the ground. I couldn't have lifted it bare-handed for long, but a binding spell was just the thing to secure the loose end of the rope around it.

"Screeeeee!"

It was spitting mad. Who wouldn't be, after receiving a sonic smash and getting dragged off like a fish at the end of someone's line? But the hard part for us was over. I dealt the critter a quick deathblow and cast a spell to reel us back up onto Iris's back.

"I found us something tasty."

"That does look like a main course. Though that was a rather spectacular approach to the hunt," admired Iris.

"I mean, that's just how you have to procure food from up in the air," I said. "Lurie, can you work with this?"

Suddenly, I realized that we had indeed missed a meal.

"How about we do some cooking?" I said.

"But we only brought those no-cook gray sticks of yours, right?" said Alma.

"Yeah. And only a minimal supply, at that. Outside of emergencies, I'd rather we procure ingredients on-site."

Storage magic consumes a huge amount of MP, and given that we were heading off to fight demons of unknown strength and ability, I'd decided to conserve energy by packing light. The emergency rations were only for dire situations in battle. Otherwise, I'd planned to forage and hunt.

"Oh yeah... You were trying to avoid bringing too much, huh?" said Alma.

"Ahem. Shall I land somewhere?" ventured Iris. "I could squeeze myself into one of the clearings in those woods."

"No, too much time waste. I've got another idea," I said.

I took out my special rope—strengthened with magic and essentially impervious to breakage—and tied it to one of Iris's dorsal spines. I'd only brought about 200 meters' worth (again, packing light), but it would do.

"Iris, could you descend to an altitude of 100 meters?"

"Um... At 100 meters, I could easily crash into the ground... Will 200 meters do?"

"Sure, that works," I said, grabbing the loose end of the rope. "Lurie, you mind casting another fortifying spell on the rope for me?"

"Wait, when you say 'procure on-site,' you couldn't possibly mean..." said Alma.

"You got it. I'm gonna lower myself down and snag a monster off the ground."

Iris began her descent.

THE STRONGEST SAGE REPLENISHES HIS STORES WHILE AIRBORNE

by **Shinkoshoto**

As Iris flew us at nearly the speed of sound to the demons' hideout, a curious noise fell on our ears.

Gurgle...

"What was that?" asked Lurie. "It seemed to come from inside this barrier spell."

"Something amiss in there? I can slow down if you would like," said Iris.

Without the soundproof barrier I'd materialized on the ancient dragon's back, the thunderous roar of the wind would've made it impossible to converse. Heck, at that altitude and speed, our eardrums might've burst. The sonic boom was just another deadly weapon in Iris's arsenal, but my spell was there to protect us from it and any other noises outside our bubble. This meant the gurgle must have come from within.

"Erm... No prob with the barrier, so no need to take it down a notch..." deflected a blushing Alma just as Iris had begun to slow.

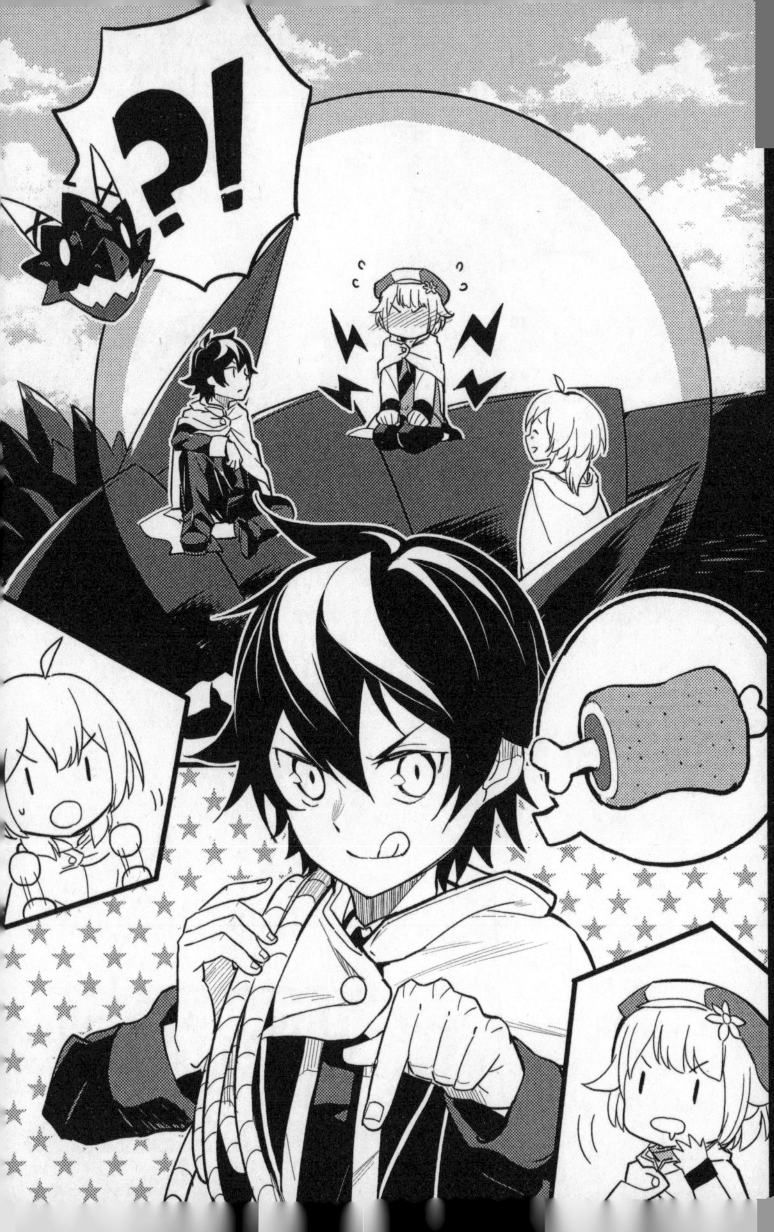
?!

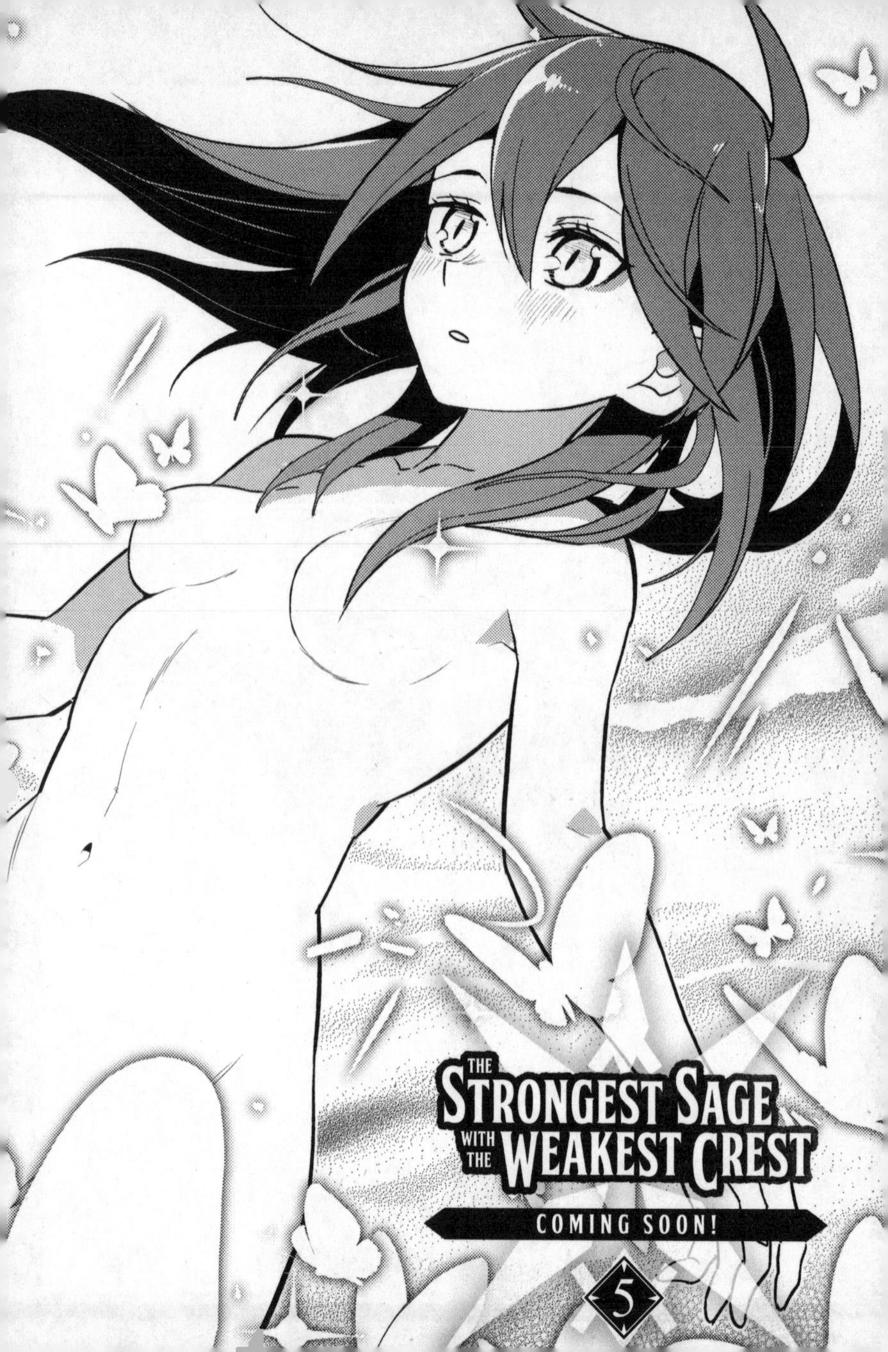
THE STRONGEST SAGE WITH THE WEAKEST CREST
COMING SOON!
5

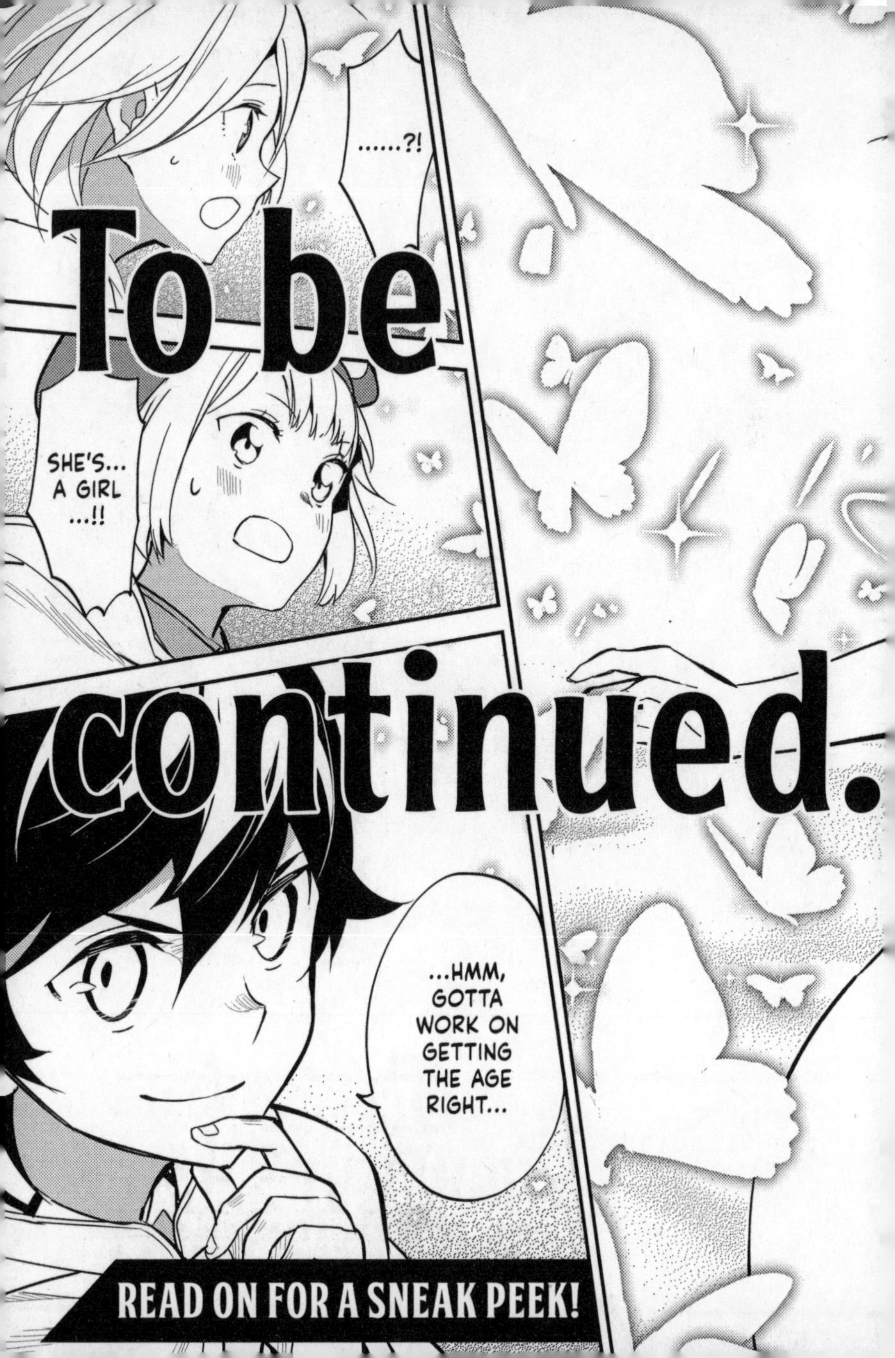
......?!
SHE'S... A GIRL ...!!
...HMM, GOTTA WORK ON GETTING THE AGE RIGHT...
To be continued.
READ ON FOR A SNEAK PEEK!

THE STRONGEST SAGE WITH THE WEAKEST CREST

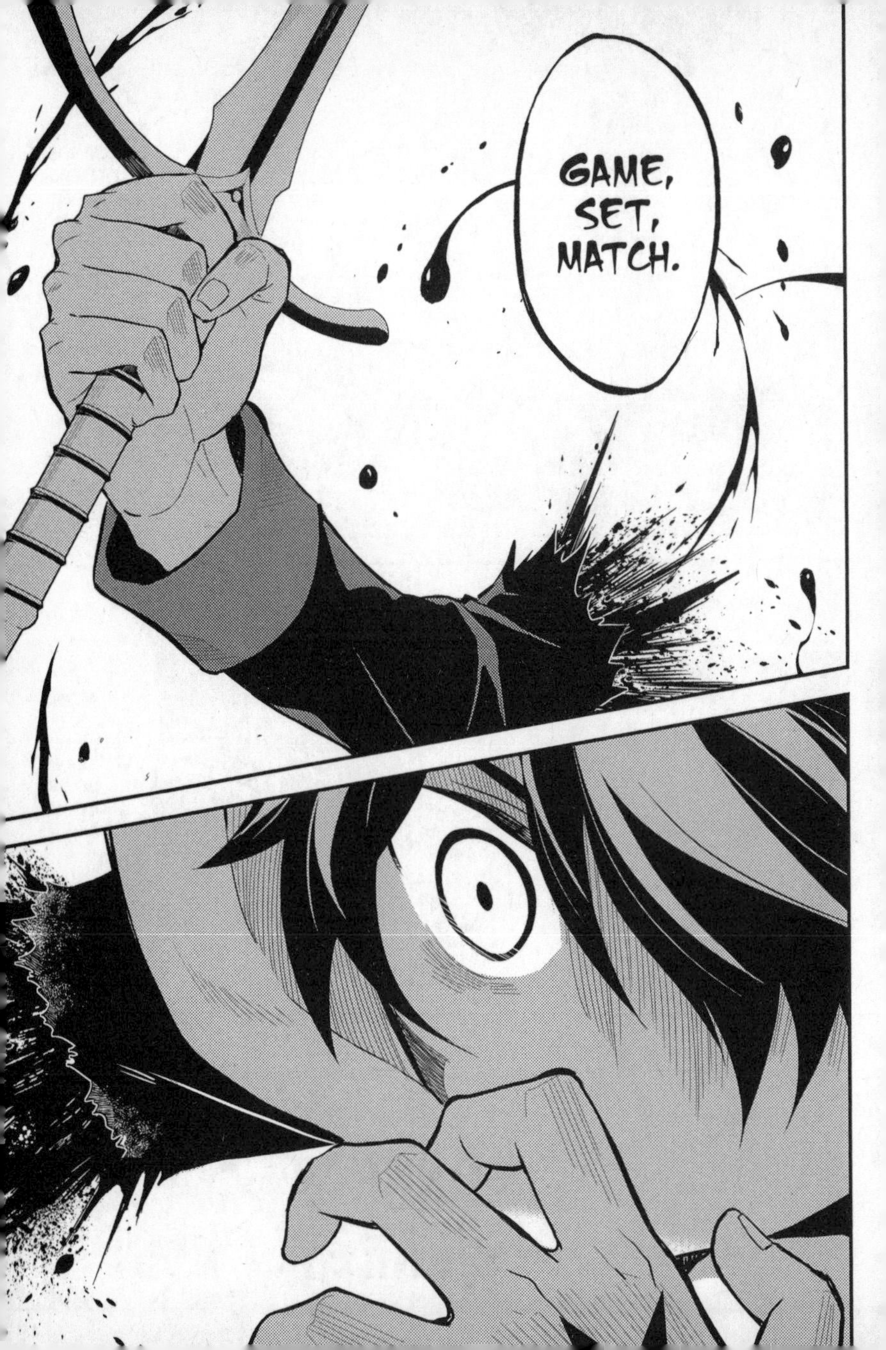
GAME, SET, MATCH.

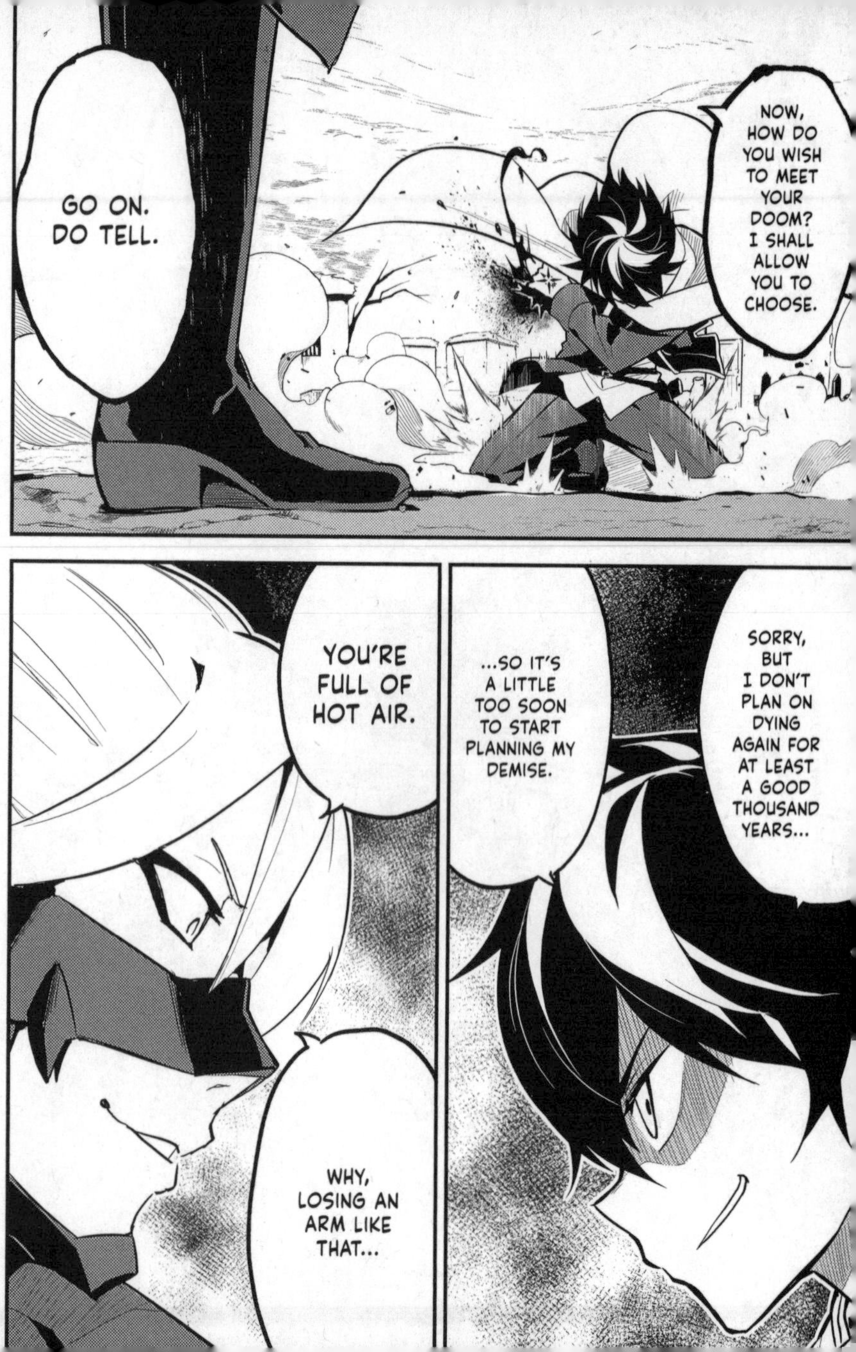
NOW, HOW DO YOU WISH TO MEET YOUR DOOM? I SHALL ALLOW YOU TO CHOOSE.
GO ON. DO TELL.
SORRY, BUT I DON'T PLAN ON DYING AGAIN FOR AT LEAST A GOOD THOUSAND YEARS...
...SO IT'S A LITTLE TOO SOON TO START PLANNING MY DEMISE.
YOU'RE FULL OF HOT AIR.
WHY, LOSING AN ARM LIKE THAT...

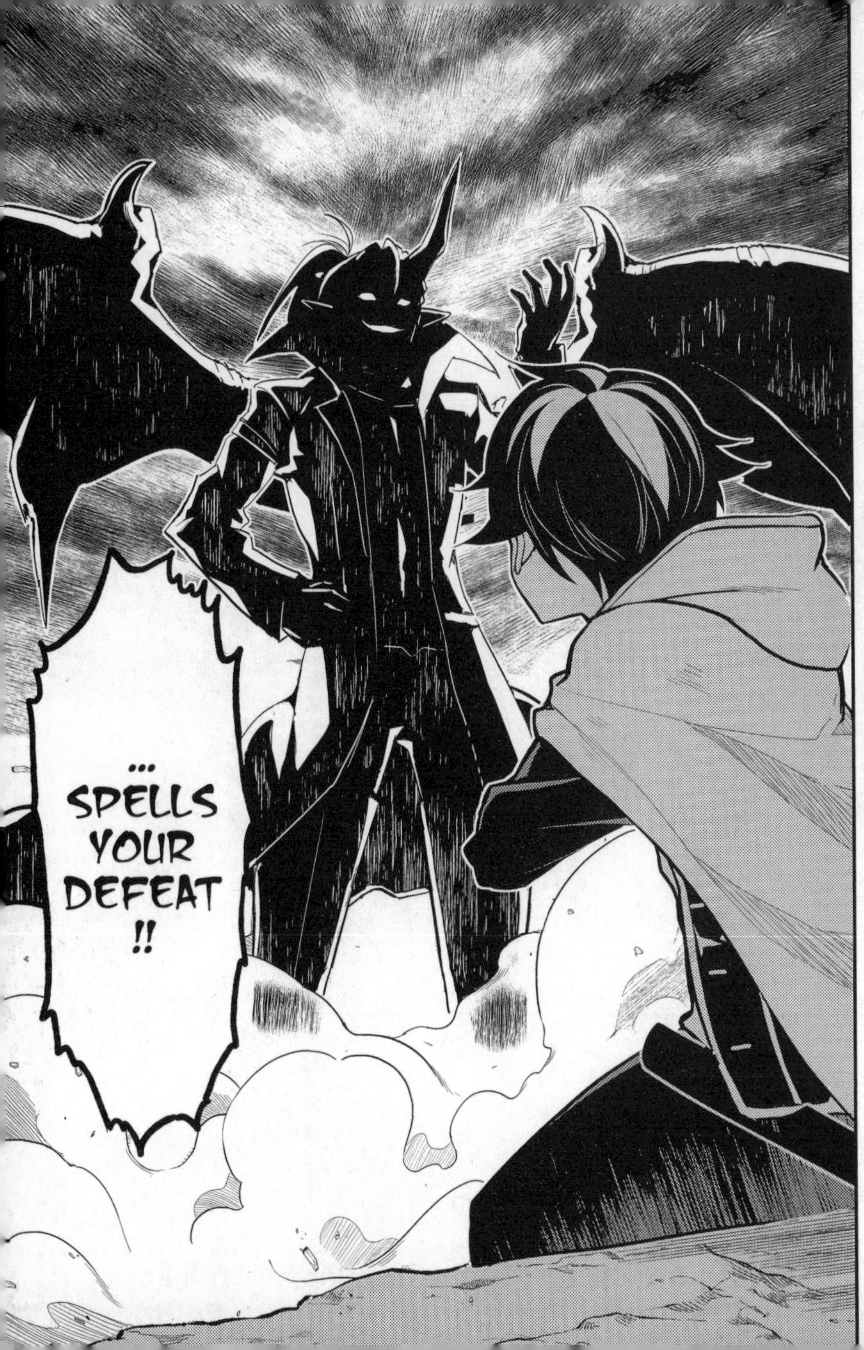
... SPELLS YOUR DEFEAT !!

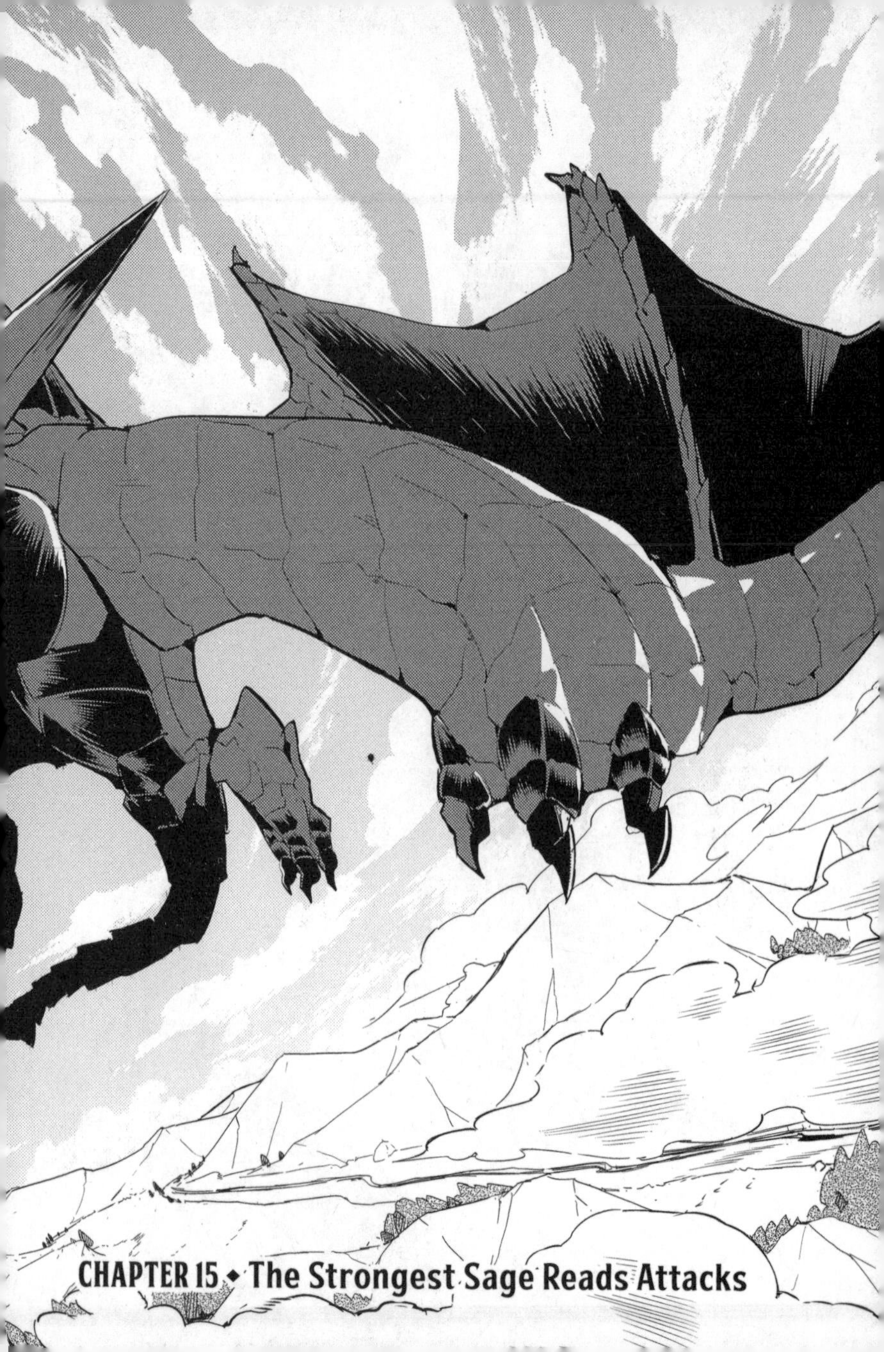

CHAPTER 15 • The Strongest Sage Reads Attacks

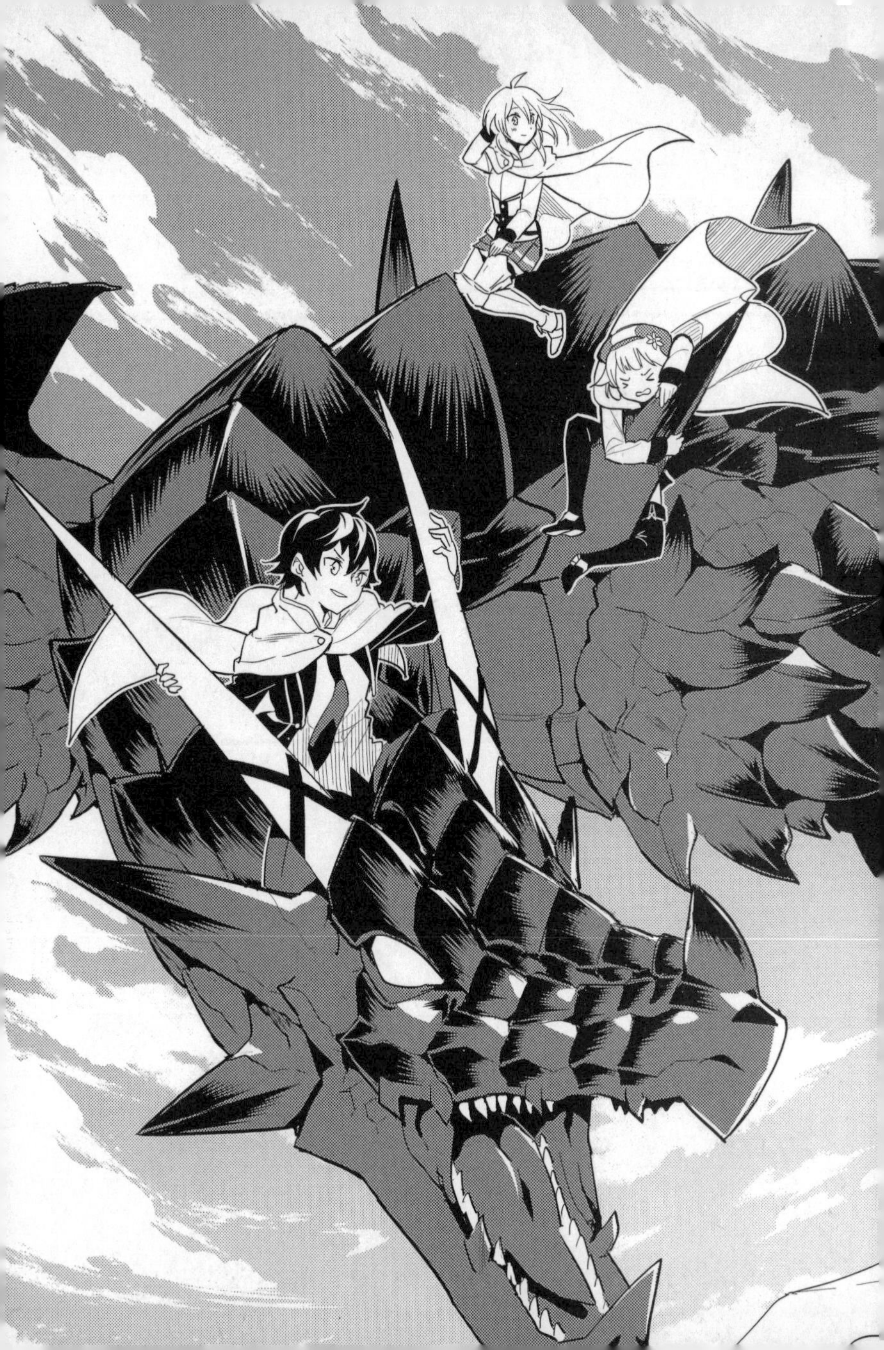

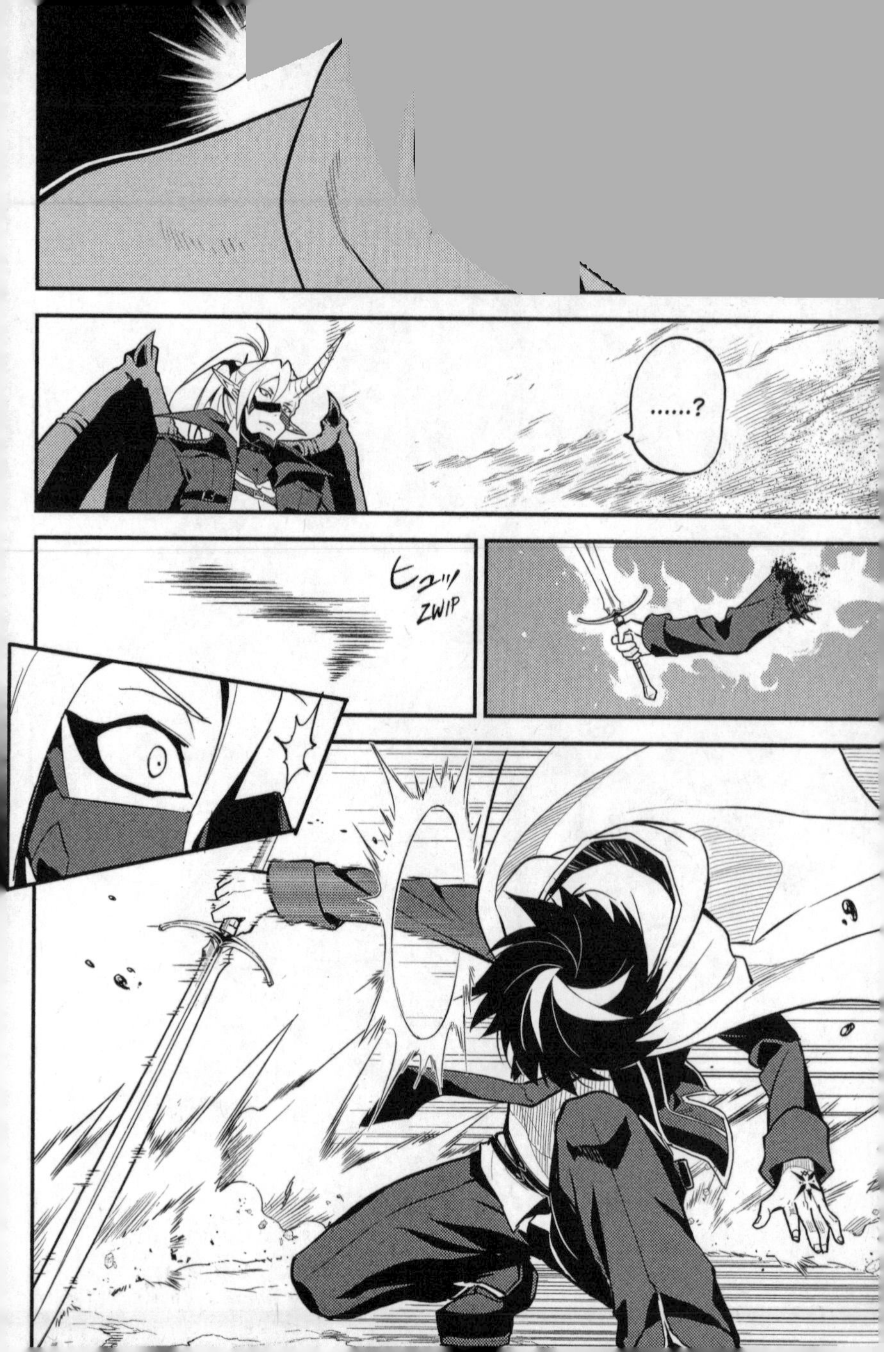
......?
ヒュッ
ZWIP

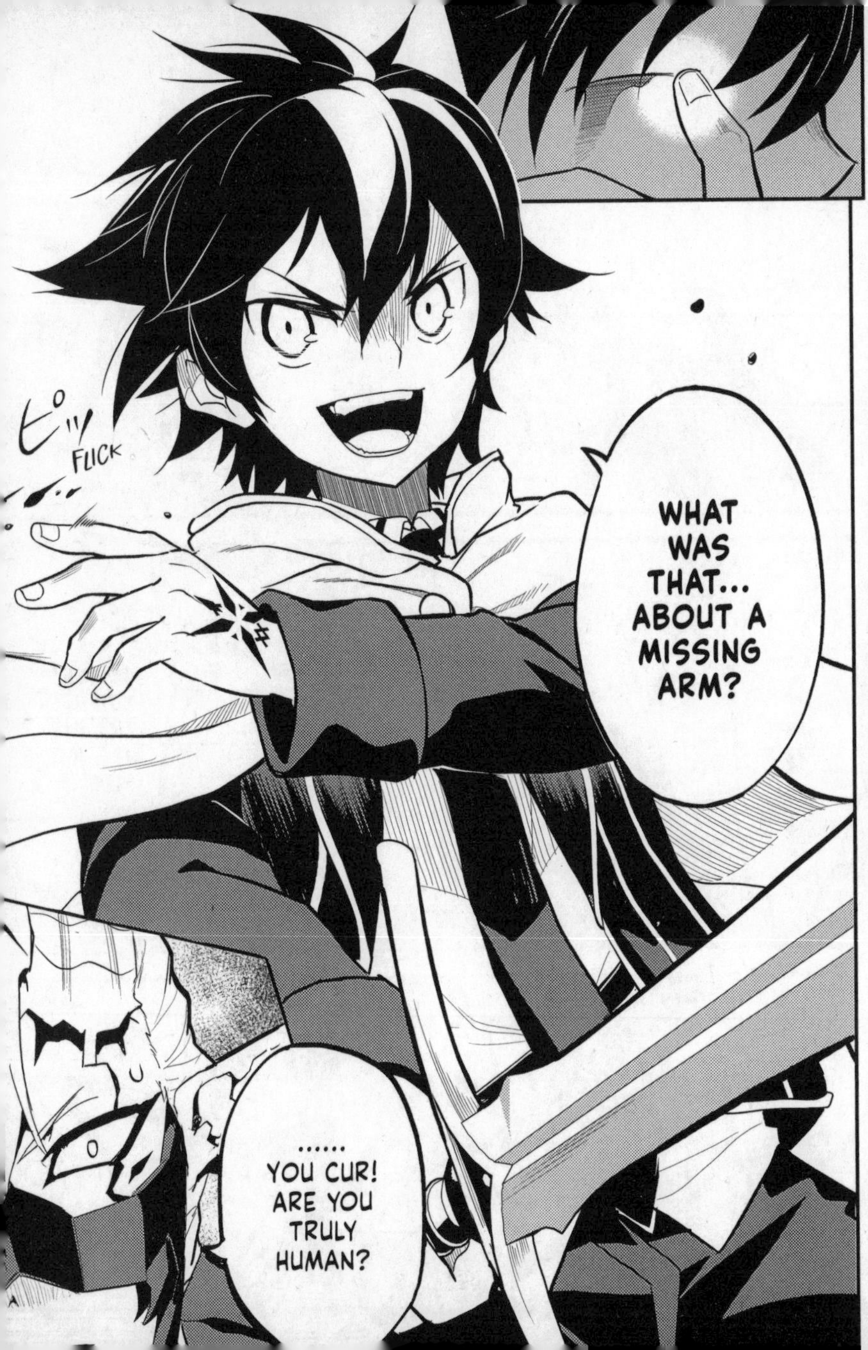
WHAT WAS THAT... ABOUT A MISSING ARM?
ピッ
FLICK
...... YOU CUR! ARE YOU TRULY HUMAN?

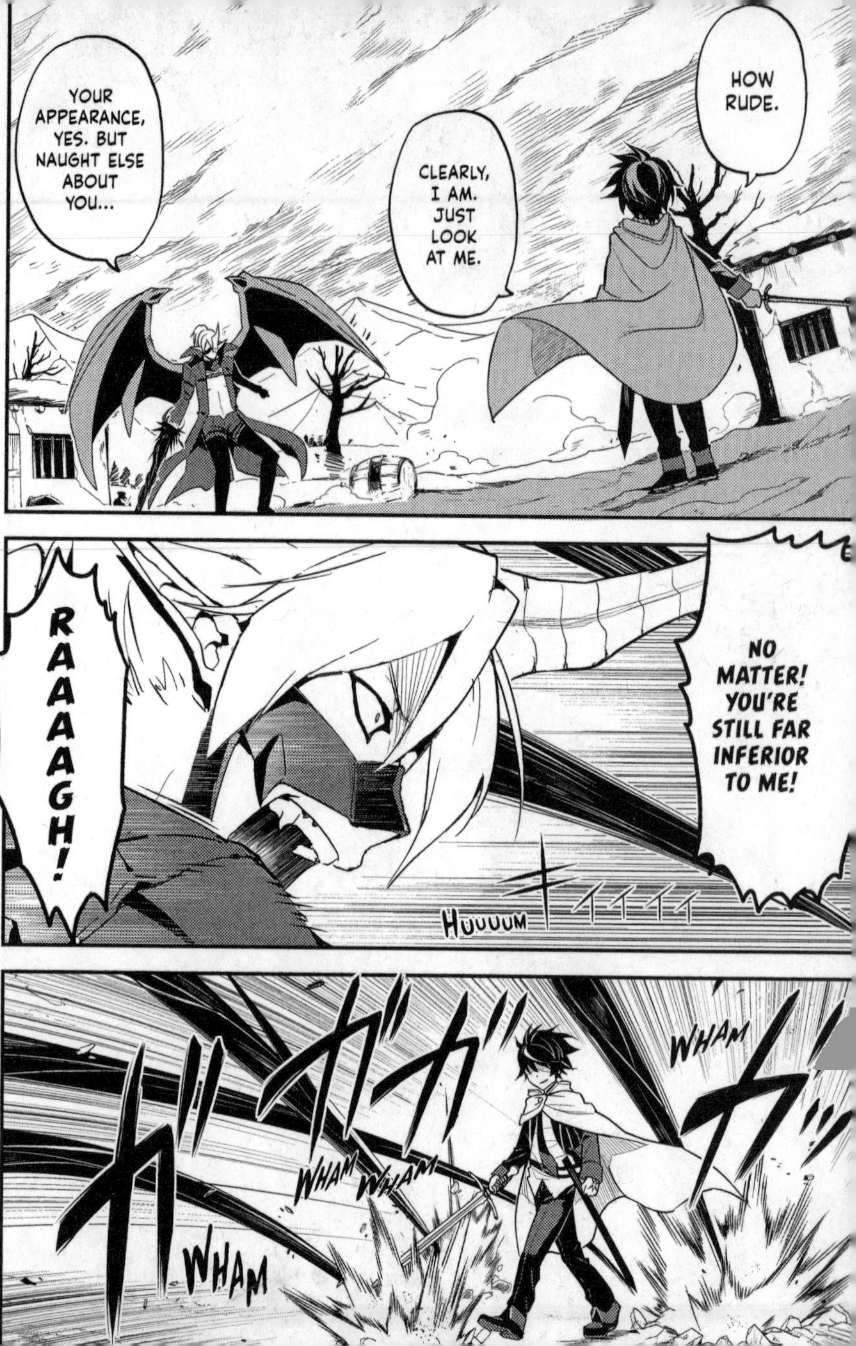
HOW RUDE.
CLEARLY, I AM. JUST LOOK AT ME.
YOUR APPEARANCE, YES. BUT NAUGHT ELSE ABOUT YOU...
NO MATTER! YOU'RE STILL FAR INFERIOR TO ME!
RAAAAAGH!
HUUUUM
WHAM
WHAM
WHAM
WHAM

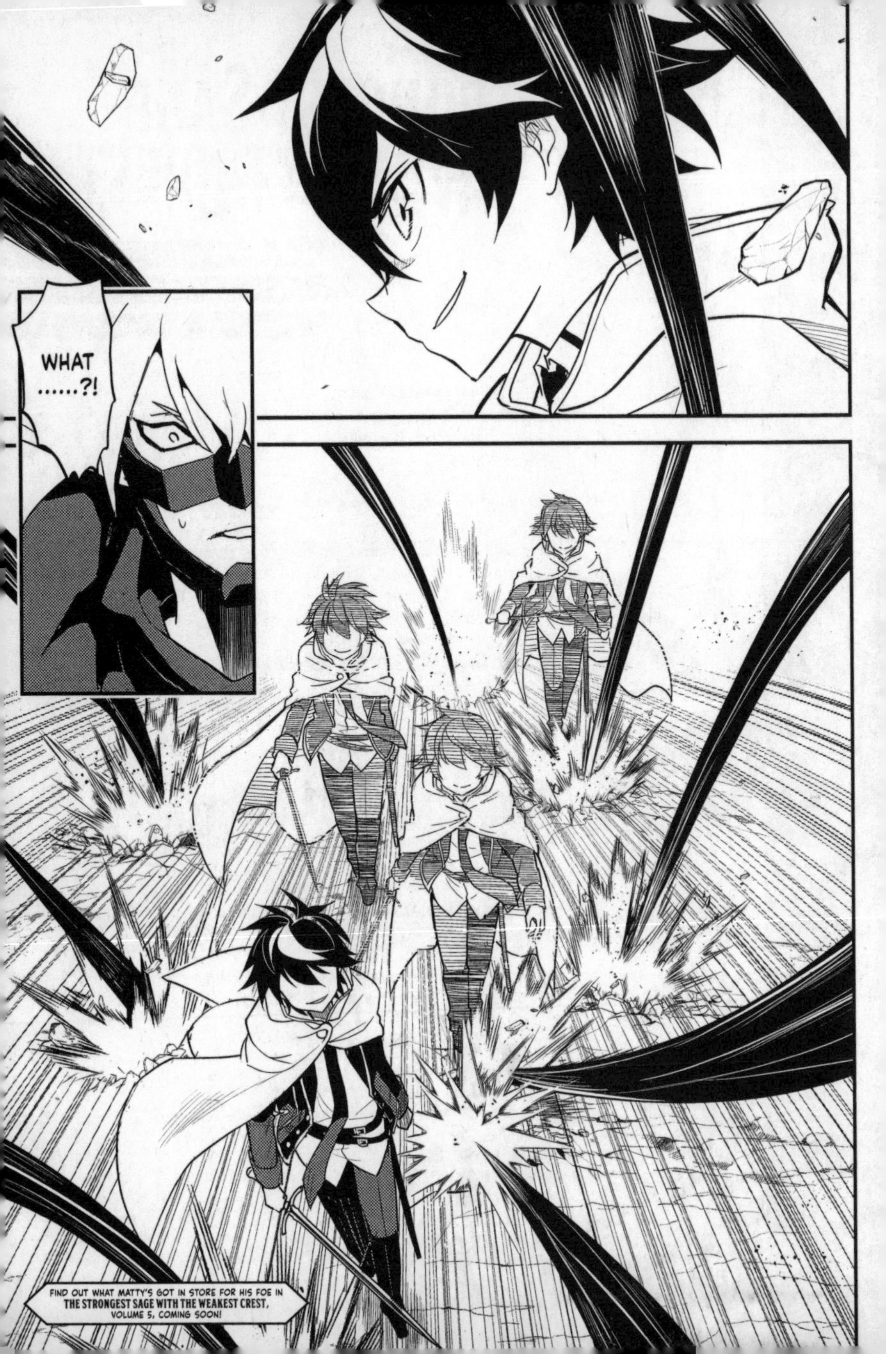
WHAT ......?!
FIND OUT WHAT MATTY'S GOT IN STORE FOR HIS FOE IN
THE STRONGEST SAGE WITH THE WEAKEST CREST,
VOLUME 5, COMING SOON!

THE STRONGEST SAGE WITH THE WEAKEST CREST

Story | **Shinkoshoto**

Art | **Liver Jam & POPO** (Friendly Land)

Character Design | Huuka Kazabana

Translation: Caleb D. Cook
Lettering: Ken Kamura
Cover Design: Phil Balsman
Editor: Tania Biswas

SHIKKAKUMON NO SAIKYOKENJA Volume 4
©Shinkoshoto/SB Creative Corp.
Original Character Designs:©Huuka Kazabana/SB Creative Corp.
©Friendly Land/SQUARE ENIX CO., LTD.
First published in Japan in 2018 by SQUARE ENIX CO., LTD.
English translation rights arranged with SQUARE ENIX
CO., LTD. and SQUARE ENIX, INC.
English translation © 2021 by SQUARE ENIX CO., LTD.

ISBN: 978-1-64609-046-4

Library of Congress Cataloging-in-Publication
Data is on file with the publisher.

Printed in the U.S.A.
First printing, July 2021
10 9 8 7 6 5 4 3 2 1

SQUARE ENIX
MANGA & BOOKS
www.square-enix-books.com